Lamu: History, Society, and Family
in an East African Port City

Dedication: To the memory of Sheikh Ahmed Jahadhmy, whose own quiet determination to unravel Lamu's past with accuracy was a beacon over the years.

And for Edward Rodwell

LAMU
History, Society, and Family in an East African Port City

by
PATRICIA W. ROMERO

Markus Wiener Publishers
Princeton

Back cover photo: Ahmed Mohammed Jahadhmy and two of his children.

For information write to: Markus Wiener Publishers
114 Jefferson Road, Princeton, NJ 08540

Library of Congress Cataloging-in-Publication Data

Romero, Patricia W.
    Lamu: history, society, and family in an East African
port city/by Patricia W. Romero
    (Topics in world history)
    Includes bibliographical references.
    ISBN 1-55876-106-3 hardcover
    ISBN 1-55876-107-1 paperback
    1. Lamu (Kenya)—History.   I. Title.   II. Series.
DT434.L35R66 1997
967.62'3—dc21   96-45647
                                            CIP

Printed in the United States of America on acid-free paper.

Contents

Preface

So many people and institutions contribute to any research project. My debt is more than considerable because of the long years involved in studying Lamu's history. There is, however, one person who stands out among the multitudes. This is Dr. B. E. Kipkorir, formerly Director of the Institute of African Studies, University of Nairobi, and a friend of some years standing. It was he who introduced me to Lamu, and suggested I study the history of that small but still important island community. Dr. Kipkorir has had a long love affair with Lamu, and was aware that although Marguerite Ylvisaker had written a very good economic history that centered primarily on Lamu's relation to the mainland, no historical study has been undertaken of the town itself. I hope I have managed to capture some of the Lamu that is so fascinating and intriguing.

The considerations of financing the many field trips to Lamu come into play. Among several sources of support, Towson State University's Research and Development Committee deserves special mention. I received three travel grants that enabled me to return to Lamu for additional research. Without the 1994 grant, I should not have been able to complete this study. I am grateful to the Committee as well as to the Guggenheim Foundation which provided my round trip airfare in 1980.

Professors Thomas Spear and Carol Eastman read a draft of chapter one and made helpful comments and suggestions. Professor Charles Beckingham generously read two chapters, and corrected some errors regarding Oman. Jeff Romero, who earned a master's degree in anthropology at Yale with an interest in coastal East Africa, and Lamu, read and criticized several drafts, and made many helpful recommendations for revision. In addition I would like to thank Usam Ghaidan, Guy Wolf, and Peter Hinks. I am grateful to all the above for generously sharing their time and expertise. No one, however, invested as much time and interest in this project as did Sheikh Ahmed Jahadhmy. He read drafts of every chapter and corrected factual errors, but never attempted to alter my interpretations and inclusions. I am saddened that he did not live to see the book in print. He knew that it was being dedicated to him before he died in August 1995. The manuscript is much enhanced as a result of the combined input of these critics. Whatever remaining errors in fact and interpretation are mine alone.

Scores of Lamu people from all ethnic groups have opened their homes, their minds, and their hearts to me over years. This is true, too, of generous and willing informants in Mombasa, Mauritius, LaReunion, and Magadascar. With the exception of living Lamu women, I have named the many who aided me in the notes. I thank them collectively and sincerely.

"Mama Khadija" was dying of cancer when I last visited her in June, 1994. She never wavered in her religious faith and, consequently, drawing on her own goodness and decency, sought to share all that she was able to recall whether that pertained to slavery, traditional medicine, or her own rather complicated life. I mourn her, as do the myriad family members to whom she was devoted. Sharif Abdalla Salim al Hussein in Mombasa was equally forthcoming and generous with his time and his knowledge. He, too, has died, and is missed by many, including me.

In Mombasa, Edward and Olive Rodwell showered me with hospitality. In fact, they probably saved my life by taking me in and then, for over a week, delivering me daily to their doctor when I was very ill in 1991. Edward Rodwell freely shared his extensive archives with me from May 1980, when I first visited his Mtapwa Creek office. Over the years he has been a constant correspondent, sending me tidbits pertaining to Lamu or lending me documents. Before his sight failed, Rodwell read several chapters of this book. After that, friends and family members read them to him. Despite his inability to see, however, Rodwell's critical faculties did not desert him and he offered very welcome criticisms for revision. My thanks to both Olive and Roddy are profound. James de Vere Allen assisted me during my first several months in Lamu. Unfortunately he has died. I am certain he would have had innumerable comments—and criticisms—to offer had he lived to read the final product.

Mention of these specific people in no way diminishes the incredible debt I owe to so many, especially the women who helped me arrange introductions, set up interviews, and who also shared their traditions and memories.

Having been tarred with the brush of an earlier, and unpopular study of Lamu, the family of Habib Saleh were reluctant to help in the beginning.

But after a few months in Lamu, some members of the Jamal al Layl family agreed to taped interviews. I have tried to present them as fairly as the facts I obtained allow.

This brings me to Abdul Hamid M. el Zein's *The Sacred Meadows: A Structural Analysis of Religious Symbolism in an East African Town* (Evanston, 1976) which was published before I began my fieldwork there in 1980. This study is controversial, not only in Lamu, but among scholars as well. In 1982 I published a critical essay on the volume, and refer to both the book and the criticism in the notes in the text that follows. el Zein was dead at the time I wrote the essay, making it difficult indeed to criticize someone who could not respond. Nevertheless, I do not retract from my earlier criticisms. Much of his analysis switches from "story telling" to recorded history, without clarifying which is which.

With a focus on symbolic and structural anthropology, el Zein's work is hopelessly ahistorical. In addition, by employing these tools of analysis, el Zein presents what I view to be a warped and thus inaccurate picture of Lamu—although there are, of course, areas in which we are in agreement. His interpretation of slavery in Lamu is highly impressionistic and does not concur with my findings. My views, based on long years of careful fieldwork, are included here. For those who are familiar with el Zein's interpretation, the differences will be obvious. For those who are not, I recommend that they read *The Sacred Meadows* and draw their own conclusions.

Some in Lamu will find fault with this book. This is to be expected in a multiethnic society where some voices are heard more than others. I view this work as a trail that I urge others to expend into a major highway leading to more knowledge about the Hadrami community and the Bajun community in Lamu. More relevant still, is the need for archaeologists to concentrate on Lamu's distant past. Histories of the other island communities in the Lamu archipelago also need to be researched and written. Pate island, in particular, cries out for the professional historian's attention.

Grace Egan exercised a firm hand in editing the final copy of this manuscript, in process making it more readable as she also caught some omissions that otherwise would have slipped through. Carolyn Westbrook used her considerable skills to unravel the genealogies and place them in coherent lines of descent. She also drew the maps from the outline created by Bettina Jenkins, while Nana Henderson offered considerable input into earlier drafts of the genealogies. Anne Thurston helpfully supplied some research materials from the United Kingdom. I extend my sincere appreciation to all of these talented women.

In conclusion, I humbly thank every one—literally hundreds of kind, helpful, and unselfish women and men in Kenya and elsewhere—who have made this book possible. This includes the staff at the Institute of African Studies, University of Nairobi; librarians and archivists, especially at the Kenya National Archives, Rhodes House Library and at the the Institute of Commonwealth Studies, the Public Records Office, and the India Records Office and Library in the United Kingdom. The interlibrary loan personnel at Towson State have provided generous and courteous assistance since I began teaching there in 1989.

I also wish to thank the family of John Haggard for permission to quote from his papers, which are on deposit at Rhodes House library, Oxford.

Patricia W. Romero
Great Cacapon WV

Introduction

Located on the northern coast of Kenya, Lamu is a romantic port city that travel agent brochures describe as "exotic" and "medieval." Lamu island features long white and mostly deserted sandy beaches that have become an increasingly attractive lure to tourists. The major town (Lamu) is located on the northeastern coast of the island and has, over time, enjoyed migrations from "Africa"[1] on the mainland as well as from communities within the Indian Ocean complex. Some claimed that Indonesians came to Lamu before the birth of Christ, bringing with them the stately palm trees that dot the island and that serve as a major economic backdrop to the people living in the town. But the claims for the Indonesians are just the tip of the iceberg as to who from the Indian Ocean beyond came, traded, and may have been responsible in helping create those who are called the WaSwahili (pl). people.

Who are the Lamu WaSwahili? The responses to that question are almost as numerous as the numbers of people who refer to themselves as Swahili. The meaning of the name has changed over time. Informed and respected elders say that today the Swahili are the lower classes who are not "outsiders" meaning Bajun, Pokomo, Galla, Somali, Giriama, Arabs, or Indians. To some being Swahili meant persons of slave ancestry, as well as those who were alleged to be the "original" inhabitants, and who, in turn, were called the Yumbili.[2] When Britain began to extend her governance down the Sultan of Zanzibar's ten mile strip of the East African coast, officials themselves differed in defining the WaSwahili. In 1912, a British district commissioner described the KiSwahili speakers as "a somewhat mixed quantity. There is . . . an absolute distinction in actual fact. The pure-bred Swahili are part of the aristocracy of the Protectorate. Some of the families are people of considerable social standing and have

1

behind them a long pedigree."[3] Still, the British referred to outsiders who married Lamu women, as "Arabs" or other terms marking their original homeland.

According to two modern scholars, Alamin Mazrui and Ibrahim Noor Shariff, "the Swahili today are a living expression of an African-Arab process of intermarriage" that began centuries ago, perhaps before the birth of Christ.[4] This definition is all encompassing and satisfactory for Lamu was well as other areas of the Swahili speaking world. Yet, to the African-Arab component, must also be added Indian, Egyptian, and Persian, as well as a blush of Circassian.

Scholars are still arguing over who were the first Swahili. Anthropologists, linguists, and historians are divided on the subject. Carol Eastman attempted to solve the riddle in 1971, but later, reversed herself. Walter Arens sees the change in the meaning of Swahili over time, but rejects the Arabness of those who lived on the coast for several generations and places them under the rubric of "Swahili".[5] Early visitors seem to have lumped all the Swahili speakers together since the term implied people of the coast. The original coastal peoples themselves, however, may never have regarded themselves as Swahili, although they came to speak a trading language called KiSwahili.

Our knowledge of how the Swahili came to speak a language that differentiated them from other Africans who lived on the northern Kenya coast is still fragmentary. But for Lamu, we will adopt archaeologist Mark Horton's model for nearby Shanga. Horton suggests that trade between the northern Kenya coastal islands and the world beyond had existed for centuries before Islam was introduced. He reads the first century A.D. *Periplus of the Erythaenan Sea* references to Rhapta as "probably in the area of Lamu." The author of this early volume is thought to be "a trader or perhaps a shipmaster" with the account itself a "traders guide to the coasts of the [Indian Ocean]."[6] Trade was with African people from the mainland who brought ivory, elephant teeth, rock crystal, hides, and other items to the coast, where, though originally land loving, the coastal people built small craft and sailed up the Red Sea to trading centers. As word spread about these trade items from the coastal communities like Lamu, maybe Greeks, but certainly Indian Ocean traders who had long connections with the Red Sea, turned their attention to the northern Kenya

2

coastal islands, and came directly to buy and sell. Horton's model includes seasonal trade fairs on islands where mainland Africans, including women, moved with their merchandise during the *kaskazi* monsoon season—November to March—and erected temporary dwellings.[7] Traders from the Persian Gulf, from India, from the Hadramaut, and from the Red Sea areas stayed at these island locations for the duration of the monsoon winds, sexual relations occurred between them and the African women. In time the children of these relationships, with other Africans from the mainland, established permanent settlements—small independent city-states on the islands.

With a semipermanent trading class of people living in port cities like Lamu, and with a growing number of Africans—some now of mixed ethnicity based on earlier liaisons—a new group of people emerge. Their language is Bantu dominated (proto-Sabaki) but also includes words spoken by the traders from whom this new group of people are descended.[8]

In terms of the composition of the Swahili language, G. S. P. Freeman-Grenville points out that "20 to 30 percent of the [language] is composed of loan words" that come from such disparate areas as Persia, Hindustan, Gujarat, Turkey, Malaysia, Portugal, Germany, and of course, England. (Portugal comes into Lamu's history in the sixteenth century, Germany and England in the nineteenth). Some words, too, are from "special Arabian dialects." All of the words referring to Islam and religion, of course, are Arabic.[9]

The Swahili language gradually developed, as traders who were posted for periods in these coastal communities were speaking that during their periods of residency, the progeny of the African women and traders spoke mostly KiSwahili so that they could communicate with both of their parents (and no doubt also learned the Bantu language of their mothers). Each new trader who arrived in communities came to learn bits of KiSwahili and, over the centuries, it took precedence over the home language of the Africans who became permanent dwellers in the port cities.

Before the advent of Islam, trade from the northern East African coastal areas to the Red Sea meant the introduction of ivory from that area into Europe by way of the Mediterranean Sea. East African coastal traders also sailed into the Persian Gulf during the *kusi*, the northwest monsoon, which blew from April to October. Trade extended all the way to China, although probably indirectly through India. Imported ceramics from the "Far East" were unearthed on Pate island by Thomas Wilson who dated them back to the ninth century. Neville Chittick, on nearby Manda Island, found shards from China dating back to this same time. J.E.G. Sutton, who also referred to the Indonesian connection with coastal East Africa, mentions slaves in China who were called "zanj," the Greek word for black. By the ninth or tenth century Swahili were exporting ambergris and slaves and conducting trade with Africans on the mainland, as they also sailed directly into the Indian Ocean-Red Sea worlds beyond.[10]

Islam arrived on the Swahili coast probably in the ninth century. Horton found caches of coins on Pemba Island (near Zanzibar), the earliest of which he labeled "Abbasid 810/11." Others were from Cairo 969. However, the locally minted coins Horton found had Muslim names imprinted on them and were dated between 1050-1080, establishing without doubt that Islam was in place there by the eleventh century—which was also when Islamic conversion may have begun in Lamu.[11]

Indians were on the East African coast by the first century A.D. (and probably earlier). They left behind children from liaisons with local women, as well as examples of their material culture.[12] A. A. Skanda, a Lamu woodcarver, believes that many traditions and much of Swahili material culture derives from India—including plasterwork decorations in the Lamu houses, and the designs used in carving wooden doors that are found all over East Africa, including Madagascar.[13] Peter Hinks argues that the jewelry designs found on Pate island (and in Madagascar) are "definitely influenced by South India."[14]

The Indians may have been preceded by traders from the Red Sea who, Horton believes, influenced early house design on the northern coast. These traders, including those from today's Yemen, also left behind their genes in children they fathered during their stay.[15] With the rise of Islam, any numbers of different ethnic groups from Persia, Arabia, Oman, the Comoro Islands, and the African mainland resettled in these coastal communities. They, too, contributed to the gene pool of the Swahili people.

The polity that developed in Lamu ranged from a king (or queen in at least one instance) to one where neighborhoods elected their representatives who served as elders over the town. These neighborhoods, which encompassed only those who lived in the stone houses, were sometimes divided. Indians, though long in residence, seem to have stayed out of the political arena—at least in terms of the oral traditions currently available.

After a sweep through what we can conjecture about Lamu's early history, this study will concentrate mainly on the impact of migrations, including slaves from central Africa, and on, the effects of British colonial policies in the nineteenth and twentieth centuries before Kenyan independence. We will see how Lamu rose to dominate the northern coast after the neighboring island, Pate's defeat at the Battle of Shela (1813-14), and how Omani migrations then played a significant role in the economic expansion of Lamu town as well as the mainland. Slavery had existed for centuries in Lamu, but during the period of economic expansion in the nineteenth century, the numbers of African slaves increased dramatically. We will look at the material culture of owners and bondsmen—before and after British attempts to abolish the institution in Lamu. In addition, we will see that, despite internal squabbles between various groups, Islam was the commonality almost all shared. (The exception being the Hindus, who are peripheral to the study). This was, however, complicated because of divisions between Shi'a and Sunni, and then between factions of the Sunni community including the Hadrami and Comoro Islanders. European competition in East Africa and in the Indian Ocean concern us where their struggles for hegemony have a direct impact on Lamu. Thus, relations between France and Britain in the nineteenth century have a bearing on the Lamu slave trade, as do disputes between Germany and England later.

I have tried to interweave the human factor in Lamu's history through a series of case studies that include all of the major players from the nineteenth century and on. Although most of the text is paraphrased, the voices behind the scene are those of the patricians, descendants of slaves, various British officials, the Hadrami, and a few of the Shi'a Indians. In reconstructing Lamu's past, I collected traditions and memories from knowledgeable elders. In order to present as comprehensive and accurate a picture as possible, I turned to a wide selection of women from all groups for their input. Altogether I gathered more than one hundred hours of taped interviews that were then combined with notetaking. The women were more willing to share their knowledge of social history and material culture, while the men were anxious to set the record straight in regard to the more negative aspects of British colonialism. There were, however, exceptions and some elders contributed immeasurably to all facets of Lamu's social history.

Although now a part of Kenya irredenta, during the colonial period, the WaAmu (pl). patricians continued to look towards Zanzibar. The Zanzibari appointed liwalis (governors) were often caught between their loyalty to the Sultan and the British government agents posted in Lamu. Furthermore, most married local women, worked plantations, owned slaves, and tried to protect their own economic interests and those of their extended family, while maintaining a facade of cooperation to the authorities who paid their salaries. Colonial officials were tied to policies handed down by the British government and passed through a chain of command that directed the actions of all district commissioners stationed in the Kenya colony. Nevertheless, the British government was less concerned with the northern coast than with implementing policies, and pacifying Africans in the hinterland, especially in territories surrounding the railroad from Mombasa to Lake Victoria. Life for all Lamu's inhabitants was seriously altered because of the collision between European culture and that of the locals. Public health, for instance improved for most during the colonial period. Western style education came to be regarded as essential for upward mobility by the Indians, later the patricians, and ultimately by the Bajuns who became a significant presence after World War II.

The abolition of slavery was a mixed blessing for slave owners and many bondsmen. As we shall see, some preferred to remain in what they termed slavery to their masters in spite of British efforts to emancipate. Others fled the mainland even before the official proclamations were issued. Relations between master and slave were complicated and, in this volume, most of the emphasis rests on those who stayed or, at least, those who maintained good relations with their former owners. Here again religion played a dominant role in determining interpersonal relationships.

Yet despite the imposition of colonialism, most WaAmu—old families and newcomers alike—maintained a modicum of freedom to pursue their own interests even as, for some, fortunes waned. And for others, poverty gave way to prosperity. This was especially true of the Hadrami community. The Indians, with few exceptions, left in search of better business

6

opportunities elsewhere. As a port city, however, Lamu collected new arrivals who arrived with little or no money and, following the paths of those who preceded them, made a fresh start in hopes of climbing the economic ladder.

In order to avoid the ongoing confusion (not to mention controversies) as to who were "the" WaSwahili, most references to the various ethnic groups in Lamu will be along these lines: the Afro-Arabs are those who claim Arab descent but whose ancestors have long included Africans as well. The slaves and ex-slaves are almost all of purely African descent, although some Circassian women did come to Lamu as concubines of Omani men. Both of these groups speak KiSwahili as their first language, although both include those who are at least somewhat fluent in Arabic. Then we refer to the Hadrami, some of whom still speak Arabic as their first language, although they, too, intermarried with slaves and ex-slaves (and others). Their children almost all spoke KiSwahili as their first language. The Indians, most of whom came from Gujarat, all spoke Gujarati, but were and are fluent in KiSwahili. The other ethnic groups all learned KiSwahili, if they did not speak it on arrival. Migrants from the Comoro Islands spoke a patois of the language, but soon learned KiAmu (the Lamu dialect).

Family history is important in surveying Lamu's past, at least from 1813 on.[16] Through the inclusion of a series of genealogies, including all the major ethnic groups in Lamu, we will see how fluid social structure was among the Afro-Arab, the Hadrami, and later the ex-slave communities. For the most part, the Indian sects chose to marry among themselves because of religious ties. Nevertheless, some Indians did intermarry with Afro-Arab, Hadrami, and ex-slaves. It was this fascination with the changing nature of the social order that attracted me to focus much of this study on that topic. Previously scholars, including me, have indicated that social structure was rigid and unchanging. As we shall see, what people said about their inflexible social order is not what they practiced.

In the past two centuries the port city of Lamu has served as a melting pot. Lamu patricians bowed to economic and/or social forces in their time, just as the first Africans from the mainland did earlier in welcoming and incorporating traders—Egyptians, Indians, Persians, Turks, Arabs—who came there from the Red Sea and Indian Ocean.

7

CHAPTER 1

The Lamu siwa and its keeper
Courtesy of the National Museums of Kenya

Chapter One

A Glimpse into the Far Past: Contradictions and Traditions

"Guide us to the Path that is Straight"
The Qur'an

For nearly every group of settlers who came to Lamu, there is an oral tradition explaining their arrival, or that of those whom they claimed preceded them. Unraveling Lamu's pre-colonial past is further complicated because traditions were collected by early British officials or by Omani agents of the British government who were newcomers to the port city. In the case of the British colonials, their failure to cite their informants presents a dilemma for anyone wrestling with various, but mostly incomplete, traditions. Nevertheless, incomplete, contradictory, and even seemingly fanciful reflections are touched upon here.

Although we are not now able to discern who among the WaAmu were the informants, many of the people who claim long residence in the town still repeat some of the traditions that follow. Conflicting accounts in no way diminish the fact that these traditions reflect what were passed down as *history* from some of the WaAmu to younger family members over several generations.[1] The "ancient city of Lamu (population 7,000) . . . [consists] of a labyrinth of narrow streets with a number of stone mosques and a fort . . . ."[2] Ancient city correctly describes Lamu but the question is: How old? No one will know precisely until archaeologists undertake a systematic study of various parts of the town, and the seafront leading to the nearby hamlet of Shela. Imprecise dating comes in the form of observations made by Mark Horton, who noted "at least three ninth century sites at Lamu." Also, according to Horton, Lamu may have been a "pair of settlements during the twelfth and thirteenth centuries."[3]

Of these, one is located between the small settlement of Shela and Lamu town (at what today is the Lamu Ginners) and the other at the extreme northern end of the town at what was the old butchery. The final site, at Hidabu hill, currently the residence of the District Commissioner, confirms several oral traditions about the earliest settlement, and lends credibility to "The Chronicle of Lamu"—the only written documentation pertaining to early migrations.

"The Chronicle of Lamu" is suspect for several reasons. First it was collected by Abdalla bin Hamed, a newcomer and the Sultan of Zanzibar's appointed liwali at the end of the nineteenth century. His source was Shaibu Farji bin Hamed al-Bakari, a member of the patrician class whose own ancestry was Omani. The al Bakari (or al Bakri) are mentioned in another unattributed tradition as those who constructed the new town (see below). But in terms of the Lamu Chronicle, we know that Abdalla bin Hamed had intermarried into the then ruling class and can only assume that Shaibu Farji was a reliable elder. Written documentation from British sources indicate that Abdalla Hamed was instructed by colonial officials to collect Lamu's past history. His 1897 handwritten text was edited by William Hichens and published in *Bantu Studies* in 1938. As we shall see, the "Chronicle of Lamu" differs substantially from various versions of "The Pate Chronicle", especially in terms of the rivalries between these city-states.[4] But the following partial traditions collected by various British district commissioners also offer conflicting accounts of Lamu's pre-Colonial history.

Going back in time to pre-Islamic settlement, one administrator speculated that North Africans "once inhabited the town, the ruins of which are seen about 3/4 mile south of Lamu, [who] worshipped a gold cow 'Ngombe ya Thahabu.'" This, he thought, pointed to "the earlier immigrants being Phenicians [sic] as the present ruins [1912] are certainly those of Mohammedan people. The Phenicians traded and had a settlement in what is now Rhodesia from 1500 to 1000 B. C. It is not at all improbable that they had settlements along the East coast of Africa at which their ships watered . . . on their way south. What is now Lamu may have been on of those settlements."[5] This is, of course, a Eurocentric view and not given credence by contemporary elders.

Another partial narrative concerning pre-Islamic inhabitants is more relevant: they were "known as the Kinamte and lived in a town, now buried under the sand of Hidabu hill, the name of which was Mrio. The Kinamte now claim to have originated in Arabia [and] to have introduced the coconut. Legend has it that they were wrecked on the island [and] that their dhow's cargo consisted of seedling coconuts." Actually, the Kinamte were a group of residents in the stone houses of Lamu by the time British commissioners began collecting traditions. This official accepted that Mrio might have been "buried by a sand storm in a single night," but caustically added for 'Sodom and Gomorrah' reasons.[6]

Still another partial tradition collected by a British administrator leaves us unclear was to who the immigrants were but says Lamu was "the place of the quarrelsome people. Later inhabitants changed the name to Tambwi Ndeo, or in the Arabic language, 'town of the graves.' When the Arabs came they named it Lamu, which is LAMMU or 'blame' because people soon blamed themselves for having given away their town. The Swahili, who did not speak correctly rendered this as 'Amu'."[7]

But, according to some informants in the early 1930s, Lamu's name was originally "Kiwandio" until early settlers from Oman and Yemen arrived in the seventh century in the wake of the Prophet Mohammed's death. Among those who came were the Banu Lami section of "Il Bakri Arabs who built north of the former town [Hidabu] and gave their name to Lamu."[8] But a conflicting account of the Banu Lami, was that they were the "first Arabs . . . now called Yumbili and the town was at the place where today is the Jumma Mosque [north end of town]. Then came many of the El-Hasa, and their tribe was Bani [sic] Lami, and they made a town and called it Lamu, the name of their tribe." Following them "came the Bani Makhzumi and they are Kureish [a province in the northeastern Persian empire]." Then, in the year 128 [A.H.] was the arrival of Sayid Khalifa bin Mohamed bin Ali bin Hassan bin Ali in East Africa." (Identified as an al Hussein sharif from Hadramaut). And, "in 290 Hijriya arrived el Hasa Arabs in Mogadiscio and developed it . . . .[and then] went to Lamu."[9]

The Lamu Chronicle tells us that the first non-African settlers "were Arabs who came from Damascus. . . ."[10] Conversely, historian Randall Pouwels believes the first settlers from across the ocean may have come from Qarmation in the ninth or tenth centuries.[11] Abdul Nassir, whose male ancestor came to Lamu from Siyu in the late nineteenth century, recalled the legend of "Hassen bin Ali [who] arrived in Lamu over seven hundred years ago." Hassen bin Ali founded the town now buried under Hidabu Hill, when "Lamu was called Amu then before the name was changed."[12] Here current traditions reenforce the earlier claim of the 128 A.H. arrival of Sayid Khalifa bin Mohamed bin Ali bin Hassan bin Ali (the al Hussein sharif). Furthermore, the seven hundred years mentioned by Abdul Nassir crop up several times in other contexts, including the following story collected by John Clive in the early 1930s.

This account concerns war between the WaAmu and those who lived on Manda Island just across the bay, but unfortunately no dates are included. Interestingly, however, in a society where women were generally important only as sexual objects or in linking the patricians in marriage, one figures in this story as the bait and the trickster. "The cause of the dispute being certain Persian ceremonial accessories, which were coveted by the Arabs. These were a brass trumpet, a chair, a drum and a wooden dish, reserved for the ruler's food, and they had been brought from Persia. The Lamu Arabs tried to take them by force and, having failed, resorted to strategy. A particularly lovely Lamu woman was selected and instructed to ingratiate herself with the ruler of Manda.

This presented no undue difficulty and after allowing a suitable length of time to elapse, forty picked youths were chosen and sailed over one evening to Manda, where they were met outside the town wall by the lady. She disguised three of them in women's clothing, armed them and escorted them into the town and thence to the ruler's house. The remainder of the Lamu force remained concealed outside the town. The woman and her accomplices were challenged by the guard who, recognizing her and knowing that she was persona grata with the ruler, allowed them all to pass.

"Once inside the Arabs killed the ruler, stole the coveted trophies, slaughtered the guard and made their way out of town, joining their main body.

A hue and cry was raised and they were chased by the Manda Persians, who caught up with them as they reached the shore opposite Lamu town. Those Arabs who survived took to the water and, with two exceptions, all were drowned."

13

The story continues with the deaths of all the WaAmu involved, except "there is no record of the fate of the 'heroine.'" Since the WaAmu are telling the story, they have to justify the loss of their men. Thus, later, "to revenge the forty slain the people of Lamu" a force against the Persians of Manda returned with "the ornamentation of a mosque, which can still be seen in the Jamaa [sic] mosque at Lamu and which bears a date seven hundred years old."[13]

Beyond the narrative, we find more evidence legitimatizing some Afro-Arab claims to seven hundred years continuing residence in Lamu. Among the oral traditions I collected in 1980 were those that pertained to a book that had been kept in the Jumaa Mosque. This volume contained recorded genealogies of the al Bakri and al Maawyia families, linking them to Lamu for the seven hundred years that, according to Clive's tradition, is the same time period that the ornamentation from the Manda Mosque signifies. Both of these symbols have disappeared, although Clive claimed that the genealogies were still in the Jumaa Mosque in the early 1930s. Again, referring to the Lamu Chronicle, another tradition tells us the Arabs who first arrived from "Damascus" met with the Weyuni (locals) who assigned to the outsiders the name "Wayumbili." But, today, the Yumbili are the people who are said to be the original African inhabitants of the town and who were placed at the bottom of the social ladder where they were forced to wash the bodies of the dead. As a caste, they were also consigned to marry other Yumbili.[14] The following brief account also features the Yumbili as the original inhabitants. Furthermore, it leads us back to the earlier story of "Lammu or blame . . . for having given away the town".[15]

> A long time ago, when the Arabs arrived in Lamu, they found local people there. The Arabs were received with friendliness and they wanted to stay on. The local people, who are called Yumbili, offered to trade land for cloths the Arabs had in their possession. But the locals were not very smart—they knew nothing about the worth of the land. They marked out sections of cloth for sections of land. Before the trading was finished, the Arabs had all the land, and the Yumbili had all of the cloth. So it remained.

Persian descent crops up in some of the traditions pertaining to former residents of Manda and of Pate island. In addition, a few WaAmu people

14

claim Persian ancestry, based on the arrival of the Bani Makhzumi from Khurasan.[16] But no one of the accounts refer to Indians as early settlers. There are at least two reasons for this omission: first, those who were recalling the histories were people who regarded themselves as of Arab ancestry, and were justifying their own relationship to and descent from the Arab groups they describe. Secondly, Indian traders did not regard these east African port cities as their permanent homes. All were sent out by their families to establish trading networks.[17] Still they contributed to the gene pool of the WaAmu if not to the oral traditions.

By shifting to traveler Ibn Battuta and his 1330s visit to Mogadishu and Mombasa we can draw some parallels to Lamu at that time. The meal Ibn Battuta was served in fourteenth century Mogadishu might today be placed in front of a visitor in most Lamu homes: rice, chicken, meat, fish, and vegetables. Ibn Battuta mentioned butter which was probably ghee (clarified butter) and "curdled milk in another vessel with peppercorns, vinegar and saffron, green ginger and mangoes"—a yogurt chutney that may have originated in India as well. The people were dressed in loin-cloths, which were fashioned around the waist and "of drawers they were ignorant." Everyone he saw there "went barefoot."[18]

The first published account we have regarding Lamu as a Muslim town comes from a fifteenth century source. During his pilgrimage to Mecca in 1441, Abu el Mahassan encountered a Lamu qadi, who claimed to have been born in that port city in 1383 (780 A.H.) The qadi's reference to a "town buried under the sand" suggests that settlement at Hidabu Hill may predate Horton's thirteenth century hypothesis. By the fifteenth century, Lamu was ruled by a sultan whose wealth in part was derived from ambergris which was "thrown on the coast" (washed up by the waves). Clearly orthodox Islam was well established as the qadi was "well advanced and learned in religion and jurisprudence."[19] This is important because over time word spread into parts of East Africa that Swahili religious beliefs were synchronic. This was the case with slaves who were poorly instructed in the religion and with some outsiders who trekked in during the nineteenth century.

Another fifteenth century document refers to a king presiding over a town which was "almost buried in sand" that nevertheless abounded in banana trees. Taken together these two sources confirm a monarchy was in place, and that the early settlement was either disappearing or possibly part of it had already been covered in sand, leaving behind the second town that Horton speculates existed. Ibn Taghribirdi also mentions a mosque—that is Pwani, still in use—which carried an inscription dated 1370.[20]

Most of the coastal city-states were governed by a monarch by the fifteenth century. And in contradistinction to Ibn Battuta's observations in the fourteenth, the aristocracy had turned from loincloths and barefeet to imported finery. When Vasco de Gama stopped in Malindi he discovered the king wearing "a robe of damask trimmed with green satin, and a rich *touca* [turban]." Seated on two "cushioned chairs of bronze, beneath a round sunshade of crimson satin attached to a pole" the king was attended by a page who carried a "short sword in a silver sheath." Musicians performed on "two trumpets of ivory, richly carved which were the size of a man." These were the *siwas* that had ritualistic significance in city-states like Lamu and were found along the coast as far south as Kilwa.[21] In a little over a century material culture had taken on an Asian flavor in East Africa—an African "borrowing" indicating the influence of increasing numbers of Arab and Indian settlers.

In the fifteenth century, contact with the Mediterranean world included importation of Venetian beads. According to female informants, Venetian beads were used as currency. The Indian Ocean trade provided dates from Oman, silks from India, and possibly gold from Sofala to the south. Exports from Lamu included always, ivory, as well as ambrigris, rhino horn, skins, slaves, and mangrove poles.[22]

It is a matter of conjecture as to who built the fifteenth century pillar tombs. Their purpose also remain a mystery. Some speculate that they are African in origin. Others believe the concept and design came from the Ottoman Turks or from India. The tombs were probably associated with a local person of wealth or someone venerated as a saint.[23]

But all was not peaceful on the upper Kenya coast. Oromo Galla [an ethnic group and called Orma in Kenya] for instance, caused waves of out-migration when they attacked these island communities, or waves of in-migration when they attacked African settlements on the mainland. Although at times the Somali lived peacefully in the area of Shela on the northern tip of the island, on occasion they attacked Lamu town.[24] Lamu

16

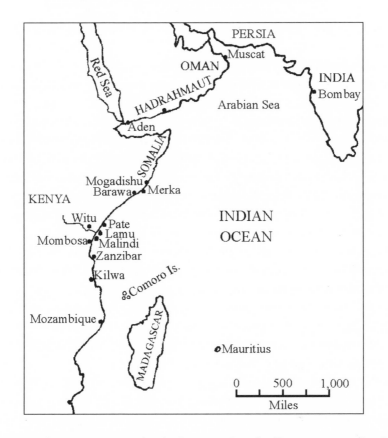

was not an important port city before or after the Portuguese arrived late in the fifteenth century. Mogadishu in the north and Kilwa in the south remained dominant. During the Portuguese occupation, Lamu's neighbor and rival, Pate, was the dominant island in the archipelago.[25]

Still in Lamu, the Portuguese found a "Moorish king" and "inhabitants" who are "for the most part Arab and regard themselves as more noble than those of Pate. . . ."[26] The Portuguese were never heavily represented on the northern coast. They did, however, attempt to establish a Christian foothold with "vicariates in Lamu as well as Faza and Siyu."[27] Conflicting accounts as to the Portuguese reception include one that suggests the king acquiesced and paid tribute without opposition. More likely, the islanders attempted an alliance with the Somali and Orma to keep the Portuguese out. But in the event they were unsuccessful and the island city-states were forced to bow to the superior armed forces of the invaders.[28]

The Portuguese did not exercise as heavy a hand over the northern coast as characterized their hold over Mozambique and vicinity. But they were considered tyrannical and racist in their rule over the Swahili.[29] Nevertheless, some Portuguese men took local women as concubines and possibly even wives. Perhaps a few women even converted to Christianity, if only for the period of the marriage. Some children were born of these alliances. During the Portuguese occupation, according to oral tradition, the Yumbili undergo yet another metamorphosis. "The Yumbili . . . claim descent from the intermarriage, as often as not compulsory of the Portuguese and Arab and African women."[30]

We know that Portuguese factors collected slaves that were shipped out of Lamu along with "amber, tortoise, shell, ivory . . . ." One Portuguese source noted that "in these lands [there are] many palm trees and fields of millet and rice. They build many ships and manufacture ropes which are made of fine straw [from coconut fiber]."[31]

At the end of the sixteenth century, the Ottoman Turks became a threat to Portuguese hegemony in the Mediterranean, the Indian Ocean and on the east coast of Africa. They raided the coast in 1542-43. In 1552, the Turks sacked Muscat, overthrowing the Nabahany dynasty (some of whose descendants ruled Pate), and by 1585, sailed into "East Africa under the command of Amir Ali Bey." Pate and Faza (a town also located on Pate island) surrendered to the Turks.[32] Then the king of Lamu offered protection to the Portuguese, who fled to that island. The Pate king returned home after the Portuguese surrendered to the Turks, and the alliance with Lamu ended.

Turkish soldiers (and no doubt accompanied by WaPate men) arrived in Lamu town, attacked one of the houses in which the Portuguese were resident, and took them along with the king as prisoners. The fate of the king is unknown—although current traditions state that all were killed.[33] The Turks maintained that they only wanted Portuguese cargo and a ship, but they stayed in Lamu from 1585-87.

We have no documentation regarding the Turkish occupation during the two year interlude before the Portuguese returned. In a show of gratitude they installed the wife of Lamu's king "on a throne" where she pledged her allegiance to the Europeans—along with the annual tribute that the WaAmu had been forced to pay earlier. But Portuguese gratitude extended only so far: those Muslims who were "guilty of murdering Christians" were punished, including loss of some heads that were "then taken to Goa." Or so the story goes. We are still dependent on traditions, even if written down by Portuguese sources.[34]

What the Portuguese documents fail to reveal is that Indian merchants were pushing the Omani "to extend trade" in places like Lamu (and elsewhere in East Africa) where "the resident Omani communities were resisting Portuguese domination." Thus the Omani overthrow of the Portuguese was based on economic as well as political motivations.[35] When the Portuguese empire in northern coastal East Africa crumbled in 1729, they left behind little beyond the memory of their occupation and a few half-caste children. Further south, they presided over the destruction of the gold trade from Sofala to Kilwa, which then caused the decline of that major Swahili civilization.[36] Later in the century the Dutch attempted to acquire a foothold on the northern coast. They made an unsuccessful approach to Pate island, which was still dominant in the Lamu archipelago, but heavy winds combined with the narrow passageway prevented entry to the channel.[37] For most of the rest of the eighteenth century the islands were free from outside interference. The French and the Americans traded with the northern coastal communities, including Lamu. Ivory and animals skins were the major trade items of interest to both. "Amerikani" cloth began to compete with the rougher hewn Indian cotton and was much in demand in Lamu. The Americans wanted to trade but the French intermittently attempted to establish hegemony in the city-states of Mombasa and Pate from the 1770s and into the 1860s.[38] From the time the Portuguese withdrew from the north of Mozambique, the Omanis expanded their power in Zanzibar and Mombasa especially. (In the 1730s the Mazrui arrived as appointees of the Omani imanate, and soon became ambitious for power in their own right. Mombasa moved from a colonial outpost to become the personal domain of that aggressive family). The Mombasa Mazrui and their allies on the northern Kenya coast engaged the men of Lamu in much of the warfare that occupied them during the eighteenth century.

In the political realm sources indicated that one leader held sway over the town for a certain period, perhaps as long as three or four centuries. Despite the written documentation, some traditions still being recited suggest otherwise. Many older residents of Lamu believe that the government was in the hands of a group of elders who represented all of the stone house dwellers. By the end of the eighteenth century, these homes of the elite extended beyond the area of the fort, and decisions regarding the town were made at the Yumbe, a palace that crumbled into ruins sometime before the British established a permanent presence in Lamu in the 1880s.[39]

The Yumbe was located on a winding sand path back from the seafront in what was then the extreme northern end of town. It was enclosed on both sides by a wall of stone houses, and beyond them mud huts covered with thatch roofs. The free but poor, and some of the artisans who were also slaves lived in these huts.[40] Lamu town was completely surrounded by a stone wall which, as time went by, and the port city grew, had to be extended. Reports on material culture in coastal East Africa may have some relationship to life in Lamu in the 1770s. In the Comoro Islands, the Turks had heavily influenced male attire, including turbans. The opulence of the rulers in Comoro was mirrored in Zanzibar as well. Porcelain, gold and silver jewelry, and Persian carpets dominated the homes of the wealthy, which were full of slaves carrying on a multiplicity of domestic tasks.[41] But what of the women in this period? Charis Waddy speculates that in Muslim port cities, women married sailors or other itinerant visitors (Ibn Battuta married women in many places he visited), and then when the men moved on, they were divorced.[42] Thus the custom of temporary marriage in Lamu may have its origins in early coastal history (although some argue that this practice of briefly taking a wife without registering the marriage was carried in by the Ithnasharia traders).

Waddy believed that the Persian influence of the eighth century Abbasid dynasty "severely restricted" the movement of women and resulted in the organization of the harem. The separation of the sexes may have reached the East African coast with the introduction of Islam, only to be abandoned before being reintroduced later.[43] According to Waddy, women did not veil and as late as the fourteenth century were uncovered down to their waists. By the 1770s, women in the Comoro Islands were in seclusion, however, and women in Zanzibar in the nineteenth century were said to be jealously watched by their husbands.

We know that wealthy families had slaves who were responsible for the care of the children. We know, too, that children were the joy of their mothers, and, in the African context, we can assume that fathers played almost no role in the lives of their daughters upbringing, while they served as models and teachers for their sons.

Relations with Pate remained voluble. The two rival island city-states may have occasionally formed alliances when under siege from outsiders, but their political relations were often strained, if not marked by armed conflict. In the middle of the eighteenth century, oral traditions mention a Pate sultan, who was born to a Lamu woman. He spent much of his time on that island instead of Pate, where he was ruler, and was said to have "loved Lamu very much"—so much so that he also married a Lamu woman. But love for the woman and her town did not preclude continual drains on the treasury. Pate sultans demanded taxes on grains and goods from the WaAmu throughout this period. This policy was heavily resented, especially by the patricians on whom the taxes fell most heavily.

Still, the Lamu Chronicle joined another late eighteenth century Pate king in matrimony with a Lamu woman. King Bwana Bakari wa Bwana Mkuu took his wife to Pate, where she bore him a daughter. When she came of age, this daughter was "wed by Bayaye wa Shiye and begat Fumo Luti wa Bayaye." By then a new king ruled in Pate but he ordered Fumo Luti wa Bayaye be chosen as his successor. After his death, however, the king was succeeded by someone else. Then "the men of Lamu went to Pate to assist their kinsmen; and war went on for a long time."

In fact, and according to the Chronicles of both Lamu and Pate, this war led to the major and decisive battle between the two island communities—the Battle of Shela (1813-14). Each turned to outside sources for support. The WaAmu sought and received aid and troops from the Sultan of Oman.[44] Earlier, in 1801, and unknown to the WaAmu or the Mombasa Mazrui, the Sultan of Pate had thought to strengthen his hand through an agreement with the British. Cleverly, he requested that they build a fort "in return for half of the island's produce." The British counsel at Bombay evidenced interest but the proposal was turned down by his government, leaving the wedge open on the northern coast for the Omani/Mazrui/Pate conflict to be played out with Lamu as pawn/participant in the next few decades.[45]

21

Siyu women sitting on the carved chairs described by John Haggard.
Courtesy of the National Museums of Kenya

Chapter Two

War and Material Culture after Lamu's Ascendancy
on the Northern Kenya Coast

"Every nation hath its set time"
The Qur'an

By the beginning of the nineteenth century British interests had expanded from India to the Persian Gulf and to coastal East Africa. Having been approached by the ruler of Pate regarding the possibility of working out an economic agreement, an officer at the Bombay office developed an interest in aspects of coastal East Africa. Anxious to learn about exports and imports, and the prices of assorted items, he requested that naval officer Captain Thomas Smee sail to several East African ports and report to Bombay on subjects ranging from trade to houses that had been "built of masonry" where the "inhabitants now reside in dwellings of much meaner construction." Smee was charged with surveying the places he visited, and with "reporting the current prices in the local currency with the equalivance [sic] value in Bombay rupees . . . of woolens and metals, the produce of England, such as how much more trade Britain can profitably conduct." And the rates of customs duties at each port.[1]

Earlier, in 1800, another British sailor had investigated the ports of Mogadishu and Barawa on the Somali coast, noting that clothes are imported from "Gulph [sic] of Kutch, Moccha, Mukula and Judda [sic]. Dates, rice, cotton cloths, tin" are traded along with "copper, ghee, myrrh, coffee, elephants teeth." Similar goods would have been going in and out of Lamu, as was the case ten years later, when Smee visited Mogadishu. The houses he wrote, "resemble those seen in the towns on the coast of

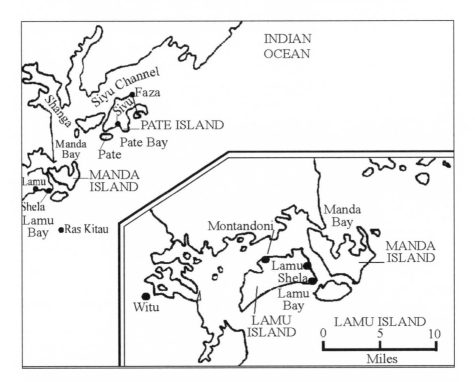

Arabia and Persia and are apparently built of stone and mud of a low square form with small doors."[2]

By 1810, British officer Lt. Hardy sailed into Pate Harbor where he observed that, "this part of East Africa appears rich in all the charm and luxuriant vegetation and striking contrast with the barren coast north of Juba. Nearby islanders came to trade and "were anxious to possess whatever they saw. They begged to be presented with muskets, pistols, powders, cloth, rice. . . . After much trouble I pacified with a little coarse cloth, some cutlery and sugared water of which they are extravagantly fond." Hardy also reported on the "rivalry of two cousins" and trouble brewing in Pate as a result.

But Hardy was unaware of the recurring conflicts revolving around Lamu, Pate, Siyu, and the Mazrui at Mombasa. The Mazrui were at odds with Sultan Said of Muscat, who wanted to reestablish his hegemony over that large and prosperous city-state. The Siyu leaders, on occasion, took the side of Pate, with whom they shared the island; and, with the Mazrui when it suited their purpose. The Lamu leadership was openly receptive to Omani friendship and harbored the Sultan's soldiers, possibly even welcoming the Sultan himself, if he came to nearby Manda Island soon after beginning his reign in Oman.[3]

Oman was nominally overlord in both the island of Zanzibar and the port of Kilwa. Custom duties in Zanzibar were heavy. The French who were active in the slave trade circumvented that island in favor of Kilwa on the mainland. A dissident member of Said's family in Oman, grandson Saif, hoped to curry the favor of the French but was rejected. He then turned his attention to trying to oust the Omani Liwali (governor) of Zanzibar. Unsuccessful in that attempt, Sayf was exiled to Lamu, where he died a few years later. Lamu, still under the control of the locals, was already settled by Omanis, who were a significant enough presence to act as jailers for the outlawed grandson of the Omani ruler.[4] In accepting Sayf at this time, the leadership in Lamu displayed a pro-Omani perspective that served them well when they summoned help for their war with Pate-Mombasa.

Problems with succession to the Pate sultanship brought matters to a head sometime preceding Hardy's visit to Pate island. The cousins to whom Hardy referred, were the claimants to the throne. One of them was Fumo Luti wa Bayaye, the son of the Lamu woman and grandson of King Bwana Bakari wa Bwana Mkuu. The conflict "which went on for a long time" broke out between the men of Lamu and the people of Pate in early 1807.[5] Abdalla bin Hamed al-Mazrui came from Mombasa ostensibly to reconcile the factions. Fumo Luti wa Bayaye took office as chief of Pate, and the Lamu men returned home. Soon thereafter, a group of men in Pate "seized . . . Fumo Luti and bound him and took him to Mombasa and put him to death." Another WaPate was installed, but was seen in both Pate and Lamu as a pawn of the Mombasa Mazrui family. Then, according to Lamu oral traditions, the men of Lamu began to build a fort behind the walls of the town. Drawing on the "Chronicle of Lamu" which is the only Lamu document bearing on events at the time, the Afro-Arabs of Mombasa conspired with the WaAmu men to build the fort—the purpose of which was "a guileful scheme." The idea was to put Abdalla bin Hamed Mazrui, who was a "constant companion to the new ruler of Pate," in Lamu as a spy, reporting back to Pate, with whom the Mazrui main-

26

tained the forced alliance. Retaliation against Lamu and her defeat were behind this strategy.[6]

What the Mazrui leaders of Mombasa and their Pate allies had not counted on was Bwana Zaidi, then a leading Lamu elder. Bwana Zaidi tricked Abdalla bin Hamed Mazrui into admitting his treachery by way of a set of letters written by Bwana Zaidi, but purportedly sent from Pate. When Abdalla bin Hamed responded to the letters, they were delivered to Bwana Zaidi, who "had done all this without advising any man. . ."[7]

The "Chronicle of Lamu" mentions two separate factions during this time: those who supported Bwana Zaidi; and those who opposed his plans for war with Pate and Mombasa. One group favored dealing directly with the Mazrui to deflect their alignment with Pate. The other faction, led by Bwana Zaidi, called for direct confrontation with the enemy. The Suudi faction went to Mombasa, where they asked for protection against the WaPate, while the Zena faction prepared for war after Bwana Zaidi caught the Mazrui envoy in his trap. When the Suudi bloc returned from Mombasa, Bwana Zaidi revealed the letters to both groups. The joint response was to order the Mombasan away. Abdalla Mazrui went directly to Pate and that "was the beginning of the Battle of Shela."[8]

Still according to oral tradition, Bwana Zaidi was of Yemeni ancestry but his father's line had been in Lamu for a long time before he rose to become the most prominent of the Lamu elders during the Battle of Shela.[9] Bwana Zaidi lived in a stonehouse in Mkumoni, the area inhabited by members of the upper class who now referred to themselves as *waungwana*.

The town leaders assembled at the Yumbe palace and agreed to continue building the fort, making plans for the defense of Lamu as well as for the forthcoming war against the joint forces of Pate and Mombasa. Recognizing they were outnumbered, the elders agreed to request aid from the Sultan knowing he was anxious to see the Mazrui defeated. Here the Indians became invaluable. They had relatives living and trading in Muscat and Zanzibar and were known for their "cash and carry" policy. The small local Indian community could be counted on for cash to pay for weapons and gun powder. In Zanzibar, the Bhattia Topan family may have provided the ships as well as some men to help Lamu in her war against the joint Mombasa/Pate armies.[10]

While the dhow containing Lamu messengers, including the then

Omani governor, Hamed Mustaha, sailed into the Indian Ocean, others worked to secure homes, to stockpile existing weapons and powder. They put smiths (probably slaves) to work making cutlasses and knives. *Mtepes*, the small hand sewn, matted sailing ships, which usually carried trade items up and down the coast, were prepared as men-of-war. These boats were close hulled and could sail effectively against the winds, especially as they usually hugged the coastline. The *mtepe* were built in considerable numbers in Pate, Siyu, and in Lamu. In preparation for war, as many as possible were assembled by the opposing sides.[11] There may have been anywhere from forty to sixty *mtepes* locally owned.

During much of 1812 the men carried on their preparations, including emptying storerooms in which to place their women and children for safety. Rape and assault were not unknown and had been a factor in earlier skirmishes between the various island communities.[12] Prominent in the preparations for war was Bwana Zaidi. According to family legend, Bwana Zaidi poured a circle of gunpowder around himself, his wife, and his children in the second story courtyard of their home. If Lamu failed to win, he said, he would rather "they all burn up together than be taken prisoners by the Mombasa and Pate people." "We are going to win, or die."[13]

The war began in 1813—sometime between January and March. The first battle ended in a draw. Within a few weeks a second and decisive battle was fought resulting in the loss of at least eighty four freemen of Pate and unknown numbers of slaves. Both battles were fought outside the walls of Shela, a small community of people from Manda who, according to legend, had been driven from their homes by the WaPate.

The combined forces of the attackers were large, coming as they did in eighty boats and spreading out over the southern and eastern ends of the island.[14] The Lamu Chronicle played down the Omani participation in the Battle of Shela. There are at least two possibilities for this. The Omanis may have been so integrated into Lamu by the late nineteenth century when the Chronicle was compiled, that those who fought and stayed on were considered Afro-Arabs in retrospect. The Chronicle may be accurate in stating that the Omani's arrived after the battle of Shela, although it is difficult to understand how the smaller Lamu contingent could have won against the combined forces of Mombasa and Pate without Omani reinforcements.

Because the WaAmu feared the Mazrui would attack again, another mission was sent to Oman, urging the Sultan to send more troops for garrisoning in Lamu. Gratitude was overwhelming and "the men of Lamu built for him [Sultan Said] a fortress and [he] placed his men there and appointed a governor with . . . a total of five hundred men; and they remained there."[15]

With this page in Lamu's history we begin the political ascendancy of the Omanis, followed on their heels by the British, joined briefly by the Germans, but consistently dominated by the aristocracy who were already in place by 1813. At this juncture, too, Lamu began her rise to prominence on the northern coast while Pate's eminence faded into memory.[16]

Earlier relations between Britain and Oman need to be discussed since they ultimately affect Lamu. Back in 1798 the BuSaid government of Oman concluded a treaty with Britain which, in turn, led to a policy of increasing interference with Omani rulers until the family was split into two separate factions—one in Oman and the other in Zanzibar. Britain's early interest in Oman was based on her extension into the Persian Gulf. Muscat was a thriving port city. The Omani navy was considered supreme in the Persian Gulf area. Piracy along the coast was a thorn in the side to British shippers as well as to the British navy. An alliance with Oman, it was hoped, would mean greater strength in dealing with the pirates. Very soon after the 1798 treaty, Britain embarked on her mission to end the slave trade throughout the world in which she traveled.[17] Oman was a major player in this trade—as were the East African possessions, including Lamu.[18]

From early in the century, Said became increasingly involved in developing his East African possessions, concentrating his interests on Zanzibar and Pemba where he augmented cultivation of the clove plantations. Since clove production was labor intensive, slaves were required in increasing numbers to fill the labor demands as the numbers of plantations multiplied on both Pemba and Zanzibar. With peace finally a reality, Lamu's wealthy were also able to rapidly expand the plantation economy on the mainland. This required increasing numbers of slaves, most coming from the central African areas of today's Malawi and

Mozambique. These slaves were marched to the interior, loaded on ships and then ostensibly carried to Zanzibar, where they were either sold into the market there, or transshipped to the northern city-states or elsewhere in the Indian Ocean world.[19] The profits from customs flowed into the Omani coffers in Zanzibar; the profits from the Omani-owned plantations flowed directly into the hands of the Sultan and his countrymen.

Prosperity blossomed in Lamu, including among some of the Sultan's subjects who avoided contributing to his enrichment by shipping contraband slaves in directly, thus avoiding the customs levies in Zanzibar. In 1822 Britain pressured Sultan Said, still residing in Oman, to sign the Moresby Treaty, the first in a series of treaties that eventually ended the iniquitous slave trade, and later slavery, in the Sultan's domains. The Moresby Treaty required the Sultan to stop all trade in slaves to European colonies—especially to British-dominated India; and forbade the sale of slaves to "Christians" (Europeans). Of equal importance, through the Moresby Treaty, Britain finally gained a consulate in Zanzibar "for the purpose of having intelligence and watching the traffic in slaves with Christian nations."[20]

Also, through the Moresby agreement, Britain could stop her competition from engaging in the slave trade, and also turn a profit from trade with the Sultan's East African possessions. At this point Britain did not have imperial ambitions in the area. By acquiescing to British designs, Sultan Said inadvertently initiated Lamu's eminent decline, just as he aided in her ascent.

The Omani community in Lamu began to grow appreciably. Omani immigrants came from various parts of that country and joined Omanis already settled in Lamu, including the Jahadhmy and the al Busaidi.[21] As was the custom in the past strangers arriving on dhows were accommodated in the homes of relatives, in mosques, and in the homes of people who hailed from the same country.

One group of people who were brought in is somewhat elusive in terms of total numbers, how many stayed, and what happened to their progeny. These are the Baluchi soldiers who were the backbone of Sultan Said's army. There were never more than four hundred Baluchi mercenaries in the Sultan's East African possessions. (One source indicates that even in Zanzibar, where they were in the largest number, there were fifty-sixty

Baluchi in 1815; thirty in 1843; and about eighty between 1848-56.[22]) Some Baluchi were stationed in Lamu from about 1813 to at least 1824—long enough to have fathered considerable numbers of children during their stay. And, gossip—taking the form of oral tradition—suggested that some prominent members of the old families were actually descendants of Baluchi soldiers.[23] Among the scarce documentation concerning the Baluchi soldiers are references to them as slave traders while they were in Lamu. One old informant remembered that they made excellent halwa. At least one man recalls hearing that the elders contacted Sultan Said and asked him to remove his Baluchi forces. This, according to tradition, was accomplished forthwith and was associated with undefined "immoral acts."[24]

Said's liwalis brought in Omani administrators to assist all who came to Lamu town in order to begin trade, to seek work, or to stake out land where they established plantations. The earliest record regarding administrative disputes in Lamu is a document dated 1825 in which Said sent Saleh bin Abdulla bin Saleh as his liwali. Two "cadis [sic] Said bin Sasir and Muhidin" approached the liwali regarding a controversy over rents that were owed on shops jointly owned by "Binta Khalaf, the widow of Saif bin Hamed" and "her sister, Fatuma binti Khalaf."[25] (Women's properties were always handled by men in their families).

East African society at the beginning of the nineteenth century was freer than that experienced at home. Women "in particular lived a much freer life." The "matriarchy" for which some of African societies are known, and which was transported to the coastal areas by slaves from the interior "rubbed off on the Arabs" in a few generations. African art forms also made their way back to Oman: Liesl Graz described a "Zanzibar wedding" in Muscat: the dancing was "pure African" and the "music was as African as the dance."[26]

The world of the *wanawake* [kiSwahili for women] maintained many of the African traditions that slave women brought with them into marriage, according to Carol Eastman. Boys, however, followed the Muslim "Arabness" of fathers—even though they were raised in the same households as their sisters.[27] The exception to this interpretation is in marriage patterns established by the Arab men for daughters born of these relationships. Because of the stigma concerning African wives (mostly concubines) as sexually knowledgeable and of easy virtue, daughters were raised according to strict codes including class barriers erected by their Afro-Arab fathers, which distanced them psychologically, if not physically, from the slave society of many of their mothers.[28] Furthermore the Arab custom of brothers binding with and caring for their sisters served to reenforce "Arabness" in sisters. This practice was thought to help boys grow into patriarchs when they married and produced their own families.[29]

In the narrow, sunshaded streets of Muscat, slave women roamed about freely. So too, did slave women in Lamu move about openly. As to the *ideal* relations between men and women and attitudes pertaining to slaves, we rely on the writings of the renowned Swahili poetess, Mwana Kupona.[30] Mwana Kupona was born in Siyu of a Lamu mother. In her mature years Mwana Kupona lived in Lamu. (Despite the internecine wars, intermarriage and movement between residents of these city states continued).

To the Swahili, poetry was another mode of keeping alive the historical past. According to one authority, the "women of Lamu, in the past as well as in the present, have been the custodians of Swahili poetry; in fact some of the best verse literature has been by the pen of women," and Mwana Kupona's *Utendi* is cited as the finest example extant.

Ailing, and expecting not to live much longer, Mwana Kupona dictated her advice to her daughter while they were living in Lamu. The verse is in KiSwahili but written in Arabic script.[31] In her poem, she touched on social distinction for girls: "learn how to behave before people of rank when you see them at any place hasten to pay them respect" and "Do not associate with slaves except during household affairs they will draw you into disgrace. . . . Go not about with foolish people . . . as to persons who are immodest avoid any contact with them."

Mwana Kupona referred to a charm that she passed on to her daughter—one that should be cherished. People often wore small amulets that contained verses from the Qur'an. In this case, Mwana Kupona strung a necklace of pearls and coral to mark her daughter "as a beautiful woman." Lamu women were said to be especially beautiful and beguiling, but modest in their comportment. Thus she counselled "be of good behavior with a discreet tongue that you be as one beloved wherever you enter." We can

32

read something concerning the fragility of marriage relations at that time (and continuing until the present) when Mwana Kupona advised her daughter to let the husband leave without interference; and when he returned "greet him then set ready for him a place of ease-taking. When he rests do not betake yourself off, draw near to him, caress him . . . let him not lack for someone to fan him."

Mwana Kupona's advice aimed towards keeping the husband at home and the marriage intact: "be like me, your mother I was married ten years yet we did not quarrel one single day. . . . we did not abase our mutual respect all the days that we lived together." Finally, "Read, all you women so that you may understand that you may bear no blame in the presence of God the Highest. Read, you who are sprouts of wheat. Obey your men-folks so that you may not be touched by the sorrows of the after-life or of this" (such as replacement by another or divorce). "She who obeys her husband hers are honour and charm wherever she shall go her fame is published abroad."[32]

Although the later editions of this poem refer to the *shiraa* [an umbrella like covering that upperclass women traveled under in public], it is highly unlikely that it was in existence and in use in Lamu in mid-nineteenth century. The poem was revised over time. As styles changed, particularly as they involved increasing modesty, revisions in the poem reflected change in customs. In fact, the *shiraa* seems to have been used off and on in Lamu from sometime in late nineteenth century and into the late 1940s.[33]

While it is important to keep in mind the bias of most British observers, not to speak of their relative ignorance of female behavior, Sir John Kirk's observations reflect a modicum of accuracy. Kirk believed that the women followed the sort of advice proffered by Mwana Kupona while their husbands were present. But when the Arab husband was away on business the "wives kick up high jinks both in his house and out of it."[34] Colonel C. P. Rigby, a most unsympathetic observer, noted in the early 1860s that the women in Zanzibar never went abroad by day. They went out at night, always veiled at this time, accompanied by their slaves. While they were influential, he agreed with Kirk that they were "much given to intrigue and love adventure."[35] A Frenchman resident in Lamu in 1878, referred to those he encountered as "depraved." Mwana Kupona's advice against following the ways of slaves suggests that M. Greffulhe, who lived in a Lamu stone house and possibly owned slaves himself, described these women who had much to gain and little to lose from depravity, since they had no control over their bodies where owners were concerned.[36]

Negative attitudes toward women are also contained in the works of some Swahili poets. According to Lyndon Harries, "women are usually less respected, if not actually despised. . . . "Ye, do not commit the (evil) work of despising your mother, remember how she brought you up: in two ways she nursed you." The poet continued to talk about the roles of mothers in providing food, dress, and "all that she has done for you." Women, Harries wrote, "are at best treated with condescending friendliness [and they were] confined to their quarters unless their husbands give them consent to leave."[37]

Matters of hygiene were also addressed in Swahili poetry. Shabeen Robert called on women to keep "Your home tidy, No dirt nor dust be found. Insects and creatures should never in it find abode."[38] These instructions would be practically impossible to carry out entirely. In these island communities people coexisted with bedbugs, fleas, roaches the size of small mice. Rats inhabited storage areas and possibly even the homes of the poor at times. Bats and birds entered freely through the open windows of Swahili stone houses (where upperclass women lived). Cats with mange, an assortment of illnesses, and full of insects, jumped through the open windows at night, often landing on furnishings and clothing. Hyenas frequented outlying areas, feeding off the garbage thrown openly into the streets, and carrying their own assortment of pests and insects. A household containing numbers of slaves and dedicated to the proposition of eradicating "insects and creatures" could accomplish this feat—but only under the sternest and most dedicated of mistresses.

A nineteenth century visitor to Lamu noted the problem of insects burrowing into the locally made coconut frond furnishings. He described "an amusing little sideshow of a woman, generally an old one, the household drudge, appearing with a bedstead of wood and skin or rope on her head, and after wading a short distance [into the Lamu Bay] chucking it down legs upwards, and then weighing it down with a few chunks of coral to prevent it from being washed away; it was to kill bugs and lice."[39]

Women from mid-nineteenth to early in the twentieth century wore long flimsy Turkish style pants that fastened at their ankles. In Zanzibar, to which Lamu was closely linked, they liked silver ankle bracelets and bangles, and gold pieces in their pierced noses. Shoes were wooden and many were coated with layers of silver. Gold coin necklaces were worn by female members of Sultan Said's family. Often these women wore gold chains around their heads, from which coins danced on their fore-heads.

Richard Burton claimed he never saw the aristocratic women in Zanzibar, but he was told in the 1850s the current cosmetics for women were "oil, kohl, henna and saffron." Lamu women probably did not have access to the expensive jewelry of upperclass women in Zanzibar, although wealthy Indian women wore heavy gold and silver jewelry. To expunge the stench that wafted up from the streets below, and to cover body odor women burned incense, sprinkled rose water, and applied the essence of sandelwood.[40]

In mid-century, Zanzibari men dressed much like those in Oman. Considering Lamu's tendency to borrow material culture and fashions from elsewhere, the styles would have been much the same for the wealthy. Men wore the fez, itself borrowed from the Ottomans, turbans on their shaved heads, or skull caps. Arab style long and heavy coats that reached below the knees were held in place with a silk sash. In the sash was the traditional Omani dagger *[khanjar]* often with a jewelled or gold-en handle. The synethis with Africa called for the "shield most Arabs carry . . . of rhinoceros hide" slung over the shoulder while a "long light spear completes the equipment."[41]

A visitor to the principal shopping district in Lamu in the late twenti-eth century would see sights that were characteristic of Muscat and other Muslim cities earlier in time. Narrow streets were lined on each side by dark, recessed shops most of which measured about ten feet across. In the southern end of town small platforms still dot the street, standing out as they do from the shops behind. Sunshades made of mats overhang some of these shops, again especially in the southern end of town.[42]

Shops and skill in making specific crafts were handed down to sons and grandsons. Tanning leather and the design of crude sandals was one craft practiced in all the islands of the Lamu archipelago. Lamu was noted for the creativity of its silversmiths, especially in the making of knives: "All the people round Lamu wear dirks [knives] and ghastly gashes they give each other with them, a heavy one will take a man's arm off with a blow; they are never used for stabbing, in bush fighting they are invaluable."[43] Hand embroidered kofia (Muslim caps for men) were made in Lamu and sold locally as well as exported. Indian goldsmiths trained slaves to do the work but kept the business tightly under their control.

After the advent of the clove plantations in Zanzibar and Pemba mat bags for storing and shipping became a big business in Lamu.[44] In addition to their use for shipping, they were decorated, sewn, and used by local women for pocketbooks. Men and women used local dyes to color branches of the duom palm, which were woven into rugs and bedcovers. Poor people almost always had a woven palm mat on their dirt floors. Most mosques used locally made mats to cover their floors rather than the expensive oriental carpets which did not long survive the sand, dust and dirt which characterized Lamu in this period.

Mangrove poles were used in house construction and often painted bright red with a local vegetable dye. From early in the nineteenth century, the sale of these poles rested in the hands of Lamu merchants. Wood from Lamu was purchased to provide planking for decks in slave ships—not only Arab dhows, but also French owned ships outfitted for the trade.[45]

Ivory from the mainland, mostly provided by the ethnic group, the Pokomo, continued to render profits for local merchants. Lamu merchants acted as middlemen for Somali and other ethnic groups from the mainland. Cattle and hides were an important and profitable export commodity. In 1850 an American merchant came into Lamu port to trade. "It is quite a large place" the captain reported. On this occasion he was unable to load the skins he sought, but departed with "22 husks of ivory." In the following decade, a Zanzibar official noted that items "of import" to the East African coast included "opium" along with cotton cloth, china glass, "12,000 arms and 7,000 beads." Opium continued to be a popular import. A British traveler mentioned "many in Lamu smoking opium" in the early twentieth century. By 1864 Lamu was referred to as "the commercial capital of the District."[46] It is important to note that, whether tied to Zanzibar through transshipment of trade items, or as a free port, Lamu was part of a trade network that spread all the way to Muscat, Bombay, Mukala,

Madagascar, the Mascerene Islands, the Comoros, and indirectly even with the United States. Also trade continued up to the Red Sea, and later extended down to South Africa.

The American consul at Zanzibar reported on a ship that took out $8,830 worth of goods in 1888, but no specific items are listed. Cottons worth $3,100 were traded in Lamu along with "specie" valued at $2,750. Orchella (for dyes), millet, and sesame (for oil) were all exported to Europe from Lamu's seafront.[47] Wealth was accruing, especially to planters and traders, thus allowing many of the families to compete with each other in conspicious consumption.

When an important event occurred in Lamu, such as a wedding, the Swahili New Year [*Siku ya Mwaka*], or feasts celebrating the end of Ramadan and the end of the pilgrimage to Mecca, musicians playing the carved *siwa* led a procession through the narrow Lamu streets. The *siwa* was made by local artisans by hollowing out the ivory tusk of an elephant, or by casting in bronze. When blown, it produced a long, eerie blare like a ram's horn.[48]

Clans built their houses and occupied separate neighborhoods [*mta*] of the town. During the major Omani immigration, they intermarried and moved directly into their wives' neighborhoods, often into their homes. Two documents, dated respectively 1860 and 1885, refer to gifts of houses made to Omani relatives of the Sultans. First, Said bin Hilal wrote Majid of "the gift to Binti Said bin Hameed [sic] from Lamu woman Binti Khalaf bin Mohamed bin Khalaf Ejashmia, a member of the "Elmawhali" family.[49] Then, in 1885, the children of "Ahmad bin Mohamed bin Athman El Mazruian" documented that "our house situated in Lamu, given our master Seyed bin Sultan given to Said bin Hamed bin Hamis Elbuzaidi [sic] a true gift and proved before us."[50] Later, Arabs from the Hadramaut and Indians occupied special sections of the town, but gifts of houses to them were not forthcoming from the old families.

The old market, where slaves were sold along with produce and livestock, was located near the seafront. The fort was nearby, and next to it was Pwani Mosque. The butchery was located at the extreme northern end of town (although some families butchered in their side yards). Gardens of flowers and tembu [betel nut] helped break the monotony of an otherwise continuous flow of stone houses. These houses were made of coral stone, dirt, and lime mortar. Inside were rough lime plaster walls and ceilings, which were held up by locally cut mangrove poles. The one constant was the fine dust caused by the lime plaster, which flaked almost continuously.

The two-or-three story houses found in Muscat during the period before the Omanis arrived were similar to those built in Lamu. Some old Gujarati residents in Mombasa hold firm to the belief that this type of architecture originated there. Later, the building styles were carried to Oman by Indian residents, as they were also brought to Lamu (and coastal East Africa) by Indians from Gujarat.[51] According to an authority on eighteenth and nineteenth Lamu architecture, many "features of the Swahili town show similarities to prototypes in Arabia, Iran, India, and other regions of the Indian Ocean." Archaeologist James Kirkman attributed some characteristics of the stone house arch to India.[52] As usual in port cities, a combination of immigrants over time influenced the town itself, and its architecture. In the southern end of town, and in areas of the seafront, African huts with coconut frond roofs housed the poor. When the city was walled, these houses (or those that preceded them), were located outside.[53]

Cemeteries were also located outside the town. In time, each religious group had its own. The Sunni Muslims share a large, open cemetery to the south of town. From the late nineteenth century and on, slaves and their descendants were buried near the *waungwana* [upperclass]. Some informants claim that before the arrival of the British, their bodies were thrown on the seafront and left to wash away. Christians, those who came in from the late nineteenth century, were put to rest in their private plots on the northern end of the island.[54]

The current stonehouses in Lamu were built from mid-eighteenth century and on. Most of the houses were originally one story. As the family grew in numbers, the houses grew in size. Since they were all interconnected (like townhouses elsewhere) the only direction in which a house could expand was up. Often married daughters were accommodated by building a separate apartment onto the preexisting structure—always going up. Even today informants talk about "going up" which means a third story addition, often across the open courtyard from the kitchen.[55]

In the early 1800s, an immigrant would have walked from the seafront into a narrow passageway enclosed by houses on both sides. At the dark entrance were usually stone seats on which men conversed or children played. A long flight of steps led up to the house proper, providing security for the occupants inside.

The interior design of Lamu houses are not identical but almost all have large open courtyards. Some contain a storeroom on one side of the courtyard. Almost all stone houses have an open kitchen area, which traditionally was covered with coconut frond thatch. Beyond the courtyard, leading back into the interior of the house, is a central room in which the family eats (historically women and children ate separately from the men), and where the women and children spend much of their day.

Leading off the main room are bedrooms and baths including the enclosed pit latrine and large coral and limestone tubs. These were filled daily by local water carriers. In some of these residences several families may occupy the central living space. Private and separate bedrooms provide an intimate hideaway for the adults. Many dwellings contain spare bedrooms usually located away from the family quarters. Servants (slaves) slept downstairs if there was a separate living area or in covered sections around the courtyard if no room was available on the lower level. The numbers of domestic servants working in these houses during the nineteenth century ranged from five to seven slaves for a two story house, to as many as twelve slaves working in more palatial dwellings, such as those occupied by the Zanzibari governor, the Qadi, and the extremely wealthy WaAmu. As prosperity increased so too did the numbers of slaves.[56] A nineteenth century feature that has mostly disappeared in recent years is that of the cement bridge, which linked houses across the narrow roadways. An earlier example of this was the home of Bwana Zaidi (Lamu plot 488). From the early nineteenth century until the mid-1960s, Bwana Zaidi's house was linked to five others, three of these through the overhead bridges.[57]

Nineteenth century wealthy families had "large beds of rosewood" carved by Indian craftsmen aided by slaves. These beds were always high and required carved steps or a chair to get into them. Woven coconut fronds were tightly wrapped around the four posters as a form of mattress. Small fourposter stools with woven coconut frond seats were the major furnishings, along with woven mats on which the family sat to eat.[58] In the late nineteenth century samples of earlier imported china could still be found in the houses of wealthy WaAmu. "The date of its arrival is unknown" but quantities were "in the possession of the well-to-do Swahili and Arabs" who used china plates for decorative purposes and "in some cases almost plastered their walls with them."[59]

It is the Lamu chairs, however, which provided the most fascinating link with the Portuguese occupation of the sixteenth and seventeenth centuries. Described as "very heavy *lignum vitae* [with] fitted arms, foot-stooles, and very high backs" the chairs were "bottomed with string instead of cane and are much in-laid with bone, ivory or mother o' pearl, but usually the former. The workmanship is crude . . . [but] you would not pass by them without stopping to look at them even in a museum." Their designs were "very curious" in that in "the ornaments on them, you often see the Maltese cross inlaid in bone or ivory. The Mohammedan workers probably don't know it's a cross at all but simply perpetuate the old pattern and fashion which was originally Christian."[60] The locally made knives were also attributed to past cultural interchange: "Sizu [Siyu] knives with ivory handles inlaid with gold" which are "a combination of steel and iron an art practiced here which is a *relic* of the old Persian civilization."[61]

Some have speculated that the Lamu houses were designed to keep women in strict seclusion: the rooms leading back from the courtyard to ever darker interior quarters. As a port city with numbers of merchants visiting between November and March each year, privacy for the women would have been desired. It is likely the rooms were designed to keep women out of the flow of traffic and to enable men to conduct business with merchants from abroad.[62] The decorative plasterwork within the Lamu houses has also been noted in Hadramaut as well as in Gujarat. Ghaidan speculated that in Lamu talismans were placed in the recessed niches that later held verses from the Qur'an or imported items such as the China plates. Similar recessed niches in Zanzibar were used to hold a "handsome cut glass, a plate beautifully painted, or an elegant tasteful jug. In addition, many homes featured ivory carvings and brass trays."[63] As fashion changed over the centuries, so did the types of displays in the recessed niches. The model for the famous "Zanzibari" doors that are found in the coastal East African cities, probably originated in India but contained local motifs as patterns changed over time. Wealthy merchants hired carvers to make their doors. Designs varied but usually some quotation from the Qur'an was inscribed across the top of the door.[64]

The carved chests that were found in most homes of the wealthy were known by Europeans on the mainland as having been created in Lamu, but are believed to have originated in Persia and India. Made of teak, they were often painted red to preserve them. Some of these chests show "through the perforation of the plates a copper-coloured foil such as the Swahili women used to wear in their ears." Joining the chests on display were also "Arab coffee pots."[65]

Coastal Omani immigrants would have found some similarities in diet. In both Muscat and Lamu, fish and fruit were almost daily fare. The banana trees noted in the fifteenth century gave way to an island full of coconut palm trees. Rice, which was exported to Oman, grew on the mainland across the bay. It is possible that the Omanis brought grapevines with them. Grapes became a staple on nineteenth century shambas (small farms behind the town and large plantations on the mainland). Dates were important to the Arabs and date trees soon dotted the island shambas. Goats and calves provided meat for festive events. Chickens roamed over the town, scratching for insects or eating the garbage that piled up outside the townhouses. In the nineteenth and until mid-twentieth century, camels and horses resided on the island. The Muscat donkey was long employed in carrying heavy items including chunks of coral used in house construction. No carriages or wheeled vehicles were in use until early in the twentieth century. The British brought the cart. Slave men and animals carried all incoming freight on their backs.[66]

After 1814 the boom in the Lamu area was no less real than in Zanzibar. Material opportunities were available, and the Omanis took advantage of them. The town leaders were grateful to the Sultan and did not oppose his appointed governors—until the British intervened to wind down, and then close, the slave trade.

Constructing a jihazi on the Lamu seafront (ca 1907)
with slave quarters in the background

Courtesy of the National Museums of Kenya

Chapter Three

Lamu Before and During the Age of Creeping Imperialism

"We allow thee . . . the slaves whom thy right hand possesseth"
The Qur'an

Lamu's linkage to Zanzibar was facilitated by the inflow of Omani men who, in turn, married local women.[1] The Omanis married in and through their marriages to especially Omani administrators, the local ruling class married up. Due to their connections in Zanzibar and Oman, the newcomers provided some exclusivity in trade that would otherwise have gone to the Indian and Hadrami merchants already resident in Lamu.[2] The early Zanzibar sultans also visited the island frequently. An American trader stranded in Lamu learned that his country and Zanzibar had agreed on a trade treaty when "Sultan Said bin Seyyid of Zanzibar and Muscat" paid a visit there in November of 1833.[3]

The Omani immigrants were mostly Ibhadi Muslims. The local WaAmu Muslims followed the Sunnah, the sayings of the Prophet Mohamed. The major difference between the Shi'a and Sunni centered on the early succession after Mohammed died. Traditional Sunnis believed that any of Mohammed's clan was eligible for succession as long as he met with the approval of the Muslim community at large. Soon after Mohmamed's death, splits occurred resulting in three major divisions within Islam. One group became known as the Shi'a and many Lamu Indians fell within this camp (but had divisions among themselves as well). The Ibhadi were an outgrowth of the third splinter group and were founded by Abdallah ibn-Ibad in the seventh century. They were "the most moderate branch of Khawarij, whose distinctive doctrine was that

44

any Muslim, even a slave, could be deposed if he fell below their standards of rectitude."[4]

Although the founder of the BuSaid dynasty was both Sultan and Imam [religious leader], Said never claimed religious leadership because of discord between the factions there. He was not a zealot, and was known in Zanzibar for his advocacy of the religious toleration already in existence in Oman. In addition, the people on the coast of Oman were not as wed to the conservative Ibhadi faith as those in the interior. Most immigrants came from coastal Oman.[5] While the Zanzibari Omanis continued to follow the Ibhadi tradition, those who came to Lamu and intermarried with the local women, did not. They either converted to Sunni Islam, or allowed their children to be brought up in that persuasion.

Lamu was recognized as a religious center by the time most Omani men arrived. For centuries itinerant sharifs [descendants of the Prophet] had come to live there. In Lamu there were already divisions between those who followed the Sunnah. Some elements of sufism were introduced by the various sharifs and by newcomers from the Hadramaut. *Madrassas* [religious schools] taught the Sunnah. One factor which *may* have been instrumental in Omani conversion was that under Ibhadi law a slave could inherit. Under Sunni law slaves could not inherit property and if they had any, it reverted to their owners.[6] The superiority of religious knowledge on the part of WaAmu may also have been a consideration in conversion. Otherwise, the locals quickly adapted the Arab ways of the newcomers.[7]

Lamu men had a long tradition of going on pilgrimage to Mecca. It is uncertain when women began to accompany their menfolk but certainly long before the mid-nineteenth century. Oral traditions recall many people dying while they were on pilgrimages. Before steamships, "it took one year to go to Mecca. Later, the trip took about three months." Some women recall hearing that early pilgrims had to ride camels once they reached the Arabian shore. Others remembered hearing about the extreme difficulties that women suffered shut up in the bow of a dhow before steamboats facilitated their journey.[8]

Local qadis had been chosen by the ruling class in Lamu before the Sultan began appointing them (and then they were Sunni). These unpaid qadis were often as subject to the pressures of those who selected them as they were to their commitment to Muslim law. According to a religious authority in Lamu, the Omani presence there meant standardization of Muslim law [the *Shari'a*] because Sultan Said appointed religious authorities who were then responsible to no local ruling body.[9] The Omani appointed qadis were also paid—their salaries being collected by the local elders but under the Sultan's provenance. The qadi was supposed to judge in matters pertaining to religion; the liwali ruled on secular law. But the qadi seems to have been the court of last resort in some cases. In 1860, litigation pertaining to two women, and for which details are otherwise not available, was decided by the Liwali of Lamu. The women protested and the case then went before the qadi, who found in their favor.[10] Earlier, in 1844, a Lamu qadi was sufficiently well regarded by Sultan Said that he brought Khamis bin Othman to Zanzibar to negotiate with the French consul.[11] Perhaps any man who could survive the religious maze in Lamu was determined to have extraordinary negotiating skills.

The French were still trading in Lamu at this time. M. Loarer described the people then as "being more Swahili than Zanzibar" with a mainland population of 20,000 and 40,000 slaves. The island "has commerce directly with India" and was exporting sesame as well as cattle. In the 1840s, problems again developed with the Orma, who a contemporary described as "savages who were given over to amputations." [Castration]. Omanis and their slaves were both found working in the shambas, with slaves especially susceptible to mutilation but "who survive even without European medicine." There were the ongoing hostilities with Pate and Siyu where Sultan Said had stationed troops. These towns are "fortified in the Arab manner and are in revolt against the Arabs . . . . [the] black population has repelled three important expeditions, with the last one being conducted by the Imam [Sultan] in person. At this time, in Lamu, as well as on Pate island, "there is much opposition to the government of l'Imam."[12]

In an attempt to quell some of the quarrels between the various northern island port cities, Said traveled to Manda where he worked out another agreement with the WaPate and where he also met with Lamu elders. In 1849, Said banished his oldest son Hilel to Lamu when he was discovered to be drinking alcohol to the point of drunkenness. Hilel fathered at least one acknowledged son during the period he was confined within the town walls. No memory of the son exists in contemporary Lamu but the fact that he was born there, and seems not to have played a part in any of the subsequent disputes over succession in Zanzibar, leads to a phenomena in Lamu that needs to be addressed.

Clan names were important to Arabs and were kept through recorded (or earlier recited) genealogies. While genealogies and descent are also important to the WaAmu old families, many clan names were dropped in favor of some more recent male relative who was recognized for accomplishments of his own. Conversely, in the case of Said's son, Hilel, the BuSaid surname may have been dropped because of the disgrace he brought to the family before his exile. In that situation, his son would have carried his own name and that of ibn (or in Lamu bin) Hilel.[13]

Enemies of the Zanzibar sultans were also exiled to Lamu. In the 1850s a member of the oldest and wealthiest pre-Omani clan was sent there by Sultan Majid. Abdalla bin Salim was involved in a plot with Majid's brother Bargash, who attempted a palace coup.[14] Another Bargash supporter, Adballa bin Othman of the el-Harith Clan was also banished to the northern island community. In his case, the British agent intervened, requesting that the prisoner be returned to Zanzibar. Instead the liwali, acting under orders from Majid, ordered him put to death and, in the process undermined the growing sense of authority that marked British officials in Zanzibar.[15]

The sickly Sultan Majid visited Lamu several times. Local women remember a story about one visit. On his arrival in town, Majid was provided with a beautiful, seductive slave woman. The Sultan was so captivated by her beauty that he instructed her owner to send her to Zanzibar where briefly she joined his harem before slipping away to her slave lover back home.[16] Later nineteenth century sultans were less interested in traveling to the port city in the north, partially because they were involved in controversies in Zanzibar, where the British were garnering considerable power.

Through a series of treaties (including the Moresby Treaty) with the Zanzibar sultans, the British applied pressure to close down the slave trade. In 1845, with his capital now in Zanzibar, Said caved in to British demands and legally prohibited the importation of slaves to Oman (who were then shipped there illegally). Then, in 1847, Said signed the

Hamerton Treaty, which further reduced the slave trade by prohibiting export of slaves to Arabia, French controlled-Madagascar, the Mascerene Islands, and elsewhere beyond the Sultan's own East African holdings.[17]

Said died in 1856. Majid played cat and mouse with the British, pretending to support their attempts to stop the trade in slaves while at the same time supporting the Indian and Omani traders in their endeavors.[18] At Majid's death in 1870, Bargash took the throne he had earlier tried to wrest from his brother by force. When he died, his elderly brother, Khalifa, ruled from 1889-90. After that, Sultan Ali reigned briefly.[19] The successive sultans capitulated to the British on the one hand, while continuing covert support for the Indian Ocean trade.[20] (Britain was still searching for illegal slaves on ships into the 1920s).

In spite of the efforts of British consuls in Zanzibar to close the port to slave ships, Lamu remained a major player in the illegal trade. The rigid and authoritarian Colonel C. P. Rigby, anti-Arab through and through, devoted himself to the abolition of the trade, including monitoring vessels sailing to Lamu. Rigby hounded the weak Majid, forcing him to submit to the various treaties that actually kept the Zanzibari government afloat. Rigby himself noted that Majid and his subjects thought his actions whimsical, and in 1861, at the end of his term in Zanzibar, wryly noted that "they were bitterly opposed to my interference."[21]

Not only did Rigby and his successors have to cope with the cunning sultans and their Indian and Arab supporters, they also had to contend with the Americans, French, and even for a time, with the Spanish. Both the French and Spanish were directly involved in the slave trade. The Americans were indirectly involved for the most part, since they allowed Arab and Indian slavers to fly their flag until they were legally prohibited from doing so in 1863.

The French had been a threat to British interests in East Africa from the 1770s. One ploy that Said used in stalling British efforts to suppress the trade was to plead fear of the French. In the 1840s, France had been denied consular privileges in Zanzibar because they refused to outlaw the slave trade, and they ignored the Hamerton Treaty altogether. Slave traders, including the French, could fly that flag and thus escape search and seizure from the increasingly active British patrols. Each time the British authorities protested, Said countered that the French would take

48

over his possessions. During the reign of Sultan Majid, large numbers of slavers flying the French flag plied the waters of the Indian Ocean with Majid reiterating his father's lamentations in response to growing complaints from the British consuls. By the 1850s, over the protestations of the British in Zanzibar, the French had gained their consulate but still did not agree to sign the treaty outlawing the slave trade. As Majid saw it, the problem rested between the two European powers and not with Zanzibar.

During Majid's reign, a Lamu liwali actually discussed the possibility of France taking over the government there.[22] No action was taken, but the British were uncommonly worried that France might move into Lamu and then to Zanzibar. The Germans, too, proved to be an annoyance to the British agent in Zanzibar, although their interest was centered on legitimate trade. Nevertheless, the other European powers at one time or another sided with each other and against Britain through the period of Majid's rule. The French, Germans, and Spanish had agents in Lamu, although again, the Germans were not involved in the slave trade.[23]

In November, 1859 a Spanish ship sailed into Zanzibar harbor in search of slaves. The captain wished to sail to Lamu but, under pressure from Rigby, Majid overtly denied him (although covertly he may have agreed). The next morning, "The Spanish brig sailed for Lamoo with the Spanish agent on board in spite of the Sultan's prohibition."[24]

In 1860, when another vessel was caught in the Lamu waters and brought to Zanzibar, Majid refused to be involved in the disposition of this ship, referring the problem back to "Her Majesty's Government." He tried to defend the rights of his "countries" to stay in the slave trade, later arguing that his people "needed their slaves. . . . if I stop the traffic in slaves it will ruin these countries and it will ruin my subjects."[25]

In Lamu, the French licensed firm Vidal hired Salim Jubran, an Arab slaver, who worked with the slave agent Buena Ventura Mas, to obtain slaves for Vidal. Jubran, however, turned coat and also became a spy for Rigby, going on the British payroll. He became involved in one of the horror stories that marked the slave trade. A boatload of slaves picked up in Kilwa ran aground. Jubran ordered that they be disembarked and marched by overland route to Lamu. Less than half survived the arduous journey. Those who lived were subsequently shipped out, leaving Rigby further incensed.[26] Rigby managed to get Jubran to Zanzibar before the

Arabs could punish him, holding him in protective custody until the liwali of Lamu, a nephew of Majid, intervened. Without Rigby's knowledge, "Saood bin Hillal" abducted Jubran and returned him to Lamu where he was put to death for "having given . . . information regarding the trade carried on at Zanzibar, Kilwa, and Lamoo." Then, despite complaints from Rigby, Majid appointed his nephew liwali of Lamu.[27]

In light of his many frustrations, it was not surprising that Rigby had to leave Zanzibar for medical reasons in 1861. The American consul who stood in for him reported that the British were patrolling the coast of the Sultan's domains from "Ebo to Lamoo" in search of slaves. However, he was critical of their procedures: "British are in the habit of boarding every native craft they meet and robbing them of anything they may happen to want." Evidence of this, he said, "was very strong."[28]

The British subjects to which the American referred were the Indian community. Although differing in religious practices, almost all members of this community were involved either directly or indirectly in the slave trade. In their early efforts to control the trade, the British had persuaded Sultan Said to issue a proclamation in 1843 forbidding the Indians in Zanzibar from buying or selling slaves. That same year, Britain outlawed slavery in British India.[29] During Rigby's tenure a great deal of pressure was placed on the Indian community to keep them from being directly involved in the trade. Nevertheless, Indians financed it, owned slaving vessels (captained by Afro-Arabs), and profited considerably from both these activities in Zanzibar and Lamu.[30]

Rigby was replaced by Captain Playfair, who was more sensitive to economic matters in the Sultan's domains, and who recognized the Rigby's highhandedness had only increased smuggling. Ironically, it was during Playfair's period in Zanzibar that a revolution of sorts occurred among Her Majesty's subjects. The Indians declared themselves citizens of the Sultan. Majid, still living at the time, agreed and allowed all those who wished, to consider themselves subjects of Zanzibar.[31] Playfair was unable to resolve the issue of citizenship, but his replacement, Henry Churchill, bent every effort to recruit once again the "Sultan's subjects" back to Britain, and thus to British law. Churchill complained that "The subjects of the Rao of Kutch are the slave traders. In point of fact they are regular slave dealers." These "Kutchees" who had their counterparts in Lamu, were selling directly "to the northern Arabs from Muscat and Persia, and the price of slaves was rising, with Kutchees forming the wealthier class of the trading population."[32] In 1873 when Sir John Kirk visited the coastal areas, including Lamu, he discovered large numbers of the "Sultan's subjects" holding slaves.[33] Eventually under Kirk's watch, the Indians reverted to British citizenship. This act did not deter them from continuing their involvement in the slave trade, nor did it stop them from owning slaves. In 1873, during Kirk's residence, Sultan Bargash issued the proclamation that ended the slave trade completely.

That year naval officer G. J. Malcolm, who was patrolling the coast, reported on a lengthy meeting he had with the then Liwali Suud bin Hamed. "[A] woman named Zema waded off towards the boat. . . . she was fearfully scourged from blows inflicted with a whip" and asked for British protection. She said "belonged to . . . Drahaman, a Borah [sic], who . . . . purchased her in the Mozambique from a Comoro man." Drahaman had gone to Cutch about four months previously "and had left her in charge of his wife, who treated her so badly she ran away." Suud bin Hamed was sympathetic to the plight of the woman, but "asked me to return" the small captured dhow "as it belonged to a poor man." Malcolm refused, lecturing the slave holding liwali on the iniquities of the slave trade, and stressing Britain's determination to end it altogether. The liwali was affable and "we parted good friends. I suppose he had often heard the same [lecture] before. Sudi bin Hamed was very pleasant, he seems intelligent, and I heard that he was a good cultivator and importer of fruit-bearing trees, even working with his own hands at his shamba." But when Malcolm inquired "if there were any Hindoos or Banians who owned slaves?" the liwali coolly replied, "No."[34]

There were never enough sailing ships available for the British to cover the northern coastal waters, yet those on patrol in the area were diligent in tracking vessels they suspected of carrying slaves. In September, 1873, Sub-Lieutenant Marcus McCausland sighted a dhow near Lamu. He gave chase but lost sight of her. Next morning he entered the town and learned that fifty slaves had been landed. After McCausland destroyed the dhow he located its cargo. Finding that the slaves were emaciated he demanded the Banian customs officer provide them with food. McCausland may have paid with his life for this humane act. He was subsequently murdered in what is now Lamu District.[35]

Frederick Holmwood visited Lamu in November 1874 and found "much illicit trading in northern ports, including Lamu." Despite a break in the ranks between some Indians and some Arab traders, the old coalition of Indians providing the finance and the Afro-Arabs obtaining the slaves, continued. In fact, chaos developed in Lamu in the wake of the 1873 treaty. While an Indian was murdered (possibly for reporting on slaving activities), the Afro-Arab families had to protect their shambas from Somali raiders who were bent on stealing their slaves.

Captain Malcolm later carried out an extensive investigation into the slave trade on the east coast of Africa. He reported to Kirk that "subjects of Her Majesty on this coast are *bona fide* owners of slaves and [they] are the principal promoters of the slave trade, supply a very large proportion of the capital required to combat the traffic. They are slave dealers to an equal, if not greater extent than the Arabs." In Lamu, "there may be about 100 Banians and Hindoos, and these will own between 250-300 slaves."[36] Even though Suud bin Hamed had provided cover for the Indians in Lamu when Malcolm had queried their ownership of slaves, considerable evidence exists that they, like the Arabs, played both ends against the middle. In fact, the customs agent, Kimdjee, had "never heard that Her majesty's subjects" could not own slaves.

In Lamu, the slave holders were furious that Bargash had caved in to British demands to end the trade. For a variety of reasons, including loss of revenue in Zanzibar and the need for British financial aid to continue payments to Oman, Bargash capitulated in 1873. In order to protect the Sultan from potential uprising by his Lamu subjects someone, probably Suud bin Hamed, invented an excuse for Bargash. According to a Lamu informant, and based on traditions still told by elderly Afro-Arabs, British squadrons bedecked in disguise as Turkish men-of-war had threatened an attack on Zanzibar. Bargash was "frightened when the Turks" who were said to be moving in on the nearly defenseless island. But the British consul quickly offered to defend the island, if Bargash would sign the treaty. Thus, the WaAmu believed the British tricked the Sultan into submission.[37]

The wily BuSaid liwali, Suud bin Hamed served from 1870 into the

1880s, but not without considerable controversy. He was fired three times, but successively managed to gain reappointment. He was, as Malcolm described him: affable and agreeable. Nevertheless, Suud bin Hamed was a complex individual: remembered as having profited from the sea trade in slaves, he was thought to have been a financier of the overland caravan trade that took its place.

The economies of the Sultan's possessions were largely dependent on the slave trade and slavery, but in human terms it was an abomination. Many died before reaching the sailing ships on the southern African coast. Many more died en route to their final destination. Two instances relating to Lamu illustrate something about the deplorable circumstances victims often endured and especially after the British patrols stepped up their activity on the northern coast. One dhow being chased off Lamu Bay was rid of its cargo when "Arabs began driving the slaves overboard with drawn swords" to avoid capture.[38] A dhow full of slaves was reported to have pulled into one of the small hidden anchorages off Lamu island and dumped the entire cargo; presumably some or all lived and were recaptured, and were either sold away or put to work in the Lamu area. It is also important to note however that slaves themselves were active participants in the trade. Many worked on dhows carrying *watuma* [slaves] directly to Lamu (and elsewhere). A British report on the slave trade in the early 1870s pointed out that "after a short time these slaves became for all intents and purposes freed men."[39]

In 1875, again under pressure from the British agent there Bargash ordered that all slaves brought into Zanzibar be confiscated. The decree, however, was merely another piece of paper to the slave traders, who continued surreptitiously to move slaves onto the island. If caught and questioned, they claimed that the slaves were free men who they were bringing in to work. This was also the approach taken by slavers caught on the open seas.[40]

It is impossible to ascertain the number of slaves passing in and out of Lamu harbor over the centuries in which the trade lasted.[41] Certainly a large number of African slaves were forced up the treacherous interior path beyond the coast line. Henry Churchill had reported in 1865 that traders were anxious to get their slaves to an island setting where escape was less likely. Lamu, another and smaller island, became a major entrepot for slaves coming in by land and then being shipped up the coast to ports like Barawa, or whipped off in ocean-going dhows to the Persian Gulf.

Some documentation does exist pertaining to the conditions of the trade into the Lamu area. Slaves gathered in Nyasa or elsewhere in central Africa were forced march long distances: 300-500 miles, often carrying trade items that were secured on their backs. One British authority put the numbers of miles that some marched at 1200-1500.[42] Men were usually shackled together with chains attached to a yoke, like a team of horses forced to pull together. The women and children were either left to walk in groups by themselves or were tied to ropes. There were considerable problems feedings slaves during these long trips. One contemporary observer noted that some subsisted on an ear of corn or something equal to that every five days.[43] While slaves were undoubtedly poorly fed, it was in the interest of the traders to keep them going to their destination so it seems unlikely slaves were provided with such miserly amounts of food. Nevertheless, the slave traders did not lavish luxuries on their captives.

In 1885 Sir Frederick Jackson visited John Haggard in Lamu. A naturalist bent on gathering specimens and a hunter interested in shooting big game, Jackson ventured into the mainland area where he found evidence of the slave trade. "As I sat waiting for [a] storm to pass, I noted that the log of wood as I thought it to be, was really two logs, one on top of the other carefully adzed and fitted together, hinged at one end, and with a large iron staple and hasp at the other, but of course no lock and key. At regular intervals were slots, forming holes from side to side just large enough to receive a man or woman's ankle, and wide enough apart to allow those so held to lie down in close to each other. Furthermore, there were two of those stocks, lying end to end, down the centre and clearly the whole length of the shed [in which he took shelter]." Jackson observed that these objects of the trade had "not only been well used, but quite recently."[44]

Descendants of slaves captured in the trade also have their oral traditions. These include memories from the mother of one informant regarding her experiences including the long march, and the exhaustion suffered by the Africans en route north. Another woman remembered hearing that "Africans who were roaming around in small parties" were grabbed by the traders. These small bands of slaves were taken to Lamu, where they were delivered to the homes of the wealthy. Those who were rejected were taken to the market, where upon inspection, they "were sold like chickens."[45]

Coastal traders took their own slaves, and with capital from Indian merchants (at the very high rate of 12% annually), set off for slaves in journeys that kept them out, sometimes as long as a year. Slave porters were given merchandise to trade as enhancement. Upcountry Africans who provided slaves and ivory (and skins on occasion) derived little in the way of useful goods from this trade. Often they were paid with trinkets or luxury items; and, with few exceptions, their lives altered little from the mostly subsistence agriculture on which they existed.[46] On return to the coast, profits were shared on a basis of how many men each Arab provided: a percentage, plus goods, to the porters and, of course, the payments on the loans to the Indians. Women and perhaps children were still coming from nearby areas into Lamu at the time slavery was legally abolished—or between 1907 and 1910. Galla women, for instance, were much desired because of their purported beauty, and some cattle keeping Galla were raided in order to obtain their women. Somalis—more often enemies than allies—stole slaves from the mainland plantations, as well as "stealing from the badly guarded shambas at the back of Lamoo" [island].[47] Conversely, the Afro-Arabs sometimes stole Somali women whom they brought to town and took around to individual houses after the open slave market was closed down in the 1880s. Pokomo women, who Beachey says were not thought to be very attractive, also became slaves and concubines to Lamu men.[48]

Regarding the fate of slave children who entered Lamu, we know nothing at all. When slaves were plentiful, their children helped herd the goats and sheep in the *shambas* behind the town. As the supply dwindled, some slave children were put to work as herders as well as other light agricultural duties. Those children entering into homes with their mothers probably played with the free children until they were old enough to acquire skills such as assisting craftsmen, or helping in the local shops. No separate market existed for domestic slave children. Swahili, like other Africans, were tolerant and mostly kind to small children. Although punishment, as we shall see, could be cruel.

Lt. John G. Haggard, whose brother was the adventure novelist Rider, arrived in Lamu in January 1884. He was the second known European to take up residence there. But Haggard was only the first of a string of British agents, and later district commissioners, who attempted to impose British policy on the WaAmu over a period that lasted seventy-nine years. The new Age of Imperialism did not catch the people of Lamu unaware. They had been indirect victims of British rule in Zanzibar. Having only come into their own economically some fifty years earlier, the WaAmu were not willing to succumb to British rule. At times they cooperated with Haggard. At times they opposed him and so, too, did Suud bin Hamed, who also worked in opposition to some of the Sultans' decrees.

In the matter of the slave trade, the planters in Lamu were in direct conflict with the British (and ostensibly the Sultans). Activities relating to shutting down the trade were much resented as the locals depended on increasing numbers of slaves to farm the mainland plantations, as well as the garden plots behind the town. Haggard's tenure 1884-85 represented the period of transition from prosperity and the good life for the wealthy Afro-Arab community to what, by the end of the century, turned to an economy in shambles, leading to the decline of the port city. Haggard's letters to his family during his Lamu residency provide an inside view of the slave trade. Sir John Kirk spent a month with him, in the process visiting Suud bin Hamed to whom he issued a warning that the "new slave traffic must be stopped." The "Governor was willing if the Sultan would send him arms and men" as the locals could not be counted on. Their hostility was directed towards the Sultan, his liwali, and indirectly felt by Haggard.

A few months after he arrived, Haggard wrote about the slave trade reopening "from the Wanika country, about 150 miles south of Lamu." The Somali "suddenly came down with cattle to exchange for slaves. . . I nailed a couple of the slaves in their possession and sent them to the Governor of Lamu (liwali) for their case to be investigated, and the Governor detained them. . . . There were sixty armed Somalis. The Somalis threatened to kill Lamu people if they couldn't get their slaves." Liwali Suud bin Hamed sent the Somalis back to Her Majesty's servant. Haggard allowed two unarmed Somalis to come into his quarters and had armed guards surround the others outside. But once the agent realized that

Suud bin Hamed was not going to back him up, he referred the Somalis back to the Liwali. According to Haggard, "They departed." But we do not know if they departed for the Liwali and got their slaves, or if they departed Lamu.[49]

Lamu plantation owners were beginning to feel the loss of income due to lack of labor. This was especially true regarding the extensive cultivation on the mainland. Reports to Zanzibar suggest that much of the time he was in Lamu, Haggard was forced to deal with rebellious landowners, some of whom actually took to arms in the back of the island. They were, however, kept under control by Suud bin Hamed who, accompanied by a force of the Sultan's guards, met with them and cautioned against violence.[50] But the liwali also proffered advice as to how to circumvent the British patrols on the seas, as he also joined some locals in funding expeditions overland.

In the matter of the Somali, however, Haggard noted that both he and the liwali were afraid of these outsiders. On one occasion, Haggard decided to confine himself to town because "the Somalis are in a furious rage with me and if I went out now I should probably be killed." Admitting that he knew there were some new slaves in Lamu, Haggard noted that he was not going to "go about running my head against a stone wall and exasperate the people of Lamu against me." At issue was the future of the trade and that he intended to keep a watch on, if powerless to do much about it.

One problem was that "the Wanika people are starving, and parting with everything they possess for food, the chiefs are now selling people and even mothers with children." Selling mothers and children into slavery meant they had a chance to survive. The Giriama, further south, suffered famine and sold themselves into slavery. By 1885 Kirk reported that they were getting in crops while the Digo "were starving" and were "selling themselves into slavery." Beyond those who chose slavery over starvation, "man stealing still goes on."[51] After the famine ended, the price of illegal slaves rose from an average of forty dollars on the Somali coast to "$50-$60 per head."[52] Otherwise, the price per slave was variable depending on supply and demand, the supply being increasingly small and the demand ever larger.

Ironically, as it was Haggard's mission to stamp out the slave trade, he was in the compromising position of owning at least one and he had several others attached to his household.[53] While his letters frequently, if somewhat inaccurately, referred to the peace he found in Lamu Haggard assumed considerable credit for changes he urged on the town. Some of these alterations were compellingly humane. In the matter of the slaves "their condition has been enormously ameliorated. When I came you never went out without seeing slaves in chains and very heavy ones too sometimes, now you never see chains at all." The slaves told him that "they can now work as they like."[54]

Shipping home a set of chains and poles, Haggard wrote "About the slave irons, they are of the description used *generally* for punishment of women and children . . . .[the poles] are used any length from a foot long to twelve or fourteen feet long. They are put round the neck of the slave who is then ordered to lie down and the end of the iron pin is burred by a blacksmith. They are then worn for as long as the master chooses (often many months) with the pole hanging down the back. . . . The other day I noticed a boy in the water in front of my house with one at least twelve feet long and as big round as a clothes post. He could hardly drag it after him . . . so he remained in the water all day long . . . [doing] this for two or three days when I couldn't stand it any longer so simply sent for a blacksmith and had it cut off."

Later, Haggard also saw a girl "with one quite as large, but as a rule they only hang to the ankle, that I see every day now; other kinds of chains are not to be seen as often as when I first came. As a rule slaves deserve their punishment, however, and although I have heard many pitiful stories I have never requested the Governor yet to take off one of these irons if they were only of a decent size. . . . I have generally found they were put on for stealing, long continued misbehavior, public immorality and so on. They are curious things and peculiar to Lamu."[55] Jackson also commented on the "pitiable sight of small slave children dragging about the streets a great pole fastened by a ring to their necks as punishment . . . ."[56]

"I have a slave woman I am training . . . [who] has the itch very badly she is now better after a month's treatment of carbolic." Haggard noted that he had discovered what he thought was a sulphur spring on the mainland and would like to have taken the woman there to treat her "except for the slave stealers of whom there are plenty in the area." The only physical reference Haggard made to female slaves was in recalling a dream to his brother, Will. After consuming a bottle of champagne, Haggard engaged in a night of fantasy that included intimacy with a beautiful slave woman. He did not mention if the woman was one of his, but he stressed his great relief in having only dreamed of this alliance.[57]

But European men did assault a slave woman while Haggard was in Lamu. In a letter to his father he wrote about "first class passengers on a mail boat" who were all drunk when the incident occurred. "Good thing she was only a slave as there was a fearful row in town." The liwali summoned Haggard as the locals had surrounded the house where the Europeans were holed up. Together with an armed guard they got them on a boat and out of town. "Even here there is considerable prejudice against a European speaking to a woman." And thus he reported the "natives behaved admirably" under the circumstances.[58]

In his letters to England, Haggard referred to his health and emphasized his enjoyment of big game hunting on the mainland. Beyond these, the dangers he faced in "this peaceful place" and in the district cropped up repeatedly. Haggard's assessment of the liwali matched that of Malcolm. He was " a dear old boy, most polite, and sends me any amount of fruit, but as cunning as an old dog as ever wore a turban." But, "I am suffering from suppressed indignation against the Governor in this town." The liwali, in turn, suffered from hostility that the locals felt for the sultans. As the appointed governor, he often bore the brunt of the anger they could not express directly. Suud bin Hamed was "a big upstanding [weighing 214 pounds], black-bearded, smiling faced, and altogether splendid-looking man." His home on the seafront was among the largest in Lamu. Here he handled the Sultan's affairs in "a reception chamber [which was] the usual long, narrow, high ceilinged room with a row of chairs on each side."[59]

In addition to clamping down on the slave trade, Haggard's instructions included opening legitimate commerce with the interior. He was anxious to increase the customs receipts in Lamu—which were still farmed out to a Hindu and were still paid in part to the Sultan of Zanzibar. Haggard devised several strategies to carry out his mission. Intending to sell elephant hides to South Africa, he decided to initiate trade with the

WaBoni [pl]., a semi-nomadic group on the mainland who were noted for their expertise in hunting elephants.

Haggard wrote his brother Will some of the problems he encountered with the liwali in the matter of the WaBoni: " He has behaved well to me here on the whole . . . but in this Waboni business he thought I should clash with his interests [and] with a little underhand work, has put a check on any idea of opening up the country." Haggard discovered that "from every elephant they kill, the Waboni have to give one tusk to the Governor of Lamu. . . [who] is afraid if trade opened up profit for the Waboni will be good and they won't want to give him the tusk per elephant." Suud bin Hamed invited the "headman of the Waboni" to come to Lamu "where he has held him" making it impossible for Haggard to go into WaBoni country until "he is released." And, that release would not be forthcoming until Haggard abandoned his own plans with the WaBoni.[60] He intended to put the matter before Kirk but before he could do so, the WaBoni made an alliance with the Sultan of Witu, a problem that preoccupied both Suud bin Hamed and Haggard during 1885.

The simmering resentments towards Haggard as agent of the European power continued, especially as Britain increasingly dominated the sultans in Zanzibar. Haggard repeatedly referred to feeling unsafe to walk the streets in Lamu, despite the presence of his four bodyguards imported from Zanzibar. He was concerned about "intrigue, fanaticism, and indignation" on the part of "leading Arabs of the town [who] are jealous of my traveling about and so is the governor [on the mainland, because of the ongoing slave trade] but they are. . . [mostly] civil in their manner, the lower Swahili approve of my being here because I have checked the incorrigible cheating of the Hindus."[61]

As the sole British official in Lamu, Haggard was officer in charge of the Indian population. The Indians, he wrote, "resent me because I have stopped their swindling" and in their "opinion I have done them a cruel wrong." He had not, however, managed to clamp down on their clandestine activities involving the slave trade. Lingering worries about his safety moved Haggard to hire a new chief *askari* who was "said to be capable of driving my effete debauched and lazy Comoro men. . . I trust to hear the sound of my stick being used amongst them pretty freely."[62]

His greatest political problem, Haggard thought, was going to be "the

Masai of Zulu race, who live 300 miles inland from Mombasa and frequently devastate the land right down to the coast."[63] Actually his greatest problem turned out to be Witu Sultan Ahmed bin Fumo Luti, known as Simba [lion]. Witu was located about forty miles across the mainland from Lamu. Although it is not possible to delineate exactly the areas on the mainland controlled by Lamu planters, the area claimed by all planters in the Lamu archipelago (including those from the Bajun Islands) was the vast stretch of cultivated land that ran from the Tana River in the south to the border with Somalia and therefore included Witu.[64]

The impending conflict with Witu was related to Britain's continuing determination to close down the slave trade and to abolish slavery altogether.

Omari bin Mohammed O.B.E., Sultan of Witu after hostilities ended
Courtesy of the National Museums of Kenya

Chapter Four

Outsiders and their Impact: Witu, Watoro, the Germans and the IBEA

"My wealth hath not profited me! My power hath perished from me!"
The Qur'an

Simba of Witu posed a threat to Lamu landowners because of the large runaway slave *(watoro)* army he possessed. These *watoro* roamed the mainland at random, disrupting operations on the plantations by capturing and selling the slaves belonging to the Afro-Arabs. Not only did *watoro* activities cut deeper into the already decreased work force, they sent a wave of fear throughout the area they stalked. Slaves on the mainland who were loyal and who had their own farming plots and families living on them, often ran away when the *watoro* approached. Women and children were sometimes deserted and left to the wiles of the *watoro*.[1]

With the slave trade curtailed, Lamu planters could not afford the loss of the remaining slaves. Cries from the locals continued regarding the cessation of the trade. Labor shortages existed, and even the British agents pressuring the Sultan on this matter recognized the possibility of ruin to the planters "because they will have to pay regular wages." Amid doubts that the "planters will be able to continue planting if slaves were not available," British authorities were optimistic as to the "opportunity for European energy to step in and our British Indian subjects, who own so much of the land, are anxiously waiting for a chance it bring it under cultivation."[2]

The Holmwood Report of 1876 indicates that the Lamu Indian merchants were beginning to take over a small number of the mainland plantations. They were able to do so because the Afro-Arabs felt the economic pinch from the loans they had made and had difficulty repaying. Also, the planters were hampered in their efforts to do so by the dwindling numbers of productive slaves on the *shambas*. The final assault came from the *watoro* menace and the imperial ambitions of the Sultan of Witu. By 1885 the combination of Simba's hostility to the Sultan of Zanzibar, and his *watoro* army on the loose "is now preventing people of Lamu from cultivating in the direction of Witu as they intended this season."

Older former plantation owners believed that the Sultan of Witu purposely seduced slaves into his army "to get back at Lamu for the defeat of the WaPate." Feelings between the WaAmu and the defeated Nabahany family ran strong throughout this century. On the other hand, contemporary sources claimed that because of the Sultan of Zanzibar's repeated capitulation to British demands, "there can be no doubt that in Lamu many of the most important people sympathize with the Patta refugees collected under Simba."[3]

Here was a major conflict for the old families of Lamu. Often at odds with Pate, the ties that frequently bound them were resurrected in terms of British efforts to end the trade. Simba was the last of the Nabahany chiefs—the family that had ruled Pate for several centuries before it was eclipsed by Lamu in the early 1800s. Even though Pate was no longer the major port in the Lamu archipelago, some people there still owned large plantations on the mainland. Their fortunes were on the ebb. Simba, with his base at Witu, represented a threat to the ruling faction in Lamu, who were seen by some as having surrendered to the Sultan's obsequious submission to the British.

In the early years of his reign in Witu, Simba was able to control the *watoro* by paying them off, thus enabling them to buy weapons. This trade was handled by the Hadrami merchants since the *watoro* were as resentful of the Indians as they were the old families.[4] Relations between the Hadrami community and the Afro-Arabs chilled and, as a result, new frictions developed between the already divided members of the Lamu community. This new trading contact was short lived, however, as the British shut down the Hadrami importation of arms and ammunition.

Haggard wrote to his brother Will who was in the Foreign Office in London, about the problems Lamu owners faced with the mainland *watoro*. "Most shambas in Mpecatoni [just across the bay from Lamu] have been abandoned in consequence of the Watoro." The Governor was afraid of them. Sultan Bargash was "so busy wallowing in the tub with his women" that he failed to send armed troops to deal with the matter of Simba and his band. A local Afro-Arab told Haggard that "the *watoro* are the curse of the country and no trade can be carried on so long as they continue independent."

In April 1884 Haggard visited the mainland to find that another hamlet had been "sacked by the *watoro.*" Later, they captured "90 Pokomo slaves" who were sold into slavery in Lamu.[5] There were frequent complaints from the Pokomo about "Swahili raiders" who came into the Tana River area, threw down a spear, and demanded women. The *watoro* took these women from the hapless Pokomo and used them as concubines.[6] An ex-slave, Salim Kheri, remembered the *watoro* on the mainland as fearsome indeed. Robbers, rapists, and thugs is how Salim Kheri described the runaway slaves with whom he came into contact late in the nineteenth century.[7]

Germans came along and further complicated matters between the WaAmu and the Sultan of Witu. German interest in East Africa was an outgrowth of early missionary activities that led to explorations in the area of Mt. Kilminjaro in the 1840s. And, of course, the long time presence of the Hamburg merchants in Zanzibar had whetted the appetites of some to establish bases on the coast. It was, however, the competitiveness between the European powers in Africa as a whole which led to Germany to cast a furtive eye on the Sultan's northern coastal dominions. Dr. Karl Peters, an extreme racist but also an inveterate explorer, traveled around in the Lamu area in 1884, signing treaties with various chiefs, including the Afro-Arab leaders in Lamu (without the knowledge of John Haggard). Two German brothers appeared in Lamu in the spring of 1885 in the guise of scientists intent on exploring the mainland interior. Haggard suspected the motives of the Denhardt brothers immediately and made it difficult for the brothers to acquire porters. Eventually, however, the Denhardts made their way to Witu, where they established friendly relations with Simba, from whom they purchased land.[8]

On return to Lamu, the Denhardts claimed that their scientific instruments had been broken during shipment, and they required new ones. They were actually importing arms which they intended to give Simba as gifts in exchange for protection in the Witu area. The Denhardt brothers took a house in Lamu, which today is located on the main street.[9] There they were joined by other Germans, including Karl Peters, who issued a charter that put some of the Sultan of Zanzibar's territory under German protection, including Sultan's Ahmed's Witu, but not Lamu.

The Sultan of Witu was using the Germans to break the Sultan of Zanzibar's hold on the Witu area. Conversely the Germans were using him to establish their claim to that part of the northern coast. The British worried about the Zanzibari flag not flying over Witu, while more realistically Suud bin Hamed was concerned that Ahmed was using the Germans to expand his empire to the Lamu plantations on the mainland.

Suud bin Hamed led a force of Lamu men to Witu "without instructions from the Sultan and without sufficient arms for fighting." Many of these Lamu men were killed in the battle of *Vita ya Katawa*.[10] The Lamu leaders complained to Bargash who, in turn, "dethroned" Suud bin Hamed, but shortly thereafter reappointed him to office.[11] With the situation between Lamu and Witu now worsened, Suud bin Hamed convinced Sultan Bargash to send him a force of men—700 soldiers—but Bargash cautioned that they not be used for purposes of invasion and should be kept at the coast in case Simba's army invaded Lamu.

The Germans sent four armed men into Lamu where they obtained arms and ammunition and stole a small sailing ship. Soon thereafter, the Denhardts alleged that one of their Lamu servants was missing. Gossip suggested the liwali had murdered the servant. Fears continued among the WaAmu regarding the German presence on the mainland, especially because of the German alliance with the expansion minded Sultan of Witu.

The Zanzabari Sultan should have used his governor to keep the Germans in check. Instead Sir John Kirk, following orders from the Foreign Office, pressed the Sultan to remain aloof in the matter of the Germans in Lamu and Witu. Suud bin Hamed neither denied nor acknowledged complicity in the murder of the servant. But he was sacrificed on the altar of European imperialism, as well as his own considerable failings with the people of Lamu. While Britain and Germany worked out their territorial claims on East Africa, Kirk persuaded Bargash to send for Suud bin Hamed. On reaching Zanzibar the liwali was again fired. Abdalla bin Hamed, who was not related, was appointed in his place.[12]

Abdalla was an even more controversial figure, kindly remembered by descendants, and disliked by contemporary Europeans. Jackson, who had known him for several years was repelled by him. And the "dislike developed as time went on, into downright loathing which abated only when I learned that he had retired into private life . . . . An arrant coward, a pastmaster in cruel and low-down intrigue, his lust for power, his abuse of it when gained, and his greed generally were limitless. His character was stamped on his face, particularly in the expression of his shifty goggle eyes, and a large drooping, flabby, and sausage-like lower lip, that was incapable of hiding an irregular, discoloured, and very prominent row of teeth."[13]

Abdalla's father Hamed bin Said, a relative of the Sultan, moved from Oman to Zanzibar, then to Lamu where he took a second wife, Mwana Shee wa Shee Wapate, an upper class woman from the al Hussein sharifan family. Mwana Shee and Hamed bin Said produced a distinguished set of progeny whose descendants have formed the backbone of the twentieth century Lamu aristocracy, many of whom descended directly from Abdalla bin Hamed.[14] (see Appendix)

At the time Suud bin Hamed was retired from the Sultan's service, Kirk merely noted: "The Sultan appointed a new Liwali whose instructions seem to have been to obtain Simba's submission through negotiation and peaceable means.. . .The Germans run to the whole of the region now known as the Sultan of Zanzibar's dominions."[15]

After he was fired Suud in Hamed returned to Lamu where he was called back into service briefly as liwali in 1888. Then he incurred the wrath of the local WaAmu by taking the bodies of deceased people "by force" and requiring their heirs to provide him with some portion of their property. Oral tradition in the matter of robbing estates for personal gain is supported by British testimony in Zanzibar. Suud bin Hamid was "very rich having confiscated under various pretences the property of many residents and a large share of deceased estates . . . ." A stern governor who "cut off the hands of all thieves . . . everything was safe except from him."[16]

Kirk, who was forced to deal with his mendacious replacement, later hypocritically lamented his displacement: "the governor who was thoroughly respected and feared. . . whose will was law in the district he governed; this man was feared by Simba . . . .[and] his removal was in a way unworthy of the ruler of an important country."[17]

In the meantime, the Sultan of Witu was being "manipulated by the German imperial designs" with Clemens Denhardt serving as political agent and advisor to Simba. The Sultan of Zanzibar, however, was still the tool of the British, who continued promoting their own imperial designs in the mainland interior. Competition between the two powers reached the level of the absurd when Haggard and Frederick Jackson first decided to send back to England skeletons of two dugong, or sea cows, they arranged to procure through local fishermen.[18] Then "the German 'naturalists' managed to get two more at once," which were subsequently shipped to a museum in Berlin.[19]

In addition to the ludicrous competition between the German consuls in Witu and the British consul in Lamu, political matters continued to be serious. German influence in Witu affected the Lamu planters, and, in turn, contributed to their waning fortunes. Simba opened a series of customs houses in the Witu area. Any trader or planter who attempted to move his goods from the mainland territory claimed by Simba was forced to pay customs duties to his henchmen. Already forced to pay customs to the Sultan of Zanzibar, and suffering from lack of workers in the mainland, this added financial burden was resented, especially by "British subjects . . . whose position is serious." Indian traders were not welcome in Witu itself. One had already been killed. To keep trade in the hands of the Denhardt's German Witu Company, taxes levied on them were so heavy that only one courageous Hindu lived and worked there.[20] After Haggard's departure, the locals complained bitterly about the customs being levied on them on the mainland by the Sultan of Witu.

Between 1885 and 1888, the British kept no permanent agent on duty in the Lamu area, although the liwali reported to the Sultan who, in turn, was supposed to report to the British consul in Zanzibar. But events in Europe at that time had an impact in the Lamu archipelago. Sir William Mackinnon, a Scots businessman and philanthropist, founded a trading company that would open free trade in East Africa. In the time the Imperial British East Africa (IBEA) company operated in Lamu, however, one unfortunate incident followed another, until in 1895 the Foreign Office took over and the IBEA faded out of the picture.[21]

The Germans established a post office that forced British subjects to pay double postage—postage already paid at the source of origin, and postage again when their mail packets reached Lamu. This dragged on and added to the hostilities between the locals, the Germans, and the hapless British who were unable to do more than write numerous letters of complaint back to the Foreign Office. The Foreign Office in turn, sent a myriad of protests to the German government. The British government was at that time unsure of their plans for the Lamu area: the possibility was that Britain might withdraw in favor of Germany, depending on the compromises the powers made regarding their African claims.[22] For a time it appeared that the Germans were actually going to occupy Lamu, and George Mackenzie, Imperial British East African agent in Mombasa, conveyed the locals' complaints to his boss, William Mackinnon, that "Germany occupying Lamoo would go against the peoples wishes."[23]

At one point, the Sultan of Witu planned to seize Lamu Island, but in August 1886 the Germans and British worked out a compromise giving Lamu to the Sultan, who ceded it to the IBEA company. In July 1890, by the Anglo-German Treaty, Germany abandoned her claims on Witu. However, the German subjects who had moved into the area, including the Denhardts, stayed on to present problems for the British government over the next decade. The treaty granted the British the inland northern territories; the Sultan was left with his island dominions and a ten-mile coastal strip. Bargash was consulted only after the fact. With reluctance "he bowed to the inevitable" and signed in December, 1886.[24]

Important to Lamu was that the Sultan of Witu was officially recognized by the treaty. According to a later, sympathetic British official, "this was heavily felt by the people of Lamu, who owned much of the Witu cultivation."[25] This also meant that the customs houses along the newly dug Belazoni Canal, which linked the Tana River with the Ozi, continued to drain the Lamu planters and merchants. The town was isolated from both commerce and food supplies coming up from the Tana River. Despite protests that the area fell within the Sultan's domain until 1890, Witu refused to abandon the customs houses until armed forces arrived from Zanzibar two years later.

The Anglo-German treaty forced Witu to recognize the Sultan of Zanzibar's "powers" over the Belazoni Canal—meaning the German government gave up her protectorate in the area and completed her shift in emphasis to the south. By that time, the Lamu mainland plantations had fallen even more into neglect.

Despite the considerable setbacks for the Sultan of Zanzibar who died a few months later, the new Lamu liwali said of him in "The Chronicle of Lamu": "While he reigned he set all affairs in good order and did everything that was needed to be done throughout his kingdom."

History shows that Bargash lost much of his territory by failing to fight the Sultan of Witu when Suud bin Hamed was pressing him to first send troops and, then, to attack the mainland. Liwali Abdallah bin Hamed, however, saw events another way. "And he never ceased to press war upon Witu until they got into difficulties and he (the Sultan of Witu) sought aid of the Germans."[26]

By the last decades of the century, Europeans became an increasing presence in the Lamu area. The German community expanded to include Kurt Toeppen, sometime manager of the German Witu Company; and several missionaries who, finding themselves unwelcome in Lamu, moved to the Tana River area where they found a more receptive atmosphere among the Pokomo. A smattering of German settlers established sesame and cotton plantations on the mainland, enjoying the patronage of Simba whose political agent remained Clemens Denhardt. Despite the Anglo-German treaty, clearly the German Witu Company was encouraging settlers along with their practice of trying to lure German traders to the area.

In 1888 the IBEA sent Stuart Sandys to Lamu as agent. The IBEA agents wore two hats: acting as British consul in the area—taking care of business, and reporting activities in Witu involving the increasing numbers of Germans. Their IBEA roles called for them to supervise collection of customs, thus replacing the Indian agents who had served Zanzibar sultans from Said through Khalifa.

As agents for the antislavery IBEA and the anti-slave trade British government, they followed the earlier instructions to Haggard: eliminating the slave trade in the Lamu area. In the Mombasa area, the IBEA was

71

actively attempting to emancipate slaves by paying a set fee to their owners, causing Lamu slave owners to doubly resent the British interference
in their area. Witu, on the other hand, was not paying compensation but
was continuing to take in runaway slaves, further crippling Lamu plantations on the mainland.[27]

Problems then developed within the German community. Kurt
Toeppen, in whose Lamu residence the "post office" remained, was
accused by "the Denhardt faction of tampering with letters carried in one
of his dhows."[28] The Denhardts wanted the "German Post Office"
removed from Herr Toeppen's control. The British, who refused to recognize the existence of the German post office, were the recipients of the
Denhardt complaints. Clemens Denhardt was finally packed up and
detained in Bombay when World War I broke out in Europe. The Germans
worked actively to stir up opposition to the British on the mainland, keeping up that ridiculous facade of a post office, while turning to the British
consul/IBEA agent for aid whenever misfortune fell upon them. And misfortune came calling repeatedly in the few years that the IBEA company
operated in Lamu.[29]

Simba was still acting as self-appointed customs collector in various
strategic locations, including the Belezoni canal where both the Pokomo
and the Galla were financially disadvantaged. Sandys complained to
Denhardt, who promised to take up the matter with Simba and never did.
Again, the Germans were importing arms. Since they were listed as
engaging in "retail trade and boats" the British consul saw no need for
arms. These weapons were a payoff to Simba, whose *watoro* army then
sacked more Lamu mainland plantations, raped and robbed Africans elsewhere in the mainland, and frightened away all but the most stalwart
Indian traders. The liwali, too, was affected as he, along with Indian
traders, shipped his Mambrui products to the Lamu area. Thus, the liwali,
like other Lamu planters was caught between the devil (Simba), and the
deep blue sea (the increasing British strangulation of the slave trade by
sea and overland).

It is possible that Sandys, too, paid for his life for interfering with the
slave trade. Between July and December of that year British slave patrols
had captured fifteen dhows, restored but three to their owners and
destroyed twelve.[30] Beyond the loss of their ships, many in Lamu resent-

ed the growing authority of agents like Haggard and Sandys for other reasons as well. Zanzibari Sultan Khalifa was not as accommodating to the
British as Bargash, and may have been complicit in Lamu Afro-Arab
attempts to rid themselves of what they regarded as interference in their
affairs. The liwali, as a wealthy slave holder, could not but have experienced dual emotions when Sandys was summarily removed from reporting on the illegal slave trade into and out of that port city. In August 1899,
Sandys was found murdered by someone identified as an Arab and buried
at Shela.

Sandys replacement, R. Simons, inherited the customs problem and
complained, but this time to Toeppen. An Indian trader attempted to ship
sesame and ivory from near Mambrui to the port of Lamu. He paid the
Witu Sultan customs duties and then at Lamu, was forced to pay yet
another customs duty—this time to the Sultan of Zanzibar. Khalifa was
receiving a negotiated stipend from the IBEA, which kept the balance of
the profits. The customs agent at Lamu finally agreed to let the sesame go
duty free but insisted on levying an additional amount on the ivory. This
sent the Indian trader to Simons because he, like the liwali and the Afro-
Arabs, was being forced to pay double duty on items they wished to ship
from their home port.[31]

Keep in mind that the Anglo-German treaty was not in effect until 1890,
and thus the competition between the IBEA and the German Witu
Company (which propped up and supported Simba) was keen. The British
agents/consuls might complain in terms of their "subjects" but until the
matter was resolved between London and Berlin, all locals in that area
were pawns to both the IBEA and the German Witu Company. It so happened at the time of Simons complaint that the Foreign Office was in
process of negotiations on a much larger African stage. Thus, when
Toeppen failed to respond, and Simons sent a formal protest to Simba,
arguing that his customs houses were illegal, the British consul was rep-
rimanded by his government. In reply to the stern admonition forwarded
from Zanzibar by the consul Euan-Smith, Simons was forced to abandon
the mostly Indian traders, and agree that in future he would "never send
in protests to enter into discussion of disputed questions in correspondence with the German authorities."[32]

Because of his own dual loyalties, Abdalla bin Hamed had been briefly replaced by clever old Suud bin Hamed as liwali up in Lamu. In 1888, the interim year in which he replaced Abdalla bin Hamed, Suud bin Hamed was invited to Berlin by the German government who hoped to get the support of the Lamu Arabs. Arriving in 1889, Suud bin Hamed was presented with a gold watch by the youthful Kaiser Wilhelm II. Suud bin Hamed was by then out of office and was never again reappointed liwali.[33]

Gold watches were in. In April, 1890, the German Counsel General in Zanzibar decided to visit Simba. He arrived in Witu bearing a "watch with a picture of the German Emperor" for Simba no doubt similar to that which had been presented to Suud bin Hamed in Berlin; and "guns for all of the notables."[34] Not to be outdone, the British quickly imported a gold watch with a picture of the venerable Queen Victoria on the back which was presented to the Lamu liwali at a baraza [a gathering of local notables and British officials].

Simons single triumph in Lamu may have been the presentation of the watch. The WaAmu came close to armed rebellion in 1890 due to the joint British/Zanzibar actions against the slave trade. Abdalla bin Hamed remained involved in the trade despite his position, and protestations to the contrary to the British. During his tenure, Simons claimed, "burglary, intrigues, immorality, and incendiarism" were rampant. "Justice and equity" could only be obtained by purchase—at a price, apparently, Simons was unwilling to pay.[35]

Later that month he was fired by Mackinnon as IBEA agent, sending in his resignation to Euan-Smith at Zanzibar. Before his ignominious departure from Lamu, Simons was involved in a contretemps with Clemens Denhardt over Simba's threats to invade Lamu and over the "history of Witu" which, if it had been accurate, would have proved Witu's claim to both Pate and Manda islands. Before the "history" and the Sultan's claims were resolved, Simons departed the labyrinth of Lamu Afro-Arab-Simba-German-British politics.

Simba's death had not ended the conflicts between the Germans and the British and between the landholders on the mainland and the *watoro*. Matters for all groups worsened when Fumo Bakari took over as Sultan of Witu. The *watoro* were increasingly uncontrollable. Heretofore they had confined their pillage and rape to the non-European community. In September of 1890 they went on a rampage which resulted in heavy losses in life and property to the various Germans in the Witu area. Simon's replacement, Hammerick Douglas, was soon followed by R. W. Pigott as British agent, and it was to Pigott that the Germans turned. Fumo Bakari turned on the Germans who, he believed, had sold "him and his country to the British after encouraging him to resist the demands both of the British and Sultan of Zanzibar."[36]

First, Herr Kuntzel, a military man who had been employed to drill Simba's troops, decided to open a sawmill in the Witu area, importing ten German mechanics to work with him. Sending some of these men ahead, Kuntzel and the rest arrived in Witu to find they had been taken prisoner by the Sultan's forces. Two days later Kuntzel and the remainder of the group were murdered and their equipment stolen or broken.

A few days later, Herr Joseph Friedrich, another agent for the German Witu Company, reported that his entire crop of "coconuttress" and sesame had been entirely destroyed along with some buildings on the mainland plantation. Unable to believe that Simba had turned on them, a Lamu man was accused, with Friedrich demanding his property be confiscated, and with the consul taking no action. When the estate of Robert Ron Dorf was attacked, blame was placed on the Sultan of Witu, who was responsible for the band of men he could no longer control. Ron Dorf identified one of the men who destroyed his estate as "the head slave of the Sultan." Pigott requested all Europeans on the mainland to come into Lamu, where they would be safe no matter the damage that occurred to their property. Denhardt removed to his Lamu house, but continued to work with Fumo Bakari, although his property losses were the largest incurred. The claims were forwarded to the British government, now in control of the area due to the Anglo-German treaty.[37]

Matters between the Sultan of Witu and the Germans, and the British went unresolved, despite numerous dispatches, claims, and counterclaims between company agents in Lamu and the British government appointee in Zanzibar. George Portal's appointment as British Commissioner for East Africa marked the last vestiges of power enjoyed by the Sultans of Zanzibar. Khalifa died in 1890 and was replaced by his brother Ali. Ali's acquiescence to increasing British control was the cause for more resentment in Lamu, which Portal attempted to address when he came to the port city en route to do battle with Fumo Bakari, in April 1892.[38]

The Lamu Afro-Arabs, whose activities included continued importation of slaves, and unwillingness to accede to the financial demands of the IBEA agent in Lamu were, according to Portal, "naughty and want sitting upon and I am going to speak to them like as father—like an ill-tempered father." On arrival in Lamu he held a baraza in front of the fort, requiring that all the "Arabs" in town be present. Later, reporting to the Foreign Office, Portal said that he come to Lamu in a "Man-o-War" (prepared for large scale fighting with the Sultan of Witu and his forces, but using the ship as a kind of threat to the WaAmu as well). "I publicly arrested and put under restraint six most prominent Arabs of Lamu on my arrival. There they completely changed their attitude and we were able to break up their combination in a thorough and effectual manner without firing a shot."[39]

Portal proceeded to march overland to near Witu where he met a detachment of Sepoy troops and a group of marines he had sent ahead as a threat of what was to come unless Fumo Bakari surrendered. When Portal arrived, his military leader had already engaged in one successful battle with Witu. The Sultan and his followers had retreated behind the stockades and were barricaded with stockpiles of weapons and ammunition supplied by the Germans. Among the troops in the first contingent were men from Lamu, who were anxious to bring the Sultan down. After the victory, one of them composed the following verse which indicates that sentiments were anti-German as well.[40]

The charcoal was for fire
Fumo has got a child
Ten Europeans who died in Witu

Kurt Toeppen carried on the negotiations with Fumo Bakari for a total of six days ("not knowing whether we would have peace or war") before Fumo Bakari surrendered and released a number of hostages. Portal reported that "I had an interesting time at Lamu and Witu and managed to pacify the country."[41] Fumo Bakari, the last of the Nabahany sultans, continued to rule over Witu until 1895. His replacement was another symbol of British imperialism: Omari bin Mohammed O.B.E. was appointed by the Foreign Office and ruled until his death in 1923.

The fist of encroaching colonialism was tightening and the WaAmu were not yet pacified, despite Portal's self-congratulatory note to his wife. They were, in fact, caught in a dilemma.

CHAPTER 5

A *Nahoa* with descendant of slaves, who is unloading a dhow in the harbor.
From the author's collection

Chapter Five

The Onset of Colonialism

"Recite to them the history of him to whom we vouchsafed our signs"
The Qur'an

In Lamu, Haggard discovered malaria was a problem that all ethnic groups had to contend with. The British consul evidenced little interest in the health of the local people nor did he seem to recognize the malaise caused by malaria, although he frequently referred to the "fevers" from which various people were recovering. Part of the problem was that Haggard's personal contacts in Lamu were generally limited to the liwali, qadi, a few local elders, some of the Indian community, and his own slaves.

Falciparum malaria was endemic in Lamu, as it was in Zanzibar and elsewhere on the East African coast.[1] While falciparum malaria struck in coastal Oman, it was seasonal. In Lamu, it could and did strike any time. For the slaves, who had assigned tasks to carry out irrespective of illness, malaria was debilitating and kept any number of the work force in a weakened state most of the time.

Of his own health Haggard had ample to say. He arrived in Lamu with "fever and I was very ill at times for a week when it went away, leaving me covered from head to foot with pocks which are now nearly all gone." Yet this seems not to have been smallpox as he was vaccinated for that a few months later on a visit to Zanzibar.[2] In another letter he wrote "my only source of irritation are the fleas." And he worried about scratching fly bites for fear of blood poisoning. His major problem was his bladder. On two separate occasions Haggard spent over a month (in a period of less than two years) in bed with sickness resulting from an obstructed bladder. This was finally resolved when a doctor in Zanzibar taught him to use a rubber catheter. In the case of local people suffering with this same condition, no European counsel or medicine was available, and the only relief was if the bladder ruptured—and that might then cause more problems than it solved.[3]

Smallpox was known in East Africa for centuries. By the eighteenth century, some natives had a form of inoculation they used. Arabs from South Arabia also practiced vaccination for smallpox: "the pus is introduced into an incision in the forehead between the eyebrows."[4] Traders from Arabia brought the knowledge with them but they inoculated only when an epidemic occurred. In central Africa, and in the 1890s, a Swahili proclaimed that there was "no cure except fire." There they diagnosed three kinds of pox, "maize pox, sorghum pox, and sesame pox . . . [if anyone gets] sesame pox he is lucky if he recovers, for it is very severe." Slaves coming from that area were inclined towards fire as treatment for smallpox. But if their eyes were affected, and if they followed traditional practices, "the urine of a child six or seven years of age" was applied to prevent infection.[5]

Dr. James Christie, who spent several years in Zanzibar in the 1860s, spoke with informants who claimed that in about 1809 smallpox "made dreadful ravages all over the island." While still in Zanzibar in late 1883, Haggard wrote home about the smallpox "which hits the European population" hard but no worse, he thought, than "in England."[6] Lamu was in frequent trading contact with Zanzibar and epidemics surely spread there, too. Lack of sanitation and not inoculation, Christie guessed, was the cause.[7]

The Lamu stone houses in the past and today, have what is commonly known as "long drop" toilets. In the two story houses, most of these long drops are shafts of about fifty feet, ventilated to allow air in between the ground and the toilet up above. The nature of these sanitary facilities is enhanced by a hole in the floor (usually covered with a stone when not in use), which prohibits contact between the human body and the area through which waste passes. In the nineteenth century bathrooms, pottery jars locally made held large quantities of water brought in from town wells that served as breeding grounds for mosquitoes.

Mosques also had large water containers of well water so that the men could wash before prayer. Mosques closest to the congested town obtained the freshest water as it was replenished by the slaves. Some houses and mosques contained cisterns that held stagnant and impure water. These cisterns drew mosquitoes and larvae of different types thus to the spread of diseases throughout the community.

Among the poor and newcomers, sanitary facilities were nonexistent. During the nineteenth century, at the height of Lamu's prosperity, small mud and wattle houses with dirt floors and no toilet facilities burgeoned, including "squalid native huts down to the water's edge" even in front of the fort. Little water from the town wells was available or stored because it had to be purchased. In the nineteenth century, the task of carrying jars of water from the wells to houses throughout the town was assigned to "water-women" as no man would "do the job" in Zanzibar or in Lamu.[8]

James Christie's description of mid-nineteenth century Zanzibar matches travelers accounts of Lamu at the turn of the century. Rubbish and "filth swept to the sea by street torrents . . . animal droppings everywhere [with] superficial sweeping." Cows and sheep often penned near the houses (or in Haggard's case within the deserted house he later occupied). "Myriads of ants and beetles, millions of rats and armies of wild dogs" did help rid the city of some of the filth but these insects and rodents were also sources of plague."[9] In Lamu, in place of the dogs, were the mangy insect ridden cats.

Before concrete walkways were poured early in the twentieth century, heavy sand and filth characterized the paths along the narrow alleyways in Lamu. Between the rainy seasons (April-May; September-October), litter accumulated on the pathways and around the market. Haggard wrote home about tromping through heavy sand as he made his way around Lamu. Soon after his arrival, he was writing about the "HEAT" and the odors that wafted up from the "stinking beach," including dried mud "which extends for miles of each side of my house. The stench is truly dreadful." Actually the area was "a VERY public latrine!"[10] As the tides came in, wastes were swept up; when the tides retreated, they washed out. Donkeys, camels, and horses all added droppings to the accumulation of filth.

Elephantiasis was common in Lamu as in Zanzibar.[11] There are no oral traditions that recall incidence of mental illness and degenerative diseases. Elderly informants believe that abortifacients were long in use in Lamu. Because life for the healthy, especially the poor, was difficult enough, it seems possible that babies born with serious defects, did not live long after birth.[12]

In July of 1884, and with a drought expected, smallpox "broke out with virulence and there have been a great number of deaths. Epidemics are very frequent but they are short and sharp in Africa." In this case "many died in the native huts almost touching the walls of my house." What seemed to disturb was the "wailing of the women" but after awhile, Haggard "got used to it . . .The Negresses who have not inherited the Arab wail but think they must do something [like] stand bolt upright with their arms by their sides and roar like great babies without shedding a tear."[13]

By September of that year "smallpox raging . . . in Lamu so many died people have stopped wailing and lots of them are buried in the narrow streets to avoid the trouble of so constantly moving them to be buried out of the town. Only yesterday a Hindi came to complain to me of two dead bodies buried in front of his doorstep and not two feet from it. . . . people have been constantly dying within a few feet of the walls of my house."[14] The disease seems to have been more fatal to the Indians than the natives, and to the natives more than the Europeans. Not all died, however, and Jackson's observations indicate that the locals had developed primitive methods of treatment that included "that of women scrubbing their bairns with salt water and sand during the scaling stage. . . ."[15]

Cholera was another threat to Zanzibari and Lamu town dwellers. The cholera epidemic of 1865 did not reach Zanzibar, but it hit Lamu hard, coming in with ships on the northeast monsoon from the Somali coast. Cholera also spread to Oman and Arabia through the "slave dhows [which] very frequently took in their cargoes at the Somali ports or Patta and Lamoo." But it went both ways: Burton recorded a "violent attack of cholera" that reached from Muscat to East Africa in 1859. In 1865 another bout of cholera was attributed to slave ships and Lamu "where cholera was there in April . . . ."[16] A major epidemic occurred in 1879-80. Christie tracked this particular outbreak to the monsoon winds which blew traders from India and the Persian Gulf to the East African coast, reversing the pattern of west to east.[17]

Before Haggard's arrival and during the nearly two years he was in residence, a number of murders also took place. In 1874, a year after the official end of the slave trade, some of the Sultan's soldiers were murdered. That same year a Hindu—a British subject—was robbed and murdered. By the 1880s, Suud bin Hamed reported "a great disaffection to the Arab government there" although Haggard incorrectly believed the liwali was "personally very popular." All parties—those opposed to the Afro-Arabs and those who cooperated—were "very anxious about the Somalis who could readily combine and plunder the town." Despite the reported popularity of the Sultan in Lamu, even "more of his soldiers have been stabbed of late while passing through the narrow lanes alone, and the few who have been detected are the people of Lamu."[18]

In Lamu British attitudes towards local Afro-Arab men were generally unfavorable. This was especially true concerning the young adult men. Jackson's words were the harbinger of what was to become almost a litany from British colonial servants posted in Lamu. "I had taken a violent dislike to the people of the better class as a whole, and more particularly to the young men of about my own age. Their pale faces and blackened eyes [kohl], their betel-nut-dyed lips and teeth, their limp and rolling gait, their infernal swagger, in fact everything about them, repelled me; they were parasites. . . . for practically every pice of the money I had paid to the slaves on the mainland for moving me from village to village, went into their clutches." In his case, Jackson noted that he was "almost rabid on the question of slavery, but I did not know what a cesspool of iniquity the place really was; I only learned that some years later."[19]

The refrain "iniquity" and "immoral" crops up in Foreign Office reports in District Commissioners accounts and in various travelers memories of Lamu and in Zanzibar. Colonel Rigby blamed the Omanis who he referred to as "sodomizers. . . . These degraded wretches" he wrote, "openly walk about dressed in female attire with veils on their faces."[20] It is true that homosexuality was tolerated between young unmarried men (and increasingly so, after slaves were no longer available). One elderly BuSaid remembered that in his youth his father forbade him access to the seafront when ships from Arabia were in port. It was widely held that visiting seamen assaulted young boys for sex: "They used to spoil local boys long ago . . . the Arabs would give them gifts to tempt them. This was especially true of *watuma* [slaves]. But it was kept quiet."[21] Rumor at the time, and later, suggested that homosexual men [*washoga*] often served as pimps for Lamu prostitutes. These were mainly slave or poor women from the mainland who had no other source of support. Transvestites and transsexuals, who associated primarily with women and who also served as pimps, were in Lamu earlier as they are still today. As a thriving port city, Lamu, like all ports, had its full compliment of sexual and erotic services.[22]

But there are no nineteenth century medical records pertaining to venereal disease. British officials do not comment on it: no doubt because they had no direct contact with the prostitutes (male and female). There were, however, traditional medicines that local used to combat these sexually transmitted diseases.

After the peace agreement in 1890 the "history of Witu" has little direct bearing on that of Lamu but it does have relevance to the chronicles that were collected when the IBEA took over the Sultan's possessions. George Mackenzie, Mackinnon's manager in East Africa, ordered that histories be collected in all of the island communities. "The Lamu Chronicle," collected by Abdalla bin Hamed, liwali of Lamu, therefore was done at the bidding of the IBEA agent. Mackenzie's instructions to record the histories of Pate, Lamu, and other northern island communities was to solidify the IBEA contractual relationship with the Sultan of Zanzibar. As we have seen, "The Lamu Chronicle" celebrates the current leading families of the port city, the descendants of Abdul Malik bin Marwan the original "settler," as the other "histories" collected at that time, including Denhardt's, do as well.

Denhardt claimed that he spent twelve years collecting the "history" which, by showing the relationship of Sultan Fumo Bakari (who replaced Simba) to the Nabahany rulers of Pate, solidified their claim to that island. Since at one time Pate had defeated Manda, Fumo Bakari claimed that island as well. Thus this "history" is an attempt to legitimize the rule of a single family in these island communities as well as establish Fumo Bakari's claim to them.[23] Denhardt's "history" is also the first written compilation of oral traditions on the northern coast.

As an outgrowth of Denhardt's efforts to miscontrue history for political purposes, Simons was ordered to send Mohammed bin Hamed

BuSaid, a British employee and a brother of the liwali, to Pate to collect "the history" of that community. Within less than a month, Mohammed's research was complete although it was hardly a contradiction to that submitted by Denhardt. Mohammed bin Hamed, as much an outsider in Pate as were the British in Lamu, managed to find a "Mzee of Patta," who justified the Nabahany connection between "Witu, Siyu, Pate, and Manda." When totaled and subtracted from 1890, the dates of rule provided by Mzee "Nab ah Ahani" take the Nabahany claims to rulership in Pate back to about 1680.[24]

At this time, too, the British began to categorize people in these northern coastal communities into "tribes" such as the Pokomo, Galla, Somali, and others with whom they were involved in what is today's Kenya.[25] The Swahili "tribe" appears to have been the name assigned to persons whose first language was KiSwahili, in spite of their ethnic origin.[26] In the following example we see some of the confusion in identity that resulted in boxing the coastal peoples into "tribes."

In 1890, T. Hammerick Douglas reported that a "Swahili" from Shela murdered a Somali. The enmity between these coastal peoples and the Somali was nothing new but, in this case, Douglas worried that large scale retaliation was about to occur on the mainland which might extend all the way to Lamu. All but one Somali then in residence on Lamu island fled to the north, to lands traditionally occupied by the Somalis. Word had gone out that the Somali were going to attack the "Swahili" in Merka and Douglas rushed to the liwali, imploring him to look into the matter and report back to him.[27]

The situation was resolved without bloodshed, but what concerns us is that KiSwahili speakers in Merka and in Shela were now identified as a tribe. We have no way of knowing if the "Swahili" in Merka were Hadrami traders, Afro-Arabs of either Hadrami or Omani patralineage, free Africans of local origin whose ancestors had been Swahili speakers, Mijikenda who had adopted Swahili as their language, slaves who were KiSwahili speakers, or a combination of any and all of the above. As to the "Swahili" in Shela, they may have been descendants of the Manda islanders who had fled during the Pate attacks in earlier centuries and who were Swahili speakers, perhaps descendants of the first group of Africans who developed the trading language in concert with outsiders. More likely the KiSwahili speakers in Shela were composed of all the mixtures that marked the Lamu dwellers, including a preponderance of slaves at the time of the Douglas report.

British officials on the northern coast had no problem identifying the liwalis and qadis as "Arabs." But lack of familiarity with the cultural antecedents in these areas gave rise to the amorphous grouping of the unknown into the known, *e.g.*, the "Swahili." Later, this tribal identification backfired, and especially when the British Colonial Office took over in 1895 and launched the native hut tax, which all ethnic groups were forced to pay. The Afro-Arabs who regarded themselves as "Arab" because of their patralineage were dismayed at being referred to as "natives" which to them implied animists, such as the slaves that they had long imported from Africa. Or, the indigenous people like the Yumbili in Lamu who were Muslim, but who had been relegated to the bottom of the social ladder among the free people in the port city.

Later, the British encountered yet another "tribal" grouping—in this case invented by the different social classes to differentiate among themselves for purposes of identification by the outsiders. In addition to Hadrami import, the social hierarchy that has characterized Lamu in the twentieth century seems to have had some of its roots in British attempts to categorize and tribalize. The WaFamao (originally from the ruling class in Siyu) became a "tribe." The WaYumbe, the *waungwana* who claimed to have taken the title of Haji Said who was said to have come to Lamu with Abdul Malik from Damascus and who identified with the Yumbe palace (or the leaders in the town at that time), were a "tribe." So, too, were the WaKinamte, meaning people of social position. These groups emerged to join the Yumbili (the lowly washers of the dead) as members of various "tribes." Yet they distinguished themselves from the WaSwahili, whom they regarded as slaves and ex-slaves of African origin. Both the WaKinamte and WaYumbe groups were composed of Afro-Arabs. The Hadramis remained (for the most part) Hadrami; and the Indians kept their own identity.[28]

According to Lamu elders, and the *Tarikhi ya Amu*, the names were groupings of neighborhoods in which various members of those who considered themselves the aristocracy lived. Their leaders were chosen from the among the elderly males who were regarded as worthy of the title.[29]

Before the Colonial office took over, and while the conflicts drug on between the British and the Germans, the WaAmu received an unwelcome lesson in imperialism. In 1892, the IBEA issued a proclamation at Mombasa, requiring the locals to register the names and residences of every one in town.[30] Every shamba owner was compelled to register his land holdings. All the merchants and traders and ship owners were ordered to register, and state the "nature of their business." For this requirement on the part of the IBEA, each person, business, or land owner (or a combination of all) was then charged a fee that ranged from one to three rupees. If the people did not comply, they were fined Rs. 100/. In return, the IBEA pledged that the fees would be applied to "the establishment and efficient management of police protection and administrative supervision."[31]

The IBEA was never able to force payment of the various fees. Furthermore, no one could provide a title or deed to their homes or their shambas because of the system of land tenure that prevailed at the time. No member of the community had any deeds to register.[32] The proclamation, however, stirred the collective anger of the patricians, the Indian merchants, and the few Hadrami who had opened small shops in the southern end of town.

In 1889, the German scholar Oscar Baumann came through Lamu on his way to Witu. He commented on the various ethnic groups he observed, including "Hadrami Arabs, Omani-Arabs and black slaves." Lamu, Baumann noted, "is the capital of East Africa," which reenforces the view that Lamu was dominant on the northern coast at this time.[33]

The British biologist W. W. A. Fitzgerald left the lengthiest account of flora, fauna, and animal life on the mainland of the northern coast.[34] As to Lamu, Fitzgerald supported Baumann. It "is, after Mombasa, the chief port of the coast and is connected with Europe and India as well as Zanzibar" by steamships run by the IBEA and the sailing dhows "owned by Arabs and Indians. The town . . . contains 5,000 inhabitants; it is a mass of crowded houses." By the 1890s Europe had brought progress of a sort to Lamu. The town was connected by a telegraph line, which "went by cable" to the mainland and as far down the coast as Malindi.

86

The Lamu mainland planters were at that time growing "short stapled cotton" that was "very poor stuff, dull, rough, uneven, and native ginning bad," which resulted in a low selling price. Women were "busy occupied in cleaning it with primitive ginning machines." The cotton seeds, which were very difficult to remove, "cleaned by means of a small wooden implement . . . called *kitoko* . . . which consists of two sticks placed in a small frame, turned in opposite directions by means of a wooden handle at each side." This difficult process resulted in "one basket a day from one *kitoko* machine. . ."[35] Coconut plantations were located on both Pate and Lamu islands, and Fitzgerald encouraged locals to create more on the mainland, where Herr Denhardt was busy clearing land and developing large plantations.

A major crop continued to be sesame. The mainland plantations had begun the mass production of sesame at the demand of the French, and this product continued to enjoy a good market until the plantations were all but abandoned in the early twentieth century.[36] Rice, a major staple on any Lamu table, also grew on the mainland but, again, not of the quality Fitzgerald considered equal to the long grain variety grown elsewhere. Hunting, which preoccupied most of the British who came to the area, was "reported to be plentiful" although Fitzgerald noted "at present there were only buck and 'pah' [a small antelope]. The elephant hunter "carries only his gun and a little food and marches from sunrise to sunset."

Although Fitzgerald did not refer to the WaAmu as hunters, many members of the aristocracy spent considerable time hunting. Often Afro-Arab youths went on several-day safaris, accompanied by a slave or several slaves, and hunted elephant, hippo, and other animals. Necessity at times dictated killing wild game as otherwise plantations were destroyed by their foraging. Monkeys constituted a problem on the mainland and slaves were often commanded to wipe them out. The *watoro* menace resulted in curtailed hunting for both sport and to preserve crops. Slaves—those who had not deserted—were still instructed to keep the animals at bay, although many killed for skins and ivory, selling them at Witu, and keeping the profits for themselves.[37] "Deer" [antelope], giraffe and "leopard" were valuable for their hides which the IBEA company bought and sent to London. One Lamu planter had a large shamba filled with only banana trees. The Arab "kept his slaves constantly cleaning and weeding plants, which looked remarkably well. The fruit he exported to Lamu."

Between Lamu and a small village on the other side of the island, Fitzgerald found "very little cultivation—indeed there seems hardly any in the centre of the island."[38] Yet elderly informants remember the center of the island as the garden of the port city. Assuming Fitzgerald's observations are accurate for the 1890s, it is likely that, as the mainland plantations crumbled into the earth from which they emerged, the locals began to develop the island. House building was going apace when Fitzgerald visited. Imports from England consisted of white cloth from the Manchester mills and umbrellas, which the men used to cover themselves from the midday sun.

By 1903 when A. Whyte went to Witu to "examine the rich and fertile district," it was still sufficiently prosperous to be hailed as "one of the most important towns on the coast." His observations differ from those of Fitzgerald, suggesting that in just over ten years the slaves and their owners had been busily engaged. Whyte reported that "Lamu may be called an island of coconut palms . . . the island is composed entirely of sea sand and is unsuitable for the raising of grain crops. Apart from the coconut growing and kindred industries, the manufacturing of mats and mat bags is the principle work of the country people. Fish is good and plentiful and is the staple article of food."

Overtapping the coconut trees seems to have begun about this time. Whyte alludes to "palm wine" being in great demand. Fresh palm juice is not considered "wine" and was widely consumed by the local people (as, of course, also was fermented juice by some few of the Muslims). In some areas the trees were "considerably weakened" as a result of overtapping. Shambas "belonging to enlightened Arabs" used goat manure for fertilizer, which "paid off" in terms of "numbers of products" from the coconut trees.[39]

Land tenure on the mainland was based on the Muslim concept that "the world belongs to God, and man is a life tenant." Hence, those who cleared the land occupied it. According to British officials who came on the scene later "cultivation possessed of permanent signs of occupation . . . [was] sufficient to produce a hereditary right. The rest of the land being held as in wafq or trust by the community as commange."[40] Later, this concept of land tenure presented almost unsurmountable problems to the mainland shamba owners when, after the abolition of slavery, they attempted to claim compensation from the British government.

This policy was complicated by conquest on the part of both the Galla and the Somali, who in earlier centuries often drove the island people away from their lands. In the 1880s, the Germans staked out and declared certain holdings, although they seemed not to have claimed land that was occupied by the Lamu planters.

The missionaries were tolerated as long as they moved elsewhere to practice conversion. W. H. During attempted to locate a mission station there but was soon dissuaded by the liwali, who sent him to work among the Pokomo.[41] The group of outsiders who made a considerable, if brief, impact were "The Freelanders" who arrived in the late 1890s due to British attempts to encourage European settlement in East Africa.[42] The British government, however, had not intended settlers quite like the Freelanders, who were described as an "association composed of Europeans of various nationalities [who] endeavored to create, on what would presumably be regarded as more or less Socialistic lines, an international colony. . . ."[43]

Their leader was an Austrian professor and "its members represented many different countries: one of them, a Mr. Scavenious, was the son of a Danish cabinet minister; another, Captain Dugmore, an English officer; and there were also several ladies of advanced political and social ideas, one of whom I was told, had publicly assumed in a speech on her landing at Lamu, the title of 'the African Louise Michel' . . . . In as much as they or anybody else seemed to have a clear conception of their aims, it was not very easy to deal with them."

The Freelanders did not stay in Lamu long but their presence was frowned upon by the leading elders. The locals complained of their behavior to the liwali who, in turn, berated the IBEA agent. To the staid and straitlaced Muslim population, the Freelanders were symbolic of but another unwelcome example of British colonialism. Arthur Hardinge, who received second hand reports in Zanzibar, recalled that soon after their arrival, they "hired one of the few buildings in Lamu suitable for European habitation, which they named Freeland House but several of them, in the tropical climate of their new utopia, got frequently dead-drunk, and offended Mohammedan feeling by taking liberties, in the name of free love with native women, some of whom being of Persian descent and fair complexion, were far from unattractive and numerous quarrels and scandals . . . ensued . . . In a few weeks, however, their funds ran short, and most of them returned to Europe." The women of Persian descent to whom Hardinge referred were probably Circassian concubines from the Black Sea area who were popular among the Omanis, and some were brought into Lamu from Zanzibar.[44]

Britain continued to ride herd over the locals in both Zanzibar and in the administrative districts that were created from the Sultan's possessions. Earlier, the IBEA had contemptuously removed the Sultan's sole prerogative to appoint or fire his liwalis, insisting that all appointments be jointly decided. This policy was continued during the colonial period.[45] With increasing responsibility in these areas, more local staff was required. A British dictated bureaucratic structure gradually emerged in Lamu. We saw that the IBEA Company hired locals, like the brother of the liwali who recorded the "history of Pate." The two or three clerks and few askaris [police] who served Haggard were, by 1895, increased to include mudirs [magistrates] sent to small towns like Faza, and Siyu to represent British interests and to articulate colonial policy.

The hierarchy which evolved from 1895 when the Foreign Office took over until 1905 when the Colonial Office became responsible for governing the Sultan's possessions, was along these lines: instructions from Whitehall went to Zanzibar where they were forwarded to provincial commissioners. Hardinge, the first FO appointee to Zanzibar, created the provinces that put Lamu at the head of Tanaland Province. In Lamu the provincial commissioner (PC) was responsible for districts who were headed by more commissioners (DC). These men were all British, coming mostly from the middle class at home, lacking the experience that many, such as Portal, had earlier brought with them from other parts of the empire. The mudirs, who reported to the DC's, were locals. Under them were the clerks, also locals, although by the early 1900s, a number of Goans were brought in to serve in place of the Afro-Arabs whose loyalties were often in question.

Thus, increasing numbers of Afro-Arabs joined the ranks of the British bureaucracy, while others among them were distancing themselves as far as they could from their new colonial masters. As was her policy, Britain required her subjects to subsidize her rule. Taxes, such as the hut tax, were levied and local mudirs were expected to collect them from their peers. Public works projects, some much needed for improving sanitation, required not only money from the poll tax, but also employees. In this way, the local WaAmu joined the British cash economy from 1901.[46]

Jointly appointed liwalis were no less sympathetic to their Afro-Arab brethren than those chosen by the sultans. They tried to walk the fine line between their own interests as slave holders and the colonials who, from the 1890s, paid their salaries. G.S.P. Freeman-Grenville remembered meeting a son of Adballa bin Hamed, who was reappointed Lamu liwali in 1891 and served in that capacity until 1909. This son, liwali of Dar-es-Salaam after World War I, was a young boy in 1903 when Queen Victoria died. Nonetheless, he remembered that her death co-incided with the end of Ramadan—meaning the beginning of Idd-al-Fitr and the feasts that marked the end of the long fast. Abdalla bin Hamed, anxious for an occasion to display his loyalty, sent his young son around the town, "ordering that the New Moon be ignored for twenty-four hours, and that an extra day's fast be observed in mourning the death of the Queen."[47]

There is no doubt that the liwalis and others employed by the British government displayed outward symbols of loyalty. Nevertheless, as slave holders and as land and home owners, who through tax levies, were forced to support the imposition of a government they did not want and whose policies they abhorred, anger seethed below the surface.

CHAPTER 6

Hadrami men converse on seafront
From the author's collection

Chapter Six

The Hadrami, Comoro Islanders, and Indian Communities
at the Turn of the Century

"Verily, God will not wrong men in aught,
but men will wrong themselves."
The Qur'an

The Hadrami sharifs had been migrating into the Lamu archipelago for centuries. Some stayed in the island communities trading on the high regard with which descendants of the Prophet were generally regarded. Oral traditions in Lamu recall that men claiming to be sharifs (as indeed most were), came into these coastal towns offering to bestow their holy powers, and demanding food, sometimes a man's daughter, or even his wife. Poor Muslims were their prey. These traditions are complemented by the observations of a German in Tanganyika at the turn of the century. There sharifs were "begging" and trying to use their "baraka" to get money for themselves as well as to yield influence among the local Muslims.[1] A few of these sharifs were actually trained in Arabic medicines and settled in places like Lamu where they established practices. While many of them were welcomed by the Hadramis who proceeded them, others were regarded as pariahs by the local ruling class. This was especially true in Lamu in the nineteenth century when the Omanis were busy ingratiating themselves with the ruling class.[2]

General impressions always lead to exceptions. The leading family in Lamu, descendants of Bwani Zaidi, had their roots in the Hadramaut, which by the late nineteenth century, was an anathema to the aristocracy. According to family traditions "seven hundred years ago," two brothers fought at the death of their father, and "the one who was defeated" came to Lamu. Longevity of residence with no ties to the Hadramaut, combined with their position as wealthy landholders descended from the leader of the Battle of Shela, caused a collective amnesia as to their place of origin by the time the new arrivals drifted in.[3]

The first recorded reference to *madrassas* in Lamu comes from Captain Thomas Boteler who traveled there in the 1830s and noted that there were "four Koranic schools," which he said all the boys attended.[4] Perhaps the renowned Hadrami scholar, Shaykh Munyi al Din bin Shaykh bin Abdallah al Qahtani al Wa'ili (1790-1869) was then running one of the schools. Born in Barawa, he "lived for long periods at Lamu and Mombasa" where he wrote poetry praising the Mazrui rulers in Mombasa but "employed Lamu poetic conventions." Sharif Munyi's migration from Somalia into Lamu, and then going further south is typical of many Hadrami in the nineteenth and early twentieth centuries.[5]

Because of the long controversy over the identity of the Shirazi, who many claim were early Persian migrants to East Africa, Gill Shepherd's research and findings present an altogether convincing argument that they were sharifs who were in Mogadishu when Ibn Battuta visited during the fourteenth century. Later, the sharifs were rulers of Kilwa, during that port city's period of prosperity. Shirazi was a *nisba*, and therefore not a conglomerate of Persians settling here and there on the coast. A Sharifan family, the Mahdali, claimed to be of Shirazi descent, but recent findings suggest they came from the Hadramaut.[6] According to Shepherd, the much older "Kilwa Chronicle" is a family history of the Mahdali in that old Swahili trading port as much as "The Chronicle of Lamu" is primarily a history of the combined al Maawyia-BuSaid families of the nineteenth century.[7] Several families also claimed close relationship to the Mahdali, including Sharif Abdalla bin Salim, whose female ancestor he said, took the Mahdali qadi Mywene Abdalla as one of her husbands.[8]

One of the most renowned Swahili poets, Sharif Abdalla bin Ali bin Nasir, lived on Pate island, but his family roots were in the Hadramaut.[9] His grandfather, Nasir, is named on the Pate tombstone of Sharif Talib, a second cousin, whose father and his brother were sent to assist the WaPate against the Portuguese.[10] The Swahili proverb that "a having a daughter is like having a tree with no branches" is paradoxical since all legitimate descendants of the Prophet Mohamed trace their lineage to his daughter, Fatima. But not all those who came to the northern coast actually had the documentation to prove their line of descent. The al Hussein sharifs were already integrated into the Lamu aristocracy, even though as the nineteenth century unfolded Hadramis became increasingly unwelcome.[11]

As a port city, Lamu also drew itinerant sharifs for brief periods of time. The family of Sharif Taib bin Ali of the Baskut clan migrated to Mombasa from Somalia at the end of the nineteenth century. Then they went to Lamu where Sharif Taib engaged in business. There he married his second wife, Zam Zam, who was a Jahadhmy. Of their many children, Abdalla, eventually married a Lamu woman who became the mother of Sharif Nasir, an important political figure in Mombasa in the late twentieth century. Sharif Abdalla took as his second wife, Jahi (a sharifa), whose daughter by her first marriage was Aisha Suud, the first female Muslim member of the Mombasa County Council in the 1980s.[12]

But not all the early arrivals were sharifs. Some Hadramis served in Sultan Said's army as early as 1812-13, and were posted in Lamu as soldiers. These men may have had wives back home but, they too, married local women. A few who drifted in during the nineteenth century started out as fishermen. This type of work was easy to finance on a small scale. A few scratched and saved so they could purchase small fishing boats, then they acquired slaves, expanding their businesses. Some Hadramis followed the pattern of the Baskut clan by shifting trade from one port city to another and gradually established coastal family networks similar to those that marked the Indian groups. But these were on a smaller scale. In the case of the early nineteenth century Hadramis, however, the families were created in East Africa and few, if any, carried on trade with those who remained in the Hadramaut.[13] By the nineteenth century, the Sunni Shaf'i school of Islam was prevalent on the northern Kenya coast. Some authorities attribute this to the Hadramaut, where the Shaf'i school was dominant.[14] Certainly the sufism [saint worship] that came to play a major role in Lamu's religious history had its source in the Hadramaut. But like any major religion, orthodoxy was tempered by local traditions.[15]

In the 1960s, Lamu born Abdalla Bujra returned to the land of his forefathers for fieldwork on social stratification among the Hadrami. His study was limited to the small town of Hureidah, on the eastern coast of the Red Sea.[16] It appears that the highly stratified society that characterize the Hadramis, carried over to East Africa where many immigrants settled. The sharifs were the highest caste (the caste system being somewhat similar to that of traditional India); followed by sheikhs, or men who were "the scholars and the tribesmen." The third, or lowest caste, were the poor.[17] Members of all three of these groups left—out migration was another characteristic of Hadrami society over time. In Lamu the sharifs came first; later, members of the learned classes, followed by the poor. Migration picked up momentum from mid-nineteenth century until early in the twentieth when they were encouraged by the British. As the inflow increased, so did the numbers of poor men from the bottom rung of Hadrami society.

The political divisions and rivalries that have been described by some scholars may have their antecedents in the Hadramaut characterized by Bujra. Political divisions, mostly along class lines, existed in Lamu. But those described by el Zein, James de Vere Allen, and others, are of a more recent origin and reflect the Hadrami patterns carried with them when they migrate.[18] Socially, the Hadrami in Lamu could not have been more different. The sharifs, whose legitimacy is based on their descent from the Prophet Mohammed, were believed by other Hadramis to possess supernatural powers (baraka); and the poor, who paid little attention to genealogies, possessed no supernatural powers at all.[19] The poor Hadramis followed the patterns they had known back in Hadramaut, requiring their children to follow the teachings of these sharifs, and elevating the sharifs to the position of direct intermediaries to Allah (and/or the Prophet). B. G. Martin pointed out that on the southern Swahili coast, Mohammed was "alive" to Muslims there, when, in fact, Mohammed is supposed to be God's last Prophet and among the Sunni, not deified.[20] This concept was somewhat true in Lamu, with the sharifs, as lineal descendants of the Prophet, believing what they were taught about themselves as part of the continuim in the "deity"; and with their followers, who continued to emulate old religious traditions from the Hadramaut.

Men came alone, those who were married left their wives and children behind. Most lost contact with their families after they settled in East Africa. But Hadrami marriage patterns came to be influential in Lamu: men could marry down in status; but women could not. Because of the poverty that affected small town Hadrami dwellers at home, few men took multiple wives. The divorce rate in the Hadrami community was high. Children most often remained with their mothers, who seldom received support from husbands once they had been abandoned.[21]

Men coming directly from Hadramaut arrived with almost no personal effects, and some came off the ships with only the clothing on their backs.[22] As it was a Lamu custom to keep mosques open at night, when ships were in port sailors as well as new arrivals often took refuge in them. In some cases, sympathetic Hadrami men, including those who had married local women and who had managed to obtain quarters, brought the newcomers to live with them until they could find work. In other cases, wealthier men of the aristocracy offered employment to the new arrivals, although it was always of a menial sort.[23]

Even if the Hadrami men had wives elsewhere, most married local women, and like the Afro-Arabs, took concubines who were later elevated to *suria* after the birth of a child. No Hadrami immigrants married into the aristocracy. Because they were poor, or thrifty, the Hadrami men chose to marry women who cost them little or nothing in bride price, the amount of money potential grooms were expected to pay the bride's family at the time of marriage. After they were established however, these men preferred to marry their daughters into other Hadrami families. They mostly followed the tradition established in Hadramaut, taking only one wife at a time and were not regarded as generous providers or as supportive fathers. Some, especially, the sharifs who traveled around, kept a wife in each town where they traveled for trade.

The Comoro Islanders were also among the poor who migrated during the late nineteenth century. Their major occupation was that of tailoring. During the nineteenth century there was "petty strife" among the Comoro Islanders which resulted in out-migrations to not only Lamu but Zanzibar and elsewhere in the Sultan's domains.[24] Comoro Islanders spoke a form of KiSwahili that was not always intelligible to Swahili speakers in Lamu and Zanzibar. That may have accounted for why they distanced themselves from the locals. James Christie noted that in Zanzibar the Comoro "are not admitted on terms of equality by any class of Arabs; they nearly all occupy huts which are extremely filthy. . . their abodes are abominable, worse even than those of the negroes. They are extremely attentive to each other during illness, and are also careful regarding their slaves, although possibly they may have no higher motive than self-interest."[25]

Hadrami sharifs had settled in the Comoro Islands. Some of them earned their living by teaching at *madrassa*, through the practice of Arabic (and traditional) medicine, and some combined selling their baraka with actual employment. One saintly but by this time, much extended group of the Prophet's descendants, founded a sufi brotherhood in the Comoro Islands, which through the life of a young male scholar from the 1880s and on, had profound implications for Lamu.

The Alawi sharifan family had long been in East Africa. Possibly the first member of that family crossed the Red Sea and settled in Mogadishu with his descendants moving down to Barawa, on to Pate island. Later the family fanned out to Madagascar, the Comoro Islands, and as far afield as Indonesia.[26] By the 1860s, one of the Jamal al Layl (a branch of the Alawi clan) Mwene Seyyid Ali, migrated there, establishing himself as a tailor.

Accounts differ as to when his nephew, Saleh bin Alwi bin Abdalla, first arrived in Lamu. One tradition put Saleh Jamal al Layl in Lamu in 1873, saying he came for a year to study with his tailor uncle. Other informants state that Mwene Seyyid Ali was not a religious sharif, and did not therefore provide more than room and board for the young sharif. Peter Lienhardt, who wrote perceptively on Saleh and the mosque he later founded, judged that Saleh arrived in Lamu in "1885 at about the age of thirty." After his initial stay in Lamu, Saleh returned to the Comoro Islands, where he first married. When the sharif came back to Lamu, he left that wife behind.[27]

Ironically, John Haggard was the British official then in residence but like those administrators who immediately followed him, remained remarkably ignorant of the Comoro community that Saleh joined, and of his subsequent activities within the town. Religious matters were, however, the affair of the qadi. Saleh resettled into the home of his uncle, but was soon appointed Imam of Sheikh Bilad Mosque and given a home next door. Described as "dark, not very tall, of medium height" Saleh was "an attractive man." He was also pious and "not dramatic nor like his descendants" whose influence was great in Lamu.[28]

Saleh established a *madrassa* that included the Hadrami and Comoro communities and possibly a few ex-slaves, as well as some slaves who were able to seek religious instruction. Sharif Saleh owned a few slaves, and these no doubt were part of his religious congregation as they also were his work force. Some claim that Saleh "tired of town" but others say that due to the ethnic composition of his student body, he was provoked into moving to the shamba area in what is today Langoni at the southern end of Lamu.[29]

In about 1891, Sharif Mansab Abdulrahman, a wealthy al Hussein, gave Saleh a parcel of land where he could carry on his teaching of the mostly poor and illiterate men who by now were his followers as well as his students. First, Saleh built a small shed where "he could pray when the rains fell." Later, through the use of slave labor, he constructed a sort of open air temporary structure of mangrove poles that rose to cover the coconut frond mats resting on the heavy sand. Thus the name Mat Mosque came to be attached to Saleh's first congregation, which performed the "Maulidi ya Daiba" every Thursday. This lengthy praise to the Prophet was accompanied by tambourines—a most unorthodox musical accompaniment and a source of almost immediate friction between Saleh and the Sunni aristocracy in the town, which included Sharif Mansab, his patron for the land.[30] Because Saleh was highly regarded as a learned man, some members of the aristocracy sent their children to study with him first at the Mat Mosque and later at the Riyadha Mosque, again constructed with slave labor, and completed in 1901 or 1902.[31]

Around this time Saleh introduced the "Maulidi al Habshi" which was another praise poem to the Prophet, composed by a distinguished holy man in the Hadramaut. The "Maulidi al Habshi" caught on with the Hadrami community and has been associated with the Riyadha Mosque since about 1910. To accompany this Maulidi, drums and flutes joined the controversial tambourines. But older informants say the swaying and dancing that has come to be associated with the Riyadha Mosque in the later twentieth century did not then exist.[32] One elder however, recalled that some male congregants performed the *uta* dance outside Saleh's home (which is still danced at celebrations commemorating him although Saleh's original mud and wattle house was destroyed in a Lamu fire in the 1980s).

Saleh met not only spiritual needs, but also temporal ones. Noting that sweet coffee was "endowed with God's blessing" Saleh introduced the custom of serving coffee after the weekly Maulidis. Later the Hadramis convinced him to serve a feast of "rice and beef" which presumably they paid for since Saleh remained a poor man throughout most of his life.[33] What emerged was weekly religious entertainment, followed by refreshment. And, of course, the ongoing *madrassas,* where increasingly large numbers of students came for instruction.

Ali Skanda recalled being a student at the newly built Riyadha Mosque. Later, Ahmed Jahadhmy, born into the wealthy Omani-Afro-Arab aristocracy in 1910, was a student of Saleh, who by then was called Habib (beautiful or loving and a word that was derived from the Hadramaut). As his reputation for religiosity, scholarship, and piety grew, students from elsewhere began to arrive in Lamu to study with the sharif. Finally, the Riyadha, under his leadership, became renowned as a religious center and was called the Mosque College.[34]

Habib Saleh married several times during his long life in Lamu. The first Lamu wife, another Comorian, gave birth to a son, Badawy. His second wife, a woman from Siyu, provided him with another son, Idaroos. A third wife, also from the Comoro Islands, gave Habib Saleh two daughters; and the fourth wife, whose family traveled between the Comoros and Lamu, gave birth to a daughter who was still living in Lamu in the early 1980s.[35] There was at least one other legal wife, too, whose relationship with the renowned scholar remains clouded in controversy. According to some family members, Habib Saleh suspected this wife of adultery and divorced her before she gave birth to a son. This action is in contradiction to the Qu'ran, which prohibits a man from divorcing a pregnant wife. Considering his reputation for goodness, kindness, and generosity, his actions in initiating divorce under the circumstances suggest he did so only because he believed he was not the father of the child in question.[36] None of the women were from wealthy families, and considering the growing reputation of this sharif, not to mention the obsequiousness with which the Comoro, Hadrami, Bajun, and other outsiders regarded him, it is unlikely that he paid bride price for any of his wives. [See Appendix]

The controversies over activities at the mosque continued, despite Habib Saleh's growing fame. Playing the tambourines, and later the drums, within the mosque itself caused a continued outcry from members of the old families, and especially in conjunction with the Hadrami composed "Maulidi al Habshi." Musical instruments were not unknown in Lamu and had long been played in conjunction with religious ceremonies in East Africa. Elderly members of the old families recall musical instruments, such as flutes, having been played during religious ceremonies at Pwani, the oldest mosque in town. In contemporary terms, it seems to have been the "jazzing up" of the more staid and ritualistic maulidi ceremonies that had characterized early celebrations that inflamed passions on the part of the aristocracy. That, and the elements of sufism which were growing by leaps and bounds in the form of adoration of Habib Saleh, as well as a growing number of sharifs who drifted into the town. These factors led to the clash between the old and familiar ways of the "insiders" that were being challenged by the mostly poor "outsiders."[37]

The Hadrami and Comoro Islanders settled in the Langoni section of Lamu. By 1901-02, with the British presence increasing, more jobs became available for especially the Hadrami, who were considered "grasping" but hard working. Hadrami men replaced the women as water carriers. They vied with slaves for jobs on the waterfront, serving as *hamalis* [porters] and as able bodied seamen on both sailing dhows and local jahazis. As their numbers increased, so too, did problems with their health. Poor, filthy refugees from Hadramaut often carried leprosy in with them when they arrived on Lamu's seafront.[38]

Overcrowded housing in the small mud and wattle homes where they lived also contributed to sickness and disease, including cholera. Haggard's reports and letters did not specify what groups were hardest hit by smallpox. Nevertheless, the Hadrami, the poorest of the poor, boxed together in the southern end of town, must have suffered heavy losses from the ravages of that dread disease. Many of them stowed away on ships at Mukula or Aden, remaining hidden until they could jump off board when they sailed into Lamu. Already weakened from lack of food and water, the Hadramis were prone to disease before they arrived at their destination. The Hadramis, like the Omanis, were not accustomed to the East African climate. In Zanzibar, Christie discussed the large numbers of slaves owned by members of the Hadrami community mid-nineteenth century. Lamu Hadramis were never significant property owners, nor did they compile much wealth at this time. But, they did buy slaves, whom they hired out, and whom they stuffed into their tiny quarters as they did in Zanzibar.[39]

The author of the *Periplus of the Erythaean Sea* mentioned the presence of Indian traders in East Africa. When Vasco de Gama sailed from Malindi to India, he was guided by an Indian pilot. The long term trading relations between India and East Africa have, as noted, influenced all aspects of the material culture. Said encouraged Indians to come to Zanzibar and his East African possessions, adding to the numbers already in residence and engaged in trade, including the slave trade.[40]

By 1870, there were approximately one hundred and thirty Indians in Lamu. In 1887 the Indian community had increased considerably although the numbers of Hindus remained about the same (33). The Bohra Muslims were up to 142 while the combined Ismaili and Ithnasharia communities totalled 55.[41] The Bohra claim to have been in East Africa longer than any other Muslim Indians, although the Khoja (Ismailis) preceded them by several centuries. But the Lamu Bohra Mosque was originally built in the mid-eighteenth century indicating that the Bohra Muslims were a presence in that area for over two hundred years—and possibly have the longest record for permanent residency in Lamu.[42]

Religious differences among the Shi'a Indians are more complex than the splits within Lamu's Sunni Muslims. After the death of the Prophet's son-in-law and cousin, Ali, Islam became fragmented. Followers who believed that succession should stay in the family split away from those who believed in electing a religious leader. The concept of Imam or holy leader developed among the former group. At the death of the sixth Imam in 765 A.D., the Ismailis (followers of the Aga Khan) broke away and formed a separate group. Following the death of the twelfth Imam, there was a further split among this group, giving rise to the "Twelvers" or, as they are known in East Africa, the Ithnasharia.

Other Muslims dispersed into many areas, including Yemen. Among this small minority there were further divisions, including one that followed the death of the twenty-first Imam in 1030. Stories differ as to what happened to his son Abu' l-Qasim Tayyib, in the immediate aftermath of his father's probable murder. But all agree that this Imam went into occultation and either he, or his descendants, will return in the period of *zuhur*, which the Bohra believe is the time of his visibility physically and spiritually.[43]

Soon thereafter, a small number of Yemini followers of this sect of

Shi'a Islam moved to India, where they joined other missionaries already active in converting a caste of traders who were known as *vohrwu* or *vohorvu*. These converts were then referrred to as Bohra, a corruption that may have been made by the Yemini who joined their ranks. Another split between the Bohra over doctrinal matters produced those who referred to themselves as Dawoodi Bohra. These are the majority of Bohra who came to East Africa and who claim the longest residence at the coast.[44]

Historical records indicate that the Bohra got to Madagascar in 1750, oral traditions suggest that they spread out from there to Zanzibar as well as various ports on the coast. They may also have reached the Comoro Islands in the sixteenth century and possibly were responsible for conversion there.[45] Most were sent to East Africa after Said moved his capital to Zanzibar and were responsible for establishing and/or carrying on trade with the local people or they transshiped merchandise from western India to other locations up and down the coast. The Indian traders were not permanent dwellers and, as we have seen, rarely brought wives and families with them. Many carried on sexual liaisons with local women, some eventually marrying. Others left behind concubines and children when they were transferred elsewhere. The Indian traders (including Ismailis, Ithnasharias, Hindus, and Bohra) introduced the rupee to East Africa, although it was not official currency until the British took over in 1895. The traders also brought to East Africa the Indian system of weights and balances, possibly as early as the eighteenth century. And they introduced concepts of architecture to the Swahili.[46]

In addition to the Bohra there were the Bhattias, a Hindu trading caste; Jains, a Hindu sect resembling Buddhism that is devoted to non-violence; and orthodox Hindus. Since the Hindu faith did not prohibit lending money for interest or making profit from the sale of gold and silver, they were the local bankers and jewelers. After the British became more established in Lamu, Goan civil servants arrived to work for the British, and a few Goans competed with the established Comoro Islanders in the tailoring business.

Indians in Zanzibar had suffered harassment from the local leaders until Sultan Said relocated his capital there. Then his advocacy of religious toleration for all enabled them to prosper without difficulty. The Sultan continued to use Indians as his customs agents in both Muscat,

Zanzibar, and to collect his taxes in his coastal dominions.[47] The individual Indian religious groups had their own trading specialties that they imported from India and distributed throughout the Sultan's domains. Textiles, for instance, were mostly imported by Muslims who advocated that their customers cover themselves. The Bohra were "tinsmiths, locksmiths, watchmakers, ironmongers. . . ." giving rise to the hardware businesses in which most Bohras specialized in the twentieth century. Hindus, on the other hand, were noted as owning dhows and engaging in much of the wholesale trade there.[48] However, Bohras (and other Indian groups) located in outposts such as Faza and Siyu on Pate island, were the middlemen between most Indian merchants in Lamu and the local consumers.

Abdul Hussein remembered that Lamu was the center for the northern coast. Bohra merchants in Faza, Siyu, and Kismayu served as general wholesalers buying ivory, ghee, animal skins, and coconuts. The goods were shipped to Lamu, then to Zanzibar where sales extended to Germans, French, and, until mid-nineteenth century, American traders.[49] Abdul Hussein's great-grandfather, Ebrimjee, and his grandfather, Yusuf Ali, both conducted business in Lamu for decades—and both were buried in the Bohra cemetery.

All of the Muslim Indians had separate mosques along with private burial grounds. As opposed to the Sunni Muslims, whose wives were forbidden entry to mosques, the Shi'a women attended but were separated from the main hall where their men worshipped. The Dawoodi Bohra had a shrine in Kismayu to which they journeyed from the late nineteenth century and on. Ismaijee bhai Saheb, an Indian known for his goodness and generosity, died and was buried near Kismayu. Visitors to the site noted a stream of light falling on his grave, and proclaimed him a saint. Word spread throughout the Bohra community that a visit to his grave would cure those afflicted with mental illness especially, although healthy pilgrims went to his tomb as well.[50]

Earlier, we noted that Indians were financiers of the slave trade. Some claimed that Hindus alone financed the trade because they were able to charge interest on their loans. Oral traditions, and other documentary evidence suggests that the Bohra also engaged in the slave trade. Nossy Be on the northern Madagascar coast was a well known slave trade port. Dr. Kolchoy Firoze, in LaReunion, and Akbaraly of Madagascar, both recalled their respective family histories, which included participation in the slave trade into and out of Madagascar.[51]

In the mid-1980s, one elderly man referred to as Lamuwalla, spoke of his grandfather who had left Kutch for Lamu in 1860. After forty five years as a trader there, he was transferred by the family to Nossy Be. By then, other family members had already spread down the Madagascar coast. Ironically this man was dressed in much the same way as his grandfather would have been back in the mid-nineteenth century, wearing a long white cotton tunic over tight fitting white jodhpurs. His full gray beard was similar to the nineteenth century model of the Bohra Indian male. He referred to the bush wives of his ancestors and to their involvement in the northern coastal slave trade.[52]

Husseinali A. Hussein was an antique dealer in Mombasa who married a Lamu woman. Her grandfather was a merchant who compiled sufficient wealth to underwrite the restoration of the Bohra Mosque which was completed in 1921. From the 1890s on this family bought and shipped ivory, mat bags, and dried fish. "The Lamu people were mostly happy" and were connected to extended families all over the Indian Ocean, with Zanzibar serving as an important center until the growth of Mombasa in the early twentieth century.[53]

By 1890, there were a number of Ithnasharia in Lamu, along with a sizable Ismaili community. When, in 1899, a split occurred among the Ismailis in Zanzibar, some Ismailis converted to Ithnasharia and went to Lamu. African families had been welcomed in the Ithnasharia sect, but apparently not in other Shi'ite Mosques in Lamu. One informant said that his father had gone there about that time and had joined the Ithnasharia community, engaging in various enterprises before he specialized in extracting oil from the coconuts which he shipped elsewhere, including to India. This family came to be one of the most prosperous in Lamu where they lived for over fifty years.[54]

There are no written records that attest to the material culture of the early Indian communities in Lamu, therefore we are again dependent on James Christie for what he observed in Zanzibar mid-century. While the Europeans favored furniture of Indian design, the Muslim Indians preferred rickety bits of European style furniture. The carpets and matting in the Omani houses were mostly absent in the Muslim Indian homes. In

Lamu, as in Zanzibar, the Indians lived in separate areas, some along the seafront in apartments built above their shops. Others dwelled in the southern end of town, with small shopkeepers using a room or two at the back for eating and sleeping. The Ismailis, according to Christie, were the most susceptible to disease and to this he attributed the numbers of Africans in their households as well as their lack of personal hygiene.[55]

Each of the respective Muslim groups in Zanzibar was a closed society, as was the case in Lamu. Each Friday night (Thursday in the case of the Bohra), the congregations met for a communal meal. Each sect came together to celebrate weddings and to mourn at funerals. These customs, however, had the effect of "making people more careless concerning the comfort of their own homes. . . . They take care of their own poor . . . . Members who are a disgrace [to the congregation] are expelled and generally sent away."

Family ties were very important. Relationships "no matter how remote" were recognized "and poverty, or lowness of station, is no reason for anyone being discarded." The old and the ill were the joint responsibility of the entire congregation. "A wife during illness is under the care of her mother and other female relatives" while the husband is "looked after in a similar manner . . . . In no class of society, civilized or uncivilized, Christian or Mohammedan, have I ever seen so much kindness and genuine affection displayed towards each other as I have constantly witnessed" among this [the Indian] community.[56]

The various castes of Hindus received a high rating from Christie as to their personal habits: they always carried their own clean water with them (even to mixing with prescribed medication); and they were vegetarians whose food was carefully washed.[57] Hindus could be seen in front of their shops each morning cleaning their teeth with tooth sticks and washing their mouths practically in concert. Hindus were careful of their health and seldom sick. To be confined to bed was to be in a "state of unmitigated misery, being deprived of his only source of pleasure, business." "Their houses are the opposite of clean . . . . They delight in having a number of cows about . . .and where there is a central court it is filled with them at night. They often prefer to sleep in cellar-like rooms adjoining [the court] that they may enjoy and derive benefit, as they suppose, from the odour of the cow-dung."[58] Older WaAmu remembered Hindu cattle sharing close quarters but with donkeys parked outside on the narrow streets, and with goats tethered to doors, the Hindus were hardly to be singled out for the proximity of their livestock.

At the turn of the century, public health measures were far down the list of British priorities for Lamu. They were still attempting to eliminate the illegal trade in slaves and to abolish the institution of slavery.

CHAPTER 7

Slave women dancing on a rooftop at the turn of the Century

Courtesy of the National Museums of Kenya

Chapter Seven

British Penetration Increases and Slave Culture in Lamu

"O Prophet, fear thou God, and obey not the unbelievers
and the hypocrites...."
The Qur'an

Beyond the crash course in colonialism, the wealthy Lamu residents were continuing to learn about British tenacity. In 1890, while Britain still ruled indirectly through the Sultan, Khalifa was reminded of his promise to free all slaves brought into his possessions after 1 November 1889. He was also expected to commence the gradual emancipation of slavery in Zanzibar and Pemba—freeing all children born to slaves as of January 1. The Sultan, recognizing that Germany and Britain had still not resolved hegemony over his possessions, balked. Understanding the economic needs of his people as well as their mentality, Khalifa explained that he had not actually intended to issue these orders. In the case of freeing newly born children, the Sultan argued that in so doing, he would be responsible for the deaths of many. With the parents still enslaved, he argued that few slave holders would willingly support these freeborn children.

Lamu slave owners were not slow to recognize that what was policy in Zanzibar and Pemba would soon be law in the northern province as well. Khalifa was not in sympathy with the British and resented their attempts to rule through him. In this case, however, the British consul in Zanzibar was also reluctant to act on the proclamation that had been the joint policy of the IBEA and the Foreign Office: "their condition in the great majority is not an unhappy one." As to the slaves brought into his territories, Khalifa remained mute. Despite prodding by the British consul in Zanzibar, "the *decree* is *known* at no single place along the coastline." Lamu Afro-Arabs, when they heard about it, simply ignored the decree as they also ignored the later proclamation to free the newborn slave children. Instead, they continued to import, and pretended those they brought in were captives they long held.[1]

Late twentieth century values dictate a harsh reassessment of the East African slave trade and of the institution itself. But contemporary observers mostly agreed with the Lamu IBEA agent in suggesting that once slaves had survived the hardships of the illegal caravan trade, "there seems little doubt that . . . in captivity the slaves were usually well treated, being a valuable asset."[2]

Nevertheless, there were incidents of cruel treatment. One case study at this time involved a slave woman owned by the daughter of the liwali of Malindi, which in retelling also illustrates the high level of hostility towards the British on Lamu island. The woman managed to escape to Lamu and sought the help of the IBEA agent. At the time she arrived in Lamu, the slave woman was "pregnant by a man from Mambrui." IBEA agent Simons turned to the local qadi, who sold the woman to "Famou bin Mbarak" of Matondoni (another hamlet on Lamu island).

Soon after the child was born the woman returned to Simons this time to complain that "the child was taken from me and I am never permitted to see it. My master beats and ill treats me to such an extent that my life is unbearable and I would rather die than return to him." The woman showed Simons "scars, wounds and welts on her person, evidently caused by beatings and which proved that she had evidently been badly treated."

The liwali was out of town. Simons was at a loss as to what to do, especially since there were already problems with the men at Matondoni regarding their inability to procure new slaves. At the same time, the WaAmu were looking at Witu with an eye towards linking up with the Sultan, despite his rapacious *watoro*, because he continued to stand up to the British.

When the liwali returned, he admitted that the man was known to be a brutal master. He summoned his brother to return the woman to her former owner in Malindi. The woman was left in the custody of a local askari. Two days later, her Matondoni master arrived and Simons request-

111

ed that he "act as I considered best." The man denied beating his slave and left to return the next day with "a party of men armed with swords and knives." All came directly to Simons' office. Simons declined to "surrender the woman" to "threats and insulting expressions towards me." The liwali was sent for and, like his slave owning predecessors, Abdalla bin Hamed tried to stand on both sides of the fence. His sympathies were with the slave owners, while he expressed criticism of the brutality the woman had endured.

But since his job required that he act in concert with the British consul/IBEA agent, Abdalla bin Hamed appeared supportive to Simons to whom he also "pointed out reasons for not further antagonizing the Matondoni people. . . . First, that the general bad feeling against us is due to our actions with regard to the suppression of the slave trade. Second, that the present situation is not confined to the Matondoni people but . . . [Lamu people too]."

By interfering with first the slave trade, and now with the institution itself the locals feared that "[slaves] can come with complaints and thereby obtain their freedom, in which case the owners would lose their means of subsistence." The third reason the liwali offered was much more serious. "In the event of a rising taking place [the liwali] would be unable to suppress it, as most of the people taking part therein would not fear the consequences, knowing that they could immediately proceed to the mainland and place themselves under Witu protection."

Finally, the liwali made clear that his "sympathies were with the slave owners and also with the people but his duty compels him to act at times contrary to his inclinations . . . ." In this case Abdalla bin Hamed decided to go to the Lamu elders and enjoin them to "make a show of leading an armed party to attack and punish the Matondoni people." Instead, the elders decided to send for the owner so that he should spend a night in jail. Unknown to Simons, they also arranged for the woman to be returned to his Matondoni shamba the morning after his release from jail.

"The following morning the Governor called upon me and stated that the Elders of the town" had sent for him. Stressing the ongoing resentment to the British, Abdalla accompanied Simons to meet with the elders who, "explained that . . . if the soldiers had not returned the woman to her owner, riots would have followed" and no one in Lamu would have moved to contain them. This incident was the first near fatal collision that the IBEA agent experienced with the increasingly angry Afro-Arab community. Simons was forced to release the man who "rode back to his village on a donkey provided by the Governor."

In his report to Zanzibar, Simons referred to the "treacherous Liwali [whose] object no doubt was to stand well in the eyes of the people. He was more anxious and desirous of making a settlement to their satisfaction and his actions throughout show him to be biased in their favor, either on account of his fear of a riot or to prove his sympathy with them on the question of slavery." The liwali had clearly explained to the British officer his own sympathies, as well as his fears that matters would grow out of hand if Simons persisted in interfering in what was regarded as a local matter. In fact, later in his report, the IBEA agent referred to "five *watoro* who had come into Lamu on their way to Siu [sic] . . . consequently the people more or less demoralized" and there was "some reason to fear that the Liwali was correct in his apprehensions that the Matondoni people would have gone to Witu."[3]

The outcome was that Abdalla was temporarily recalled through pressure on Khalifa. His replacement was one of his brothers, who continued behind-the-scenes support to the local slave owners (of whom he was one) and at the same time, attempted to placate the British official.[4]

Among the myriad causes for Lamu's rapid decline, the imposition of British colonialism cannot be ignored. The *watoro* played their part, of course, in driving the Lamu owners away from their mainland plantations, and in seducing other slaves to abandon their masters and join ranks with the Sultan of Witu. British interests in Mombasa and the beginning of the Uganda railroad, too, were instrumental. But abolishing the slave trade and later slavery itself were overriding reasons for the downward spiral in the late nineteenth and early twentieth centuries from which Lamu never recovered.

Frederick Jackson returned to Lamu in 1903 when slavery was still legal and found much change there from his last visit in 1883. "Perhaps the most noticeable change in the better class of Swahili element was the number of young men listlessly roaming about on the [sea]front, in the streets, and in the Customs House compound, singly, in couples, or three or four together; well-dressed idle loafers with nothing to do. The reason for this was not far to seek, directly we set foot on the mainland—the mainland was derelict—almost dead." The slaves who remained were "worn out." Jackson believed that the blame was not altogether the end of the slave trade, and later slavery, but that "incidentally deprived the sons of slave owners of their congenial work as supervisors, and converted them into Lamu loafers."[5] An elder, however, testily responded to these British complaints, exclaiming that one man could not do the work of ten or twenty.[6]

According to Jackson, those able bodied slaves on the mainland who could, went south to Mombasa: "desertions on a wholesale scale took place, able-bodied men bolted and were soon lost in the camps scattered along the [railroad] line, women and girls sneaked away and soon attached themselves to Indian coolies; nothing could stop the exodus, and only the old and worn out were left."[7] Some few Lamu slaves ran away to the Christian missionary station at Rabai down near Malindi. And, as Sultan Khalifa had predicted, once owners were forced to free children born to slave parents, the Rabai United Methodist Free Church Society picked up numbers of those who were forced away from their parents. One such child, a four year old male was there "while his master lived in Lamu."[8] At Rabai, and briefly at Lamu, compensation was paid for slaves who were freed and sent to live with the missionaries.

As the mainland plantations were deserted, some Pokomo, a few Giriama, and some Orma moved in but, since they were squatters, they were reluctant to plant trees or long-term produce. They also had the *watoro* to contend with. The areas they occupied were soon overrun with bush, thus attracting elephant herds and other wildlife. Complications arose over ownership when both Europeans and Asians tried to unravel problems of land tenure. Some Afro-Arabs mortgaged their lands to Indians in order to maintain the life style to which they were accustomed in Lamu. The Indians bought the land on speculation, and especially while the Germans were still in the Witu area, but soon ran into difficulties when the Afro-Arabs could not produce titles.[9] Then, too, there was the ongoing hostility to the Indians in the Witu area.

Slaves on the mainland had also engaged in other enterprises when they were not slashing and burning to clear, plant and weed, or later harvesting their crops. Some moved to the coast where they collected bechede-mer for the Chinese market, or cowrie shells and, on occasion, tortoise shells. In addition, ambergris continued to be in demand as an export product. Slaves were forced to pay their masters part of their profits on these export goods. In most cases slaves were supervised by a *nohoa* [overseer] who were loyal to their owners and therefore diligent in driving their charges to work and in collecting their profits from side activities.

The largest slave owners in Lamu at the end of the nineteenth century were the Jahadhmy, al Hussein sharifs, al Maawyia, al Bakari, and Mwyene Shee Hamidi. One source referred to a slave, Jumaa Mja, who he said owned 600 slaves on the mainland. Slaves did own both land as well as other slaves.[10] Other sources noted that Abdalla bin Hamed owned over 500 slaves, while a qadi who married locally was another large slave owner on the mainland. Almost all of the liwalis appointed by the Zanzibari sultans staked out large land holdings which they worked with the labor of several hundred slaves. Saif bin Salim, an Omani from Zanzibar, was also a large slave holder. The Skandas, who had moved from Siyu, and intermarried with a local family, owned a moderate number of slaves which they worked on their mainland shambas. But names are not so important as status. It appears that almost all of the Omani men who intermarried with the Lamu Afro-Arab families involved themselves with the ongoing shambas, or staked out and farmed large parcels of land. The labor was carried out by the slaves, supervised by the *nohoas*, with the master or his sons overseeing all.[11]

The Lamu Afro-Arab families, land-owning slaves, and some other small Lamu landholders acquired their holdings in any numbers of ways. If their claims actually went back seven hundred years, some of the land had long been taken away from them by the Orma who came in from the north. Muslim Bajun who resided on the mainland provided land through marriages that were arranged with Lamu women, who, in turn, married their children back into the Lamu families. These alliances were sometimes sources of conflict, with the WaPate claiming the same land that Lamu residents declared was theirs. In fact, some of the hostilities between Lamu and Pate were based on disputes over landholding on the mainland.[12]

An illustration of how these families became intertwined in the nineteenth and, later, the twentieth century is provided in this capsule family history. Abdalla bin Hamed, the liwali, was descended from Hamed bin Said, an Omani who first married in Zanzibar, and then came to Lamu in about 1870, taking Mwana Shee wa Shee WaPate as his second wife. Mwana Shee was an al Hussein sharifa and, "when Abdalla bin Hamed proposed marriage, the sharifs refused to entertain the idea. . . . How can anybody from Zanzibar marry a relative to the Prophet?" Hamed bin Said "then sent word to the Sultan: the al Hussein in Pate have turned down the proposal of marriage." But before the Sultan could act "one of the sharifs dreamed that the Prophet said the marriage should take place between the sharifa and this man [an Ibhadi]. They sent a message saying the marriage would take place. He became a convert and left Ibhadism"—in this case pragmatism took precedence over religious differences.[13] The two married and Mwana Shee began producing the offspring who, in their turn, joined Bwana Zaidi in contributing to the genes of every member of the contemporary Afro-Arab community in today's Lamu. It is true that these families trace genealogies through male ancestors. Nevertheless, when the mother was a free born member of the old Lamu families, such as the al Hussein Mwana Shee, lines are traced matrilineally as well. For instance, Mwana Shee's daughter, Fatuma, became the mother of several children. In order to trace their line back to Hamed bin Said, these descendants go through their female progenitor, just as the sharifs go to Fatima to get back to the Prophet Mohamed.[14]

About Hamed bin Said, who owned vast tracks on land in Mambrui, people at the time were in such awe of his wealth and prowess that he is still memorialized in verse:[15]

> *"The gate of the lions*
> *Hamed went to Mambrui*
> *with his sons as*
> *a big strong man."*

Although some claim that slavery has been a constant on the coast from time immemorial, conditions changed as did the demand for the types of crops produced. From the mid-nineteenth century, mainland slaves had their own quarters, including parcels of land that they farmed for themselves and their families. During this period, slaves also constructed mosques, the ruins of which are still to be found at various spots on the mainland.[16] Conversion to Islam was said to be mandatory, although many African slaves clung to their own traditional beliefs, which they passed on to their progeny. They, in turn, were also instructed in the Qur'an by slave teachers and the occasional sharif hired by slave owners for that purpose. Sharif Abdalla Salim al Hussein, however, stated that little in the way of religious instruction took place. "The *nohoa* was not instructed, nor did he teach Islamic religion. On some of the larger mainland shambas, with a large labor force" the Sharif doubted if "religion was stressed beyond teaching prayers, if that." Traditional religion, he said, included witchcraft and that prevailed on the mainland plantations.[17] Little or no instruction in the Qur'an meant that many slaves, especially the men, felt no compunction in running away from their masters. These runaways formed the backbone of the *watoro* menace on the mainland. On Lamu island, most slaves received religious instruction along with the children of their owners. They tended to be more tied to the Muslim faith and therefore, less likely to run away. Also, it was easier to run away from the mainland than from the relative isolation of a small island.[18]

Their huts were sparsely furnished with a few mats and some rudimentary cooking utensils. All cooking was done outside, and despite the heat or during the rains, was accomplished by wood fire. Women, with the help of small children, gathered the wood. Women alone cooked the food. Slave women also helped in planting and in cultivating grains and rice. Men took care of coconut tapping and climbed the tall trees to scatter the produce below. Most slaves worked five days a week during the off-season, and six days when planting or harvesting.

Dances were a major form of entertainment, especially at the time of religious holidays. Possibly the *maulidis* to which descendants of slaves are so devoted are rooted in the mainland slave experience. Religious fervor presented a positive outlet for slaves, and served to impress owners with the outward manifestation of solid conversion. On occasion, owners manumitted slaves and, if one was perceived to be especially devout, he or she stood a better chance of freedom than those who were believed to be still practicing witchcraft or other forms of religious worship unacceptable to orthodox Islam.[19] But most manumissions occurred on the island where slaves worked and lived in closer proximity to their owners.

Long accustomed to traditional medicines in their own areas in Africa, they learned to use local herbs, roots, and fragments of tree bark or leaves for medicinal purposes.Ghee and coconut oil became medical properties. Arabic medicines which the sharifs produced from various powders was also much in use on mainland shambas.[20]

After the mainland plantations were abandoned, the Afro-Arabs shifted attention to the center of Lamu island, where they staked out shambas and placed slaves bought illicitly. The deep sandy interior of the island gradually was turned into a lush tropical paradise as a result of extensive slave labor and through the use of irrigation. While the mainland plantations served to provide export produce that, in turn, yielded considerable profits for the slave holders, the island shambas mostly yielded fruits and vegetables for local consumption. The exceptions were coconuts and mangoes, which were exported.

A single Afro-Arab family owned two to three parcels of land of variable sizes. Each had its own complement of slaves. Every large shamba contained poultry, goats, sheep, donkeys, and cows. Until the 1930s, some Arabian horses were bred for local use. Camels provided power for grinding grain and extracting oil from coconuts. Donkeys were used for transporting heavy loads into town and carrying produce from the shambas to the owners town houses. The coconut was vital to Lamu's economy, and trees were planted on all of the shambas, large and small. Every conceivable part of the coconut palm was used—from the frond, which was dried and matted for bags, rugs, and roofing, to the nut itself, which was used for cooking oil, medicinal purposes, and finally for fuel. Every slave family was dependent on the coconut for food, furniture, work, and fuel. When fruits and vegetables were ripe, slaves enjoyed the same nourishing diet as their masters. But they worked very hard. During the harvest season men, boys over ten, and sometimes wives, labored from sunup to sundown. When the coconuts were ripe men did the hazardous work of climbing the tall trees; and later they gathered the coconuts which they bundled up and either carried to town themselves, or piled them on donkeys backs that they then drove into town through the heavy sand— always in blistering heat—the cool breezes of town not extending to the low center of the island.

A trusted older slave served as *nahoa* on each large island shamba. His job entailed cajoling the work force into unceasing activity during har-

118

vest; and into repairs and building in the off- season. Except during the heavy rains, which normally occur in May and June, and then the lighter rains in September and October, either the master or one of his sons visited the island shambas frequently. As the years wore on, and fewer new slaves came in from outside, contacts between masters and slaves often created a rapport that was not possible on the larger and more distant mainland plantations.[21]

The work week varied on the shambas. Most slaves worked six days a week on the large island shambas; on the smaller ones, some worked five days, their labor being used for other purposes on the "off day."[22] On Friday men were free to attend mosque. The slaves performed all the labor attendant to upkeep and functioning of the mosques.[23] In Lamu, as in Muscat and Zanzibar, women were not allowed to attend mosque.

Lamu town had no army at the end of the nineteenth century. Each wealthy family, however, had a slave army. Men armed and drilled their slaves on the island shambas to create a militia in case of further problems from Pate, or difficulties with the Somali, who were still regarded as hostile and warlike. At least once in the 1870s, Lamu men took their slave armies to the mainland to recapture a village of *watoro*. The runaways, joined by local allies, defeated the Lamu force with a "rain of arrows" forcing it to beat a hasty retreat to Lamu. As Frederick Cooper found elsewhere on the coast, slave armies were unreliable in recapturing other slaves.[24]

Slaves and free men alike were armed with bows and arrows, spears and swords, and when available, muzzle loading muskets. Slaves carried bows and arrows while their masters were armed with the more sophisticated weapons. Lamu was noted for the quality of "swords, knives, and spears" produced by its craftsmen—usually slaves or Indians.[25] Both ex-slaves and former masters still drilled on the island shambas at least until the 1930s, although the British presence eliminated warfare between island communities. Because of a history of cattle raiding which then led to feelings of hostility in Lamu, Somalis were compelled to leave their weapons on the mainland "where they can pick them up" although, after the British took over, "some chiefs were allowed to bring their arms into Lamu to keep them in good humor."[26]

The burden of work fell more heavily on the female shamba slave than

119

on her town counterpart. Informants disagreed about how marriages were contracted among Lamu's shamba slaves. Some said marriages were approved by their masters, as in the town, but were hazy about details. One woman remembered walking from a plantation near the Tana River to the coast, a distance of about twenty-five miles, to Lamu, where she was placed on a shamba where she met and married her first husband, also a slave. Permission for this marriage was granted by the master, who had nothing to lose since he owned them both.

Another woman born in Lamu town, married her first husband, also a town slave. In this case an arrangement was made with the husband's owner. She moved to her husband's residence, disassociating herself permanently from her former owner. Later, her previous owner, a BuSaid, was compensated when a female slave owned by the al Maawyia, a relative, married one of his male slaves. The exchange of persons was even, with no money involved. In fact, since all of the patricians had by the turn of the century intermarried with each other, exchanges of this type were common. It is was only when outsiders or Lamu men outside of the charmed circle, wanted slave women for wives that the issue of compensation was addressed.[27]

Washambala [new slaves] were considered outsiders, even if they came from the mainland plantations, and were not eligible to marry *wazalia* [old slaves]. Female *washambala* were often "sold off" into marriage with men who did not qualify as members of the aristocracy. Otherwise, the *washambala* were tested for work habits and loyalty. They also had to learn KiSwahili. In these ways they and their progeny were gradually incorporated into the slave society on the island shambas.

Among the slave women's duties was herding animals on fenceless shambas, being pressed into service during the harvest, gathering firewood for cooking. The women tended the family garden plots. They ground rice, maize, or millet each morning, and carried all water needed daily from the well to the house. Because slave families worked hard in the intense heat, their few items of clothing required frequent washing. That burden, too, fell on the women as did the sole care of their children who, when old enough, helped out with family chores.

British authorities believed that slave women had a low rate of reproduction. Some descendants of slaves claim that their mothers and grandmothers were more able to produce children than their female owners, whose birth rate was also said to be low. Others claimed that suckling babies inhibited conception. Abortion, as noted earlier, was practiced. It is possible that new born babies who were severely crippled or otherwise deformed, may have been quietly disposed of. Furthermore, slave women were subject to frequent miscarriages because of the heavy work load that marked their lives from childhood through menopause. Venereal disease also restricted conception.[28]

With little contact beyond the shamba, slave women there knew even less of Islam than their menfolk. While the men enjoyed a Friday break from labor, the women's duties to their families, and their households continued without letup. They dried palm fronds and made brooms that they used to sweep the dirt floors of their small mud and wattle houses. They dried beans and peas to tide them over during the dry months. Women on the same shambas, or even women on neighboring shambas, sometimes helped one another, which not only lightened individual women's burdens, but also provided opportunities for visiting. According to one old ex-slave, no matter the time of the day, or the day of week, it was *kazi, kazi, kazi.* (Work, work, work).[29]

The one avenue of escape for town slaves was concubinage. On the shamba it was a bit more difficult to tempt a master into bed until after the aristocracy began the construction of large residences to which they often brought their town wives and children on weekends. Here, these slave built homes, which were kept tidy by female slaves, offered both master and bondwoman the opportunities to engage in sexual intercourse during the former's regular visits to his landholding. The progeny born of these liaisons, however, did not always became free—especially as the supply of slaves was limited to mostly reproduction from the 1890s and on. Masters might, however, allow them privileges such as the ability to keep the income from tasks such as making *kofia* (small caps worn by Muslim men) or mat bags and rugs. Most of the income they derived was also theirs to keep—except, of course, when owners were greedy, in need of extra cash themselves, or just mean spirited. There were those kinds of masters, too.[30]

Shamba slaves occasionally joined their neighbors for festivities and dances. In their few free hours, women visited neighboring shambas and gossiped while matting bags and rugs or stitching hats. On special days of the year both town and shamba slaves celebrated with feasting, song, and dance. One old man remembered a special African dance, *dandoro*, which slaves performed in an open space near the southern end of town. Usually dances were performed to music played on instruments made of cow or buffalo horns, and on a *sikweya*, a special drum that resonated so loudly that everyone in Lamu town could hear it. Slaves also fashioned drums from gourds covered with animal skin and tied with coir—one of the few relics of their African past.[31]

Health problems plagued the slave community. As we have seen, malaria was a problem for the African slaves who were often forced to work despite raging fevers. Respiratory problems were especially severe, no doubt because of the poor facilities to which they were relegated for sleeping. Trypanosomiases, jigger fleas, famine, and drought, plus the dread leprosy had their effects on the slave community at one time or another. And, in the 1890s the rinderpest epidemic which wiped out whole populations of cattle in East Africa, struck Lamu island. Herds on which the locals depended died. Costly replacements came from the Somali, whose own herds had also been reduced as a result of the epidemic.[32]

Town slaves, whose close proximity to masters and mistresses enabled them to enjoy more intimacy, were, on the whole, better treated than their shamba counterparts. Some young men began their service in business or in shipping and rose to positions of importance, often keeping most of their earnings. A trusted slave who started as a seaman on his master's dhow on occasion became its captain, sailing with his crew of other slaves to ports as far away as India. (Few Indians allowed their slaves to serve as captains—preferring direct control over the trade themselves.[33]) Slave captains enjoyed the authority to conduct all negotiations in their masters' interest and were said to be well rewarded when they returned with ample profits.[34] Empty-handed captains or those with low profits were likely to be punished on return.

Masters' perceptions of their slaves ranged all the way from invisibility—or "nothingness" as one old informant put it—to something resembling extended kinship. Racism as characterized by western standards barely existed in Lamu. A member of the aristocracy born to a slave mother might be as dark as a newly arrived African. While the Zanzibari

122

Omanis preferred women who were from the Black Sea area or the wide-eyed light skinned Ethiopian women, Lamu men were drawn to the sensuous African women of darker complexion.[35] There was, however, the rigid class consciousness that put the slave (and then ex-slaves) at the bottom of the social ladder.

The living informants who talked about their experiences, or the experiences of their parents and grandparents were those who stayed on in Lamu, many of whom continued in subservient relations with former owners in what they termed as "slavery" long after official emancipation.[36] We do not hear the voices of those who left—speaking as it were with their feet.

One old ex-slave woman recalled hearing that slave traders "used to sew eyes and mouths [of captives] to keep them quiet and subdued." Also, there was the recurring litany among former slaves owned by the Afro-Arab patricians that the Indians were cruel and that as soon as possible, those who could, left them. Laws governing slave behavior on Lamu were not so harsh as stipulated in the Shari'a. But, if a slave killed an Afro-Arab, he was condemned to death by torture. His master was then forced to pay a sum of money in the amount determined by the qadi, to the family of the deceased. The leg irons Haggard referred to were still in use. Hadrami slave owners were remembered to be especially brutal. Or they whipped their slaves if they were negligent or late in performing assigned tasks. Concubines were especially ill treated.[37]

Ex-slaves remembered "good masters" and "bad masters." Ahmed "Boke" [Jahadhmy] caned his slaves when they were slow in getting to the shamba [or] slow in household work."[38] The "nothingness" that characterized the attitudes of some owners towards their slaves thus carried over to the slaves as an example of their lack of humanity. Also, some owners "used to treat their slaves like donkeys, driving them until they dropped from exhaustion."[39]

Afro-Arab men, however, often preferred their slave concubines to their legal wives, especially Orma women, who they purchased in the town market. Later, Orma women, and others, were taken to the homes of Lamu men where they were purchased for household duties, which often included sexual intercourse with their masters and who, once they gave birth were elevated to suria.[40] Fathers often gave young sons concubines for pleasure and to ward off homosexual activity. We do not yet know enough about the heart versus the pocketbook (or politics) in arranged marriages at other times or places to compare the success of sexual alliances in Lamu, but there is some remaining evidence that illustrates that true love relationships were formed between masters and their concubines. My Lamu informants—male and female, free and ex-slave—all believed that the special concubine, not the wife, most often captured the heart of the master. The extremely high divorce rate from the first, arranged marriages seems to bear out the assumption that these alliances were often unhappy.[41]

Every household had its head female slave, usually an older woman who had been raised as a member of the household. Among her functions was to provide sex education to slave girls, and to some extent, the daughters of owners. The training for free girls was, however, tempered by fathers who were anxious for their daughters to be chaste. The *unyago* [puberty rites] that Margaret Strobel found in Mombasa, did not exist in Lamu.[42] Sex, for free women, was for procreation and for the pleasures of their husbands. For slave women, sex with masters often put them on the road to freedom.

Although upper-class women supervised male slaves, they were most often in the company of female slaves. One respected patrician woman remembered her mother sitting for hours, stiffly erect, on one of the Lamu chairs with inlaid with ivory and gold, issuing strict instructions, pointing her finger to emphasize her commands, and sending her slaves scurrying in different directions on their various tasks. Of special irony here, is the fact that this particular mother was a *suria*. Furthermore, it illustrates an example of how, once they gave birth, concubines successfully coped with their metamorphosis.[43]

Although informants expressed different opinions on women's treatment of their slaves, most believed they were treated kindly, especially those born into the household.[44] A few slave-owning women were, however, capable of extreme cruelty. An incident recorded by a British district officer illustrates:

> Until quite recently an old woman used to perambulate the streets of Lamu begging. She had no eyes, nose, or features and no fingers or toes and her body was a mass of scars. I once inquired what disease she had, but was told that long years ago she had taken liberties with her mistress, who thrown her on the fire and held her there.[45]

CHAPTER 8

Homes of slave descendants around the Riyadha Mosque (background)
From the author's collection

Chapter Eight

Abolition of Slavery and Direct Rule

*"Therefore on ill-omened days did we send
against them an impetuous blast that
we might make them taste the chastisement of shame in this world:—but more
shameful shall be the chastisement
to come; and they shall not be protected."*
The Qur'an

As the first decade in the twentieth century unfolded, the people of
Lamu faced inward toward their homes and shambas. In the case of the
commercial sector, merchants burrowed into their businesses, hoping to
deflect government interest from their affairs. Throughout this decade,
British officialdom increased its hold over what was now called
"Tanaland Province" with headquarters in Lamu. Both the provincial
commissioner and the district commissioner for Lamu, were located in
the town. Their staffs increased, and so, too, did their demands on the
local people. During this period, too, British influenced decisions by the
Sultan of Zanzibar began to affect the WaAmu severely.

The Afro-Arabs continued to drift along, maintaining their rituals and
customs in spite of waning fortunes. A great-grandson of Liwali Abdalla
bin Hamed recalled that the mansion built and occupied by his family on
the seafront still housed the Zanzibari sultans on their infrequent visits.
"Lamu had the reputation for entertainment—beautiful dances, singing, a
cultural center. Zanzibar had been the political center and became the
educational draw for many members of the upper classes, but Lamu com-

bined both culture and religion." Even though the economy was in decline "the Sultans and leading Arabs of Zanzibar went to visit, and sometimes to marry. The Lamu women were noted for their grace and beauty. . . . [The] men were recognized for their hospitality and piety."[1]

At the turn of the century the Hadrami community increased as some Indians, especially the Hindus, began to move further south. The Hadramis created "certain problems in that they elevated the sharifs to high positions—thought they were blessed."[2] The Hadrami, accustomed to a low standard of living, remained thrifty, and contributed to capital formation which they used to acquire small stocks of goods for sale either on the streets, or in small dukas in the very southern end of town.[3] Not only spatial divisions separated the old families from the new Arabs: social distance between the groups continued over the years. The Comoro Islanders, still mostly tailors, were beginning to adapt to the culture of the Afro-Arabs and a few men intermarried with less prosperous members of the old families, meaning that the social structure was again showing elasticity. At this time, too, some male members of the aristocracy started to slowly drift away from Lamu. Most went to Zanzibar and a few moved to Mombasa.

The Afro-Arabs had "high status" among the European newcomers slowly making their way into the Kenya colony. Early white settlers recalled coastal Muslims as "civilized" and desirable as opposed to the "animist Africans" upcountry.[4] This view contrasted with opinions held by the civil servants who were posted in Lamu. The chorus of complaints now included *fatina* or political insubordination.

There was every reason for the Afro-Arabs to react negatively to further imposition of British rule in Lamu. A final blow fell on them when the "Abolition of Slavery Ordinance" was proclaimed by the Sultan in 1907. In Lamu, the effects of the Ordinance were not much felt before 1909-10 when the slavery commission began in emancipate slaves on the island.[5] (Many Indians had held on to their slaves although legally required to emancipate them back in the 1870s).

When the commission set up offices in Lamu, all slave owners were ordered to the seafront with their slaves. Notices were posted about the town in which slave owners were warned that they would be punished if they did not produce their slaves on the appointed day. The notices also promised fair compensation to the owners. Lamu slave holders, however, were paid less compensation than those further down the coast or in Zanzibar and Pemba.[6] There, compensation for an able-bodied slave was equal to the five months wages a slave earned for his master. In Lamu compensation was equal to only three months pay. In all, a total of Rs. 150,000 were paid to Lamu masters and mistresses.[7]

Many actually refused to free their slaves. A few others believed the compensation so small that they refused to apply for it, and simply kept their slaves anyway. Those bondsmen who were freed seem to have been the troublemakers and the aged. Compensation actually relieved them of the necessity of meeting their previous responsibilities towards the elderly men and women slaves.[8]

The British government provided money to the District for upkeep of the "old infirm slaves with no income." In fact, many able bodied slaves who were let go also went on the government dole claiming "they were incapable of work and few of them have savings or relations who can support them." Some went to live in the southern end of town where missionaries set up stations to provide them with care and, of course, attempted their conversion to Christianity.[9]

What was a slave in Lamu? Slavery, as defined by former owners and those whose forebears had been in bondage, meant that owners had all rights in and to the persons who were their slaves: including their labor; their children; and their possessions. Even slave inheritance legally went to the owners. An argument can be made that once the Legal Status of Slavery Ordinance went into effect, whatever remaining relations that existed between owners and slaves was no longer *slavery*. In fact, District Commissioner Talbot-Smith noted that after emancipation "the difference between the labourer and that of the slave is that he is permitted some say in respect to who shall purchase his service. Further he is totally unprovided for in his old age. . . ."[10]

Talbot-Smith, however, was expressing the British view of post-emancipation relationships between some owners and some slaves. In terms of *status* as defined by slaves who elected to *remain* in the same form of bondage that characterized their existence before the Ordinance (which was a British law despite the Sultan's having been coerced into signing it) they were *watuma*. Even though district commissioners were remarkably ignorant of actual practices and beliefs in the town behind them, they recognized that "in the end the master was as dependent on the slave, as the bondsman on his master."[11] There was one major difference after legal emancipation in Lamu: masters could no longer sell their slaves. Because of growing labor shortages, few would have wanted to do so had it been possible.

It was mutual dependency, among other reasons, that kept slaves and master tightly bound. Even the Sultans of Zanzibar continued to hold slaves and into the 1950s, compelled them to back out of the Sultan's presence on their knees. This practice was witnessed by any numbers of Afro-Arabs; and over the years, quite possibly observed by British dignitaries.[12]

Religion was the most important tie between masters and slaves. Most town slaves learned parts of the Qur'an by rote and were taught enough Muslim law to know that only masters had the right to free them. The Riyadha sharifs, too, played a significant role in convincing slaves that they were bound by the Qur'an, not by secular law. Habib Saleh and his two sons, Ideroos and Badawy, maintained a significant influence over many domestic and shamba slaves because of their association with the Riyadha mosque. A grandson of Habib Saleh recalled that "the British bought slaves but according to Muslim law, as interpreted in Lamu, slaves belonged to their owners until the owners freed them. Slaves were taught this, too."[13] In this case, more than legal abolition was involved. It was also a power struggle between the growing authority of the Riyadha sharifs with their Hadrami allies, and the British.

For many, owners and slaves alike, the admonition of "Allah's will" helped assuage the sea of change in which they were forced to swim. Sharif Abdalla bin Salim remembered Lamu as "much more religious" than Zanzibar and Mombasa. Ali Jahadhmy believed that the "religious sentiments in Lamu were so strong that they lent equality between master and slave" which, "helped bind the ties that kept many of them together after legal abolition."[14]

When the British attempted emancipation in Lamu, they succeeded in freeing those who wanted to be free, or those whose owners were glad to part with them. One very old and decrepit female remembered: "The British went away. Then another came but didn't succeed" in separating *watuma* from their masters. (She seems to have meant the District

Commissioners who followed). "A long time ago, people used to work inside the houses where no one could see them. They worked on shambas and . . . . [lived] in the shambas. Slavery kept going." But, "another European bought them and others let me go free."[15] Those who stayed on seemed to be those who accepted the teachings of the Qur'an and the Sharia. Furthermore, according to informants, house slaves who grew up in their owners' homes felt stronger ties than those who lived on the shambas.[16]

Any slave who wished to, might report his master and subject him to a fine of Rs. 1,000 or imprisonment. Yet few brought claims against owners for continued enslavement. Concubines were excluded from the Ordinance: "Concubines shall not be deemed to be slaves . . . and nothing in this ordinance shall alter the law relating to . . . the rights and duties of concubines." But, if a concubine was mistreated and brought charges against her master, she was freed with no compensation to her owner. Free men, especially Afro-Arab youths, continued to take concubines in Lamu up to and through the 1930s. This was said to be "common practice, a sort of trial marriage." Some of these relationships, like those before emancipation, not only produced children but resulted in long term unions in which the women were elevated to *suria*. Their children were granted the same status as the children born to most slave mothers and free fathers of previous generations.[17]

It seems clear that in the case of many Afro-Arabs and their slaves, public "emancipation" on Lamu's seafront was mere theater for the British Commissioners who, having fulfilled their assignment to emancipate disappeared. In 1919, and in complete ignorance of events in Lamu (and Zanzibar), the British issued a decree that stated that slavery no longer existed in East Africa.

The small number of missionaries in Lamu seem not to have interacted with the majority of the Muslims any more than did the British colonial servants. The missionaries—including by 1910 five women and four men—educated some young children and held services "on Sunday at the mission and in the slave village" which was located in Langoni. However, contrary to their position in Mombasa, where "near rioting" was reported because missionaries took in ex-slaves, they seem to have secured no following among that group in Lamu. They were virtually ignored by the

130

Afro-Arabs and other slave holders. Consequently, the missionaries were as poorly informed as resident officials about the continuity of master-slave relationships on Lamu island.[18]

But what of those slaves who wished to be free, who did not allow injunctions from the Qur'an to interfere with the Ordinance? According to informants, many ran away "as soon as opportunities presented themselves." Some stowed away on dhows and a few even went to Arabia, where they formed a small Swahili speaking community. Some went to Mombasa, ran into hard times, and came back to plead with their masters for day work.

Former owners recalled some incidents regarding those slaves who opted for freedom, or were freed by the owners for compensation. In the case of Ali Abdalla, he sold his "slaves to the government agent and they were rebellious afterward." They "were belligerent about being referred to as former slaves"—as they often were by those who let them go. Class lines continued to be strong, and "upper class men taunted their former slaves." Before emancipation, some slaves married "in the traditional way" and they continued to do so after they were freed. "Those slaves did not follow the religion"—the assumption being that is why they opted for freedom. Continuing, Mzee Ali said that after they were free, they walked up to people, such as himself, and "were insulting. If a slave knew he was talked or written about (reported), he would beat that person." They also "robbed people." His mother owned a few slaves, he said, and his father had about one hundred. "Now [in the present time] they are high and they don't like you to tell them they are a slave."[19] Another informant talked about slaves choosing names upon their freedom. Some, he said, tossed names in a *kofia*, and assumed the name he drew. This was practiced to rid themselves of names that were not associated with Islam, because some slaves were given Swahili names for the day of the week, or names that ridiculed, like *sumaki* [fish]. Others were named for the occupations in which their father engaged.

Lower class women, and those who still regarded themselves as slaves, traveled to Mombasa as finances allowed. Some moved down there temporarily, but "we always came to back to Lamu and many us of returned to live when we had enough money or could do something to earn a living." While the trip up and down the coast was not so arduous or so potentially dangerous, dhows did sink. One ex-slave woman remembered that several of her female friends drowned—being stuck as they were behind the heavy mat in the lower section of the dhow. Few of the Lamu women knew how to swim.[20] Some poor women, who feared the dhows, trekked to Mombasa through the heavy bush on the mainland. The lure of the city in those days was primarily limited to jobs—or at least the hope for employment that would enable them to send money back home "to our masters and to our families."

Omi Shee's mother remained tied to her former mistress, who had given her a plot of land on which to build a house. With Omi Shee's help from money she earned during the Mombasa years, her mother retired to the house in Langoni. "Some slaves in the town families stayed on until the old ones died, and even some of their children stayed on until they died. Our master had to leave Lamu to earn money elsewhere and that is why my mother retired." At the end of her working life, Omi Shee also retired to the tiny sparsely furnished home where, joined by her own daughter, her final days were beset with drudgery and hardship.[21]

It is to Ralph Skene that we look for the only documentary evidence pertaining to African influenced traditional dances and to evidences of spirit possession and witchcraft in this period of the twentieth century. The *dandaro* that Salim Kheri remembered dancing was "essentially a slaves dance." With "men and women together occupying one part [of a circle] facing inward the drums being in the middle." The dancers, he wrote, "place the right hand on the left shoulder and the left hand under the right elbow, in this position they bend the knees slightly and sway the body in time to the music while progressing very slowly sideways round the circle to the right." In fact, many of the dances that Skene observed in Zanzibar, Lamu, and elsewhere on the coast were imported from Nyasaland, and practiced only by those of African ancestry.[22]

There was a great deal of spirit possession practiced in Lamu during and after slavery. Whether the practice was imported by the African slaves is unknown but "both Arabs and Swahili" believed in the existence of evil spirits. In light of research on spirit possession as a means by which women gain power, Skene's findings confirm that "the great majority of the people who get *pepo* are women." To Skene, however, the reason for

132

this was "these ills are due to a disturbance of the nervous system of imaginative and highly-strung individuals."[23]

In Lamu, when an evil spirit had been cast on one by a sorcerer, Fatuma Abdalla recalled that a woman was supposed to hold a sword while she chewed a betel nut and danced. The combination were sufficient to break spells. Evil spirits lurked in rural areas of the island and on the mainland. A *Shatani* called *ngoloko* inhabited the mangrove swamps but "fortunately its members are limited." The spirit looks "like a human being but has a cloven left foot" like a donkey. The *ngoloko* waited for tired travelers who "it" flattered by offering refreshment with "its right arm behind its back." As the traveler tilted back his head to drink, *ngoloko* brought out its right hand and "the long pointed iron fingernail on its forefinger pierces his Adam's apple so that he dies." Lamu people "knew and feared *ngoloko*."

They also feared a bird spirit, *nyuni wayu*, who looked like an owl but "was no ordinary bird." The *nyuni wayu* "are exceptionally malevolent towards newly born children. In consequence, when a mother's time draws near, a gourd is balanced on a stick to which a bow is tied, and sometimes a decorated cow-skull as well, and the whole contraption is placed on the roof of her house." Because the *nyuni wayu* do not have good eye sight, they "mistake this for an archer and the child is untroubled by them."[24]

Fear of danger from these particular spirits (or similar ones) permeate all the major ethnic groups in Lamu. Afro-Arab join descendants of ex-slaves, Indian, and Hadrami in protecting their babies eyes from "the evil eye" or the *nyuni wayu*. Beyond the measures taken to divert the spirit's attention to the house, mothers uniformly smear burnt *udi* [incense] over their babies eyes. Some—Afro-Arabs and Indians—also draw various designs on babies faces as a further preventive against evil spirits.[25]

Spirits invaded the homes of Swahili and Indian alike. Women of both groups believed that these spirits talked through them, although they did not engage in the spirit possession ritual. In many homes, incense was kept burning to "cleanse and purify the house of spirits." Many of the women at all levels of society, believed in diviners. One Lamu woman was famous for her ability to forecast the future, depending on "seven stars" for her predictions.[26]

An ex-slave woman in Lamu confided that "a long time ago *kayambi* was a dance that witches performed when the 'evil eye' had caused someone to be ill." *Kayambi* means a rattle usually containing pieces of grain. Thus the dance is named for the rattle which serves as accompaniment. "In those days, a big fire was built . . . big smoke from the fire . . . to give healing to chase the jinns away." Jinns, according to her and to other women, come "from the sea" and are believed to be called in by witches.[27]

According to another ex-slave informant, "a man could keep another from having sex by witchcraft. A husband can cast a spell to keep another from having erections." Men tended to rush to have spells cast on their wives if they found them guilty of adultery, "but the women were cool. They waited. There was a woman here known to be a witch. If a woman wanted to put a spell on someone, she could go to that woman. Men could not go." This witch was also capable of creating impotence through "her spells." Most of the spells this particular female informant recalled involved divorce, and the various ways men and women attempted to control one another.[28]

In Lamu, and elsewhere among the WaSwahili, wedding celebrations are separated by gender. Men have their special dances, as do the women. Preceding weddings, women assemble in an enclosed area where they sing and dance. The description provided by Skene is still in vogue: "The women sing in chorus to the sound of buffalo horns beaten with short sticks. No men are allowed to take part in the procession."[29] This *vugo* ceremony heralds the bride's transition to adult status. Songs are sexually explicit and the dances parody sexual intercourse. In Skene's time, only slave and ex-slave women would have performed the *vugo* in public.

Fears and superstitions surrounding the sea proliferated in Lamu. One Swahili legend regarded a curse that went into effect in the last month of the 360 day year when "someone will be lost at sea." The patricians did not allow their boys to play at the seafront during that last month, and many others followed suit. Women grew increasingly concerned about their menfolks who were traveling by dhow; seamen themselves feared shipwreck and death as the end of the year drew closer. According to oral traditions, "numerous times in Lamu's history tragic loss has come to those who are sailors, traders, or traveling by ship at this time."[30] Yet slaves and ex-slaves accompanied their owners on sea voyages to Mecca. "They cherished it" despite people dying from "ship wreck, disease or illness."[31]

In the natural world, complaints about lack of labor echoed from all classes of former slave holders, leading us to believe many slaves opted for freedom in 1910. British officialdom continually reported that "former slave owners" would not work. If they did work, they insisted on "fifty cents a day or more" which was more than the British were willing to pay. District Commissioner reports from 1910 and through into the 1930s (with very few exceptions) lament "the rising generation of Arabs in Lamu, having lost their slaves, seem averse to work, some inclined to drift through life in an aimless manner, although fond of comfort and little luxuries they would appear to prefer being without than to having to attain them by work. They may be seen walking about town in the most spotless clothing and yet seem indifferent to the filthy conditions around their dwellings."[32]

The Afro-Arabs did not work for a variety of reasons. Some did not need to while they still had numbers of slaves working for them. For those who possessed no slaves, the several district commissioners observed that many were supported "mainly by the needlework for their women folk who embroider caps and also make matting bags."[33] This was true and British officials also correctly depicted the lack of income among this group of men after they "frittered away" the compensation for their slaves. The economy prospered further down the coast, but Lamu's economic decline had turned into stagnation.[34]

Down in the Malindi-Mombasa area, a wage labour system was introduced, and public works that had been initiated by the IBEA were taken over by the British government. Although the Afro-Arabs (and others) in Lamu were being forced to pay new taxes, only a small amount of the money collected was put back into the local economy. As compensation ran out and much that could be mortgaged was, the Afro-Arab families began their own form of emancipation. One old woman from the aristocracy remembered that when she was a child—in the early 1920s—numbers of slaves were freed by her family and went to the mainland where they joined the squatters and attempted to cultivate crops. Those who were friendly with their former owners sent them grains and fruits.

135

Others, she recalled, consumed what they needed and used the surplus to buy necessary goods for survival. However, these ex-slaves soon abandoned their plots because, she thought, WaBoni and Somali raiders drove them out. Reports of roaming bands of *shifta* [bandits] came from many informants and *shifta* seem to have been a major barrier to later attempts to reopen the mainland farms. The *shifta*, unlike the *watoro*, had no base from which to operate. They were nevertheless a serious threat to the ex-slave communities on the mainland. Some older informants remembered hearing about robberies, including even the few livestock the ex-slaves (and other Africans) managed to secure for themselves.[35]

Another Afro-Arab reported that, contrary to British reports, some members of her family attempted to work on the mainland, restoring shambas and attempting to weed out and save remaining coconut trees. The former owners, she said, were even more vulnerable on the mainland than their slaves and after a few incidents in which some men were injured as well as robbed, most retreated permanently to the island.[36]

While masters who could, clung to their slaves, and attempted to carry on the semblance of life as they knew it during the nineteenth century, the British were busy introducing direct rule over Lamu and the northern coast as a whole. The bureaucracy which earlier had consisted of a few civil servants, and a few African (and later Goan) clerks, grew appreciably after the Colonial Office took over the administration of the area. In 1902 the first medical officer, Dr. Waters, "a character of whom innumerable stories are told" started a six year posting in Lamu. The physicians who followed came for tours of only a few months, the exception being one who stayed from 1913 to 1916. In 1922 and then the post was downgraded. From that time until after World War II, Lamu was served by a series of Indian "sub-assistant surgeons" with occasional visits from doctors in Mombasa. During the years actual physicians were in attendance, the majority of the cases they saw dealt with malaria, digestive problems, bronchial aliments, and neuralgia with "the last appearing endemic" brought in by ship.[37]

By 1909 Tanaland Province, administered out of Lamu, required additional local staff, as did Lamu town and its hinterland. In Lamu District alone under European supervision "were the Arab staff of the Sultan of Witu, a Liwali and Qadi in Lamu, a Liwali and Qadi in Siyu, a Qadi at

Witu, and Mudirs at Faza, Hindi, Kiunga, Wangeh, and Mkonumbi." A Commission of Enquiry looking into conditions in Tanaland "concluded that the PROVINCE HAD BEEN ADMINISTRATIVELY STARVED both as regards money and good men to guide it; that, by neglect, we had smothered a country rich in possibilities and decreased population, so as to make lack of population one of the main causes of deterioration."[38]

Part of the problem with Lamu was the "extraordinary degree of love of intrigue and immorality which predominate in the character of the Arab and Swahili population" that have "brought personal disaster on more than one officer." Declining to go into "detail the causes were in some cases the lapse from strictly conventional administration [that] was no more serious than has occurred in other Districts, but here it served as a splendid weapon for personal enmity. These unpleasant episodes have probably been the [result of province officers who] have vacillated between an active hostility and an immeasurable distrust of the Arab official and foolish confidence in him and a criminal neglect in his supervision."[39]

The commissioners report requested that more administrative duties be handed over to the liwalis . . . . and "the Government to be most particular in the selection of European Officials to posts . . . particularly in the Lamu District." The result was the strict and controlling Ralph E. Skene, who was sent to run the Lamu District in 1910. His brief administration could hardly be characterized as negligent. But his lack of empathy for the locals, and especially the *waungwana*, and his dedication to detail, launched him immediately into controversy. If Britain had hopes of winning over the local people, and in inducing them to cooperate, the Colonial Office made a problematic choice in the appointment of Ralph Skene.[40]

By 1911 Skene reported that twenty one Europeans (including a few missionaries) were posted in Lamu along with forty six Goans, most of whom were civil servants (although a growing number came in as tailors). Among Skene's responsibilities was to force the locals to pay the hut tax which had been put into effect earlier in the century. The hut tax was levied on Africans in the British colony. "Persons of Arab descent," however, "although born in the country, do not consider themselves natives, and as non-natives they are therefore exempted from taxation."

Skene, refused to acknowledge the considerable numbers of "Arabs" in Lamu, insisting that they provide proof of descent. This system worked to the advantage of the Hadrami community who, in most cases, kept the Arabic language and who were but recent arrivals. By seeming to side with the Hadramis over the old families, Skene further divided the communities. The problem of the hut tax was finally addressed by adding another category: the non-native hut tax, which included those who claimed Arab descent. In fact, neither the natives nor the Afro-Arabs could afford the levy and many simply did not pay. Skene, who was also civil magistrate over the district, ordered the recalcitrant to court where he added fines to the unpaid taxes, and sometimes sent those in arrears to jail. He established a County Council, meaning that local landowners had to vote for the leaders they had otherwise chosen by common consent. For this privilege they were forced to pay the poll (income) tax (Hut and Poll Tax Ordinance of 1910).[41]

Skene did not endear himself to the liwali, with whom he was charged to work more closely. One of his first acts was to send a terse note to Seif bin Abdalla, the liwali's son, notifying him "that your house occupied by the post office will not be required by the Government [the lease came to an end]."[42] He was high handed and arrogant when it came to dealing with Lamu women as well. He wrote the liwali that, "Owing to the riotous conduct of the women in Lamu at an ngoma last night, and which is still going on I shall be obliged if you will kindly stop the issue of all ngoma permits for a week."

KiSwahili written in Arabic script was the official language of communication between all mudirs, qadis, and liwalis in this period. Interpreters and "Arabic clerks," (some ex-slaves from Zanzibar) were hired by the government to translate documents for British colonial servants.

Licenses were issued for every conceivable activity: porters were required to pay a fee; game hunters were licensed; palm wine tappers were required to obtain licenses. Each shop owner also needed a license. The enterprising entrepreneur who sold bits of food in the street was subject to a license charge. All dhow captains were obliged to pay the government a fee of two shillings (Rupees earlier) for every ten passengers on board their ships. Stamp duties increased. Auctioneers (mostly

Hadrami) were forced to purchase licenses as were gold and silversmiths. Court duties—including probate—were levied against the locals. There were fees for marriage licenses and divorce decrees. For this reason, many marriages and divorces were not recorded with the government. Nevertheless, as these figures illustrate, divorce rates were high in relation to marriages.[43]

	Marriages	Divorces
1910	2826	1865
1911	2541	1861
1912	2540	1863
1913	2430	1862

The imposition of unwanted British colonialism was a very costly measure that all but a few of the locals attempted to avoid as best they could. It is no wonder that after these burdens had been unceremoniously levied on the locals, a former district commissioner noted that "the unsavory reputation of the District has frightened the individual Officer who, generally speaking, has pursued a policy of *laissez faire* and prayed he would get away without personal damage . . . . those who adopted this policy have been the most popular with the people of Lamu."[44] In Skene, the locals got what Freudians refer to as an anal personality and the *laissez faire* practices that existed before his arrival were abruptly halted.

In his first year of residence, Skene confirmed that he had filed "568 charges for recovery of hut tax in the island of Lamu alone. A large number of summonses issued were not obeyed and warrants for arrests had to be issued." One old Lamu man remembered being brought before the district commissioner for failure to pay his hut tax. He said no one explained what it meant, nor the purpose insofar as Lamu was concerned. He was just told that "it was the law [and he] must pay." Many of his peers were equally resentful and refused to pay until "some started getting sentenced to jail and so they paid." Nearly seventy years after the fact, this man recalled that he told the DC "when we get to the next life God will avenge."[45] Ironically, soon after the non-native hut tax was put into effect, many Afro-Arabs decided to become "native" after they learned their taxes were higher. Indians, too, were forced to pay the non-native hut tax which most did. As to the Afro-Arabs, a DC reported that it "not easy to fix the amount each should pay as we have no means of estimating a man's income."[46] Hut taxes ranged from Rs. 3 for a native to Rs. 13/ for non-natives and increased over time in spite of the waning economy.

The Qadi handled cases of a religious or personal nature. The magistrate dealt with civil cases, although it was Skene who meted out punishment on eighty court cases ranging from theft to failure to pay the various taxes. Rioting (Skene's designation) not surprisingly took place in both Lamu and elsewhere on the island. In fact he sat in judgment on seven cases where rioting was alleged, acquitting some of the over two hundred men brought to trial. Before Skene took over, the Lamu liwali had successfully decided 286 criminal cases of which 280 dealt with avoidance of the hut tax. The qadis, Skene noted, "were not corrupt as the natives are very well aware that they can appeal to the High Court in the event of their being wronged in any way." Nevertheless, in Lamu from 1910 and on, it was the British who handled cases involving taxes, not the qadis.[47]

When the locals were put in jail for failure to pay their taxes, they were also forced to pay for their subsistence while there. An example of justice under the newly imposed colonial system involved a woman, "a pauper who was imprisoned as a debtor" and who was therefore "too poor to pay in advance the subsistence allowance of the Judgment debtor while in goal . . ." Unable to waive the rules, Skene turned to the High Court in Mombasa to inquire whether "an order of imprisonment can be made without payment in advance. . . ."[48] While the British had every right to criticize the horrors of the slave trade as well as cruelty to slaves, their own policies towards prisoners left much to be desired. Some were ordered to be whipped as well as fined (a few sentences called for as many as twenty lashes). Leg irons were used on those who presented problems. And, a cat-o-nine tails was among the relics the British left behind when they turned over the jail at Kenyan independence.

Among Skene's myriad activities on behalf of the Colonial Office were those that dealt with the health and welfare of the Lamu citizenry. Considerable correspondence dealt with two "lunatics" Skene eventually succeeded in removing from Lamu. One man was guilty of applying a white powdered substance on his body, and running about town "raving and ranting." The second, had been involved in a criminal action and was judged insane. Both were exported to Nairobi where they were placed in an asylum. Before the arrival of British humanitarianism, they would have been kept at homes under the observation of their families. Later, a leper gave pause. He, too, was shipped out of the District.[49]

The following case study reflects on Skene's sometimes ruthless handling of the patrician class. Deciding to locate a karosene oil store and slaughter house on the walkpath to Shela, Skene contacted Mama Furutuna, the property owner whose plot he desired. In her reply, Mama Furutuna advised that she "did not wish to sell her land and will therefore bring no evidence to prove its value." Skene worked out the approximate value based on a scale tied to appraisals made in 1893. Between 1893 and 1907, he decided, land had risen at the rate of about ten percent a year. After 1907 (the year the Ordinance went into effect further down the coast) land values had dropped thirty percent, therefore Mama Furutana's land as worth approximately "Rs.0.0193643 per square foot."

By the Skene initiated "Lamu Acquisition Act" Mama Furutuna's land was confiscated. Although Mama Furutuna pled for the opportunity to be heard (through a male relative) Skene put the matter to rest. Sheikh Ahmed Jahadhmy identified the woman as either a "Beraki or Lami" who owned a great deal of property in Lamu. "I do not know for what reason all her property was confiscated, even the plot on which now sits a church (the Catholic church on the seafront). That land and the land behind it all belonged to her."[50]

One of the more unusual licenses was for ostrich feathers issued to a European ostrich farmer near Witu. Among those who purchased hunting licenses were the liwali, Seif bin Salim, a Denhardt brother, Mohamed al Maawyia, and Ali bin Mohamed who was a grandson of liwali Abdalla bin Hamed. He was also the father of Mohamed bin Ali BuSaid, later a big game hunter and then government game warden. Mohamed al Maawyia became an esteemed chief of Lamu in the 1930s holding that position until his death in the mid-1950s. He was also a direct descendant of Bwana Zaidi Ngumi, the hero of the Battle of Shela.[51]

Squabbles over estates, and especially over probate charges marked the early years of colonial administration in Lamu. Many Indians circumvented probate by shifting their money to family members during their lifetimes. One deceased Indian left "effects over Rs. 100." Considering that "adult laborers" earned Rs 15 per month, this was a rather small sum for a member of the mostly merchant Indian community. By comparison, a poor widow, Motti Jessa, received a total of Rs. 14/07 "as her portion of her husband's estate."

Skene reported that "money is the only medium of exchange in this district" yet informants remembered turning to barter to offset lack of income. Coconuts and mangoes were exchanged for sandals. Or various fruits and vegetables were traded for palm fronds to mat into bags and rugs. "Silver is used for making ornaments" Skene wrote in his annual report, but in fact silver and gold were traded on occasion, and the case of the most destitute, both were pawned to Indian moneylenders for needed cash.

Skene, and district commissioners who followed him, were critical of the "natives who spend as soon as possible all they can lay their hands on." Menials in government service "usually spend all their pay during the first week after pay day" although they were paid on a monthly basis. On entering "service the employee might demand 1/2 or 1/3 of the promised wage in advance to settle his own household matters" and then some continued to ask for advances to keep their households afloat.[52] The government practiced the same type of debt bondage that characterized the former masters who, when they could, loaned money in advance. Some even transferred their laborers debts to others in return for their own indebtedness. In the case of many former slaves they were "placed in an extraordinary undesirable position as they were practically forced to work for either very small returns, or no pay and are therefore liable to be forced to thieve . . . so that may obtain food, clothes and lodging."

In comparison to the Afro-Arabs, the Indian community generally presented fewer problems to district commissioners at this time. They continued to buy up shambas and many attempted to take over mortgaged shambas on the mainland. Messrs. Ismailji Buddahbhai and Sons refused to sign a deed "on the grounds that the boundaries on the shamba are incorrect"—a problem that would recur in the decades to come. One of the largest Indian owned firms in Lamu was that belonging to an Ithnasharia family, Sheriff Jaffer and Company. This company also became embroiled in a land transfer controversy which suggests that, beyond undefined boundaries, locals avoided paying taxes on the profits of land they sold.

Charles Whitten, an eccentric European known in Lamu as "Coconut Charlie" arrived in Lamu in 1911. He bought a parcel of land at Kitau, on Manda Island. The owner of the land, Mohammed bin Athman, attempted to reclaim the title, once it was legally transferred from Sheriff Jaffer and Company to Whitten. His excuse was that "someone else had sold the land" and thus the Indians, who were required to register a deed of some kind, were not the legal owners and therefore did not have the right to sell to Whitten. The government ignored the Afro-Arab and allowed the transfer to proceed.[53] No doubt other Afro-Arabs lost their landholding by avoiding paying the government levies and in long run being forced to take whatever sums the Indians paid them under the table. Or they mortgaged their lands to the Indians, and then claimed them back when the Indians profited by their sale.

Although most of the Afro-Arabs fell on hard times after emancipation, a few managed to maintain their prosperity by going into business. Ahmed bin Abdalla "Boke" was a rich man throughout the period of economic decline in Lamu. (The term "Boke" is an unfortunate one in that the British administrators seemed not have to realized that it was not a *nisba* but a pejorative term meaning roughly "someone touched in the head." In the case of this man, however, it referred to his sometime bad temper).

In 1910 Ahmed bin Abdalla "Boke" issued a draft in the sum of Rupees 500 for merchandise from Bombay, dealing directly with the merchant community there, thus avoiding the Indian middlemen in Lamu. The firm, however went into insolvency and "Boke" lost his money. He made up for that with the later purchase of sailing dhows, and with an extension of his business into Zanzibar and later Mombasa.[54]

In 1913 conditions had not improved—nor had attitudes on the part of the British towards many of the residents of Lamu. By now "many are breaking religious prohibitions" not keeping the fast at Ramadan and drinking liquor while "notably acquiring a taste for European goods."[55] Yet, in a port city such as Lamu cultural transformations regularly occurred as outsiders settled and brought new customs with them.

One group of newcomers arrived in Lamu as prisoners of war. German African troops from Tanganyika were locked in the fort by night, and put to work on the seawall and in road construction during their brief stay. Beyond sighting the German submarine, the *Konigsburg*, that made a foray into Lamu Bay and, which frightened the locals who feared for their sailing ships, World War I had little effect on Lamu. A few men were drafted as carriers in the King's African Rifles (KAR). One, bitterly remembered being sent down to the Tanganyika border—the longest distance he ever traveled from Lamu throughout his long life.[56]

In Zanzibar, an al Hussein sharif with close ties to the Sultan, who was believed to be favoring the German cause, was arrested on suspicion of treason. The Sultan intervened with the British authorities, and obtained his release but on the condition he return to Lamu. Arriving with his son and his concubine, the sharif's activities were monitored by British authorties even though his son, Sharif Abdalla Salim, was hired as court interpreter.[57]

Ex-slaves and Hadrami competed for any numbers of the low paying jobs created by the British government in Lamu. Some were hired as porters to load and unload government steamboats. Others were employed as day labor to clean and sweep government buildings. Based on their previous domestic experiences, ex-slaves were hired as house-boys to the growing European population in the town. In the war years, Lamu's sagging economy received a slight boost. New dhows financed by "Indians, Arabs, and Europeans" were constructed on the seafront, calling for "skilled craftsmen . . . riveters, and caulkers." Here, too, ex-slaves were in competition with the Hadramis—the Afro-Arabs presumably employing their former slaves while the Indians and Europeans hired both groups, depending on their relative skills. Lamu was also becoming a "major center of distribution of goods imported and then redistributed to local islands" requiring expert sailors and crews for the small *jahazis* that plied the Lamu archipelago. The sailors "who work on shares receive too much advance for their sales and as a consequence develop problems with owners."[58]

There were still no "native" traders in the Lamu District. The Hadrami and Indians controlled trade while the "upper class continue to sit around in small circles, engaging in conversation but doing no visible work but are borrowing heavily."[59] Beyond dhow building, "the principal native industries [were] . . . rope making, sandal making, white cap embroidery, cowrie shell counting." Exports included copra, mangrove poles supplied by the Bajun, bark, ivory, matting bags, and cattle. Skins were a major source of income during the low period of the first decades of the century. In 1916, 187,314 legal ox hides were exported for a "total value of Rs. 12,975." Coconuts, donkeys, goats, beeswax, and chilies appeared on manifests exported from Lamu to the neighboring islands and down to Mombasa. Almost all of this trade was in the hands of the Indian community, which also controlled the interisland commerce.

Population figures, based on the hut or poll tax, are for the entire province but they illustrate something about the temporary restoration of prosperity during the years:[60]

1908/09	24,750
1909/10	24,795
1910/11	23,350
1913/14	30,800
1914/15	25,857
1915/16	26,238
1916/17	26,048

Counting again the entire district, 302 seamen were employed on oceangoing dhows in 1915, 305 in 1915, and by 1916 with the threat of war less ominous in Lamu, 776 sailed out. Their average wage was a respectable 12/ rupees a month without rations. They, too, borrowed against wages and were often in debt when they began their next trip.[61]

Sharif Abdalla Salim recalled that in the first two decades of the century, some in Lamu were "still wealthy. There were so many al Hussein then in Lamu—one of the biggest families. Many had island shambas, although problems arose in farming those on the mainland." By the time Sharif Abdalla's mother died (in the early 1920s), the post-war economy had gone into a tail spin. Sharif Abdalla was one of the throngs of young men who abandoned Lamu in favor of Mombasa, where he obtained a higher paying position. But not before being forced to turn over his mother's legacy to his father. Down in Mombasa, he married into the Mazrui family, and began his rise in politics.[62]

In 1916-1917 sesame seeds and coconut oil were major items of export, suggesting that the island shambas were becoming increasingly productive. Informants remember that ex-slaves had begun to return to Lamu and were undertaking paid employment for their former owners.[63]

Once the new slaughter house was opened at the northern end of town the Hadrami took over as butchers. They maintained their hold on this occupation and when the butcher shop was opened near the Fort (now relocated), Hadramis moved in as a class to small stalls where they sold to individual clients. Some ex-slaves fished for income, joining Hadramis and Bajuns who, while not living in Lamu, sailed in and sold their fish to locals on first the seafront, and later to merchants in the butcher shop. Many ex-slave men and women dried their fish on the seafront, or in areas in back of the town. These dried fish were sometimes exported, but often sold to the very poor who could make a good pot of stew from a small amount of dried fish.[64]

Even in the 1980s some Hadrami merchants pursued the age old tradition of smuggling goods into Lamu. Local police, always a small force in Lamu town, rarely were able to intercept the smuggled goods. Slipping off at night, some Hadrami petty traders met Arab dhows at appointed places, or they went directly on board dhows in the harbor to conduct business and to avoid paying the requisite taxes and duties. Luxury items especially preferred by women were most frequently smuggled in by Hadrami merchants. Although most of the Afro-Arabs had little income, their wives continued to demand gold jewelry and fine materials for the wedding ceremonies that required as many as seven dresses for the seven nightly events.[65] It seems likely that the Indians sought to avoid taxes and duties in much the same way as their Arab counterparts and especially as pertained to gold, silver, and silks. Indian dhows coming into port would have been able to cooperate, although occasional searches were conducted by customs officials.[66] Because of the government fees charged per every ten persons arriving on Arabian and Indian dhows, many captains refused to turn over their "crew or passenger lists." After their passengers had departed, there was little the British could do but conduct a head count as men came on shore. But, of course, dhows often dropped anchor off Manda Bay and passengers rowed ashore before they were in sight of the customs agents.

From the time of Skene's arrival and picking up momentum in the next several decades, a steady stream of migrants poured out of Lamu seeking better opportunities elsewhere. In the case of the ex-slaves who stayed on despite increasing economic hardships, self-determination and personal freedom were relative terms. Most ex-slave informants pointed out that after they were emancipated they were both kinless and landless. Those who remained in the owners' households or on their shambas were often better off than those who had been set free. So, too, were their masters and mistresses, who had the products from their labor to sell. Those who got away and found employment often did well. Many never returned, letting their slave past disappear from both memory and genealogy. One Lamu ex-slave served as mayor of Mombasa. Members of the Lamu aristocracy who had moved down there knew who he was, as he knew them from past days of servitude. Neither ever addressed his former status and, while he was in office he proved himself a man of considerable ability.[67]

A few of the old and ill ex-slaves pensioned off by the British lived out their lives in relative comfort in Langoni. DC John Clive reported that in 1934 there were "only fourteen slaves at the slave village" and "no more are to be admitted as all kinds of others are anxious to be ex-slaves for purpose of obtaining housing and food." In 1939 another British official mentioned the "small camp of ex-slaves who receive 8 shillings per month. Ex-slaves get two issues of clothing per year; shirts and shorts for men and *lesos* [large pieces of cloth] for women."

Regarding abolition, however, one family told of generations of slaves who had been born, married, and died while serving their grandfathers, fathers, and themselves—right under the noses of the British colonials. The last slaves of this family were freed in 1958.

District Commissioner Talbot-Smith looked back to the decades following emancipation with more insight than most:

> "It is imagined that those families will have to gradually drop to a lower social status as has happened with aristocratic families elsewhere and their places will gradually come to be occupied by others who neither know nor understand their past traditions, their past struggles, difficulties and ambition."[68]

CHAPTER 9

A funeral in which the body is being carried on the *tusi*
Courtesy of the National Museums of Kenya

Chapter Nine

Life in Lamu from the 1920s: The Government and the "Swahili"

"Lean not on the evil doers lest the Fire lay hold on you.
Ye have no protector, save God, and ye shall not be
helped against Him . . . for the word of thy Lord will be fulfilled,
'I will wholly fill hell with Djinn and men.'"
The Qur'an

A brief economic upswing in the 1920s was marked by little or no improvements on the economic front for most of the WaAmu. British colonial officials complained about the economy and issued uncomplimentary reports. One reason for the litany of negative attitudes towards the patricians was that district commissioners revolved through Lamu's door so quickly they often arrived in time to write the yearly report and then moved out again without getting to know the people or the circumstances surrounding them.

It was not uncommon for Lamu to have two or three different district commissioners within the space of a single year. Those who came in often turned to the reports of doom and gloom left behind by their predecessors, adding only the yearly statistics collected by subordinates. Their interaction with the locals was limited to the leading elders, the qadi, and the liwali, who was still jointly appointed. Most yearly reports were characteristic of the following: "The Swahili together with their neighbors, the representatives of Muscat Arab families, reached some years ago a fairly high stage of Oriental civilization. Now . . . they are on the decline, and are going from bad to worse. With all this poverty, and ruin are stalking in from every side: plantations are going into decay, houses, once pretentious, are crumbling to ruin."[1]

Yet, the Provincial Commissioner, whose base extended down the coast to Mombasa by 1920, and who arrived on the scene just in time to submit his report, provided some explanation. It was his belief that those "who can work and can find work, do so. The result is loss of over 1,000 population which is in Zanzibar. Practically every person capable of earning a reasonable wage elsewhere has migrated, excepting sailors, and a limited number of herdsmen and agriculturalists."[2]

In 1921 T. Ainsworth Dickens came to Lamu, as district commissioner for three years. Dickens interviewed some locals in order to collect a history but he seems not to have made any long lasting impression on the old families, perhaps because his attitude was similar to those who preceded him: "European officials in dealing with native officials cannot be too clean minded nor too tactful . . . . our endeavor should be to get them to respect us no matter whether we can respect them or not." He, too, noted "a decrease in production, the potential value of the land being as valuable as ever."[3] But, again, made little or no attempt to aid the locals in restoring their hold over their mainland properties.

In 1921, the official currency changed from the rupee to shillings [R1=1s.4d]. This action caused a major financial debacle for the WaAmu and the Indians as well. Many Afro-Arabs had squirreled away their rupees on the pretext that they were too poor to pay the various taxes. Indians, whose trade was tied to their home country, were put at a disadvantage because, they too, had hidden income from the tax assessors. Letters of complaint flowed in calling for the restoration of the rupee as coast currency.

Dickens believed the change in currency had an impact on the district nearly equal to the rise in the hut and poll taxes, which also went into effect in 1921. "The increase of this tax . . . Rs. 3/ to Rs. 7/ . . . " combined with the change from rupees "and the abolition of slavery was a disastrous mistake." In spite of lowered assessments, "the Hut and Poll tax is the greatest source of revenue."[4] But the locals continued to be in arrears on their taxes throughout the decade: "part of the town upkeep came from hut tax, non-native poll tax, and trader's licenses. The problem was collecting *on all 3*."

In the late 1920s, a district commissioner employed additional counters to help the liwali and his staff collect the taxes.[5]

The older members of the Afro-Arab community remember the taxes as leading to the loss of homes and of property on the island. Only a few "who could lead the good life and these men used to keep their money in their belt at home, but gradually almost all were poor. That's why they couldn't afford to pay the hut tax. So when the British threatened to put them in jail, they went to friends and relatives to take a loan, which they repaid slowly, slowly. Then they went to the Asians." But some also blamed the Hadrami who, they said, "came to Lamu when they had nothing, and started their business . . . . But they rose quickly and now are more rich than the Lamu people."[6] The fact that the Hadrami, like the Indian community, were hard working and saved seems not to have been taken into account by the patricians who had not relinquished their nineteenth century mentality despite their waning fortunes.

A *suria* whose husband had been among the very wealthy landowners in the 1920s referred to "Arab pride. . . . It was a shame for Arabs to go to each other to borrow money after slavery ended. The Hindis . . . opened shops, saved their money, and grew prosperous." After emancipation "the culture remained the same: big weddings, big feasts, all the show. The Arabs borrowed money from the Indians, mortgaged homes, land on the mainland. Those who mortgaged their land to the Hindis at least got something for it. Others let their land grow up in weeds and their houses fall down."

As for the procedures involved, "the Arab borrowed 30 rupees (and later shillings) from [the] Hindis at interest. Gave mortgage [a] on his house, or one of his houses. Most Arabs owned several houses. As he did no outside work, he could not get any money to repay. Back again for more rupees (shillings). Perhaps another small loan. Then [the] Hindis foreclosed. Took the houses. Arabs either moved out or they rented their homes from the Hindis. Some sons who went to Mombasa or elsewhere to work sent back money to help pay the rent. Some slaves sent money to help."[7]

Because of the continuing divisions in the town, Dickens established an advisory committee that consisted of a political and ethnic mix that brought together men who were light years apart socially. The Hadrami Sheikh Abdalla Hassan Bates joined Indian T. M. Jeevanjee and Afro-

Arab Issa Hasham in occasional meetings with DC's. Later, Charles Whitten was added to the committee, as was Mohamed al Maawyia.[8] Despite the cries of poverty in the district, the government bought land from several families, mostly the patricians whose houses were still standing but who were in need of cash. Abdalla bin Hamed's mansion on the seafront became the district commissioners official residence until it later was turned into the Lamu Museum.

Before the purchases were made in the 1920s, the government paid Shs. 150 per month on Abdalla bin Hamed's house. Mohamed Maawyia rented one of his houses for Shs. 150 per month, thus enabling him to meet some of the many financial burdens attendant to being the leading elder in town. Ali Mohamed Zena, another member of the family who were prominent in the Battle of Shela, rented out another house for Shs. 60/. Other Afro-Arab families rented houses to the government and obtained their monthly living allowances in this way with rents ranging from Shs. 60/ to 120/.[9]

Back in 1911 the district commissioner had purchased the land surrounding Hidabu hill on which a later one built a school. By the l920s, the building had fallen into disrepair, was claimed to be haunted by spirits of the past, and was abandoned. Later, the government chose to build the district commissioners residence at Hidabu, where it still stands.[10]

Trade was off during the 1920s and '30s. Dhows were no longer being built, and as a consequence, "dhow makers are not needed, rope and sail making off, provisions of shark oil (a local industry) down." In 1923, "coconut plantations have been unproductive and cereals have suffered from a variety of pests, the principle being the grasshoppers, baboons, pigs, and elephants." By then, five thousand (mostly men) had left the district and these were "almost entirely Arabs." Many WaAmu "are in Mombasa working on the Kilindini Harbour Works." The Lamu streets "were filthy" and in 1929 the DC worried about an epidemic if they were not washed. In this case nature came to the rescue with the onset of the rainy season.[11]

Dickens made repeated references to the affects of emancipation: "Generous but misapplied legislation in suddenly divorcing masters and retainers, produced a landed class with a small amount of capital instead of labor and with no education to qualify the former to obtain the latter.

Their very freedom was the undoing of the ex-slaves, for as landless and fatherless, they lacked initiative and dreading the responsibilities of life took fright and died while their children drifted into town."[12] Dickens words account for the reason that many of the ex-slaves returned to work for their former masters, or, chose to reattach themselves in the secure bonds of the past.

Dickens' refrain, and the ongoing laments regarding poor economic conditions, marked the two decades that followed. Inability to collect taxes, and the growing impoverishment of the locals did not, however, keep the two or three Europeans in residence from their pleasures. Employing local labor, they built a tennis court near the district commissioners home on the seafront. In 1925 "a cricket club was formed" the members being the "English residents" and the Goan clerks. A Goan also provided some of the comforts of home by opening a liquor store near the Fort. Soccer came to be a big hit "with the Lamu boys who were quite good." Eventually four teams were formed with the competitions taking place in the heavy sand behind the town. These games provided the only occasion in which men of all social and economic classes socialized and that was based on competition between them and their support for their respective teams.

During the 1920s, and continuing throughout the colonial era, Christmas decorations were strung about, including down the main street where the Muslim and Hindu traders kept their shops. Old men remembered with nostalgia the Christmas tree, near today's Coast Cinema in Langoni. Christmas celebrations were tolerated but the liquor store was the source of almost constant complaint from the elders, the Indian community, and the growing numbers of Hadrami.[13]

Dickens was accurate in his comments on the declining population. But the statistics between 1920 and 1940 are not an accurate measure of migration because as the Afro-Arabs left, former slaves returned, and an influx of people from Witu poured into Lamu town. The figures are relatively stable but they do not account for shifts within the district. We do see, however, the growing imbalance between married men and women in the 1920s and 1930s. But even those figures were skewed as they did not take into account the numbers of seamen who were away at any given time, making for a floating population. In any case, Dickens was struck by the preponderance of females in Lamu.[14]

	Married men	women
1932	3982	11,071
1933	4002	10,968
1934	4122	11,586
1935	3991	11,649
1936	4134	11,852

In 1929 the government had to advance maize to the locals in the district. Most of the WaAmu relied heavily on rice as the staple of their diet, but because of the food shortage, they ate what was available. Charles Whitten reported that "never during his twenty years of residence in the town has the price of copra fallen so low." The clove market was off in Zanzibar, meaning the market for mat bags fell as well. Imports exceeded exports mostly because of the rice shortage but there was a slight increase in exports: ghee, native caps, dried fish, raw cotton, and *boriti*. By 1930 the "American depression had spread world wide" and this was blamed for even worse conditions in Lamu that year.

Capital was not there to be invested, therefore output continued to shrink. With no labor force to produce goods and foodstuffs, no capital was acquired. The depression only reenforced these economic conditions in Lamu. The dhow traffic dropped again. Incoming dhows went from 72 in 1930 to 50 in 1931, to the lows of 36 and 28 in the years 1932 and 1933. Mohammed al Maawyia, then chief of the town, had a large shamba on the island. There he entertained in the manner to which his family had been accustomed during the days of prosperity. Mohammed al Maawyia invited dhow captains, their musicians and local musicians to play at his shamba: "The big merchants went to stay for 2 or 3 days with musicians performing . . . feasts and entertainment going on every day." Many members of the patrician class, crying poverty when it came to taxes, continued to emulate the opulence of the past, especially when visiting *nahoas* honored their homes or shambas.[15]

Nevertheless and surprisingly, in 1930, John Clive reported that "The Arabs are keeping their heads above water as evidenced by an over collected Non-Native Poll tax."[16] That was the year Clive and his wife arrived. Elders remembered them fondly—and singularly—as insightful and somewhat more sympathetic to the locals. Described as a "one armed man" Clive had a "tough and tenacious wife" who, during a smallpox epidemic, entreated Lamu women to come to her residence for vaccinations.[17] The Clives stayed until 1933. During this time John Clive was less preoccupied with administrative detail, and more concerned with revamping the economy. He also compiled a history of Lamu, building on an earlier one written by Dickens.

Like Dickens, Clive believed that "Lamu needs a mainland population" estimating that in 1932 alone the cost of running the district "exceeded income by about £500 with expenses falling most heavily on the locals who remained behind. Clive failed to reopen the mainland because of the ongoing dispute concerning land claims that were not resolved until after his departure.

Where previous district commissioners had referred to the well dressed young men who loaf around the town, and to the "immorality of this class", Clive remarked on their cleanliness and marveled that they could maintain an aura of prosperity in their dress. He was also perceptive in recognizing how many of them managed to appear prosperous. "The old families who remain are still partially supported by their slaves who stay on and by the combined labor of men and women who do the matting."[18]

Despite the overall economic plight "the first, and only, Lamu Agricultural Show which, advertized in advance, attracted 72 Europeans who filled two coastal steamers. Many Arab, Somali, and African visitors were present. . . ." This took place in 1930 and no long range benefits came from the show to establish Lamu on the road to economic prosperity. In 1936 the Ithnasharia Panju family opened the Lamu Ginnnery on the path between the town and Shela. Locals complained that the Lamu Ginnery" has a monopoly on importing and gristing maize" and this is "grossly unfair because they are violating the food rules in as much as they operate a cotton ginnery and oil extracting machine under the same roof there is an adjoining coir machine which creates much dirt and dust."[19] No action was taken, however, because the Panjus created jobs in both small enterprises.

The airstrip at Manda was finished in the mid-1930s, connecting Lamu with Mombasa and Malindi in less than three hours. Few WaAmu could afford the luxury of a plane ride, and most continued to sail in and out by dhow. A very poor quality road path offered a long and bumpy ride, but that was contingent on dry weather, and whether bandits were in the vicinity. Most supplies continued to arrive by water—dhows carrying locally ordered items; and the steamships providing government necessities.

In 1938, C. A. (Daddy) Cornell came to Lamu as district commissioner. Cornell was described as a man who believed in delegating authority, spending some small part of his day distributing tasks to his subordinates, and otherwise, paying little or no attention to detail.[20] Cornell reported that "the worst of the depression was over." *Boriti* exports were up but cotton prices were down due to "the world market and poor yields." In fact, most all exports were down, despite Cornell's optimism.[21] Trade also fell with Italian Somalia. In 1936 the Italians had invaded and mostly conquered Ethiopia. Fears of war were growing and the Fort was undergoing transformation to serve as a detention center.[22]

By 1939, the "only outlet for labor is hamali work and dhow crews" with further numbers of men going to Zanzibar, Mombasa, and elsewhere for work. But also in the 1930s, the largest dhow said to have been built in Lamu was launched. That belonged to an al Hussein sharif and his family. Some were obviously making money during this bleak period, as two more smaller dhows were also put in commission.[23]

Beyond bureaucratic matters and district commissioner reports, life within the town proceeded with few internal disruptions. In these two decades many of the ex-slaves and their descendants who stayed on, or who returned, gradually came to be absorbed as extended kin by the old families. It was "hard to distinguish the descendants of slaves from descendants of the Afro-Arabs who fell on hard times. There were always some plebeians in Lamu, like the Yumbili, and the wave of Hadrami poor. But slaves of the old families often had more privileges and suffered less discrimination then the newcomers."[24] One female member of the aristocracy noted that the "new generation of women born in the 1930s and 1940s, experienced the change from viewing slaves as belonging to the family, or as former slaves and daughters of slaves as belonging to the family. Their daughters and sons did not grow up with slaves in the house, but viewed these people as poor . . . . members of the family." While that may be true on one level, members of these families were also aware of the social chasm that separated them. Afro-Arab females argued that there is the Muslim tradition of taking care of one's own, even ex-slaves and their families."[25] As we have seen, in the aftermath of abolition, many slaves took care of their masters and mistresses, and as one descedant pointed out "we took care of their children."[26]

Ex-slaves entered into the economic arena—often in competition with the Hadrami—making and carving stools, chairs, bedsteads. They made pottery and wove mats, and tanned mangrove bark and manufactured sandals.[27] In some of these enterprises they were joined by their masters. Some traveled on ships and traded, returning to share bits of profit with their former owners "who are cap-makers, gold and silversmiths, sandal-makers, and small traders."[28] According to two old ex-slaves still living in the 1980s, men of their class worked "in their masters homes making gold and silver jewelry. Some [Afro-Arabs] brought pieces of gold to be melted down and new pieces made. Some brought money and purchased the gold and silver—earrings, bangles, necklaces. The slave craftsmen were best . . . . [although] there was also an Indian who did these things. Descendants of the slaves were not so talented and their business suffered. Local people thought the Indian were mixing gold and alloy" at disproportionate rates and eventually turned to Mombasa and Zanzibar to buy their jewelry."[29]

An old freed slave in her late eighties with stretched earlobes hanging as loosely as her sagging skin, remembered hunting trips that her husband used to take with his master in the 1930s. "The master carried pistols and the slaves carried pangas. They killed mostly for eating—topi and other animals. Hippo meat was regarded as very good and we all shared it with our masters." The British correctly noted "there was little money but there was plenty to eat." They "gave them jobs cleaning up the town, but this was usually on top of whatever work they did for their owners." Another woman talked about the island shambas, where her husband was a coconut tapper. She used to collect firewood to sell, the proceeds of which she shared with her mistress.[30]

As late as 1923 masters were still claiming inheritance of their slaves property. Although the cases were resolved by the qadi, the British legal system upheld the claims because of earlier ordinances still in effect. For instance, Juma Kirobote died and "his master Ahmed bin Abdalla bin

Mafit inherited . . . ."[31] During years immediately after emancipation, slaves and ex-slaves acquired considerable numbers of houses in the Langoni area. Most ceased building on the seafront, but those homes that belonged to them there were allowed to stand as long as they and then their descendants occupied them.

Slave and ex-slave children joined those of the old families in games along the seafront and in swimming in the debris laden bay. One former slave woman lost her only son while he was swimming with other youths in front of the town. Although inexplicable to some, to her the drowning was "Allah's will." The high infant mortality rate was also attributed to Allah as were the various ills that plagued Lamu's children.

Many children went to work in the informal economy, selling peppered apple type mangoes and ripe coconuts on the narrow winding Lamu streets. Others, girls especially, helped their mothers with household duties in their owners homes as well as in their own tiny quarters.

Long after legal emancipation slaves and former slaves who remained in contact with former owners, continued to carry on rituals associated with their past activities. Circumcision for baby boys most often occurred seven days after birth. Slaves carried the babes to the seafront, where they engaged in a ritual if questionable cleansing. Slaves and their descendants continued playing active roles in wedding celebrations. The women performed vugo, joined in past years by their former owners and their descendants.[32] Even though they were on the brink of poverty, most of the old families continued to celebrate the Swahili New Year, the Idd al Fitr, and other festivities. On these occasions they were served by ex-slaves and their descendants who sometimes also provided much of the food they consumed.

Death, too, called for specific rituals to be performed. After the Yumbili washed the bodies, slaves (and ex-slaves if they were still close to the family) prepared it for burial. Among the rituals associated with death were stuffing the orifices and then wrapping the body in white sheeting that contained perfumes and oil. In Lamu, most women made their one and only appearance at mosque when their bodies are carried there for finals prayers. (A "woman's mosque" was started by a woman from Rasini in the 1930s. The congregation was drawn almost entirely from the ranks of the slave community. Ironically, however, both sexes attended, with a curtain separating men from women[33]).

Bodies were (and are) transported to the mosque and on to the grave yard on the *tusi*, a wooden frame with poles protruding back and front on both sides that holds the body. Only men were allowed to be in the funeral procession. Women, were thought to be "too emotional." At the death of her husband, the wife went into mourning for forty days, where she remained in the house, wearing only old clothes, and praying. Ex-slaves and their descendants joined the family in mourning and, as time passed, more social barriers crumbled bringing Hadrami, and even Comoro and Bajun women into these circles to comfort the bereaved. Men, whose lives are tied to the outside, and whose notions of elitism were more thorougly ingrained, mourned three days often accompanied in their mourning by friendly former bondsmen and their sons.

On the death of Habib Saleh in 1935, slaves and ex-slaves vied for the opportunity to prepare him for the last rites. His funeral—which marked the beginning of the *ziara*, a procession in this case to his grave—was attended by almost all men of slave descent, the Hadrami community, and some members of the old families who had studied with him and who respected him still, despite their distance from his sons. In fact, some continued going to Sharif Ideroos for medical care until his death in 1968.[34]

Sometime in the 1920s, Mohamed bin Ali Zena (Bwana Zena) is said to have brought *lelemama* [a special competitive dance] associations into Lamu from Zanzibar.[35] The dance was accompanied by buffalo horns, and in Lamu, incorporated slave and ex-slave men and women. Sometimes they danced *lelemama* together, at others they separated along gender lines with the men dancing in front and the women behind. According to one old woman who danced *lelemama* in this period, Bwana Zena took some "of the slaves to his shamba where he taught them *lelemama*. It was a secret and no one could tell until the time we began to dance." Soon rival dance associations emerged, with Bwana Zena's group competing against another, also composed of slaves and ex-slaves. Mohammed al Maawyia, then a leading elder in the town, and a relative of Bwana Zena, did not approve of the "banis" [dance groups that were accompanied by musical instruments] that emerged from the early *lelemama* rival groups in Lamu, but he did allow Bwana Zena's "Kingi" group to practice on his shamba.

The second major "bani" that emerged in this period split off from the "Kingi" faction, and was called "Kambaa." This group was headed by two ex-slave men. It is possible that the rivalry became quite intense because of the underlying antagonism between the former slaves, the "Kambaa" group (called the "rotten rope by "Kingi"), and the "Kingi" who were aligned with their former owners, some of whom still regarded themselves as *watuma*.[36]

The "Kambaa" were located in Mtamvini, which later became part of the Langoni, home to the poor and newcomers. "Kingi" represented Mkumoni, the stone house area where the patricians lived. Although male Afro-Arab informants agreed that there were no rivalries between the two groups, other than their respective locations, and that "everyone just had a good time," it is difficult not to hypothesize that competition was based on more than locale.[37] In fact, "Kingi" itself carried a message that may not have come through to the British colonials in Lamu. What could be more suggestive than naming a group of slave dancers kings?

In this early phase (1920s-1930s) of the "banis" the "Kingi" group was at a considerable advantage because of sponsorship from the Afro-Arabs, "everybody contributed a little bit" including the members of the bands. Their costumes were more expensive, sometimes from cloth especially purchased for the competitions. In addition, they had the *sikweya* drum which was "so loud that when it was beaten all the of the Lamu people knew the "Kingi" wanted to hold a meeting [competition]." Practice on the shamba usually turned into a picnic, and again because of patronage, the "Kingi" were able to eat sweetmeats, drink tea, and at times, slaughter an animal. On one occasion, a former "Kingi" remembered that after they ate the meat on the shamba, they "carried the head into town, along with some of the leftovers, called the 'Kambaa' messenger gave him the head, and threw the rest of the food at the sea shore." This display indicates that the "Kingi" were not above provoking jealousies on the part of the "Kambaa" who had no Afro-Arab sponsors.

An old "Kingi" woman remembered some of the songs they used to sing back in the '20s and '30s—almost all reflective of the strong competition between these groups, where the "Kingi" poked fun at the "Kambaa" who were more in number. In retrospect, informants uniformly agreed that though the verses were provocative, they were received with good nature by whatever side was being ridiculed. But we do not have the input from the "Kambaa" competitors to weigh in balance how much resentment may actually have occurred at the time.

"We are few but we should be smart and get ready for them. Even though we are few—even if there are so many,

We should go forward: We have now got some good people on our side

They are many but we are good." (Meaning the former slaves were many).

The "Kambaa" had few musical instruments—although both sides continued to hit sticks on their buffalo horn.

("Kingi")"You are surprised to see such a drum? What have you been saying—it has cut into your hearts."

The "Kambaa" retorted:"The person has taken your money and he is not coming with a big drum."

"Don't shout any more, it is you have spoiled it [withbackbiting].

And again the "Kambaa" opposition:

"Remove your finger from your mouth and don't be surprised to see a band now.

You were shouting at us and now it has come."

One bit of universal wisdom emanated from these various verses: "The world is full of problems, so do not think you will get everything."[38]

Although locals deny that Lamu women were prostitutes in this period, district commissioner reports refer to the high incidence of venereal disease, which they attributed to "immorality and prostitution." In 1923 the provincial commissioner in Mombasa complained about "night clubs run by women. There is no counterpart on the coast except perhaps Lamu which may be described as a permanent night club." By 1929, with so many women from the Lamu District flooding into Mombasa and creating more social problems, the district commissioner called for a pass system to be introduced. By 1938, "prostitution in Lamu township is extremely common and the women remain a constant source of infection as they rarely go to the hospital for treatment." But, many WaAmu claim that the prostitutes were Bajun women from Faza who began to drift into Lamu in these years. This was reenforced by a DC who caustically noted in 1939 "20 Faza girls reported to have gone to Mombasa without parents permission and were listed as prostitutes." The Hadrami were zealous in watching over their daughters—marrying them off at puberty and promising them even earlier. The old families, with few exceptions, secluded their daughters in a similar manner. The ex-slaves, they claimed, copied the morals of their former owners and did not "allow them do such things."[39] There were, however, the multitudes of ex-slaves who separated themselves from their former owners and what their daughters did is not a question any one could answer. One old woman told the daughters of her former owners about her youth when she had a boyfriend. She used to "change her shoes to be unknown by the head of the house, and sneak off to see him and to flirt."[40]

The following excerpts from sailors songs which were sung by the "Kingi" in this period, reenforce the district commissioners views that some Lamu women did more than flirt:

> *"I am giving a message to give wings*
> *Come here and I will tell you my words to send them*
> *Please go and look for the wings of [bird]*
> *There are things in my heart*
> *I feel so bad and I am very far from Lamu.*
>
> *Lamu: there are beautiful and expensive ladies*
> *A visitor agrees that he cannot say anything about Lamu people*
> *Because he is not knowing the flesh of their bodies*
> *The generosity of their spirit*
> *And even the beauty of their figures*
> *You do not have anything wrong with the women of Lamu.*
>
> *Even if you get a woman who does not know how to lay*
> *Remember you will be puzzled and excited*
> *You do not know what to do*
> *Whatever you want to think at that time*
> *You will not remember*
> *Men have become very poor on Lamu women."*[41]

The "banis" were dorment until after World War II when they were revived. Bwana Zena, who brought *lelemama* to Lamu, was too old to involve himself in organizing competitions after the war, but turned over the "Kingi" group to his son, Mohammed.[42] The "Kambaa" also came under new leaders—two more descendants of slaves who also lived in

Langoni. These "banis" were joined by the newly formed "Scotchi" whose costumes included kilts, and whose leader was Sheikh Fadhil bin Omar, a member of one of the old families. Again, every effort went into composing the cleverest and most provocative songs, accompanied by carefully choreographed dances. Some of the upper class danced with the "Scotchi" but among the women "only the ex-slaves and no unmarried women." Mohammed al Maawyia and other elders refused to join the "Scotchi" group because some of their slaves were members. But younger men in Lamu were willing to surmount the class barriers that separated them earlier in the century. Competitions between the "Kingi" and "Scotchi" groups were less ruthless, but because of the old antagonisms between those who stayed on and those whose forefathers were set free, the "Kambaa" band was often still contentious beyond the bounds of competition.[43]

"Usually they danced from the shambas to the seafront in town." Men led the procession "dancing while the women came behind singing." The women in the front ranks "wore no veil. They covered their breasts with a *kikoi* . . . . had so much jasmine in their hair." They "wanted to look their very best." Costumes for men ranged from the kilts to "cowboy hats" to "suits and casteoff military uniforms."[44] The "Scotchi" eventually imported bagpipes from Scotland which they used to challenge the "Kingi" with their loud drum. The Afro-Arab women, often joined by the Indians, and some Hadrami, congregated in a special area where they could watch the proceedings and cheer on their favorites. They, of course, were veiled. The "Kambaa" were "always defeated" according to a former "Scotchi" woman. Conversely, a "Kingi" recalled that the "Scotchi" lost the competitions repeatedly to their group. The dances may have died out but the spirit of competition, perhaps even malevolence, lived on with these elderly informants.

Lamu Afro-Arab women remembered dancing *lelemama* in the 1950s in their houses, but as yet they were reluctant to participate in the wedding dances which took place outside in areas sealed away from view. By the time the Afro-Arab and Hadrami women began to dance at weddings, the "banis" had died out. Later, "dance competitions returned to Lamu" but they featured mostly "outsiders" at "political events."[45] The Hadrami and the Indian communities did not participate in the competitions, but

164

came out in numbers to witness the colorful ceremonies, meanwhile decrying the expenditures that neither the former slaves or the patricians could afford. This was especially the case with the mortgage holding Indians who witnessed material manifestations of their loans in the form of costumes, musical instruments, and feasts.[46]

A small boy at a Lamu *madrassa* with his leg in a wooden stock
Courtesy of the National Museums of Kenya

Chapter Ten

The Hadrami and Indian Communities from the 1920s

*"Mohamed is not the father of any man among you,
but he is the Apostle of God, and the seal of the
Prophets: and God knoweth all things."*
The Qur'an

Behind the town, at the Riyadha Mosque, Habib Saleh continued to influence the growing Hadrami community, the ex-slaves, and a few other Muslims who straggled in. Abdalla Kadara, the man Habib Saleh denied paternity, claimed that when the early shed that foreshadowed the mosque itself was built a Hadrami, Ahmed Batweh, visited there and proclaimed that "it has started to become a Hadrami mosque." He also alleged that it was Ahmed Batweh who put Habib Saleh in touch with Ali al Habshi, the Hadrami who composed the maulidi so associated with the Riyadha.[1] The family, however, dispute this as they reject much that Abdalla Kadara reported about them to Ahmed el Zein and others.[2] They argue that due to his growing reputation as a religious scholar, Ali al Habshi knew of and was in contact with Saleh while he lived in the Comoro Islands. Furthermore, they reject the allegation that the Riyadha was solely under-written by the Hadrami.[3] The facts are, however, that the Hadrami community was not involved in, or did it support, any other mosque in Lamu.

Because of lack of documentation it is difficult to gauge the extent that the Riyadha Mosque and its founder were known beyond Zanzibar and the Comoro Islands in the period before the 1920s. It is possible word of Saleh and his new mosque were spread by Sheikh Abdalla bin Muhamed Ba Kathin al-Kindi, a Lamu born scholar who made two pilgrimmages to

168

Mecca and otherwise obtained a modicum of success in religious circles beyond coastal East Africa.[4]

With the onset of British colonialism doctrinal matters cropped up that elsewhere led to political reactions that were orchestrated by Muslim religious leaders. There was, as we know, general discontent on the part of coastal East Africans as they were repeatedly forced to bow to the dictates of the British, even if these orders were issued through a succession of Sultans. Some anti-colonial resentments were acted out through religious means in Zanzibar, in the Comoros, including refusal to abolish slavery in Lamu. In general the Hadrami were favored by the British colonials and were unlikely to be politicized at this time. Furthermore Saleh was virtually unknown to the British and, had he engaged in stirring up political discord, this would have been reported by district commissioners.

A sufi brotherhood of sorts developed in Lamu, but not until after Habib Saleh's two sons became active in the Riyadha Mosque, and then not as a reaction against colonialism but, instead as opposition to the patricians. While it is true that the Hadramis brought with them the pattern of saint worship that they had known in their homeland this was not applied to locals until Habib Saleh died in 1935. The exclusiveness that characterized the 'Alawiyya tariqa' in the Hadramaut was not found in Lamu. In Lamu, however, Habib Saleh, followed by his sons, encouraged membership in the Riyadha Mosque. One of the reasons they played tambourines and other musical instruments was to encourage people to come. On the other hand, the "path to God" (tariqa) that is based on the historical links to succession from the Prophet came to be increasingly important to the followers of Habib Saleh, and later his descendants.[5]

Respected members of the old families sent their sons to study with Habib Saleh during the early part of the twentieth century. He was regarded as a learned scholar and, as such, was unique for his particular time. As his sons grew into manhood, and began to assume active roles within the Riyadha Mosque, the atmosphere changed. In retrospect, it is difficult to judge the intentions of those who perceived themselves as interpreters of the faith. Although the Qur'an contains many passages that are regarded as the word of God, it was open to interpretation by Muslim scholars. And, in the fourteen centuries since the Prophet founded the religion the Qur'an has been subjected to interpretations that led to quarrels among various factions within the Islamic community.

The question is whether Ideroos and Badawy used their positions to establish oligarchies bent on controlling their followers to build on the power base their father created through his generally good reputation? Or, did they regard themselves as theologians capable of interpreting the laws and doctrines of Sunni Islam? The Sunni Muslims became divided on these two questions soon after Habib Saleh died. As far as the tenant of charity [*zakat*] is concerned, Habib Saleh had established the precedent of reaching out to the poor. In this respect he was followed by his sons and their descendants.

Following Habib Saleh's death, the al Hussein sharifs distanced themselves even further from the Riyadha Mosque. So, too, did the other patricians. But in the 1920s and the decades that followed, the Riyadha sharifs extended their influence, although they did not then have the numbers in their congregation to exercise political leverage in the town. That came later after Kenyan independence, when Habib Saleh's grandsons ran the mosque college.[6] But as a means of keeping his memory alive, if not actually an attempt to elevate him to sainthood, Saleh's sons organized the *ziara*. This annual event was regarded by some of the patricians as heretical and was boycotted by them and the other non-Sufi in Lamu.[7]

Social stratification in Lamu in the late nineteenth century was based primarily on rules of descent carried from Hadramaut, and the criteria for marriage was defined according to ancestry. In Hadramaut, a family could get rich, but their rank was still low and marriages were kept within these classes.[8] Among the newly arrived Hadrami descent was dropped in favor of prosperity. Abdalla Bujra's father came in as one of the poorest youths and rose to be one of the wealthiest men in the district. He, like other Hadramis able to obtain low paid jobs, saved until he could buy a cow of his own. One cow led to more, then Bujra opened a small shop where he sold rice and sugar.[9] Because the Hindus wholesaled cloth some believed Bujra bypassed them by trading directly with ships. In fact, like their predecessors, many Hadrami merchants continued smuggling to obtain the goods they sold. According to one informant, "they used to meet ships anchored off Lamu Bay where they sold goods as well as bought."[10] Once he obtained his wealth, Bujra could have married his children to any of the Hadrami families, including the sharifs, and to many of the offspring in the patrician class. But as wealth began to offset class divisions, the chasm widened between followers of the Riyadha Mosque with their increasing emphasis on saint worship (which after 1935 centered on Habib Saleh), and the strict followers of the sunnah that marked the Afro-Arab old families.

The *ziara*, which in Lamu came to be associated with annual visits to Habib Saleh's tomb and later to that of his two sons, was also an import from Hadramaut. The annual procession grew in numbers of participants as the Riyadha congregation extended its influence among the poor and outsiders. Songs of praise associated with the Prophet's birth (the maulidis), that were accompanied by the clamor of musical instruments, followed by the introduction of rhythmic swaying and chanting, were alien to the Orthodox Sunni. The growing emphasis on the power of bara-ka extended now to the ex-slave community, further dampened relations between the Riyadha congregation and the Afro-Arabs. The antagonism between the two groups was increasingly based on perceived differences in religious expression, rather than class or caste—although these elements were also present.

By the time Habib Saleh died, his two sons had trained in the use of medicines imported from elsewhere in the Muslim world. Their large practices drew not only the Hadramis, but also a significant following among the Afro-Arab community despite doctrinal differences. One common misconception arose at this time, and that revolved around the so-called healing prowess of these sharifs. Some reported that they spit sali-va into food (applied "baraka").[11] According to them, and to members of their congregations, the Jamal al Layl sharifs did not spit, but blew a "puff of breath to those who believe in [their] power" as descendants of the Prophet. The temporal medicines they prescribed included herbs, roots, and Arabic powers mixed with water, oil, or laxatives. The sharifs also made amulets containing verses from the Qur'an that patients wore or hung in their homes.

It was Ideroos and Badawy who set into motion the power struggles that characterized the divisions between the Hadrami, Comoro Islanders and ex-slaves on the one hand, and the old families on the other. But, within the ultra-conservative circles disharmony also occurred. The second rupture, like the first, centered on the Comoro community. Long term

171

dissension between that group and others in the Riyadha congregation came to a head in September 1949: "After Friday prayers a fracas occurred between two rival parties—resulting in 20 injuries for both sides." One party "consisting mostly of Comorians decided to leave" thinking they would be dissuaded by other members of the congregation. The DC reported that "They left for Mombasa, Malindi, and Mambrui, among other places and when they found their departure caused a disturbance they consulted a lawyer in Mombasa." Their claims of inconvenience and injury were eventually dropped but this incident resulted in a permanent rupture between many of the Comoro Islanders and the Riyadha that extended down the East African coast.[12]

One of Habib Saleh's daughters married a learned sharif, Said al Beidh, who, after studying with Ali Habshi in Hadramaut preached and taught in Mombasa. Accompanied by his two sons, he moved to Mambrui and opened their "Riyadha Mosque." Sa'id al Beidh was originally from the Comoro Islands, and his wife's mother was one of Habib Saleh's Comoro wives. Thus after the Lamu Comoro Islanders split with the Riyadha there, many of their countrymen shifted their allegiance to the Mambrui mosque of Sa'id al Beidh, his sons, and later, the grandsons who continued to run it.[13]

But the mosque college continued to flourish, and students enrolled from elsewhere in East Africa. In the 1950s' when he was Chief Qadi of Mombasa, Sharif Ali Badawy, a grandson of Habib Saleh, came back to Lamu to preside over increasing numbers of Riyadha followers who flocked in for celebrations honoring the birth of the Prophet. By 1954, about 5,000 came in from as far away as Tanzania and Zanzibar on about 150 dhows.[14] Most were WaAmu who had gone elsewhere to work. Significant numbers who returned for what came to be known as "The Maulidi" were not associated with the Riyadha Mosque. By this time the Riyadha celebrations had taken on the atmosphere of a carnival. Stick and sword dancing were performed outside the mosque, with mostly Hadrami, Bajun, and descendants of slaves performing. But increasing numbers of the old families, especially the young, came to witness the events.[15]

In Hureidah the divorce rate was high but there were few polygamous marriages except for the very rich who had two or three wives—all living in the same house. When a woman married, she went to the home of her husband.[16] When they came into Lamu, most Hadramis took one wife, because they were extremely poor and followed the pattern established back home. Most often, they provided unpretentious living quarters. As these men began to prosper, and especially in the post-World War II period, many of them (and others who migrated in from small communities elsewhere) divorced at the same high rate that characterized the other Sunni Muslims in Lamu.[17]

The Jamal al Layl sharifs were reputed to be among the most married men in Lamu. While it is true that Habib Saleh himself, followed by his sons, and later his grandsons, took any number of wives, and divorced many of them, they were not alone in practicing serial or polygamous marriage. Many Lamu men have treated the institution of marriage lightly. Divorce statistics bear this out. One common factor was the surplus of women of all classes. Another was the increasing poverty that marked Lamu as the twentieth century progressed. The earlier model that bound men to arranged marriages to their cousins (parallel and cross) persisted. Where earlier in the century men could easily obtain concubines to satisfy their sexual desires, they now turned to serial marriages.

Divorce, while easy for a man to obtain, was often provoked by wives. In fact, among the ex-slave community, serial marriages were as common for women as men.[18] For the Afro-Arabs, a major factor contributing to the high divorce rate in this century was that of "secret marriage." Legal wives, when they learned of husband's secret marriages were outraged, and often manipulated divorce through various means such as withholding sex, or being argumentative.[19] Whereas concubinage also often resulted in hurt feelings and outpourings of anger, men tended to keep their wives and otherwise follow their yearnings. The increase in divorce, however, often found men escaping their responsibilities towards their former wives even though they were often cousins, and hence their children.

In the case of secret marriage the brides were very poor. Their fathers were glad enough to marry them off for small compensation. Regarding the Jamal al Layl clan, religious followers often believed special blessings came to their daughters as a result of these brief liaisons. The Jamal al Layl sharifs often came to parents demanding their daughters and, because of their respect families acquiesced, even though many of these girls were just reaching puberty. Some few practitioners of secret marriage supported the children they fathered. Many did not, and that has been especially true of the sharifs over time. They did, after all, leave behind their blessings while passing on the gift of descent from the Prophet Mohamed.[20] The partial genealogies of the Lamu Jamal al Layl sharifs in the Appendix do not take into account the numerous offspring that resulted from these temporary sexual encounters.[21]

Some Lamu customs that are loosely associated with the religion were not derived from the Hadramaut and were practiced by all the Muslims. For instance, when the rains are late, men went to Friday mosque to pray—special prayers for rain. When an eclipse of the sun or moon occurred, they also rushed to their respective mosques to pray. Before western culture seeped in, the WaAmu believed an eclipse meant that the world was coming to an end. Every year of the twelfth day of the third month of the Islamic calendar, the Sunnis recited maulidis in honor of the Prophet—Habit Saleh's arrival did not alter this ritual, only the manner of celebration and the verses (al Habshi) differed from celebrations carried on traditionally by the old families.[22] One custom that came to East Africa is the practice of circling a bull around the town at certain times of the year. This ritual has been associated with rain making ceremonies and some say was African in derivation. But it may have been pre-Islamic and brought in from Arabia or elsewhere as *mila* [tradition].[23]

T. Ainsworth Dickens described the numbers of Hadrami in Lamu as "not in any way considerable" in 1921. According to Dickens they "are hard workers or small traders and, to the extent of their numbers are extremely useful from the economic point of view." In 1934 W. Slade Hawkins, who found economic conditions in Lamu "deplorable" because the "Arabs won't work" praised the "new Arabs—the WaShiriri. . . [as] very different. Virile, hard working, and grasping." By this time it was estimated that there were over 1300 Hadramis in the Lamu District.[24] Dickens urged "repopulating the mainland with [them] as a way of helping with economic recovery." The old families however, were opposed to further immigrants from Hadramaut. An example of their growing prosperity in the 1930s included a stock trader who shipped on average of 125 cattle and 400 sheep regularly by steamship. In addition, there were

174

Hadrami auctioneers, the butchers, various petty traders, and those still employed in lowly capacities by the government.[25] Irrespective of their rank at home the Hadrami arrivals in East Africa came with no more than their shirts on their backs and a few items in their packs. To get to East Africa some worked on dhows jumping ship at ports like Lamu. Others settled in outposts like Ndau, Kiunga, and other small towns along the coast, before drifting in. A few members of the learned class migrated in and among them were the Noor brothers. They became involved in transportation and eventually owned a bus service that operated between Mombasa and Lamu. They were also stalwart supporters of the Riyadha Mosque.

A few of the twentieth century migrants brought their wives, or sent for them after they were established.[26] Of them, several arrived illegally. Older Afro-Arab women remembered seeing a few Hadrami women circulate around town in the early evening hours. They were different because all of their faces were covered over and only their eyes appeared above the masks they wore. There may have been more reason than custom for the masks. Several of these women were tattooed. One very old woman, who arrived illegally, was adorned in a patch of red dots tattooed on her chin. In addition she wore a gold nose ring that was a remnant of her youth in the Hadramaut. Earlier, too, the Hadrami practiced a mild form of female circumcision on their daughters, as they themselves had been circumcised back home. They ceased this practice after a few years in East Africa.[27]

When they reached Lamu, some Hadrami men were dependent on their wives for support. One old woman remembered a Hadrami family coming in to Lamu in the 1930s. This couple lived in a mud hut they built in Langoni. Because the husband could find no work, his wife baked the unleavened bread common to their homeland which he hawked on the streets. What may have had some bearing on the 1949 riot that broke out in the Riyadha was the fact that some Hadramis also turned to tailoring as a way of earning their living. The Comoro Islanders, joined by a few Goans, had almost a monopoly on that occupation, the Hadrami tailors became competitive after their wives started making women's clothes as one of the several ways they helped to support their families.[28]

While newcomers at the turn of the century mostly cohabited with slaves, by the 1930s many Hadrami were established families. As they acquired small shops and bits of wealth, the early arrivals tended to marry their children back into their group. In time, cousin marriage was preferred among them as well.[29] Later arrivals ran into a wall of opposition from those who preceded them.

The question of descent and Hadrami social stratification gave pause when some men came in, claiming to be sharifs but without proper documentation. One man arrived in Lamu, again working as a milk boy in the shambas while he attempted to establish his credentials. They were never recognized by the Jamal al Layl or any of the other sharifian clans. Refusing to seek steady employment he remained poor, married several times, producing many children including two in his old age by a much younger wife. At his death he left nothing behind but the pretenses of his descent. Their mother eked out a living for her children through cottage industries in her home. Hadrami women, she said, worked hard all of their lives.[30]

Among the Hadrami who crossed the divide that separated them from the old families was Salimu Ahmed Bassaida who went to work for Smith Mackenzie, the trading firm established after the IBEA failed, as a clerk. He married locally and moved into a Lamu stonehouse. In yet another example of how a *nisba* came to be dropped in Lamu, some of his children were called Mackenzie after his place of employment. Then there was Abdalla Hassan Bates, who served as one of the long time leaders in the Lamu community—his name also having been westernized.[31]

As the Indians gradually shifted their operations to the more profitable Mombasa, the Hadrami took over their shops. A few Afro-Arabs and some descendants of slaves also opened small shops along Lamu's shopping corridor, but the major entrepreneurs were the hard working Hadrami merchants, most of whom moved from abject poverty to a modicum of prosperity within a single man's lifetime. Or as one Afro-Arab elder acknowledged: "The Hadrami saved while the old families squandered."[32]

Throughout the colonial period, British attitudes towards the Indian community varied widely. As British subjects the Indian community was expected to obey the laws, even when others practiced avoidance. The inevitable quarrels between the merchant class, which included the majority of Indians, and others in Lamu, usually found district commissioners siding with the Asians. The Christian Goans, who formed the backbone of the mid-level administration, were especially favored. They belonged to the local British founded Club and were not segregated from the tennis court, as was the case with the other Indians. In Kenya colony, Indians suffered from several forms of discrimination. They were, for instance, not allowed to buy or build houses or shops in areas that were reserved for whites (and in some cases for Africans). In Lamu, rules governing home ownership were not applied by the colonial government but the Indians were, de facto, kept out of stone houses by the old families until their fortunes waned.

While the Indians lived in Lamu, relations between them and the Hadrami were also distant, partially because the Hadrami were thought to circumvent the wholesalers, but also because the Indians placed a growing emphasis on western education, which was anathema to the Jamal al Layl sharifs. Separate schools for Arabs and Indians were established in Zanzibar before the turn of the century. Then, after the Indians in Mombasa were successful in petitioning for a school, the Lamu contingent began to lobby the government. In the 1920s the government set up an Indian school only to arouse the anger of the patricians. The uproar continued into Clive's tenure, when he reported that the Afro-Arabs were aggrieved at the prejudicial treatment accorded the Asians.[33]

The problem, however, was not entirely lack of government support. Serious opposition to western style education came from Sharif Badawy who, Clive reported, used every means at his disposal to first prevent the school being opened, then to prevent boys from attending. Hadrami boys were forbidden altogether and otherwise "people were afraid of these sharifs" and many of the old families refused to allow their children to attend. One elder maintained that with schooling "the religion was reduced. Even the Prophet said this would happen . . . . [as] schools spoiled the religion."[34]

Badawy himself was poorly educated. His father died when he was sixteen and his instruction came from a brother-in-law but "there was no school for Arabic in East Africa" when he was young, and he was not interested in secular learning. One of his sons noted that in Badawy's day only a few people "could read, write and preach from reading religious books." His opposition to secular education was based on "no time to study religion."[35]

Over the years the Indian school received almost universal commendation from a series of district commissioners. Students worked hard. Teachers were well prepared. Instruction included Gujarati, English, and large doses of mathematics. Even though the Indian population declined considerably from the 1930s, the numbers of students ranged from a low of 32 to a high of 52 into the 1950s. But the Bohra attended only a briefly before they founded a separate facility. In 1932, Clive reported that they did not "agree with the educational philosophy" which included sporting activities. The Bohra returned in 1955, the year a district commissioner proposed the Arab and Indian schools merge to pool resources "but the Indian parents and that community *do not* favor."[36]

British officials were often irritated with various members of the Indian community because of the complaints that poured in from one group or another. The Bohra were contentious regarding maintaining privacy in the area around their mosque. In 1934 the first of several petitions appeared in the District Commissioners office, referring to the long standing quarrel over the passageway into the mosque. This particular disturbance involved members of the Riyadha congregation, whose mosque was at least a mile from the in-town Bohra mosque, but who persisted in making a mockery of the Bohra Shi'a faith by blocking the entrance to their mosque.[37]

The Hindu community also protested. They argued that the slaughterhouse was located too near their homes; they had to cremate their dead at Ras Kitau on Manda Island; and they complained about frequent requests to see their balance sheets (based on the contention they were price gouging as well as hiding profits). Once they presented a petition calling for cattle to be shipped on pontoon boats and not by dhow. They argued that lifting, pushing, shoving, and then crowding on the dhows was "too cruel" to the cattle who were on their way to the slaughterhouses further south.[38] Sometimes the entire Indian community banded together to petition the government. In 1933 a Bohra leader, Ithnasharia Jaffer Panju, and Bhattia Vallabhdas Valji complained that the depression had severely limited their incomes and requested "a poll tax exemption for the poor." They came back later to report that their safety was at stake and petitioned that another assistant be added to the police force.[39]

With the exception of the small Bohra community, most traders who had lived in Lamu had died and left little by of memory to their descendants. Among the few who survived and were able to recall something of the past was Kiki Dastoor whose Parsi father arrived from India in 1901. Cawasj M. Dastoor went to work for Smith Mackenzie and with his wife, also a Parsi raised their two sons, Homi and Kiki in traditional fashion, praying over the perpetual fire they kept burning in their home. Both boys were educated by their parents, "especially math—all traders learn mathematics" before being sent to a Parsi English speaking school in Bombay. There they were initiated into the Zorastorian *navjote*. Kiki recalled that "during the colonial period we were all one. We mixed." After leaving Smith Mackenzie their father went into business for himself importing among other things the fez cap with tassels that all non-European civil servants were required to wear. Later the Dastoor sons extended the family holdings, diversifying in process: "Asians expand horizontally and do not make big stores out of small ones." At independence, Homi and Kiki elected not to become citizens thus they had to take in a Kenyan partner— a "Swahili man from Witu."[40]

Bhattia Kesharji Ratlansey Dhutia, 85 years old in 1985, provided the following brief sketch of his family. His great-grandfather left Kutch for Muscat sometime in the late nineteenth century. In Muscat some of his children were hired customs collectors and appointed religious judges by Sultan Said. When the Sultan moved to Zanzibar, members of this family followed, again being sent out as customs collectors, but also engaging in business. Buying and selling ivory was one of their specialties. In 1901 Kesharji's father was posted to Lamu where his grandfather was already engaged in the ivory trade—they "were wallabas" meaning they spread out. By 1915 the family was engaged in "lending money on interest and in wholesale."[41] After World War I most of the Bhattias sold out and went south to Mombasa. Intercourse between the few who stayed and the many who departed was limited to efforts on the part of the former to collect on mortgages that had been foreclosed.[42]

Esmailjee Hasanbahi, a Bohra who claimed to be nearly one hundred in 1985. At the turn of the century the Bohra had shops: carpentry, cloth, foodstuffs. . . . [and] paid for the big buildings on the seafront that were built by Swahili. Before World War I, the Bohra were in the Lamu islands and northern outposts. Malindi. Zanzibar." Ivory trading was the family business, but later Esmailjee owned *jihazis* taking "goods for other people and getting money traveling to Malindi, Siyu, and Lamu. . . . . [and] three boats." As the owner, he received fifty percent of the profit from the merchandise and fifty percent rent on his boats. He also had a shop in Lamu, as did each of his brothers.[43]

As the century progressed, the Bohra came to dominate the inter-island trade, sending younger males to serve as local agents, as had been the custom when they engaged in the Indian Ocean trade. Their sights were shorter, profits fewer, but based on Lamu economic standards, the Bohra were still considered wealthy.

In 1911 Bohra Gullum Hussein died. His estate was probated in Lamu.[44] The family opened their glass-hardware business in 1892 before branching out to other enterprises, including the monopoly on boriti in the 1930. By the time of his death, Gullum Hussein went to Mauritius where worked for the Carrimjee-Jevanjee shipping firm.[45] His son, Taherally was born in Mauritius, but spent his youth in Lamu before returning to attend school in 1926. Taherally stayed on and became involved in the family hardware business which Gullum Hussein's brothers had opened in 1915, but returned to Lamu in 1938 to marry his first cousin, Kubrabai, an arrangement made by their mothers before their respective births.[46] Even though this family moved to Mauritius, they continued their clan ties to Lamu. Their son, vice chancellor of the University of Mauritius, married a member of the family that built the original Bohra mosque back in the eighteenth century.[47] (see Appendix)

Christie reported that among the Indian community in the 1850s in Zanzibar "there is a great display of wealth in female dress and ornaments, silks and satins of decided hues and patterns, massive gold bracelets, anklets and necklaces. . . . "[48] This pattern continued in Lamu until the Great Depression. Precious jewels and gold and silver symbolized wealth and they also constituted a form of life insurance for women. Hindus had their ear lobes stretched and filled them with jewel filled gold discs. All wore heavy gold jewelry over their silk saris. Some weighed down their wrists with heavy silver bangles from Zanzibar and pierced their noses so they could insert diamonds and gold.[49] With the exception of jewels, these examples of Indian material culture brought to Lamu were adopted by the Hadrami and the Afro-Arabs who, despite their relative impoverishment adorned themselves with all the gold and silver they could afford. Another Indian custom that made its way into the Muslim world at large, was that of applying heavy coats of hennaed floral patterns to the women's legs and hands—of brides and married women in Lamu.

The Bohra, Ithnasharia, and Ismailis rarely divorced. One man commented that "we cannot divorce immediately as the Swahili do. We must wait and consult with our leader." As was the case in the nineteenth century, these communities continued to be dominated by their involvement in their mosque, and by their strong family ties.[50] Among the Shi'a "the husband is the head of his family. Even the wife's parents must ask him before they give their daughter a gift. Our bride price is low. [We] believe in saving money for business, or for homes, or for emergencies."[51]

In the 1930s, twenty nine Bohra families derived their incomes from various business enterprises. Abdulhusein Sodawala ran the "fizzy drink factory." Others were tinsmiths.[52] But the Bohra also engaged in the ivory trade to support the big families characteristic of their group. As conditions worsened for the Afro-Arabs, one Bohra opened a hock shop where "a man would bring in gold ornaments if he wanted money and never come back again."[53]

The social history of the Asian community consists of the bits and pieces of memory from elderly informants. Because they were generally disliked and resented by other groups in town because of allegations of price gouging and of the high interest on loans, they tended to socialize among themselves. But even that was limited to the few affairs of a non-religious nature. One elderly woman recalled that in the 1920s the women visited back and forth. Yet there were limits: as a child, she was forbidden to eat Hindu food. Furthermore, there "was no intermarriage. . . . that was prohibited on all sides. . . . " Her recollections however, were accurate in noting that during the colonial period there was "very limited social mixing between the Indians and the Swahilis. . . ."[54]

But fostering, which was common in Lamu, led to instances of social integration. Kubrabai's mother was ill when she was born and "a friend

of my father was a Swahili man. He said one of his sister's had no children. I was taken to her and raised until I was seven years old. I spoke no
Gujarati at all and didn't want to leave the Swahili family to return home."
Conversely, an Afro-Arab woman born in the early 1960s to a family that
had many children already, was fostered by an Indian woman—one who
ran the *madrassa* attended by patrician children. Fostering included all
groups in the town. Step-fathers raised wives children, uncles and aunts
took in the children of their brothers and sisters, especially during the
hard years of poverty that marked some of the Afro-Arab families.[55]

Shi'a joined Sunni in journeying to Mecca for haj, although in the case
of the Bohra, many also paid a visit to Cairo, which is to them a holy
place second only to Mecca.[56] And of course, the Hindus had their tem-
ple. It was located behind the Goan spirit shop. The Hindus were less
integrated socially into the community. Beyond the differences in theology, the Indian community was economically competitive within itself—
each group jealously guarding respective trading items and networks. By
the 1930s only a few Hindu remained and among them were holders of
substantial mainland property on which they had foreclosed for lack of
repayment on loans. Other than their near monopoly on textiles, the
Hindu community contained a prosperous businessman who owned a
large sailing dhow, and the headmaster of the government school. Kiki
Dastoor recalled that the last two Lamu Hindus died "about 1945, before
that many simply closed their doors and went away to attractions like
Mombasa. Hindus were not foolish. When one year they made Shs.
10,000, the next year 8,000 and on down, they left."[57]

Just as splits occurred within the Riyadha community, so, too, did a
rupture come between the Dawoodi Bohra. According to Husseinali A.
Hussein, no one in the Bohra community knew "much about the Dai
[leader of the Bohra community with headquarters in Bombay] until
1937" when he came to Mombasa to bless his congregation and incidentally to pick up the annual tithes the community was required to pay
directly to him. After that, the Dai or his representatives made regular visits coupled with demands for money, but there was no accounting for the
funds collected.

Unlike the Aga Khan, who after the rupture within his congregation,
began building schools and hospitals, the Dai (and his successor) was

accused of financial irresponsibility and of interfering with their affairs. In addition there were growing questions as to the doctrine of papal infallibility, a claim made by their high priest. The reform movement picked up momentum in East Africa but the isolated community in Lamu remained loyal to their leader.[58] But the reformers, who included the Mauritius Carrimjee family and the Mohamedbhais, were declared *persona non grata* by the Bohra leader. No communication was allowed within families, or between friends of those who separated over doctrinal matters. The reformers were considered dead.[59]

In the 1930s, the Goans were also few in number, the customs officer, a baker, tailor, retailer, the liquor store owner (whose shop and house were located where Marhous Hotel stands), and a medical doctor whose tour of duty was limited to less than a year. The Ithnasharia were relatively well represented still, with a congregation of around forty-five persons including the Panju brothers who owned the cotton ginnery. Alibhai Sufi ran a sweet shop while another owned a toy store. One Twelver concentrated on stationary including books.

The Ismaili community still had more than thirty people living in Lamu in the early 1930s. These included the religious leader and his family and a few petty traders who mostly dealt in exporting and importing from the nearby islands. The community attended their own mosque, and differed from the other Shi'as in town because the Ismaili's face a portrait of the Aga Khan when they pray.[60]

During the first decades of the twentieth century considerable prosperity accrued to the Asians not only from their business acumen but also because of the economic misfortunes that effected the patricians. According to John Clive, the Indians "live to some extent at the expense of the Arabs. I cannot give statistics but I believed they own as much of Lamu island as the Arabs, on whose mortgages they have foreclosed."[61] By the 1930s, it was becoming apparent that they could not foreclose on the mainland shambas they had loaned against because of a series of complex land laws passed by the British, whose representatives were either unwilling or unable to unravel, and whose attention in Lamu focused on buttoning the colonial collar around the necks of the locals of all ethnic groups.

CHAPTER II

A.A. Skanda, wood carver, demonstrating his artistry for tourists
Courtesy of Edward Rodwell

Chapter Eleven

The Land Claims and the "Swahili" 1930s-1950s

"In the Name of God, the Compassionate, and the Merciful"
The Qur'an

The depression hit Lamu's already weakened economy hard. Especially effected were the Asian merchants. In addition to falling profits, the issue of the land claims had not been resolved. This concerned property they owned in theory from foreclosures on the mainland but had been unable to repossess. Because of the complexities regarding their concept of land tenure, the old families had borrowed but had not been able to provide deeds. It is unclear why the Indian moneylenders continued offering mortgages on land they were unable to sell or cultivate, but perhaps they believed in time they would get it all sorted out and that the land would be even more valuable. By the 1930s their economic plight was serious enough that the Asians redoubled their efforts to force the government to carry out the long awaited survey. But while the Indians were urging that a survey be undertaken in order to dispose of the land, the WaAmu were wrapped up in a series of appeals to the government.

The history of the land claims dispute had its origin in legislation passed by the British government. These laws were virtually unknown to, or ignored by, the WaAmu mainland shamba owners. Their concept of land tenure was based on the tenuous claims to property that had been cleared and used by their ancestors. Over time, families extended their holdings by ordering their slaves to clear more land around that already under cultivation. The British, and later the Afro-Arabs, referred to this concept of land tenure as Mohammedan Law. But the British were profoundly myopic when it came to understanding the Swahili system of land tenure. They did acknowledge that the sultans of Zanzibar claimed "all waste and abandoned land, and land not in private ownership" in the reserved ten mile strip that the British took over in 1895. This large amount of territory they planned to put to use and claimed it for themselves as Crown lands. Without an extensive survey, however, no one knew exactly what belonged to the Crown or what was rightfully owned by the locals.

Among the many measures marking creeping colonialism were the passage of a series of land ordinances. First, the British government passed the Registration of Documents Ordinance in 1901. The Sultan's "waste and abandoned land" was transferred to the Crown. This land had to be registered, as did all the land that was claimed by the various WaAmu, including slaves. By 1907, word had penetrated to some of the old families that the British were beginning to survey Crown lands and a flurry of activity resulted with some claiming and trying to sell what might have been regarded as Crown lands. (Efforts to survey were sporadic and completely ceased in 1920 when funding stopped).

In 1907 notification "went out that no person can acquire any title to any land which was not privately owned prior to the year 1887 or to any land that has since been abandoned." The government then claimed that land across from Lamu was abandoned because there were not enough slaves to cultivate, and the *watoro* were a clear and present danger to those who tried to work it.[1]

In the first decade of the twentieth century the locals were being forced to pay the hut tax, poll tax, license fees on every conceivable type of trade, and sometimes paying double customs duties, while they were losing their remaining mainland slaves. For the old families and the slaves who had their own recognized bits of land, the situation went from bad to worse.

The 1908 Lands Titles Ordinance required that they register titles. Registering titles required additional fees to be paid to the government— if anyone could register a title to land that had not been surveyed. In 1911 District Commissioner Isaacs held a baraza in which he asked if they would be prepared to take a tract of land for all their claims. They replied that it would be impossible to do so, as everyone owned their own shambas, and there was no such thing as joint tenure. Later, the Lamu elders recalled differently: it was their opinion that Isaacs offered "them a strip of 7 miles of land in settlement of their Witu claims."[2]

Between 1911 and 1915 no land claims were filed, but efforts were made to work the mainland, and more mortgages were placed on some of the shambas. (Ironically, at this late date the Indians seem to have had a vague notion as to what sections they were providing loans on, although few of them ventured to the mainland because of the *watoro*, followed by the *shifta*). In 1916 another land ordinance (No. 4) went into effect, and the landowners were "told to file their claims for their shambas. Most did so, but a few, fearing it would cost them money did not."[3]

In 1919, Ordnance No. 19 "granted the right" to file claims that year but "each separate claim must be supported by a separate affidavit"—meaning, to the claimants, more fees they could ill afford. According to Clive, "during that year the Arbitration Board was in full swing at Lamu, and not only Lamu Arabs, but the inhabitants of the three towns of Pate, Siyu and Faza submitted formal applications to the Recorder of Titles, but these were "adjourned *sine die* [and] . . . no other action was taken." In 1922 the post of Recorder was abolished for lack of funds, and after that the "attempt to establish a registry of title for the coastal belt . . . was abandoned."[4]

In fact, no action was taken, or if claims were made they were most often turned down. In 1980, then seventy year old Ahmed Jahadhmy, a former mudir in British government employ, could recite from memory the exact numbers of times his family claims were made and turned down: "five times between 1919 and 1933 by several different colonial governors."[5] One of the reasons for these rejections was the avowal that "the land had been in effectual occupation for over seven hundred years." The British argued that the "successive waves of people" who had swept in over the centuries invalidated the claims.[6]

Most of the British administrators in Lamu painted negative impressions of the Afro-Arabs. These views found their way into "Handing Over Reports" in which conditions in the district were conveyed in an impressionistic manner. From Skene in 1910 and continuing, there is scarcely a constructive comment in the records kept by the large number of DCs who were primarily novices, and whose terms of service in Lamu were usually limited to a few months or a year. Negatives reenforced negatives. What fears and uncertainties the locals had, we will never know. No one recorded their side of the unfolding narrative, although oral traditions reveal a great deal of bitterness.

In 1921 Ordinance No. 36 altered part of the Land Title Ordinance of 1910. This ordinance provided that "no documents should be registered without either a description or a plan signed by the Director of Surveys."[7] Yet no surveyor was available. In fact a 1922 a "survey of conditions" notes that "Lamu Island and District" had as of then "38 part unheard" claims and "1,293 unheard. Outstanding claims of 331 [heard but not set-tled] were the most in the Coast Province."

Mohamed al Maawyia, a leader in Lamu by 1923, "and other interest-ed persons" presented a claim that year, but it was not resolved. The DC reported that "the principal mover in this matter is [Maawyia] who states that the claim made in common by the leading families of Lamu town represent half the people on the Poll Tax register of 288." By then, the old families had been advised by someone in the government to file jointly.

The area for all these claims amounted to a total of 276 square miles. Mohammed al Maawyia, again on the advice of a British official, filed in the names of the WaKinamte, the WaFamao, and WaYumbe—and these were labeled by him or the British government as "families."[8] In this instance, too, he referred to the old grievance that the WaAmu had been paid less compensation for the slaves than others further down the coast. But these claims were turned down.

In 1924 the provincial commissioner for the coast declared that "in need they were not. They wish to get something for nothing in regard to future sale." In 1925 the district commissioner echoed the same senti-ments, and again the claims were rejected. Yet even Clive, who was not supportive of these claims, pointed out that the mainland "slaves would not return to their masters and no other labour was available."[9] In 1926 the last Ordinance was passed which dealt with "irregularities in the proce-dure of the Court of the Recorder of Titles which have resulted in more than one case, in the loss to the parties of their rights under properly reg-istered documents." This one also dealt with "notices concerning mort-gages, encumbrances . . . and to certain survey fees and other changes payable in respect thereof."[10] Around this time, huge sections of land upcountry were being set aside for Europeans. For instance, "100,000 acres [went] to the 3rd Baron Delamere at Njoro, nearly 200,000 acres to Powrys Cobb at Molo and Mau Narok, 500 square miles to the E[ast] A[frican] syndicate at Gilgil."[11] Of course these lands, too, were expropriated from Africans.

The British administration itself had difficulty in dealing with the various ordinances and the irregularities that developed. Yet, up in relatively isolated Lamu, with no lawyers, little command of the English language, no surveyors available, the claimants were expected to follow new procedures as they developed. (". . . it will appear that no less than four separate registrations are running concurrently at the Coast, each with its different incidence and some necessitating far greater expense than others.")[12] At this time, too, "mortgages and foreclosures" were beginning to crop up in the wording of the legislation. The mortgagees were being hounded by the mortgage holders who, though anxious to foreclose, could not determine the extent of their holdings.

In 1932, again on the advice of a British official, the claimants had dropped the "families" as a unit claim, and the claims were "presented in the names of all the landowners." In that year the Morris Carter Land Commission was established to deal with outstanding claims, and the WaAmu landholders finally got their chance to testify. Abdalla "Boke" Jahadhmy and Mohammed al Maawyia were selected to represent the combined interests of all the claimants. Each of these men was highly respected within his home community and both served on the Lamu County Council where they interacted with British officials. But neither was familiar with European style investigatory panels, and lacked the sophistication that marked their inquisitors. Nor did they possess knowledge of British land tenure policies and how these differed from traditional practices.

In the following testimonies, primarily from Abdalla "Boke", we hear something of the frustrations and anguish of on-the-scene players in the drama that was played out before the Carter Land Commission panel in 1932. "Boke" began with a statement in which he attempted to delineate the differences between claims that had been filed by the families as a whole, and those that had been filed individually. Possibly he was as puzzled as the panel since these claims had been variously filed on the advice

190

of others. When clarification was called for, he moved to what he knew: [we] "claimed the whole area . . . . There is no part of the area that we are not claiming which has not been cultivated." By that he meant over time and by many divisions of the families, but he did not so stipulate.

After citing numerous problems in attempting to file the claims, Abdalla turned to 1930 and those filed when Sir Edward Grigg, governor of the colony, came to Lamu. At that time "they were informed . . . that the Governor was not prepared to accept their petition on the whole area that they were claiming, but he would give them about 5,000 acres" to divide, meaning individual blocks of five acres. They had rejected that ungenerous offer.

Following on more claims and counter claims, the Afro-Arabs and their co-claimants felt they were being discriminated against. They "have never lost any opportunity of presenting their case to the Government . . . . Suppose it is argued that all of this land is not cultivated for a long time, the Arabs do not think that is a fair argument for the land to be taken away from them." As the claimants saw it, the "whole difficulty with non-cultivation of land for a number of years goes back to the . . . abolition of slavery, and it is clear that is not the fault of the Arabs." Not only were exports lost, but since the land was uncultivated "now it cannot grow even the food it requires." Lamu island is like a "sand dune. . . [and that] is the reason the Arabs are claiming the land on the mainland . . . because of their cultivation . . . Our feelings are increasing daily because of this land . . . . Even that right of going to the courts of law, which should be given to everybody, has been refused to the Arabs."

A panel member muddied the waters by bringing up the "tribes" (meaning in this case the designations applied to different social groups). Unfortunately "Boke" plunged ahead, agreeing that "yes it is [a] claim by tribes not individuals." Lyall Grant, chairman of the Commission, bore down for clarification (clinging to the European concept of tribe) asking if the tribes claimed they owned the land individually or by group? Here, Abdalla made the most poignant argument the families had. They were he said "all mixed up together."

"Boke" reached the crux of the matter when he testified that "Because of arrangements arrived at between ourselves, they are quite a number of people who do not know which plots belong to their ancestors, so we arranged to claim in partnership. . . . They all know that their ancestors had a right to that land, but they themselves do not know which particular area was being cultivated. . . . They were no other tribes at all cultivating. . . . Some people know that their families were cultivating there, but they did not know the actual spot on which they are cultivating. . . . [Our] ancestors lived on the land." But, did they not have slaves there, working and living on their shambas? Yes, he responded, they had "a great number. An individual owned about 200 to 400." A committee member referred back to compensation paid for the slaves at emancipation, turning Mohamed al Maawyia's complaint concerning compensation into criticism.

Based on the long held view that the Arabs spent their compensation, one commissioner inquired if they had spent the money keeping the land under cultivation. Abdalla, echoing the refrain that was repeated over and over, replied "Who would cultivate it? At the time of compensation, we had not the slaves. The slaves were stopped before the compensation was paid." Later, "Boke" pointed out that some of the lands were owned by the Wafq. That, he said, could not be sold.

Sheikh Mohammed al Maawyia added that he filed two claims and won his case "but I am not cultivating the land. The first reason is that there is no cultivation anywhere near my land: if I want to work the place, I cannot get any labour." Mohammed, too, had put in "many claims for a large number of areas of land, which I claimed as my own, but the Government told me that, if I would limit the number of areas I was claiming they would give me these two certificates." Coercion to settle for less was common, according to the memories of old WaAmu. Mohamed al Maawyia also claimed that he was "afraid lest the Government charge me the survey fees, which I should not be able to pay. . . . I could not pay; I do not know how much."

Later, the respected Mombasa liwali, Sir Ali bin Salim, testified on behalf of the WaAmu land claimants, but placed their claims in a wider context. This was, he said, a matter of concern to the entire coast and the matter stood "between the people and the Sultan." The people had no need to register deeds, or apply for surveys, they simply took the land they needed from the Sultan's ten mile strip until the "Government took it over." Sir Ali again explained the land tenure system that developed among all the coastal people under the reigns of various Zanzibari sultans. Ultimately, it was family and not individuals who inherited the tracts that their ancestors cultivated over the centuries.

"Neither the [IBEA] Company nor the Sultan helped the people."[13] The Sultan of Zanzibar was a puppet to the British and therefore powerless to help the WaAmu, although they did appeal to him. The Sultan, however, wrote "a letter to the Lamu people" explaining that "as regards your land and your property, no one will interfere with it; it is yours. You can sell it if you like; it is your property." But in the end, the Carter Land Commission turned down the WaAmu appeals on the basis of the joint claims they submitted. Further appeals resulted, but "owing to the slump when the Government couldn't afford a recorder the matter lapsed" and in 1957 it was "taken up again after thirty years." The DC reported that year the claims were mostly adjudicated although in nothing like the amount of land the WaAmu had originally claimed. Throughout this period most of the land lay fallow or grew into bush. The "Government was reluctant to lease" and those who might have worked the land were unwilling to do so because "unadjudicated claims" might have been settled, leaving the current farmer in the lurch.

As for the claims filed in the years after 1911, some of the locals who had money, either registered deeds in their own names or did so for family members. Ali Jahadhmy's uncle filed several claims in the early 1920s, one on behalf of Ali's father who was too poor to pay the fees. None of the plots were large. None were mortgaged. All remained in the family until the British government had been replaced by the Government of Kenya.[14] Some of the these claims were "filed by Lamu slaves who were themselves slave owners, and cultivated their own pieces of land on the mainland." A few of them were able to establish their claims.[15]

As with any society when change is superimposed from outside the perimeters of the culture, the Lamu Afro-Arabs had been wrenched from the life styles they created during the nineteenth century, their political system overridden by the laws and regulations dictated by the British; and their economic underpinnings knocked out from under them by the myriad circumstances we have seen after the onset of colonialism. But no economic reforms were put in place to help them ease into these substantial changes. The Indians, who mostly lost out on foreclosures, departed en masse. The Hadrami community began to prosper—as much as was possible in a stagnated economy. And the patricians clung more tenaciously to their life style, embittered over their lack of compensation for the land they hoped would restore some of their prosperity.

Before and after the unsatisfactory resolution of the land claims, Mohammed al Maawyia and others either refused to pay their taxes or begged for a reduction in the scale. "Arab pride" combined with some government income, and later the small claims settlement, enabled Mohmamed al Maawyia to entertain visiting traders at his shamba in the old style. Mohammed al Maawyia and his peers were also underwriting the education of their children. From the reported four *madrassas* in Lamu in 1830, the numbers increased throughout the period of prosperity, but declined at the turn of the century. By the 1920s, the old families had expanded their *madrassas* and increased the numbers of teachers. The pay was poor and fees were limited per child, but because the numbers of children at each *madrassa* were considerable, these teachers "earned a good income."[16]

Serial marriages and concubinage meant that most men had large families to provide for as well as educate. In the *madrassas*, male children learned to read and write Arabic in order to study the Qur'an. Some were instructed in other subjects as well. Discipline was often severe, including placing little boys legs in wooden stocks, similar to those employed to punish slaves. Religious instruction for girls was not so rigorous but was required. The daughters of many of the patricians were privately tutored in their homes. These girls learned to read and write KiSwahili in Arabic script. Some became facile in composing poetry—romantic verse and prayers concerning families and friends. As a port city, even if in decline, much of Lamu's collective attention still centered on the sea—as the following poem written by a woman in the 1940s illustrates:[17]

> *"The prayer I keep repeating (and pray and repray)*
> *All please say Amen*
> *Safety and safety for the wealth of the children*
> *May it come earlier and let us be patient*
> *Or may we be the patient people*

Let them unload at the harbor of Hadramaut, the dhow
Goods for the people, and it should not delay to come back.
May it not delay and let us be patient
All that the voyagers who come from Lamu
May God give them all that is good
Give them peace (peace be upon them)
Let them have joy, too, forever, and ever.

Some local men also composed poetry, although most of it is lost or was taken away by European collecters. The wide chasm that separates men from women in the Islamic world accounted for the gifts that men frequently requested these poets write for their male companions, often marking special occasions like Idd al Fitr. The poets were, of course, paid for their services.[18] Their poetry is an illustration of the amalgamation of the African-Arab culture that created what John Middleton refers to as "the world of the Swahili": a distinct culture composed of borrowing and blending and applying these results to local needs. Another manifestation of the this phenomenon was the practice Lamu women developed of weaving Arabic love verses to their husbands in colorful mats. Sometimes, women wove their verses in the form of riddles and some of them, when unraveled ridiculed.[19] Elite women did this as well as ex-slaves, who used to embroider suggestive messages to their masters.[20]

The limited education available to the poor centered around religion. Teachers were rarely qualified. The Riyadha sharifs were preoccupied with the mosque college and with their medical practices. Those who were employed were often Hadramis who had other occupations or itinerant sharifs who wandered in and then either started a trade or went elsewhere. The pay, based on numbers of mat bags woven by students, amounted to a few cents per pupil per week.[21]

The Afro-Arabs finally prevailed on the government to open a school for them, following the earlier one established for the Asian children. In 1929 the first class of scholars consisted of "twenty who attended evenings only, and thirty day school pupils. Many of the boys [are] from the best families in Lamu . . . . The ages vary from 12 to 30 years." Within a few weeks after classes were underway, attendance dropped: "the parents sent their children to mosque for religious instruction in the morning" and resented the lack of instruction in the Qur'an.[22] By the mid-

1930s, with attendance very low the day school was closed. The night classes continued, running for only one and one-half hours devoted primarily to reading, writing and mathematics. Attendance hovered between twenty and thirty students throughout the 1930s, and at the end of that decade, a few girls enrolled. Although their instruction was limited to domestic science, another great outcry of protest came from the Riyadha sharifs.

Because of problems attendant to obtaining an education in Lamu, Zanzibar continued to lure children of the elite in the 1930s. The father of Sherifa binta Seif al Hussein "is quite willing that his daughter should undergo four year training preparatory to becoming a teacher at the Government School in Mombasa. She trained at the Arab Girls School in Zanzibar and did well."[23] Although Ahmed Jahadhmy remained a dedicated educator to those attending the night school, he sent his own older children to private school in Zanzibar.[24] In the 1940s thirty or more boys were joined by two or three girls, until the government day school for boys reopened, then the numbers of students increased to a range of between forty to seventy pupils.[25]

Lamu had no electricity until 1968. All night school study was done under *tyawandi*, the kerosene lanterns that produced more heat than light. (Lamu's mosques contained numbers of lanterns which, before kerosene, the slaves kept filled with locally produced coconut oil. The poor mostly used *tyawandi*, with the wealthy employing the larger style which "lit an entire room.")[26]

Ali Abdalla Skanda was among the boys who enrolled in the government school when it opened in 1947. Later, Skanda went to Mombasa and sent his children to school there. In fact, Mombasa lured away many who could not afford Zanzibar, but who were intimidated by Badawy and other sharifs.[27] Skanda attended vocational school where he specialized in woodcarving. No form of vocational education was available in Lamu even though some craftsmen took on apprentices, a practice that has continued into the present. Other Lamu youths studied trades in Mombasa. Because of Lamu's sagging economy, most who were schooled in Mombasa stayed there or went elsewhere to practice their skills. After a lull in local education for girls, progressive fathers once more to enrolled them in the Arab school in the late 1950s.[28] Again staunch opposition came from the conservative factions. In fact the reaction in Lamu in this period foreshadowed attitudes towards women's education in much of the Muslim world in the decades that followed. Among the first students were the younger daughters of Ahmed Jahadhmy, a daughter of Abdalla al Maawyia, Zela and Zena Yahie, and Fatma Mohamed.[29] The Riyadha sharifs and some youthful followers led an attack on these young girls as they attempted to enter the building. They were pelted with stones and all ran home. Next day, some of their fathers accompanied them, still to the cries of infamy and to a rain of stones. Finally, police protection was provided by the government—but young boys who witnesses contended were influenced by the sharifs, continued stoning them intermittently through the 1970s.[30]

Opposition continued, too, to education for boys. But the Afro-Arab community, anxious to stay in the forefront as an affirmation of their elitism, determined that if they could not maintain their position through land and slaves, they would educate their children to enjoy the benefits of better jobs. Indeed, C. P. Lloyd, district commission in Lamu in 1954, reported that "it has not escaped the notice of some sections of the community, fortunately a majority of the elders, that in order to qualify for a good job and high salaries, it is essential these days to receive some education."[31] Another DC referred to "particularly the girls. . . many ladies quite rightly want to be attended in hospital by female nurses and attendants and this can't be provided unless more women go to school."[32]

Meanwhile, at the Lamu primary school for boys, principal Salim Khamis wrote to the BBC that in 1953 "English is still a new thing." He requested that "English by Radio" section recommend "How I could improve my spoken English . . . [and suggest] books or papers which you think could help the teaching of English."[33]

By the 1950s, Habib Saleh's grandsons were running the Riyadha Mosque. Their influence over the Hadrami community was almost total, but some descendants of slaves joined the children of their former masters in obtaining a secular education. In this case, economic opportunity took precedence over indoctrination on religious grounds. The children of the conservative sharifs "are instructed in the Qur'an, advanced theology and Arabic. The boys are expected to become *madrassa* teachers and instruct the young boys in religion. Through these sharifs, there is an almost built-in religious class in Lamu. Their daughters are rarely educated and are kept in the house."[34] This was true, too, of the Hadrami. Their education was almost entirely limited to rote recitations of the Qur'an. A few Hadrami boys were sent to school, at least long enough to learn the rudiments of mathematics, but they, too, felt the long arm of the Riyadha sharifs.

Paradoxically, many of the sharifs provided their own children with secular education. Sharif Hassan Badawy continued his father's opposition and briefly entertained establishing a western style curriculum at the Mosque College but did not follow through because no competent teachers were available from the group that were his mainstay.[35]

Leisure hours for girls were limited. Even aristocratic girls were made to work at home. After puberty most were kept inside except for escorted visits to homes in the neighborhood. Children of the poor, however, roamed about town often to the consternation of British authorities.[36] Hadrami girls were especially secluded and the Indians mainly played among themselves.

Before World War II, Afro-Arab boys were prohibited from visiting the seafront when the large sailing dhows were in port. But old rules gave way to new from the 1940s, with less supervision characterizing boys in all classes. They played games in the heavy sand, and hunted on the island until they were old enough to pursue big game on the mainland. While their sisters learned to carry out the responsibilities that would be theirs in adulthood, boys of the aristocracy rarely were taught any useful skills. Among them, the double standard of male superiority was learned at an early age.

Small children of both sexes went off in groups to *madrassas,* although they usually they did not fast at Ramadan until they reached puberty. Ritual prayers five times a day were rigorously enforced at home among all classes. Children were literally taught their prayers at their mothers' knees. Imports from the east like birthday parties called for a maulidi along with cake and cookies. Though doctrinal interpretations differed among them, religion was part of the daily life of nearly every man, woman, and child in Lamu, as is still the case today.

Poor families often used their children as street vendors. These children, especially girls, hawked trays of apple mangoes coated with pepper.

Bread and sweets were also sent out of poor homes, including those of the Hadrami, on small platters that children bounced about as they made their way through the dark winding streets. Little girls peddled mother's jasmine corsages, especially as increasing numbers of tourists trekked in during the post-World War II era. Mothers sent children to collect firewood that could be used for cooking or sold for a few shillings. Poor boys learned to herd a few sheep or cattle in the shambas behind the town, collecting small wages, that were then passed on to their parents (mostly single mothers).

Among the many changes in Lamu after the introduction of British colonialism, was usurpation of the Afro-Arabs rights over their wafq properties. Where before a group of elders at each mosque handled finances, (including inheritances left to respective mosques), by the time Ralph Skene left, the money had been shifted to a wafq Commission established in Mombasa. The accounts for each mosque were kept separately there.[37] Pwani Mosque, the oldest in town, "owns considerable area of land in the township on which many houses are built." The "Liwali Seifu Mosque was well endowed" and owned two large island shambas on which rents were collected. Beyond the mosques, the wafq documents included gifts to relatives. Bwana Fadhil, father of Mohammed al Maawyia, built a mosque in memory of a daughter he loved who died in her youth. Upkeep on that mosque, like others built by Lamu Afro-Arabs, was maintained through contributions from the families that were associated with the mosques. Due to the network created by intermarriage several families overlapped in the care of any number of the thirty mosques in Lamu by independence.[38]

Houses were deeded to mosques. This was especially true when the old families had little money to give for upkeep. Endowments included funds that had been left through inheritance in the nineteenth century when the old families were wealthy. Some of the controversial land claims on the mainland involved inheritances left to mosques, but these were almost all rejected in the end because no one could establish perimeters or guarantee to farm the land. Small tokens were placed in wafq as well. One gift of a Qur'an, for instance, was handed down from a Somali woman who "realized that the world is but a transient domain and not an enduring abode, a place of passage rather than a place of confinement. . . . "[39]

199

The custom of fathers giving houses to their daughters remained intact throughout the century. If anything, more houses passed into women's hands because of the declining male population. Some of the ruins the district commissioners referred to were owned by women who lacked the means to keep them in repair. Fathers often deeded houses directly to their daughters before their deaths—in order to be sure they were provided for, before the restrictive inheritance laws could take effect. Because in Lamu, it was customary for brothers to take care of their sisters' property, as well as assume some responsibility for sisters children, often houses were deeded to brothers and sisters in full confidence that daughters would have homes in which to live out their lives. No matter the divisions over doctrinal matters, husbands were a tenuous phenomenon in the lives of Hadrami, Afro-Arab, and the descendants of slaves.[40]

CHAPTER 12

Lamu town from the air, with the landing strip on Manda island in the background.
Courtesy of the author's personal collection

Chapter Twelve

Health and Leisure

"Whether you bring a matter to the light or hide it,
God truly hath knowledge of all things"
The Qur'an

Administrators regarded Lamu "as the most attractive coast station" although the district commissioner's house on the seafront, had "no electricity or piped water [and] a multitude of bats." These liabilities were partially offset by "wide verandas and huge airy rooms separated by curtained arches, with intricately carved wooden shutters to the windows." As they discovered on arrival, the bachelors who were posted there "roosted in one corner of it, the remainder occupied by [artisans] and by whole families claiming squatters rights by virtue of their descent from the [liwalis] slaves."[1] The house was located in front of the Bohra Mosque, near what would be Petley's Hotel but until 1946 was an Indian owned export-import business.

Smith Mackenzie's huge warehouse was down the seafront on the road to Shela. The customs office was further away—and avoided as much as possible by local merchants. Tiny shacks of former slaves dotted the seafront area between the wide verandas that marked businesses or government buildings. In the 1920s and late in the 1930s "the whole harbor was filled with *jahazis* and *mtepes*, joined by the occasional dhow." The *mtepes* came from the Bajun islands carrying both *mangati*, the better quality and heavier mangrove poles, and *boriti*.[2] The small boats anchored in the harbor dumped their slops overboard. High tide at certain times of the year washed over the seawall, stringing litter from the harbor onto the wide main thoroughfare. At low tide, the combination of filth and litter rested on top of the mud at the outer edge of the seawall sending stench wafting into the district commissioners residence as well as the other buildings located at the seafront.

Behind Lamu's small business sector, economic activities continued along much the same lines that had characterized the town since emancipation, but with considerable shifts in population. Men from the old families continued to trickle out. Their places were taken by newcomers from the Bajun Islands and from the mainland. Although some of the Afro-Arabs lived off their rents, the labors of their slaves who chose to stay on, and the income earned by their wives in cottage industries, many of the younger generation went to work. A few, like Mohammed Ali BuSaid turned avocation into employment.

Mohammed bin Ali recalled that he, and other boys, used to go on big game hunting safaris to the mainland, despite the threats of bandits. His hobby became his business and he began shooting elephants and hippo for profit. Legal exports of hippo teeth ranged from 186 pounds in 1931 to 204 in 1950. Ivory in cubic weight went from "151.31 to 191.01" in these years. Illegal exports, which went out surreptitiously probably equalled those numbers if they didn't surpass them.[3] British administrators were increasingly troubled with the widespread poaching that characterized the Lamu District. Some hunted without paying the steep licensing fees, or, as with Mohammed bin Ali, hunted illegally until they could earn enough to buy the license. One solution was to hire poachers as game wardens. This is how Mohammed bin Ali joined the government, where he remained until his retirement at independence.

But the WaBoni, experienced hunters themselves, were the main perpetrators. George Adamson, also a game warden, was posted in the northern part of Kenya moved into the WaBoni forest where he imagined that "no warden has ever visited" and that was a "hot bed of leopard poaching." He was "extremely successful and took a number of prisoners to Lamu for trial."[4]

In 1943 Lamu was still considered "the ancient port" that intrigued nineteenth century visitors. To Adamson, even then it was "more Arab than African . . . . [with] Indian influences mingled with the English and Arab in the faces of the people." With amusement, Adamson recorded a notice posted outside a shop that was a local attempt to instill a modicum of public health: "This hygene [sic] house, no spitum or other dirty business."

Despite the inroads the British made with installation of sewers and drainage systems, donkeys—who continued to join porters in transporting goods through the Lamu streets—defecated everywhere. Mangy cats remained a health problem. (The cats were so lacking in "stamina and courage that many believe the rats actually eat the cats here.")[5] All of the pests common to Lamu remained except for the hyenas who were extinct on the island. As the numbers of small cement homes burgeoned out from the center, piles of refuge grew accordingly. Most homes had trench latrines, if not the deep pits of the town houses. Even so, poor local men, joined by new arrivals, still used parts of the seafront as their toilets.

Many stone houses contained cisterns with stagnant water that attracted flying insects as well as catching the droppings of the bats and birds. British authorities attempted to educate the owners of these houses through campaigns that encouraged residents to stock their cisterns with fish. With no inspection to back them up, few locals took heed.

At the turn of the century Lamu contained twenty some wells. A few new mosques were erected, each with its own well. Urban sprawl that characterized the post-World War II era, called for additional wells in the rapidly urbanized former shamba sections south of town. Water was therefore plentiful but locally made water pots were replaced by rusty tin cans that were carried door to door by men on long poles that rested on their shoulders. Even the well water contained parasites that were a hazard to the health of those who did not boil it before consuming. In fact, few of the locals heeded the advice of numbers of European officials in this matter as they ignored advice on most other fronts as well.

The last major outbreak of smallpox was in 1922, but in 1926, the district commissioner reported twenty two cases in quarantine with about 2,000 vaccinations to locals. When it came to preventing the spread of smallpox, all segments of society cooperated, although few of the women came forward for vaccination. Because of the "considerable amount of traffic between the Persian Gulf and Lamu, during favorable weather, the passage can be made in shorter time than smallpox takes to develop." From 1926 on the sub-assistant surgeons were sent to meet all steamers and native vessels to check for persons afflicted. If smallpox was discovered the entire ship was quarantined, yet as late as 1933 the disease was still coming into Lamu—this was the year that Jane Clive vaccinated as many Lamu women as she could summon to her home.[6]

In 1918-19 the world wide flu pandemic swept across Africa and took its toll on Lamu.[7] The flu was thought to have been brought in by arrivals on dhows, and rapidly spread through the town before striking others in the district. At the time a medical doctor was in residence but he was powerless to stop the epidemic because there then no medicines available to treat the flu.

One of the major problems in studying the history of disease in Lamu concerns the frequent change in staff and the inadequate medical education of the sub-assistant surgeons assigned there between 1920 and 1935. In fact, Kenya colony did not have a consistent medical policy in place in rural areas at independence. Constant "pressure to apply sanitary measures" reflected the government's strategy.[8] A clinic was established in the 1920s, but medical supplies continued to be short. One can sympathize with the district commissioner who, in 1920, sent to Mombasa for aspirin and in return received an empty pill box.[9]

Diagnoses varied according to who was making them. A sub-assistant surgeon in 1933 diagnosed a large number of cases of pneumonia. His replacement reported very little pneumonia, but he determined that was a considerable increase in tuberculosis in 1934.[10] Falciprium malaria remained a problem, with reported cases ranging yearly at between 1100 and 3,000. The differential here probably reflects more people going for treatment as medical care improved and medicines became available. Children were rarely seen at the clinic, or in the early years, at the hospital. Their deaths from malaria were therefore only infrequently recorded. We have no way of knowing the ratio of their deaths *versus* those of adults. Diagnoses of yaws remained a constant, with cases reported at about 300 a year. One year chronic rheumatism afflicted 449 people (mostly men in 1927-28) and the next a whopping 2714 cases were diagnosed. Figures for bronchitis hovered above 1,000 most years, and constipation brought over 2,000 people to the hospital in the mid to late 1930s.[11]

The new maternity wing for Asian and Arab women was opened in 1939, but few women made use of it until the 1950s. Most preferred their traditional midwives. Births were on the rise among the Hadrami and Afro-Arabs, although still limited among the Indians and the descendants of slaves.[12] By 1959 the district commissioner reported that maternity services "were gradually gaining ground and the prejudice against seeking medical advice slowly being overcome" by women.[13] A few went to the clinic for abortions when the Asians were still in charge (three in 1937, 3 in 1938, 5 in 1942, with the numbers rising to 5 in 1949, and 7 in 1950).[14]

Another major health problem in Lamu was hookworm. In the 1950s, after decades of complaints concerning the apathy among the Afro-Arabs, officials began to realize that the high incidence of hookworm was responsible for lethargy among coastal students.[15] Leprosy decreased over the decades, but lepers were still being shipped off to the colony in the 1950s. Ulcers and other skin diseases were regularly reported over the century.

An important factor that the official forms did not address, was what were the predisposing conditions before patients came to the clinic? For instance pneumonia may have been the actual cause of death, but what about diarrhea, vomiting, weakness from malnutrition? For the more than forty years that medical records were maintained, the high incidence of one year diarrhea, and in another dysentery, indicate that the sub-assistant surgeons regarded the two as interchangeable. Yet, dysentery is most often viewed as potentially a much more serious problem than diarrhea. There was no category for cholera although it is likely that was included under dysentery on the official form.

Measles were not reported until the 1950s, yet older WaAmu said there were epidemics that resulted in some deaths, especially among children. At least a few cases of chicken pox were reported in some years, with four dying of the disease in 1915. No orthopedic equipment existed. The sub-assistant surgeons did, however, set broken bones. One even "successfully completed the removal of a cataract." Considering the folklore pertaining to the evil eye, ophthalmological problems were a major source of concern. Kwashiorkor, a protein calorie deficiency, was not a problem in Lamu, probably because of the daily diet of fish by all but the most destitute. Rickets and pellagra were not reported. Teeth problems resolved themselves by eventually falling out. Dentists were not available.

Crippled babies "who were not able to walk properly" were treated by locals through homemade "metal leg bracelets with a chain on the ankle which could be attached to a solid object." The idea was to hold the child's leg in place with the hope it would strengthen. Local remedies existed for many types of illnesses. Beyond the sharifs and their cures, the traditional healers used herbs, roots, and leaves in treatment of their patients. Some added bits of minerals to water, oil, or applied them directly in troubled areas. Before quinine was available the local treatment for malaria was considered successful. The healer heated a pan of water on charcoal, placed the steaming pan under the legs of the patient, and then draped a cloth over all. The idea—which worked—was to produce sweat and lower the fever. In fact, the locals were often skeptical of western medical treatments after they were introduced.

In the 1940s, a district commissioner, in a self-congratulatory discussion with Mohammed al Maawyia concerning the benefits of western medicine received an unanticipated response: "No. Before we had malaria we were told we just had fever. Now we are told we have pneumonia, before we were told we just had a bad cough. Having diagnoses only makes us worry. . . . Things seem more serious." More recently another town elder repeated those sentiments: "We didn't know fever was malaria. We knew we had a lot of problems with fever but we had our own treatments. We didn't know about heart attacks and cancer. We were healthier."[16]

Venereal disease became a source of increasing consternation to district commissioners. Local medicines were sometimes effective, but many times arrested the diseases but not curing them. Gonorrhea and syphilis were attributed to the "rampant immorality" of the people in Lamu. For one thing, the women refused to come to the clinic. The older scholars at the Arab night school were tested for venereal disease in 1929 with the DC caustically recording in his report that "if the incidence at this school represents the index of v.d. in an obvious form among the population, the condition must be common indeed." The male students he noted were "anxious for treatment" although some seemed to have tried "Swahili medicines . . . which was a pity." In 1930, Captain Gregory-Smith wanted to open a clinic but "the leading Arabs . . . . opposed the matter with suspicion."[17] The district commissioner in 1931 commented that "purdah . . . does little to effectively stop the control of venereal disease which is ruining the race."[18]

Over the course of the twentieth century, Lamu developed a reputation as a town where homosexuality was at least tolerated, and perhaps practiced to a rather high degree.[19] DC reports as well as travelers reports from the earliest period, reported on "widespread immorality"—it was this *thought* that homosexuality was prevalent that gave rise to the reports. Historical gossip among other whites in Kenya colony suggested that any numbers of the district commissioners were engaged in this practice with mostly young boys in the District, as well as in Lamu town.[20]

There are many factors that contributed to the practice of homosexuality in Lamu. The long period between reaching sexual arousal and availability of marriage partners motivated some young men to act out their sexual needs. Boys and young men were forced to live in an all male world, except for their limited contact with close female family members. This was especially the case after concubines were no longer available to freemen. With a disproportionate number of males among the slave population, single sex may have been the only option available to many. Rape was almost unheard of. Most of those who did engage in single sex activities settled into heterosexual relationships (often with a string of wives) as soon as they were able to raise bride price.

There were men in Lamu, as elsewhere, who were genetically predisposed to homosexuality. These men acted out with each other, or with young, unmarried men. In most of these cases "older men sought satisfaction by inserting their penises in the thighs of young boys who played the role of women."[21] Some older patrician women joined by descendants of slaves acknowledged the long history of homosexuality and pedophilia in Lamu. One commented that "Arabs used to spoil boys but it was kept quiet until the influx of the Bajun" who, these informants suggested, brought homosexuality out of the closet. Older men paid small change to boys to engage in sexual relations with them, as continued to be the case with the poor Bajun, who came into Lamu in increasing numbers in the wake of the labor shortage after World War II.[22]

Because of the natural predilection for single sex on the part of some men, and the need for money on the part of young boys, including the poverty stricken Bajun who trickled into Lamu, a limited network of male prostitution developed in Lamu. Some of this activity was promoted by a few Europeans including District commissioner "Daddy" Cornell and Nestle heir, Henri Bernier, and others. In fact, the network of homosexual activities in exchange for money was enacted to perfection by Bernier who converted to Islam, dressed in kofia and kanzu and who, because of unlimited resources could buy his way into the most conservative of Lamu families.[23]

Arriving in Lamu in the mid-1940s, Elspeth Huxley and her stayed with Henri Bernier "a middle-aged Swiss of gentle manners who lived at Shela, a crumbling town about two miles from Lamu town.[24] Actually a number of European males had settled in and near Lamu, among them Charles Whitten who had moved to town in the 1930s after abandoning his shamba. Then, there was Percy Petley who arrived in Lamu in 1913, and founded the hotel when he retired from his business interests on the mainland.

Huxley may have met Whitten and Petley, but she would not have come into the presence of both men at the same time. They developed a strong antipathy towards each other, to the point that if one walked down one side of the street, the other retreated. Neither man ever married. Whitten was openly homosexual. Petley, a big game hunter, was not.[25] Coconut Charlie Whitten came to be a great favorite with Lamu children. His Lamu house featured a balcony from which, on feast days, he "threw piles of coins . . . to the children who scrambled in the street to the amusement of Mr. Whitten."

Whitten and P. A. Petley wrote for competing newspapers in Mombasa. Their mutual dislike carried over to their reportage "causing some embarrassment for the respective editors when the same story arrived in two wildly different forms." Where Petley was rough and "looked like a baboon" Whitten dressed in "a silk suit and was a good cook." Whitten collected bric-a-brac that centered on Lamu material culture, and was "pleased if visitors asked to see his museum." Although not a single motor car existed on Lamu island, Whitten "served as an agent for motor car spares", ran an insurance agency and bought "a two-stroke generator with which he charged batteries for radios such as the local residents possessed."[26] At his death in the 1950s Whitten left his property in trust to provide bursaries to aid Lamu boys with schooling. Several of the current generation of prominent Afro-Arabs benefitted from the Whitten

Scholarship.[27]

Pamela Scott, an upcountry member of the British gentry, stayed at Petley's Hotel in the mid-1950s finding it refreshing if primitive. At that time the rooms were "a long row of stalls [with] walls only coming up five or six feet between 'rooms.'" There was only "one toilet for all the rooms. Africans used to go to the roof and pour stagnant water from a large can down for showering."[28] Edward Rodwell recalled a rather unsettling discovery during a short stay at the hotel. Petley, he said, "found the only place he could keep the butter chilled was to place it under the seat in the privy."[29]

In 1955, the acting district commissioner reported "several cases . . . in Lamu township of indecent assault on young boys. Three men were prosecuted, two appealed, and these cases were thrown out of court. The effect of these prosecutions was a marked exodus of undesirables from the District."[30] A Mombasa journalist confided that from the arrival of the Freelanders in the late nineteenth century and on, "all the hippies and *washoga* came to Lamu." Henri Bernier and "Daddy" Cornell bought shambas in the Witu area. Cornell, a small wiry man, drew extra pay from occasionally filling in as DC, and therefore kept up some of his relationships with people in the town. In 1957, Cornell was brutally murdered. Officially his death at Witu was attributed to Somali *shifta*. But rumors in both Lamu and Mombasa attributed it to a lovers quarrel.[31] Bernier soon disposed of the shamba, and moved full time to Peponi, his Lamu island paradise.[32]

Lamu was also home to the occasional transsexual and transvestite. Over time, no group was exempt, including the Afro-Arabs. Whereas *washoga* dress in men's clothing, transsexuals and transvestites often dressed in women's clothing, or as close a facsimile as they could manifest and still walk the streets. Their feminine draping of the *koikoi* often made them the objects of derision among Lamu men, although many of the women, especially family members, were tolerant. Local *washoga* often performed on musical instruments at the women's wedding ceremonies—they were regarded as safe in the harem because women knew that actively homosexual men were not going to marry their daughters. Transsexuals and transvestites, although not invited, often arrived at weddings or in the women's section at the maulidi hidden under their *buibui*,

210

the long black cloak worn by women when they went out.[33]

Lesbian relationships are less easy to detect. The Swahili have a word for lesbian (*msagaji sg.; wasagaji pl*). But contemporary WaAmu were unwilling to discuss the subject even though they admitted that they knew lesbianism existed *zamani*. My informants were Afro-Arab and descendants of slaves who, while denying any knowledge of the practice among their respective groups, referred to two well known Hadrami women who were lesbians. Homosexuality—a male activity—is more openly discussed, indeed even ridiculed by some Lamu women. In a world where women are so systematically abused, neglected, or left at young ages with no husbands, it is difficult to believe that, over time, some lesbian activity did not develop. Women, according to sexologist John Money, are "touchy feely" and they are more likely to succumb to sexual activity based on feelings of closeness and security rather than being driven by libido.[34]

Wife abuse was seldom reported by the British, whose knowledge of personal matters pertaining to the WaAmu remained limited. Hadrami men were often accused by their wives of mistreatment, and informants mentioned men in all segments of society who had engaged in wife beating on occasion. Informants claimed that the women refused to go to the British authorities out of fear or because of embarrassment at bringing shame on their families. When a husband came to the district commissioner seeking the return of his wife from Mombasa, his investigation revealed that she "complained of his ill treatment" and refused to return. The DC advised that nothing would be done: "The lady probably prefers pin money to marital drudgery, in which case, of course, she is not alone."[35]

In the Mombasa Social Survey, G. M. Wilson conducted a study among male prostitutes, including some from Lamu District. Most were rural boys who came to the city, "75% who came into this profession between the ages of twelve and fifteen years. . . ." Of the "90 male prostitutes studied 35% came from Lamu [district]." By the post World War II era, Lamu had long been superseded by Mombasa as the premier port city, and as we have seen, many in Lamu shifted to Mombasa for employment, including prostitutes. Wilson found in Mombasa that the males moved about in the same areas as female prostitutes, sometimes sharing a house with them, or renting them rooms. The males often served as procurers for the female prostitutes. In addition, the survey revealed that "they also provided the beer and bhang [marijuana] that the females sold to their customers." In order words, many of the male prostitutes extended their networks to include other forms of income. A similar type of economic enterprise continued to exist on a much smaller scale in Lamu.[36]

Female prostitution may not have been widely practiced in Lamu but as we have seen, despite the protestations of the elders, it provided a measure of support for some poor women. Janet Bujra studied prostitution among women in a Bajun town on Pate island. Lacking any skills beyond their ability to use their bodies, these women were able to make enough to buy houses, gold jewelry, and could even help support poor family members back home.[37]

When, in the late nineteenth century, the British established their rule over the Bajun, their economic status had already been altered. Emancipation of their slaves had also effected the stratified social system which was familiar to the Hadrami: "Masharifu, *waungwana*, and slaves."[38] Ali Jahadhmy, who spent the early years of his childhood in Faza, recalled that in the 1920s and 1930s "very few Bajuns had slaves. They were more a more egalitarian society because they were all very poor." In the postwar years their leaders "became obsessed with being referred to as 'Arabs' and organized to gain recognition, especially as they came into Lamu." Their women were "regarded as beautiful and many become second wives for Lamu Arab men, or after the arranged marriages. Dowry [for Bajun women] was very small in comparison with what Lamu men had to pay for upper class wives."[39] For those who were unable to marry, many went into paid prostitution as a way of earning what they termed "a gift." In the 1960s, when Janet Bujra conducted her fieldwork in "Atu" she was told that "there were no virgin girls . . . . Some women let small boys have intercourse for 5 cents."[40]

Attitudes towards sexual intercourse were different between many of the poor Bajun and those of the Afro-Arabs and Hadrami. One Jamal al Layl sharif commented that the Bajun "do not place the same high priority on virginity" that marked the older established Lamu families. Some Bajun, he said, have come to these sharifs, requesting that they engage in

212

"temporary marriages because their daughters are not virgins. Therefore, if they marry sharifs, even though very briefly, they can later marry [a non-Bajun] without stigma."[41]

The increasing Bujun population in Lamu created new divisions in town, as well as new alliances. The conservative male Hadrami, who were aligned to the Riyadha (and later Swofaa) Mosque, formed common bonds with the Bajun against the Afro-Arabs, whose disapproval of various religious practices continued. The Bajun high regard for the sharifan classes transferred to the Jamal al Layl family who, in turn, welcomed the enlarged group of followers.[42] And, since they began their substantial migration into Lamu from the end of the second World War, the Bajun proved to be strong adherents to the philosophy of ethno-nationalism.[43]

As the poor Bajun women became a significant presence in town, social barriers between Hadrami, to some extent the Indian, and Afro-Arab women slowly dropped. Wedding invitations extended ever more often between these groups. The Hadrami and Afro-Arab women almost always included the descendants of slaves (as had been the case traditionally). During the 1930s, some wedding exchanges had already taken place, but the regular incorporation of one group by the other did not take occur until the early 1950s.[44]

Wedding customs still included vugo dances, and those remaining ex-slaves and their female descendants maintained their rights to perform them. Only in the postindependence period, were they joined by the Afro-Arab and Hadrami women.[45] A few Indian women observed, but rarely took an active part in the festivities. The wealthy among them wore the most recent fashions, and those who managed to maintain their gold jewelry wore it all. Styles changed appreciably over the century, the influence coming from the west rather than the east. Older women recalled weddings in the 1930s and 1940s when they applied heavy coats of white powder to their faces, maintaining kohl on their eyelids and in their brows, and set off with bright colored lipstick. The shining dark henna designs that characterized brides and married women remained in vogue even as wedding dresses changed to feature the long white flowing gowns typical of brides in Europe and America. The major difference here was that Lamu Muslim brides donned their white wedding gowns after they had proven their virginity when their marriages were consumated. This was done on the second night, reserved for their public display before invited female guests. Wedding rings came to symbolize the vows made between male relatives of the bride and groom at the mosque, with the exchange of rings and other jewelry taking place on the night the couple met—literally in most cases—for their first heterosexual experience.[46]

After the second world war, Elspeth Huxley visited Lamu where she saw "very old ladies attended perhaps by very old ex-slaves [who] linger on amid past glories.." Here "women are chattels still" with no life beyond "the walls of their houses."[47] Even as the Hadrami community overtook most of the Afro-Arabs in the extravagance of their wedding celebrations, their young brides had little to look forward to beyond the confines of their homes, childbirth, and perhaps in time, divorce. When they did go out, usually after dark, both Hadrami and Afro-Arab women gathered under the shiraa, the tentlike cover Stigand mentioned seeing in 1912. Older women still positioned themselves at both ends of the poles that held the cover under which their mistresses glided about town. But a new twist was added when lower class women devised the one woman sharaa, and sallied around under it, often in their barefeet. After World War II, only Shi'a Asians remained. The women were less constrained in their movements about town, did not employ the shiraa, but those who were married wore a long robe with silk scarfs over their heads. They went daily to their respective mosques with most social affairs confined to their weekly communal meals. Younger Afro-Arab women gradually began their exodus from the tight controls that bound their mothers and grandmothers, joining their Indian counterparts in outside employment—especially those who attended school in Mombasa and were influenced by the more open society there.[48]

CHAPTER 13

Lamu ex-slave demonstrates the one woman shiraa for tourists (ca 1952)

Courtesy of Edward Rodwell

Chapter Thirteen

Lamu through the Second World War and to Independence

"And how many a guilty city have we broken down and raised up
after it other peoples: And when they felt our vengeance, lo!
they fled from it."
The Qur'an

Lamu's indigenous population continued its decline through the 1930s and into the 1950s. As war clouds gathered in Europe "illegal immigrants" from Hadramaut and Bajun Islands arrived by dhow, troubling the British administration through whose nets they slipped. The Asian community, including some Bohra, continued trickling out, leaving the limited business opportunities to Hadrami who were still there, or the new arrivals. Some Afro-Arabs were engaged in business during this period as well. A few opened small shops in their own neighborhoods, selling canned goods and various types breads brought by children from the homes of poor women. Poverty was relevant. Economic conditions elsewhere in the northern coastal area were deplorable.

In 1939, Italy, poised for possible invasion on the borders of Somalia, prompted the two British officials in Lamu to establish a watch with locals taking part on a voluntary basis.[1] In October and November, 1940, Italians, who were actually Somalis "looted Shakani, the village nearest the border." That incident was followed by Somali intrusions into Kiunga, close enough to Lamu to motivate a number of Indians to send their wives and children to coconut shambas at Shela. Charles Whitten and Cawasji Dastoor volunteered to work in regulating prices during these early months of transition from peace to war. With the Northern Frontier

District closed for trade cattle ceased coming into Lamu. The coastal dhow trade was off. In 1939, an Indian firm attempted to interest the Americans in buying *boriti* but failed.[2]

In the early stages of the Italian conflict, the chief of Shakani arrived in the Lamu district commissioner's office carrying what he described as "a curious article" that had washed up on the shore. "It is black. It is round like a football, but far larger, and it has a number of horns thrusting out in several directions. Can you tell me what it may be?" The DC surmised that the description indicated a mine, and suggested he journey to Shakani so he could see it for himself. "Bwana . . . so that you should not be thus troubled, we have hammered off one of the horns and (with profound salaam) here it is." It turned out to be a "German mine vintage 1939 . . . why, when soundly hammered it had not destroyed Shakani, only the Almighty knows."[3]

The district commissioner reported in 1940 that some percentage of Lamu town and the district were "sympathetic to the Italians and the position of the administrative staff was not an easy one." Because Lamu was then the third largest town in Kenya colony and located closest to the Italian border, the civilian administration was replaced by the military in late August, 1940. Local Afro-Arab and a smattering of Hadrami men were drafted into the Arab Company of the King's African Rifles, and along with others returned from training "with a machine gun platoon. . . ." In the early months of the war, a Greek "coastal schooner, armed with machine gun . . . and powered with a diesel engine was dispatched to Lamu as a guard ship and military transport." Some of Lamu's smaller dhows were commandeered by the government and used to transport materials to northern coastal positions where small contingents of men were posted. The small *jihazi* boats carried men back and forth to the northern islands where observation posts had been erected.

Local sentiment was strong divided. With the exception of the Indians, many of the WaAmu were strongly anti-British. Muslihi Abdalla, a former slave, reported that "so many slaves escaped from Lamu because they did not want to fight for the British." The war was described as a conflict "between Kenya and Somalia. . . . [and an Afro-Arab] alerted the *watuma* so many soldiers have come." Some "men and their slaves did not want to fight for the British—the fighting did not concern them. Slaves hid on the roofs of houses in Mkumoni, they hid on the shambas, and some left town." In the case of the Afro-Arab who helped the ex-slaves, and who joined others in eluding the draft, the British remained marginalized.[4] Beyond sensing some lack of sympathy, the civilian administration, and later the military leaders, were unaware that many men in their prime fled the island rather than be drafted.

Of course, many of the WaAmu did not hide away in this early but strategically important stage of the conflict. According to elders, during the early years when fears of invasion were at their highest, most of the Afro-Arabs "took their families to the island shambas for safety. It was a very hard time. Many of us took the watch coming in from the shambas each morning and returning at dark."[5] There was no business at all. Black outs marked the nights which meant the large lanterns were not lit nor were ceremonies such as those pertaining to weddings allowed.

The British troops, including Nigerian, were posted along the seafront, in the fort, and at Shela. The European troops were considered unfriendly to the locals but the Hausa Muslims from Nigeria, and later troops from the Gold Coast, intermingled with the men who otherwise had little to do beyond keeping watch at their assigned times and places.[6] The Nigerians were remembered as being dressed in colorful uniforms, and for marching in formation to and from mosque on Fridays.[7]

Early in "1941 South African Air Force were stationed on the aerodrome at Mkowe . . . . but by March the Italians had been drive from Kismayu and Mogadishu . . . . and thus ended Lamu's uneventful share in the War."[8] Still, because of their strategic location, and because many of the wealthy WaAmu had shortwave radios, fears for their safety persisted long after the Italians ceased being a direct threat. This was especially true as the Japanese inched their way west into Burma. Elders remembered that the Indian community feared that British India might fall to the Japanese.

The Muslim population was also divided when the British briefly brought a group of Jewish refugees onto Lamu Island in the mid-1950s. Led by the sharifs, the conservative Hadrami community protested. The aristrocracy was generally supportive. In order to squash some of the growing controversy surrounding the Jews, the Imam of the Friday mosque preached a sermon in support of their presence on the island.[9]

In spite of dire predictions that as the war drug on the moribund economy would worsen, business picked up. Demand for *boriti* called for dhows, and the shipbuilding industry enjoyed a brief revival with three dhows launched at Lamu although building supplies were short. Clove production in Zanzibar increased which, in turn, led to the demand for more mat bags in Lamu.[10] But gunny sacks became increasingly popular and after the war, all but replaced the mat bags—thus further cutting into the brief spurt in Lamu's economy. The switch to gunny sacks was heavily felt by poor Lamu women, and it led to the further impoverishment of most local *madrassas.*

Dhow traffic from the Indian Ocean had declined appreciably during the depressed years of the 1930s and never fully recovered. The total numbers that sailed in from Persia, India, and Arabia ranged between 28 in 1935 and 50 through the 1950s. Lamu dhows shipped tons of *boriti* to Persia and Arabia in 1943-1945 before the traffic again fell off.

In 1957 during the war in the Middle East seventy five dhows sailed into Lamu's harbor, and most of these picked up *boriti.* Problems in the Middle East also aided local dhow owners. *Boriti* exports under Lamu control expanded, and shipments included the old staples of hides, skins, and ghee. But this tide of good fortune was merely an interlude for Lamu. By the late 1950s, trade was increasingly tied to the East African coast, and Lamu was dependent on imports of rice and maize, as had been the case during the 1940s.[11]

Inflation took its toll. The cost of living rose appreciably in the 1940s. Taxes went up. Labor shortages increased, and, the government was forced to raise salaries for those locals in its employ. For the first time, in 1943, "six Arab clerks have . . . been placed on the scale of salary [and] . . . given the same terms and conditions of service as the Asians who are not members of the Asian Civil Service."[12] Day wages increased to Shs. 1/50 because "labor becoming very difficult to get."[13] District commissioners worried that the locals were producing too many "cash crops at the expense of food. This should be watched." The Indians were "price gouging and the black marketing is rife."[14] They reported that the rains were good through most of the 1950s, sometimes cutting Lamu off from the mainland and contributing to what DCs noted was a lack of visitors. Nevertheless, crops were plentiful "and due to that odious practice of mortgaging harvests, excellent profits for Asian shopkeepers." Smith Mackenzie, still in business in these years, was the agent for tobacco, mostly from Pate and sold to Somalia.[15]

In the mid-1950s taxes rose again, up by about ten percent since the war. The tax hikes could only have contributed to general feeling of support for the influx of mostly Kikuyu who arrived in Lamu as prisoners, beginning in late 1951. At this time, too, the Bajuns were demanding that they be elevated to non-native status, although most lacked the resources to pay the taxes levied on natives.[16]

The Kikuyu were "extremely troublesome. They complain of the food, demanding fresh vegetables which are difficult to get in Lamu. On several occasions they have refused to work. . . . They need firm handling."[17] As The Emergency intensified upcountry, more Kikuyu were transported to Lamu. Some were based on Manda Island, but from late 1951 and until the situation was resolved in 1956, increasing numbers were placed in Lamu. Some were boarded in private homes taken over by the government and, of course, the fort was reserved for the "really bad criminal types serving long sentences. . . . [the] political types . . . and others are difficult, aggressive, and troublesome." Again more calls for firm handling. In 1955 Lamu prison had "approximately 100 detainees . . . Pangani, approximately 100 Mau Mau." At Manda Detention Camp "approximately 200 black Kikuyu, Embu, and Meru detainees while Takwa held 210 black Kikuyu and Meru with two or three Asians." By this time a firm hand must have been applied as many detainees were "doing road work, tele-communication building, agriculture tasks and general public works."

Many WaAmu remembered there was a general sense of sympathy for the African prisoners who were living in and working around town during the day. Some found ways of passing them bits of food or other treats. Friendships developed, too, between a few of the locals and the mostly Kikuyu prisoners which suggests that the firm hand was not always in place. No member of the permanent Lamu community was actively involved in The Emergency, but anti-British sentiment continued to dominate certain segments of the Afro-Arab community.[18] This was so, despite the fact that the district commissioner in 1952 commented that the arrival of "the Mau Mau dumped on the Isle of Peace . . . aroused the very conservative local inhabitants."[19] But political activity picked up momentum among the Afro-Arabs in Mombasa, including Lamu transplants, who were divided between the supporters of the The Emergency leadership, and the conservative forces who believed their problems with the British would be dissolved only when they were reattached to Zanzibar.[20]

The detainees under The Emergency were fortunate the fort did not fall down around them. H. J. Simpson reported that by 1959 "the ceilings . . . are unsafe and things have at last been brought to a head . . . we *must* have about 130 convicts in Lamu. There is any amount of work for them to do. And also we must have the fort repaired. We cannot just allow it to fall down."[21] Some repairs were made but the fort passed over to the Government of Kenya in stages of serious disrepair. That year saw "petty crime increasing. Two bad fires in Mkumani and the owners of the houses are convinced it was arson." In addition, the government suffered the loss of "a large sum of cash and stamps from the Lamu Post Office."[22]

Arson had, in 1957, been behind the burning of the "Methodist Church which was in mud and wattle with *makuti* roof." At the end of the decade, Illegals were "still coming in by dhow." Crime increased with repeated references to children "pilfering" as well as to "drunkeness."[23]

In 1957, the district commissioner still complained about smuggling and ivory poaching. In addition, the Bajun were illegally cutting *boriti* on which the government had established limits.[24] By now, they were flooding into Lamu from their respective small hamlets and economically depressed towns. Some joined families already established. Like the Hadrami who preceded them in the early throes of British colonialism, the Bajun took the lowest paying jobs. For the Bajun social status was set at birth and that could not be altered, but after they moved into Lamu, and as some prospered, their status altered within their own communities but they were peripheral to the old families.[25] The Bajun were still praised for their prowess in sailing the small *jahazis* and *mtepes*, and for their abilities as fishermen. While the fish they caught provided for their own needs and those of their community, many sold "much of their produce to an Indian-owned company operating out of Lamu."[26] When the Bajun moved into Lamu, a few found the means to purchase small fishing boats, but their income as sailors was limited to a percentage of sales, plus rental fees, to the boat owners.[27]

Pokomo Muslims, followed by Pokomo Christians started arriving on their own initiative in the post-World War II era. Almost none of the latter-day migrants had skills or education. They, too, were forced into low paying jobs, competing with the Bajun and the longtime indigenous poor Comoro Islanders, with long term ties to Lamu.[28] But because competition for the limited employment was stiff, many men left their women and went elsewhere. By 1956 the Comoro population was composed of "37 men; 105 women; and 69 children."[29] A few set up shop as tailors, joining the other Comoro men behind their sewing machines. Again, social barriers crumbled when, in the 1950s, with an increasing shortage of Afro-Arab males, a few Comoro men with promise also married into the old families. Most, however, married into the ex-slave community as did the Bajun, and a few Muslim Pokomo.[30]

In 1956, the district commissioner listed 147 Kore in Lamu district.[31] By then, they too, had joined other newcomers as immigrants. The Kore trace their descent from the Maasai and their traditions are similar. According to their traditions, the Kore were taken from their Maasai homeland by the Somali, among whom they lived as slaves until they were freed by the British. During the twentieth century they gradually drifted from northern Kenya to Mokowe, across the channel from Lamu island.

Some of Hadrami had become shamba owners, and hired the Kore as shepherds for their flocks of livestock. Nearly simultaneous with the new demand for shamba labor, a severe epizootic wiped out Kore cattle on the mainland. The Kore, like the Maasai, are a livestock based culture whose cattle were described by one man as "are our lives, our children." Thus many Kore welcomed the opportunity to fill the void by those who had moved up or out. The early arrivals confined themselves to small shacks on the shambas in the center of the island and, although they were Muslims, generally remained apart from the town dwellers.

Some, however, allowed their children to attend *madrassa,* but only a few sent their children to secular schools. They did not affiliate with the Riyadha sharifs and tended to marry among themselves or into the Lamu ex-slave community.[32] Two examples of Kore intermarriage within the ex-slave community are found in the Appendix. In each instance, the women involved practiced serial marriages. One woman was celebrated for having married a total of sixty men which, if true, meant that she married and then shed something on the order of two a year.[33]

Lamu *waungwana* who were forced out of Lamu in the last three decades of the colonial era went to Zanzibar, and like Mohammed Jahadhmy, found professional and clerical work there. Some young men of high standing at home found work on small sailing ships, and of course, dhows. Ali bin Mohammed BuSaid, the oldest son of the hunter, became an electrician on merchant marine vessels, sailing around the world many times before returning to Lamu to open his business as an electrician.[34] Others were not so fortunate. Some young men from the most aristocratic families found themselves "working the Mombasa docks side by side with former slaves, and the children of our slaves." The Lamu community in Mombasa grew in striking proportions from the early 1950s. "We knew each other and things were different in Mombasa. Much freer. We associated with those whose families had been our slaves. But when we got back to Lamu, we knew the difference."[35]

With the outflow of Lamu men, the old patterns of leadership within families, and within the individual *mtaa* changed, or broke down entirely. Sharif Abdalla Salim, as the oldest member of his al Hussein clan, was head of the family in Lamu which, he said, by the 1950s amounted to a few men and some women.[36] Down in Mombasa, Sharif Abdalla Salim had been elected as Arab representative to the Legislative Council in 1931. He and others complained about the treatment accorded the community there. But, the Lamu community was not politicized in the 1930s, nor in the years leading up to independence: "the old unhurried routine remained mostly undisturbed."[37]

Eventually, several political parties developed in Mombasa, leading Abdalla Kadara to found the Lamu branch of the Kenya African Union (later merged to become Kenya African National Union KANU), but the majority favored federation of the ten mile coastal strip with Zanzibar. Most of the people in Lamu looked beyond the pier into the vast open stretches of the Indian Ocean, reluctant if restrained, to turn towards "Africa." Some of the WaAmu who lived in Mombasa joined the Coast Peoples Party (CPP), as did the few WaAmu who bothered to engage in political activity at all. But Sharif Abdalla focused his sites on an independant Kenya which included the coastal strip as well and this put him in opposition to the goals of the CPP.

Sharif Abdalla was less conservative than his contemporaries in Lamu although like them, he engaged in several marriages. His generation was the one that marked the shift from polygamy to secret and serial marriages because of their decrease in fortunes. In his case, Sharif Abdalla's first wife, a Mazrui, remained with him for fifty one years until death severed their bond. In the 1940s, and after having divorced several other wives, Sharif Abdalla married a Christian woman after a lengthy contretemps with her minister who opposed her liaison with a Muslim.[38] But that marriage also ended in divorce. Sharif Abdalla remained an apologist for polygyny, which had marked his generation of patricians. Islam, he said, "allows for a man's appetite, while Christian men took women in adultery or without marriage. One does not want to eat the same dish every day. . . ." No doubt speaking from long years of experience, he wryly noted that sometimes "men have to pay bribes to the old wives when they are discovered having a new one—to quiet the old . . . ."[39]

A Swahili historian who knew the old Sharif praised him as a politician who "had since his election, shown a marked determination to inject a dose of militancy into the community. . . . [his] zest for political wrangling gave the Arabs someone . . . fitted to enter the political mood of the time.[40] In those years he traveled to "Nairobi meeting with other officials: Europeans, Asians, and Africans" and twice journeyed to London where he met Queen Elizabeth II. Back in Lamu, however, he refrained from "political discussions with the *waungwana* but kicked up a fuss about those sharifs and education up there."[41]

As the colonial period drew to a close lamentations of district commissioners or officials who were posted in Lamu over the twentieth century continued to mock. J. S. Lockhart recorded in 1952 that the "Arabs, with their customary dignity and charm of manner, predominate life in Lamu town itself. They live as landed proprietors, traders, and on charity from friends . . . . their not-to-work, not-to-worry outlook of Inshallah . . . counteracts any exhortations to activity or progress in any civilization."[42]

The first local elections were held in 1961 with gender segregated polling booths. H. J. Simpson recorded in his diary that the liwali requested he give a talk about responsible voting in 1961, but he anticipated "no problems in Lamu. . . ." Two years later, with all hope of being reunited with Zanzibar gone, the combined WaAmu community turned to face "Africa" when they again went to the polls to elect the government that would lead them to independence.[43] In behavior that was reminiscent of earlier events that had altered their social, political, and economic institutions, they reacted too late.

Simpson maintained the paternal demeanor that characterized the long years of British rule: "We must make sure that in politics, and in everything else, there is no bitterness. . . . If people disagree, let them disagree without bitterness, without intimidation . . . ." He recognized what many knew all along: "some people don't want . . . government at all."

Over the centuries, Lamu was accustomed to accepting an influx of people from the sea, as well as Africans from the mainland across the bay. What bound the old families and new Arabs together, even though they quarreled over doctrinal matters, was their tie to Islam. Those who were called Swahili intermarried with Omani, prospered, and established an oligarchy. The Sultans of Zanzibar sent liwalis who, in turn, married into the *waungwana*. New arrivals came from the sea, disrupting the social order that the Omanis themselves had disturbed. The long resident Asian community kept their shops, their separate lives, and mostly co-existed peacefully as well as profitably. Then, came the British bulldog to hound them into restructuring their economy, their social order, and to exercise control over their indigenous political institutions. Still they had their respective belief in Islam to which they clung. This became the bedrock of their lives—no matter the disagreements among them. Comoro Islanders came in by the sea and, some departed that way due to further quarrels, these with a religious base. In the twentieth century, major changes swept in with the modern world encroaching through secular education and improved public health. The plantation economy was never replaced, but the WaAmu were nothing if not enterprising in finding ways to circumvent the loathsome taxes and managing to maintain a semblance of their culture, with slave and master alike conspiring. Those who stayed on did so based on belief that religious law superseded secular ordinances issued by Christians. Men of the old families turned from concubines to the serial marriages that have characterized the west. In process, they took descendants of slaves, Bajun, and even westerners as their marriage part-

225

ners, although the latter usually as converts to Islam. The Hadrami grew wealthy, and formed their own kin networks among whom they married, although they, too, developed the pattern of divorce in preference to polygyny.

Wars between local communities were replaced by major conflicts featuring the European powers, beginning with German Witu in the nineteenth century, and moving to the clash with Germany in World War I. The final major brush with war was spawned by Germany, but effected Lamu only briefly and then was relegated to Italian Somalia. The large sailing dhows that swept gracefully into and out of Lamu harbor over the centuries were mostly replaced by motor driven ships. Still the Persians, the Indians, and Arabs sent the occasional dhow, or motor driven boom to trade—tying the WaAmu with that romantic link to their past. Small *jahazis* that centuries ago sailed up to the Red Sea and down to Kilwa ply the water still. But the WaAmu sailors have mostly been replaced by the Bajun. The once majestic culture and reputation of Pate as the premier port city on the northern coast had been superseded by that of Lamu in the nineteenth century. Lamu, in turn, gave way to Mombasa in the twentieth. Lamu men, pride diminished, started anew in places as wide ranging as Arabia and America. After the revolution in Zanzibar, those of Omani descent reestablished ties to the home of their ancestors. Those WaAmu who left for Mombasa have returned to visit. Some were able to come home permanently.

After the Bajun sailed in, the Pokomo followed, including increasing numbers of Christians who settled into abandoned old ruins and went to work for the newest immigrants: the small but growing community of Europeans who bought and restored Lamu homes. A few Giriama traveled north to Lamu. If those who argue that the Pokomo, and Mijikenda were among the original Africans who sailed across the bay into Lamu's harbor centuries ago to trade are correct, then these recent arrivals have brought the past full circle into the present.[44] The Kore also arrived from the mainland, and took the places of the Hadramis, as the Hadramis had replaced the slaves on the island shambas. They were followed by a different, and sometimes pervasive invader: the tourist. Although the cast of characters has changed considerably, Lamu town, fortunes on the wane or the rise, remains a port city with all the vicissitudes and strengths that have marked her since her rise to dominance on the northern Kenya coast.

In Lamu, plus ça change, plus ç'est la même chose.[45]

APPENDIX

An example of a genealogy kept by Lamu Afro-Arab families.
From the author's personal collection

Hamed bin Said and
Mwana Shee WaShee Wa Pate al Hussein

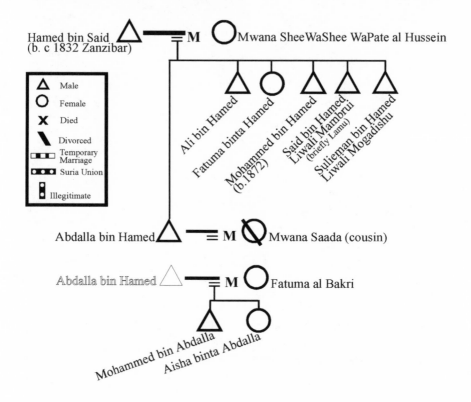

Hamed bin Said
(b. c 1832 Zanzibar)

Mwana SheeWaShee WaPate al Hussein

Legend:
- △ Male
- ○ Female
- ✗ Died
- ╱ Divorced
- ▬▬▬ Temporary Marriage
- ●▬●▬● Suria Union
- ▮ Illegitimate

Ali bin Hamed

Fatuma binta Hamed

Mohammed bin Hamed (b.1872)

Said bin Hamed, Liwali Mambrui (briefly Lamu)

Sulieman bin Hamed, Liwali Mogadishu

Abdalla bin Hamed ═ M ─ Mwana Saada (cousin)

Abdalla bin Hamed ═ M ─ Fatuma al Bakri

Mohammed bin Abdalla

Aisha binta Abdalla

228

Hamed bin Said (cont'd)

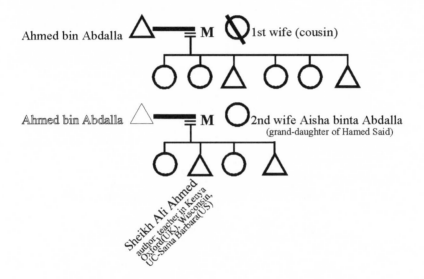

Ahmed bin Abdalla ... = M ... 1st wife (cousin)

Ahmed bin Abdalla ... = M ... 2nd wife Aisha binta Abdalla
(grand-daughter of Hamed Said)

Sheikh Ali Ahmed
author, teacher in Kenya,
Oxford(UK), Wisconsin,
UC-Santa Barbara(US))

Hamed bin Said (cont'd)

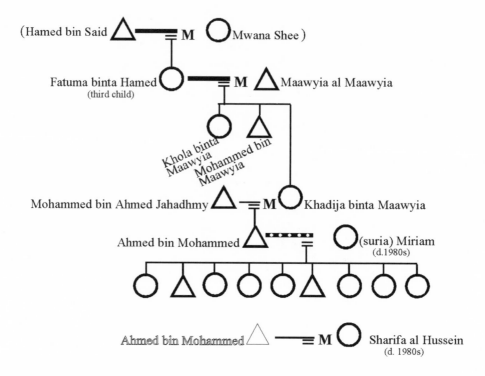

(Hamed bin Said △━━≡M ◯ Mwana Shee)

Fatuma binta Hamed ◯━━≡M △ Maawyia al Maawyia
(third child)

Khola binta Maawyia
Mohammed bin Maawyia

Mohammed bin Ahmed Jahadhmy △━≡M ◯ Khadija binta Maawyia

Ahmed bin Mohammed △━━━≡ ◯ (suria) Miriam
(d.1980s)

◯ △ ◯ ◯ ◯ △ ◯ ◯ ◯

Ahmed bin Mohammed △ ━━ ≡M ◯ Sharifa al Hussein
(d. 1980s)

Hamed bin Said (cont'd)

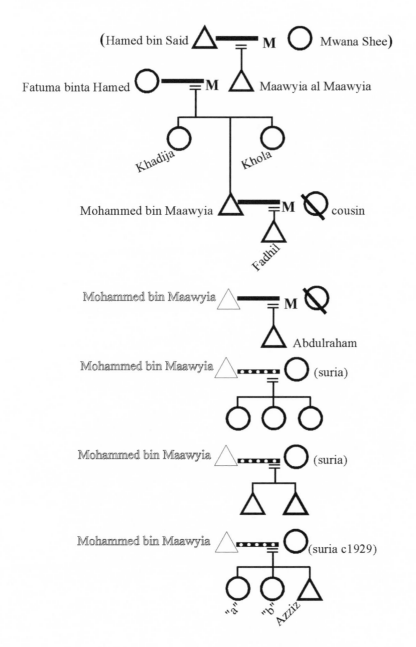

Hamed bin Said (cont'd)

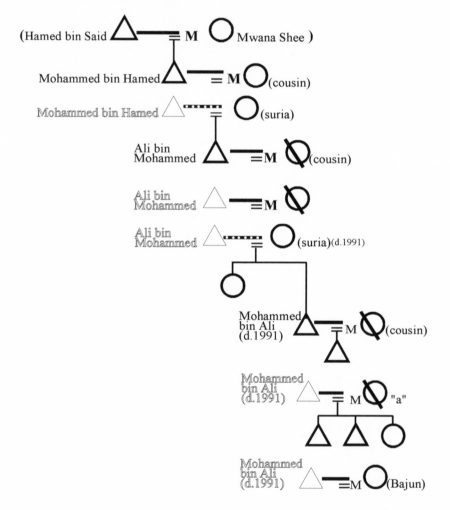

(Hamed bin Said △——= M ◯ Mwana Shee)

Mohammed bin Hamed △——= M ◯ (cousin)

Mohammed bin Hamed △····= ◯ (suria)

Ali bin Mohammed △——=M ⌀ (cousin)

Ali bin Mohammed △——=M ⌀

Ali bin Mohammed △····= ◯ (suria)(d.1991)

Mohammed bin Ali (d.1991) △——=M ⌀ (cousin)

Mohammed bin Ali (d.1991) △——= M⌀ "a"

Mohammed bin Ali (d.1991) △——=M ◯ (Bajun)

Hamed bin Said (cont'd)

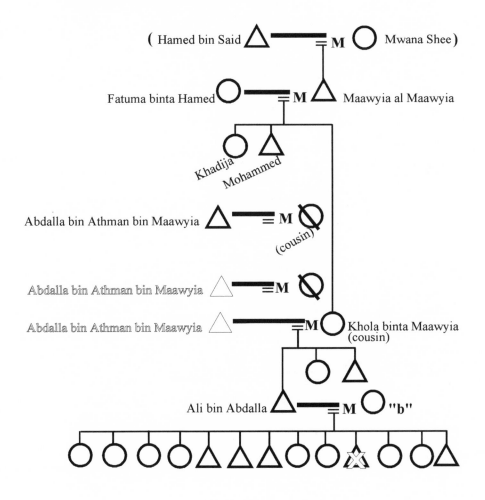

233

Habib Saleh Jamal al Layl

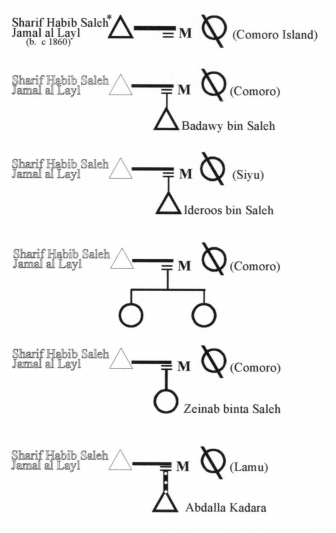

Sharif Habib Saleh* Jamal al Layl (b. c 1860) △ — ≡ M ○ (Comoro Island)

Sharif Habib Saleh Jamal al Layl △ — ≡ M ○ (Comoro)
△ Badawy bin Saleh

Sharif Habib Saleh Jamal al Layl △ — ≡ M ○ (Siyu)
△ Ideroos bin Saleh

Sharif Habib Saleh Jamal al Layl △ — ≡ M ○ (Comoro)
○ ○

Sharif Habib Saleh Jamal al Layl △ — ≡ M ○ (Comoro)
○ Zeinab binta Saleh

Sharif Habib Saleh Jamal al Layl △ — ≡ M ○ (Lamu)
△ Abdalla Kadara

* only the women by whom Habib Saleh acknowledged children (or, in the case of one, disputed parentage) are included.

Habib Saleh (cont'd)

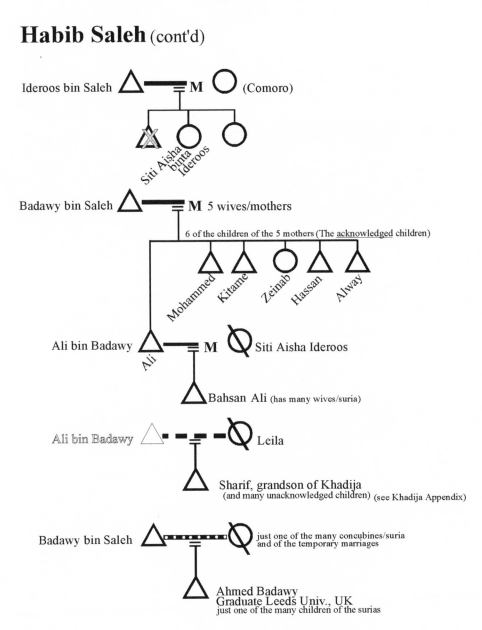

Ideroos bin Saleh △━━━M ○ (Comoro)

Siti Aisha binta Ideroos

Badawy bin Saleh △━━━M 5 wives/mothers

6 of the children of the 5 mothers (The acknowledged children)

Mohammed Kitame Zeinab Hassan Alway

Ali bin Badawy △━━M ⊘ Siti Aisha Ideroos

Ali

△ Bahsan Ali (has many wives/suria)

Ali bin Badawy △- - -⊘ Leila

△ Sharif, grandson of Khadija
(and many unacknowledged children) (see Khadija Appendix)

Badawy bin Saleh △·········⊘ just one of the many concubines/suria
and of the temporary marriages

△ Ahmed Badawy
Graduate Leeds Univ., UK
just one of the many children of the surias

235

Khadija (cont'd)

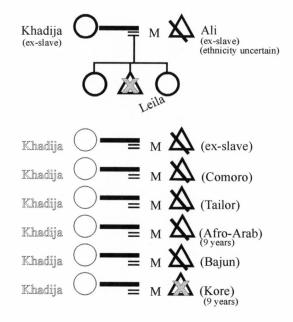

Khadija (cont'd)

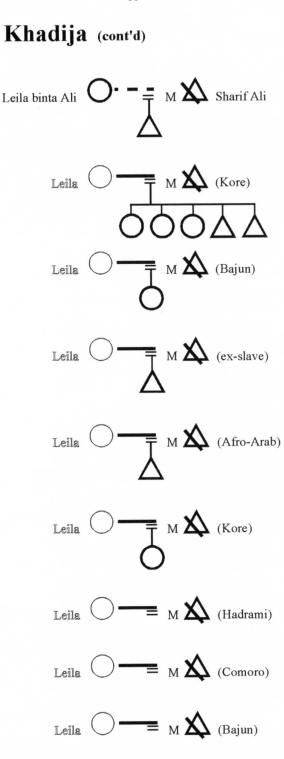

Goolamhussein

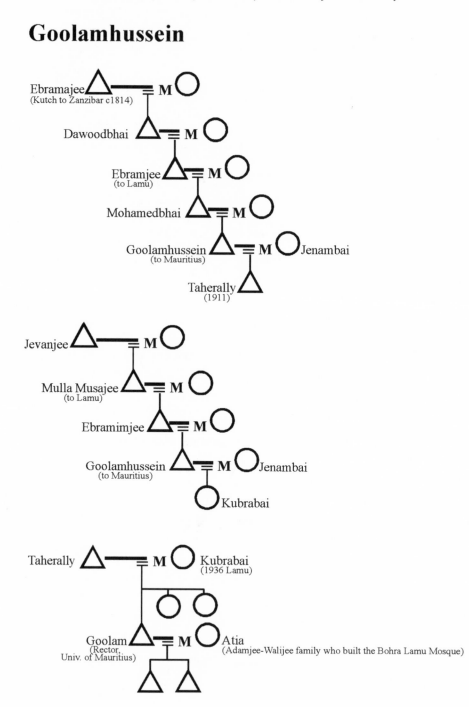

Notes

Introduction

1. Even in the present time, local Afro-Arabs and many others refer to the mainland as "Africa." Nevertheless, this position lends credence to the arguments advanced by Pat Caplan and Françoise Le Guennec-Coppens in *Les Swahili entre Afrique et Arabie,* (Paris, 1991).
2. M. Tolmacheva attempted to address how the name came into play. See M. Tolmacheva, "The Origin of the name 'Swahili'" *Tanzania Notes and Records* 77 & 78 (1976) 27-38. See chapter one.
3. DC LAM/2/3 Political Record Book, Kenya National Archives (KNA).
4. Alamin M. Mazrui and Ibrahim Noor Shariff, *The Swahili: Idiom and Identity of an African People* (Trenton, 1994), 18-19. See also Marina Tolmacheva, "Essays in Swahili Geographical Thought" in Rose-Marie Beck, Thomas Geider, Werner Graebner (eds)., *Swahili Forum* II, 1995, 1-40.
5. Carol Eastman, "Who are the WaSwahili" *Africa* 41 (1971) 228-36. Personal communication, January, 1991. W. Arens, "Changing Patterns of Ethnic Identify and Prestige in East Africa," W. Arens (ed)., *A Century of Change in East Africa* (The Hague, 1976) 65-75. Among the many articles and books discussing this topic, these few are the most pertinent or recent: John Middleton, *The World of the Swahili: An African Maritime Civilization* (New Haven, 1992), 1-26; James DeVere Allen, *Swahili Origins: Swahili Culture and the Shungwaya Phenomenon* (London, 1993), 1-19; Derek Nurse and Thomas J. Hinnebusch, *Swahili and Sabaki: A Linguistic History* (Berkeley, 1993); Marina Tolmacheva, "Sur la cote swahelie aux frontieres naturelles et culturelles et de la civilisation" (ed)., Sylvie Devers, *Pour Jean Lalaurie* (Paris, 1990), 435-47. Jan Knappert, "Conversion in Swahili Literature" Nehemiah Levtzion (ed)., *Conversion to Islam* (New York, 1976), 81. See also Wilfred Whitley, *Swahili: The Rise of a National Language* (London, 1969); A. J. H. Prins, *Sailing from Lamu: A Study of Maritime Culture in Islamic East Africa* (Assen, 1965) 31-36. A. I. Salim, "The Elusive Mswahili: Some Reflections on his Culture and Identity" Arens, *A Century of Change* (215-27); and Gill Shepherd, "The Earliest Swahili: A Perspective on the Importance of the Comoro Islands in the South-West Indian Ocean before the Rise of Kilwa" (261-81) J. Maw and D. Parkin (eds)., *Swahili Language and Society* (Vienna, 1985). A. I. Salim (ed)., *State Formation in Eastern Africa* (New York, 1985); Thomas Spear, *Traditions and Their Interpretation: The Mijikenda of Kenya* (Athens, 1982). Derek Nurse and Thomas Spear, *The Swahili: Reconstructing the History and Language of an African Society 800-1500* (Philadelphia, 1985), viii. And, although his argument mostly concerns the Shungwaya tradition, and is related to his attempts to reverse some of Spear's findings on the Mijikenda, Willis does discuss ethnic identity, which he believes was not a product of colonialism. See Justin Willis, *Mombasa, the Swahili, and the Making of the Mijikenda* (Oxford, 1993) 12-13 *et passim.*

6. Mark Chatwin Horton, "The Early Settlement of the Northern Kenya Coast" Ph.D. thesis, University of Cambridge, 1984. Mark Horton, "The Swahili Corridor and the Southern African Iron Age," paper presented at University of London, School of Oriental and African Studies, November, 1986. Horton also refers to Ptolemy's *Geography* in terms of references to the Lamu archipelago. G. W. B. Huntingford (ed and trans)., *The Periplus of the Erythraean Sea* (London, 1980), 7. Dr. Karl Peters, *The Eldorado of the Ancients* (London, 1902) suggests that in the *Periplus* the "land of Sarapionas" were actually Lamu and Witu, 316. See also J. S. Trimingham, "The Arab Geographers and the East African Coast" in H. Neville Chittick and Robert I. Rotberg (eds)., *East African and the Orient* (New York, 1975), 115.

7. Mark Horton, "Early Muslim Trading Settlements on the Eastern African Coast: New Evidence from Shanga" *Antiquaries Journal* 68 (1986) 299.

8. Nurse and Spear, *The Swahili* 40-51. For one example of local women carrying on liaisons with outside traders elsewhere in Africa, see George Brooks, "The *Signares* of Saint-Louis and Goree': Women Entrepreneurs in Eighteenth Century Senegal" in Nancy J. Hafkin and Edna G. Bay (eds)., *Women in Africa* (Stanford, 1976), 19-44.

9. G. S. P. Freeman-Grenville, *The Medieval History of the Coast of Tanganyika* (Berlin, 1962), 27. Edward Rodwell claims that in the early nineteenth century forty percent of the Swahili vocabulary was Arabic; and that Bantu input dominated the language after the heavy inflow of slaves from central Africa. Personal communication, 1994.

10. Horton, "The Swahili Corridor"; Thomas Wilson quoted in *The Standard* November 1985. Wilson personal communications, 1985-90. Neville Chittick, "East African Trade with the Orient" in D. S. Richards (ed)., *Papers on Islamic History II Islam and the Trade of Asia* (Oxford, 1970), 98-100. J. E. G. Sutton, "The East African Coast: An Historical and Archaeological Review" (Nairobi, 1966), 8-9. See also T. M. Ricks, "Persian Gulf Seafaring and East Africa: Ninth to Twelfth Centuries" *International Journal of African Historical Studies* 3 (1970) 339-57. For seafarers along the Comoro Islands with whom Lamu was engaged in trade, see T. H. Wright, "Early Seafarers of the Comoro Islands" *Azania* 19 (1984) 13-60. Malyn Newitt, "The Comoro Islands in Indian Ocean Trade Before the 19th Century" *Cahiers d'Etudes africaines* XXXIII (1983) 139-65. A good case for early Indian trade with East Africa is presented by Kenneth McPherson, "Processes of Cultural Interchange in the Indian Ocean Region: An Historical Perspective" *The Great Circle* 6 (1979) 78-92 and Reda M. Bhacker, *Trade and Empire in Muscat and Zanzibar: Roots of British Domination*, (London, 1992) 5-7. Although historians have suggested that the Chinese may well have sailed to the East African coast, few believe that they carried out active trade over time. Louise Levathes believes that not only did the Chinese trade with the Swahili coast, but they also contributed to the gene pool of the Bajun. See Louise Levathes, *When China Ruled the Seas: The Treasure Fleet of the Dragon Throne, 1405-1433* (New York, 1994).

11. Mark Horton and C. M. Clark, "Zanzibar Archaeological Survey 1984-5" Ministry of Information, Culture and Sports, Zanzibar, 1985. Horton private communication, 1987. A pre-Islamic phenomenon found on these East African coastal areas is the pillar tomb. According to James Kirkman, the pillar tombs are "evidence of African elements" in what he otherwise thought was "Arab" culture on the coast. See James Kirkman, *The Arab City of Gedi: Excavations at the Great Mosque, Architecture and Finds* (London, 1954), 4. For specific reference to pillar tombs—but nothing per-

taining to the two in Lamu—see Thomas H. Wilson, "Takwa: an ancient Swahili settlement on the Lamu Archipelago" pamphlet, n. d. See also James DeVere Allen and Thomas H. Wilson, *Swahili Houses and Tombs of the Coast of Kenya* (London, 1979), 33-34 for Wilson's finds on a Lamu tomb, which he dates as fifteenth century and says it was used as a place of pilgrimage and worship. This tomb, however, may have been the product of synchronization between African traditional religion and Islam, owing to its' late date.

12. Bhacker, 5-7.
13. Abdalla A Skanda, interview, Lamu, 1980.
14. See Peter Hinks, *The Folklore of Jewellery*, forthcoming.
15. On nearly Takwa Island, Thomas Wilson described a pot used for cooking *mofa*, which are small loaves of bread containing dates. The *mofa* type breads are said to have been brought from the Hadramaut. Wilson dates settlement at Takwa between three hundred and five hundred years ago. Thomas H. Wilson, "Takwa: an ancient Swahili settlement of the Lamu Archipelago" pamphlet (Nairobi, n.d.), 10.
16. See F. Constantin, "Social Stratification on the Swahili Coast: From Race to Class" *Africa* 59 (1989) 145-61. For some of the problems associated with family history, see Kelly William Bate, "Family History: Some Answers, Many Questions" *Oral History Review* 16 (1988) 127-30.

Chapter 1

1. While it is important to keep in mind the lack of chronology and "severe limitations" of oral traditions, it is also necessary to give voice to the collective memory of the WaAmu as pertains to their history, even if contemporaries are no longer aware of who was speaking. See Jan Vansina, *Oral Tradition as History* (Madison, 1985). 185 and *passim;* Jan Vansina, *Living with Africa* (Madison, 1994), 41-46. See also Thomas Spear, "Oral Traditions: Whose History?" *History in Africa* 8 (1981) 163-79; David Henige, *Oral Historiography,* (London, 1982); Daniel F. McCall, *Africa in Time Perspective: A Discussion of Historical Reconstruction from Unwritten Sources,* (New York, 1969); Joseph E. Miller (ed)., *The African Past Speaks.* (Hamden, CT, 1980); J. E. G. Sutton, "The Settlement of East Africa" in B. A. Ogot and J. A. Kieran (eds)., *Zamani: A Survey of East African History,* (Nairobi, 1968) 69-99.
2. Report of Arthur Hardinge on Progress in the East African Protectorate to 1897. Col. 8683 1879.8 Parliamentary Papers (PP).
3. Mark Horton to author, July, 1987. Horton's flow of articles on the northern Swahili coast are mostly unrelated to Lamu town. Nevertheless, it has been necessary to turn to his findings elsewhere in order to create a hypothesis relating to early developments in Lamu. See Mark Chatwin Horton, "The Early Settlement." See also Paul J. J. Sinclair, "Archaeology in Eastern Africa: An overview of Current Chronological Issues" *Journal of African History* 32 (1991) 185.
4. "A Chronicle of Lamu" [Khabari Lamu by Shaibu Farazi bin Hamed al-Bakariy al-Lamu] collected by Abdallah bin Hamed, Wali of Lamu, 1897, and translated by William Hichens (ed)., *Bantu Studies* 12 (1938) 8-33. Marina Tolmacheva (ed)., *The Pate Chronicle* (East Lansing, 1993). Tolmacheva has brought together the various versions of the "Pate Chronicle" and has written a long introduction in which she discusses their source (1-35). See also Randall L. Pouwels, "Reflections on

Historiography and Pre-Nineteenth Century History from the Pate Chronicles" *History in Africa* 20 (1993) 263-96.

5. DC/LAM3/2 Kenya National Archives (KNA). John Horace Clive, "Short History of Lamu" DO 1933 Mss. Afr s. 1273 Rhodes House Library.

6. Clive, "Short History." In addition Clive speculated that the town might have been deserted when its wells went dry, or because of an epidemic.

7. Lmu/8 Political Record Book KNA.

8. Clive, " A Short History." See also Ahmed Mohammed Al-Jahadhmy, *Tarikhi ya Amu* (Muscat, 1991).

9. Lmu/8 Political Record Book KNA. Clive, "A Short History" has a somewhat similar version.

10. "Chronicle of Lamu" 9. See Marina Tolmacheva, " 'They Came from Damascus in Syria': A Note on Traditional Lamu Historiography" *International Journal of African Historical Studies* 12 (1979) 259-69.

11. Randall L. Pouwels, "Tenth Century Settlement of the East African Coast: The Case for Qarmation/Ismaili Connections" *Azania* XI (1974) 65-74. See also Randall L. Pouwels, *Horn and Crescent: Cultural Change and Traditional Islam on the East African Coast 800-1900*, (Cambridge, 1987). Jean-Claude Penrad argues that the Ismailis did not convert to Islam until the twelfth through fourteenth centuries. Thus, if the Qarmations were settlers in Lamu in the tenth century, it is unlikely that they were Muslim. See Jean-Claude Penrad, "La Pre'sence Isma'ilienne en Africque de l'est" in Denys Lombard et Jean Aubdin (eds.), *Marchands et hommes d'affaires asiatiques dans l'Oce'an Indien et la Mer de Chine 13e-20e siecles* (Paris, 1988), 222.

12. Abdul Nassir bin Abdalla Skanda, interview, Lamu, 1994. The old families have insisted that some of their progenitors maintained continuing residence in Lamu for over seven hundred years, as the land claims will illustrate (chapter 10). Clive, "Short History" refers to documentation in the Friday Mosque which supports this claim. Oral traditions that confirm Abdul Nassir and others herein come from interviews with Sheikh Ahmed Jahadhmy, January 1980 through June, 1994; Ali Abdalla al Maawyia, April, 1980; A. A. Skanda, January 1980 through 1991; Sharif Abdalla Salim al Hussein, Mombasa, 1980; Various Afro-Arab women from March, 1980-June 1994.

13. Clive, "A Short History" and oral traditions from Lamu women. It is possible that the bones Frederick Jackson referred to were those that remained from this conflict, although more likely they were remains of those slaughtered in the Battle of Shela. See Frederick Jackson, *Early Days in East Africa,* (London, 1930), 7.

14. In the Lamu Chronicle the Weyuni were forced to wash the bodies of the dead, showing how oral traditions change over time. There are still Yumbili in Lamu. In 1985, while I was living in a Lamu stone house, an al Hussein sharifa who lived across the narrow street died. Her nephew summoned my houseboy, a Yumbili, who carried out all of the traditional preparations for her body. These included obtaining a long wash tub that is kept for this purpose and then washing her body. He did not perform any of the other functions necessary for preparation as these were left to women. The houseboy and another Yumbili I came to know in Lamu both agreed that they can still be called on to wash bodies when someone of importance among the old families has died. They, and their families believe they were the "original" people on Lamu island before the Asian arrivals came in—but no one would hazard a guess as to when that might have been. Viewing the Yumbili as a caste of body washers may have origi-

nated with the Hindu. Among them, the Dom were an undertaker caste who were a lowly subclan of the Untouchables.

15. My informants for this tradition were two Afro-Arab women who claim to be descendants of the earliest settlers from the Indian Ocean littoral but they believe their ancestor came from Yemen, not Damascus. Almost all of the women with whom I interacted in Lamu were quick to respond with stories of the past, some calling them legends, others referring to them as history.

16. A. A. Skanda, interview, 1980. Lamu women, 1980.

17. Ebramzee Gullumhussein, interview, Mombasa, 1980.

18. Ali Abdalla al Maawyia, interview, Lamu, 1989. A. A. Skanda, interview.

19. J. H. Stigand, *The Land of Zinj,* (London, 1913), 11-12. Three gold coins from Kilwa that surfaced in Zanzibar were minted there in the early fourteenth century. One coin, dated at between 1320-38 carries in Arabic the reference to a sultan, an "ah-Mahdali" and, according to Helen Brown, this is the first time the terms sultan was actually mentioned in the fourteenth century East African coast. Although Kilwa was an active port city in the fourteenth century, the coins from there lend credence to Lamu also having a sultan at that period in her history. See Helen Brown, "Three Kilwa Coins" *Azania* XXVI (1991) 1-4.

20. G. S. P. Freeman-Grenville, "Lamu" in C. E. Bosworth, Evan Donzel, B. Lewis, and Charles Pellat (eds)., *The Encyclopedia of Islam,* (Leiden, 1983) 655. Freeman-Grenville also mentioned the "celebrated pilot Ahmed B. Madjid" who visited Lamu island in the fifteenth century. Freeman-Grenville believed that the stone houses which emerged at a later period of time in Lamu were influenced by southern Arabian architectural styles.

21. "Vasco Da Gama's Discovery of East Africa for Portugal 1498" in G. S. P. Freeman-Grenville (ed)., *The East African Coast* (Oxford, 1962), 54. See also Patricia W. Romero, "Lamu Women, Art, and Material Culture" paper presented at the African Studies Association meeting, Atlanta 1989.

22. Great Britain Admiralty, I.D. 1189 *A Manual of Portugal in East Africa,* (London, 1920). Kirkman named a Gedi ruin "the House of the Venetian Bead" speculating that either the Portuguese or Turks brought these beads to the East African coast. Horton's thesis of early Red Sea trade suggests another trade route. H. Neville Chittick, partial untitled manuscript, Lamu Museum, refers to the inhabitants of Manda as "wearers of gold" in as early as the twelfth century but most likely by the fifteenth. M. D. D. Newitt "East Africa and Indian Ocean Trade" 1500-1800" in Ashin Das Gupta and M. N. Pearson (eds)., *India and the Indian Ocean 1500-1800* (Calcutta, 1987), 201-23. See also Albert H. Hourani, *The Ottoman Background of the Modern Middle East*, (London, 1970). Hourani refers to the spread of Turkish influence from 1516-17 and that provided not only trading opportunities, but also cultural exchange. Arab sailors, drawing on Indian and other sources, wrote descriptions of the East African coastal areas they visited in the fifteenth century. Lamu is both mentioned as a place they traded but also noted on a map illustrating ports to which the Arabs traveled. See H. Grosset-Grange, "La Cote Africaine dan Routiers Nautiques Arabes au Moment des Grand De'couvertes" in *Routiers Nautiques* XXX (1971) 9, 17. The Red Sea Trade with Europe brought Venetian beads down, while sending spices out. See Frederic C. Lane, *Venice: A Maritime Republic*, (Baltimore, 1973) 291-92. For Oman and early contacts with the Indian Ocean world see K. N. Chaudhuri, *Trade and Civilization in the Indian Ocean: An Economic History from*

the Rise of Islam to 1750, (Cambridge, 1985). See also Bhacker, *Trade and Empire.*

23. James de Vere Allen and Thomas H. Wilson, *Swahili Houses and Tombs of the Coast of Kenya,* (London, 1979) 34, 41.

24. Newitt, "East Africa" 211-12; Sutton, "The East African Coast" says the Galla were a problem to northern towns in the late sixteenth century (21). See also Thomas Spear, *Kenya's Past: An Introduction to Historical Method in Africa,* (Longman, 1981) 105-6.

25. C. R. Boxer (ed)., *Further Selections from the Tragic History of the Sea 1559-1565* for the Hakluyt Society, (Cambridge, 1968) n.3, 49. See also C. R. Boxer and Carlos de Azevedo, *Fort Jesus and the Portuguese in Mombasa,* (London, 1960). For an out-dated but still useful summary of the Portuguese period see R. Coupland, *East Africa and its Invaders,* (Oxford, 1938) 41-72.

26. "Anonymous: The Rebellion of Mombasa in 1631" in G. S. P. Freeman-Grenville, *East African Coast*, 179, 181-82. At this time the "Arab" and Indian residents may not have intermarried as heavily into the local "Swahili" community. See Bhaker, *Trade and Empire,* 68.

27. The chapel was probably built at Shela, which may have taken its name from the Portuguese "chela." See G.S.P. Freeman-Grenville (ed and trans)., *The Mombasa Rising Against the Portuguese 1631 From Sworn Evidence*, (London, 1980) xxxiii n.3.

28. Antonio Nunes, *Luiro dos Pesos da Ymdia e assy Medidas e Mohedas escripto em 1554* (Lisbon, 1868) 44-45. Freeman-Grenville, "Mombasa 1634" 179. Justus Strandes, *The Portuguese Period in East Africa* (trans. Nairobi, 1961) 66. British Admiralty I.D. 1189 from an earlier oral tradition that stated "Lamu submitted with-out resistance. . . ." At about this time Strandes reported that Indians were smuggling trade items into these Portuguese possessions, of which Lamu was one, therefore the Portuguese cannot have maintained too close a watch over this port city (100).

29. C. R. Boxer, *Race Relations in the Portuguese Colonial Empire 1415-1825* (Oxford, 1963) 41-84

30. Clive, "A Short History."

31. See Stigand, *Land of Zinj*, 51-52; Boxer and Azevedo, *Ft Jesus* 30-31. Joao dos Santos, *Ethiopia Oriental* (Lisboa, 1609). Portions of this document are in the Ft. Jesus library and have been translated. Marguerite Ylvisaker, "The Ivory Trade in the Lamu Area 1600-1870" *Paiduma* 28 (1982) 221-32. See Pouwels, *Horn and Crescent*, especially 28-50.

32. Freeman-Grenville, *Mombasa Rising*, xxiii-xxxiiv. It is even possible that the Turks left a permanent mark on Pate island in the form of the name "Faza." Feza, a Turkish name meaning flight in the sky may have been corrupted to Faza, and later further corrupted to Paza.

33. A. A. Skanda, interview, 1980.

34. Strandes, *The Portuguese Period*, 129-9; 138; 184. Clive, "A Short History" also car-ries a garbled account of the Portuguese in Lamu, based in part on oral traditions. If it is true that the Portuguese installed the wife of the Lamu "king" on his place, and considering mistreatment of Christians on the part of the WaAmu, possibly placing a woman in nominal control was a way of reacting against Islam in this instance. The hatred of the Christians for the Muslims was virulent. On the other hand, history also records a queen ruler in both Kitau (on Manda Island) and in Pate. See Bwana Kitini, "The History of Pate" in Freeman-Grenville, *East African Coast*, 251; and Stigand,

Land of Zinj, 61. See also Hourani, *The Ottoman Background,* 6-7. See also Aziz Esmail "Towards a History of Islam in East Africa" *Kenya Historical Review* 3 (1975) 147-58.

35. Bhacker, *Trade and Empire*, 32. Sheikh Ahmed Jahadhmy claimed that the Omanis were in Lamu during the period of Portuguese occupation, interview, 1980.

36. Randall Pouwels, however, discusses the rising literacy in East Africa during the seventeenth century. See Randall Pouwels, "Swahili Literature and History in the Post-Structuralist Era" *International Journal of African Historical Studies* 25 (1992) 261-83.

37. Robert Ross (ed)., "The Dutch on the Swahili Coast 1776-1778: Two Slaving Journals; Part I" *International Journal of African Historical Studies* 19 (1986) 305-60; and Part II l9 (1986) 479-506. Although he has virtually nothing to say about the Dutch in this part of East Africa, Jonathan I. Israel's *Dutch Primacy in World Trade 1585-1740* (New York, 1989) covers the African hegemony that the Dutch established during this time.

38. C. Halls, "Dutch Navigation of the East African Coast" *Tanganyika Notes and Records* 67 (1967) 46-7. The brig "Richmond" sailing out of Essex made several stops on Lamu island, as did other American trading vessels at this time. "Log of the Brig Richmond-1764" courtesy of the Essex Institute. For later trade between the Americans and East Africa, see Norman R. Bennett and George E. Brooks (ed)., *New England Merchants in Africa: A History Through Documents 1802-1865*, (Boston, 1965). For French activity see G. S. P. Freeman-Grenville, *The French at Kilwa* (Oxford, 1965), 8-10. See also Bhacker, *Trade and Empire* 37-38.

39. "A Chronicle of Lamu" 13. Yet elsewhere in the Chronicle, references are to the "men of Lamu" until Bwana Zaidi emerges once again as "chief." (see 13-18, 21). Sheikh Ahmed Jahadhmy, Mzee Mohammed Ali BuSaid, and other elders with whom I spoke in 1980 believed Lamu was governed by a council of elders even during the period of Portuguese occupation. These men, however, are descendants of the Omanis who began to come in, in some number from the late 1770s. The Chronicle refers to the Yumbe (13) where the chief presided. See James De V. Allen, *Lamu Town: A Guide* (Mombasa, n.d.) 3. Allen refers to a "republican government" and a gerontocracy—a state council ruled by old men, but adds that one or two might bear the title of Sheikh (read: sultan, chief, king). A. J. H. Prins believed that Lamu was divided into family factions who lived in neighborhoods that dictated who was ascendent at any given time. Since his major informant was also Sheikh Ahmed Jahadhmy, and because Sheikh Ahmed's small book on the history of Lamu discusses these neighborhood family leaders, I believe Prins came to his conclusion based on discussions with Jahadhmy. I also believe this form of government emerged after the Portuguese period in Lamu. See A. J. H. Prins, *Didemic Lamu: Social Stratification and Spatial Structure in a Muslim Maritime Town*, (Groningen, 1971) *et passim.* See also Jahadhmy, *Tarikhi* 16.

40. McKim believes the early coastal dwellings were round mud huts much like those of the traditional Pokomo dwellings. See Wayne McKim "House Types in Tanzania: A Century of Change" *Journal of Cultural Geography* 6 (1985) 51-78. Abdul Nassir Skanda and his father, joined by Ali Abdalla al Maawyia, all testified to the fact that Lamu was surrounded by a town wall. The Skandas found sections of the wall under their woodcarving shed at the very southern end of town back in the 1980s. Horton, too, discovered a few coins in the area suggesting that older dwellings may be under

the sand.
41. Robert Ross, "The Dutch" Part I 311, 317-21.
42. Charis Waddy, *Women in Muslim History* (London, 1980) 11, 42. For Ibn Battuta, see Marina Tolmacheva, "Ibn Battuta on Women's Travel in the Dar al-Islam" in Bonnie Frederick and Susan H. McLeod (eds)., *Women and the Journey: the Female Travel Experience*, (Pullman, 1993) 119-40.
43. See K. N. Chaudhuri, *Asia Before Europe*, 204-05. Chaudhuri's synthesis of architecture and space in Muslim homes led him to believe that women were not confined to a special quarter of the house but were kept out of areas where men did business.
44. "Chronicle of Lamu" 19-21.
45. See Bhacker, *Trade and Empire* 43 for Pate's overtures to Britain.

Chapter 2

1. S. Farish, Department Secretary, Bombay 31 December 1810, 586 India Office Library and Records (IOL). The British may have been exploring the Lamu archipelago as a result of fears of French hegemony there. In 1801 the Governor General of India received a letter from "Abubukr Sultan of Patta in Africa" asking for protection from the French. Wellesley Papers V. 551 pp. 1-17. (IOL). In the nineteenth century rupees circulated along with Maria Theresa thalers, although the rupee did not become the official currency in British East Africa until 1921.
2. Ibrahim Pirkor, 21 September 1810, 586 IOL. Smee, *Ternahi* [garbled name of ship] log, 586 IOL. Lt. Hardy, *Sylph*, ship's log, 586 IOL.
3. Stigand, *The Land of Zinj*, 81-94, collected numbers of oral traditions which purport to sketch in the years preceding the 1812-13 Battle of Shela. A major problem with Stigend's account is lack of knowledge as to his sources, not to mention the exact quotes produced from various players, including the Sultan of Oman and Zanzibar. Dates, too, are somewhat unclear. For the Sultan's visit see LAM/3 Political Record Book KNA. Bhacker, *Trade and Empire* (93) provides a list of dates for the Sultan's visits to East Africa, and has none listed between 1802 and 1828. If these dates are accurate, the DC report is not.
4. See Risso, *Muscat*; See also Freeman-Grenville, *East African Coast*, n.1., 22. M. Guillain, *Documents sur 'Histoire de l'Afrique Orientale* I (Paris, 1856) I:533-38.
5. Sigand, *Land of Zinj*, 81, incorrectly lists the date as 1233 A.H. or about 1806 A.D. Stigand seems not to have drawn on Lamu sources for his account. He claims that some Lamu people did not support the candidacy of Fumo Luti wa Bayaye while the Pate people did not want him "because of his Lamu birth." According to Stigand, the "people of Lamu poisoned" Fumo Luti wa Bayaye. This account differs from "The Lamu Chronicle" and from oral traditions of Lamu informants Sheikh Ahmed Jahadhmy and Abdalla Skanda (whose family were originally from Siu). See Marina A. Tolmacheva, "Group Identity in Swahili Chronicles," paper presented at the African Studies Association, November 1991. And, Tolmacheva, (ed)., *The Pate Chronicle*. See also Randall L. Pouwels, "The Battle of Shela: The Climax of an Era and a Point of Departure in the Modern History of the Kenya Coast," unpublished paper in the possession of the author. Pouwels leans heavily on Stigand and on the Pate Chronicle for his analysis. See also Alice Werner, "A Swahili History of Pate," *Journal of the Royal Asiatic Society* 14 (1915) 280-99.

6. See Bhacker, *Trade and Empire*, 82-83; Stigand, *Land of Zinj*, 66-68.

7. "Chronicle of Lamu" 20-21; oral traditions from Ali Abdalla al Maawyia; Sheikh Ahmed Jahadhmy.

8. The "Pate Chronicle" carries another and incomplete version of these events. The author was not privy to activities within the Lamu camp. And, as always, the "histories" of these conflicts reflect the camp in which the writer belonged. For Lamu oral traditions I relied on Ali Abdalla al Maawyia, a relative of Bwana Zaidi and Sheikh Ahmed Jahadhmy, another relative and unofficial but knowledgeable historian of Lamu. Sheikh al Amin bin Ali Al-Mazrui, *The History of the Mazrui Dynasty of Mombasa* (J. M. Ritchie trans and ed). (Oxford, 1995).

9. Some families estimate that Bwani Zaidi's ancestors had come to Lamu in the fourteenth century but there are no records to bear out these assertions, nor are there any that trace the claim of residency back to the seventeenth century. Everyone agrees that the al Maawyia family of Bwana Zaidi, however, was already well established and prominent when the Omanis began to come in, in the nineteenth century.

10. Bhacker, *Trade and Empire* (71) discusses this family and notes that they helped the Sultan in his "wars with Mombasa . . . ." But again there is conflict between the sources. Kheikh Mohammed Abdulla Kanshui, Liwali of Lamu in 1959, wrote that the Said was actually in Zanzibar in 1811 when "12 elders from Lamu" went there "to ask his help." LAM/3 Political Record Book, KNA.

11. For the *mtepe* see A. H. J. Prins, "The *Mtepe* of Lamu, Mombasa and the Zanzibar Sea" in *Paiduma* 28 (1982) 89. See also Neville Chittick, "Sewn Boat in the Western Indian Ocean, and a Survival in Somalia" *International Journal of Nautical Archaeology* 9:1980:287-309; *Kenya Trade and Supplies Bulletin* IX: 3 (1959) 9; Eva Wiesauer, "Dekortechiken und Ornamate an Holzobjekton der Ost-Afrikanischen Kuste. Ein beitrag zum Kunsthandwerk der Suaheli under Berucksichtigung ethnohistorischer Quellen" Ph.D. thesis, Universitat Wien, 1975. Copy in Lamu Museum. Richard F. Burton, *Zanzibar City Island and Coast* I. (London, 1872) 74. Stigand, *Land of Zinz*, 142. A. H. J. Prins, "Uncertainties in Coastal Cultural History: The 'Ngalawa' and the 'Mtepe'" *Tanganyika Notes and Records* 53 (1956) 207-212.

12. See "Chronicle of Lamu" 25, in which references are to made to preparations to "ward off disgrace from our sisters and children without being beguiled by what happened long ago."

13. Ali Abdalla al Maawyia, interview Lamu, 1990. Ali Abdalla, who is descended from Bwana Zaidi, and his family currently occupy the home. He showed me a secret passage leading to a tunnel between several family homes. Bwana Zaidi built the tunnel in order for his family to escape, should the need arise, during the war between Pate, Mombasa, and Lamu. This story was supported by Ali Abdalla's wife, a first cousin on their father's side, and also a descendant of Bwana Zaidi. Fadhil Mohammed, another cousin of Ali Abdalla, independently told me the tradition concerning Bwana Zaidi and his threat to burn himself and his family if they lost the war. Lamu interview, 1989. According to family tradition, Bwana Zaidi had no sons, but several daughters were born to him. By the turn of the twentieth century, several grandsons, however, were living in Lamu (including one in his house), and one granddaughter, Hadija Mohammed Tofiki, was the wife of Suud Hamed's clerk. Lmu/8 Political Record Book KNA.

14. For a detailed study of the terrain around Lamu Island, and that of Pate, see A. J. H. Prins, "The Little World of Lamu" pamphlet, 1965, copy in Lamu Museum.

15. "Chronicle of Lamu" 27-29. British sources taken from later informants said that Said sent five hundred soldiers, rifles and a few cannon. And they claimed that it was at this time that Lamu became under the domination of Zanzibar. "The first ruler after the Nabhan-Mazrui War was Mohammed Nasser El-Busaidy who was succeeded by Ahmed Mafteh el-Hinawy [of Zanzibar]." Lmu/8 Political Record Book KNA. Others, however, disagree and claim that Lamu had repeatedly accepted Omani appointed liwalis before 1812.

16. It is possible that in addition to losing the war, Pate's harbor was silting up, which would also have contributed to her decline due to the difficulty for ocean going dhows to sail close to the port. Thomas Wilson, personal communication, 1983.

17. For excellent background studies on Oman in this period see Patricia Risso, *Oman and Muscat: An Early Modern History* (New York, 1986) and the early chapters of Robert Geran Landen, *Oman Since 1856: Disruptive Modernization in a Traditional Arab Society* (Princeton, 1967). Also, for the rise of Islam in establishing hegemony in trade see Patricia Risso, "Muslim Identity in Maritime Trade: General Observations and Some Evidence from the 18th Century Persian Gulf/Indian Ocean Region" *International Journal of Middle Eastern Studies* 21 (1989) 381-92. For a pro-British interpretation pertaining to Oman and the rise of the BuSaid dynasty see Coupland, *East Africa and Its Invaders*. For British interests in Oman and by extension Zanzibar and the Sultan's East African possessions, see Bhacker, *Trade and Empire*.

18. See J. B. Kelly *Britain and the Persian Gulf 1795-1880* (Oxford, 1968), 412-13. Kelly reminds that slavery "became entrenched in the social structure of Islam . . . .[with] Abyssinia and East Africa [feeding] the markets to Arabia." Oman rose to prominence in East Africa with the conquest of Zanzibar and Pemba after defeat of the Portuguese. It was after this that the slave trade picked up momentum. Oman experienced intermittent problems with Mombasa but they are beyond the scope this study. See Risso, *Muscat*, 130; and Sutton, *East Africa*, 25-26.

19. Edward A. Alpers, *Ivory and Slaves:Changing Patterns of International Trade in East Central Africa in the Later Nineteenth Century* (Berkeley, 1975). See also Sutton, *East Africa* 27.

20. Coupland, *Invaders*, 215.

21. Bhacker, *Trade and Empire* 94-95. Bhacker lists numbers of Omani clans who were either in East Africa or came over during the nineteenth century. None, interestingly, were the al Bakri (or al Bakari) leading to the possibility that this family may have arrived in Lamu during the conflicts in the wake of the death of the Prophet Mohammed (see chapter one and oral traditions).

22. C. S. Nicholls, *Swahili Coast* 255. Guillain, *Documents* II, 238.

23. Kiki Dastoor, interview, Lamu, October 1985. Some informants alleged that Ali Abdalla Skanda, a fair complexioned old man who died in the mid-1980s, was of Baluchi origin. His family originally came from Siyu but family legend claims they hailed from Alexandria in Egypt, and hence Skanda from Alexandria. In Egypt and in Ethiopia, Askunder is a common name given to boys, and that is translate into Alexander. Abdalla Ali Skanda, interview, Lamu, 1981.

24. Kiki Dastoor, interview, Lamu, 1989. At Fort Jesus in Mombasa, Baluchi soldiers, their wives, and slaves all slept within the Fort. It is possible that in Lamu, the Baluchi, who had no wives in residence, may have brought slave women or even free but poor Lamu women into the Fort, raising the ire of the town fathers and calling for

their removal. See "Extracts from the Diary of Richard Thornton" 48. Fort Jesus Library, Mombasa.

25. DC/Lam3/2 Lmu/Political Record Book V5 KNA.

26. Leisl Graz, *The Omanis:Sentinels of the Gulf* (London, 1982) 121-23. See also Edward A. Alpers, "'Ordinary Household Chores': Ritual and Power in a 19th Century Swahili Women's Spirit Possession Cult" *International Journal of African Historical Studies* 17:4 (1984) 680. Alpers limits his interpretation to Zanzibar and suggests that women were increasingly subordinated to men during the 1870s and on. Changes in Zanzibar soon became the norm in Lamu, which borrowed heavily on custom and material culture, especially after the arrival of Sultan Said in 1840. In this context—and others—Lamu was a second port city to the major entrepot of Zanzibar.

27. Carol Eastman, "Women, Slaves and Foreigners: African Cultural Influences and Group Processes in the Formation of Northern Swahili Coastal Society" *International Journal of African Historical Studies* 23:1 (1988) 1-20. Not every example Eastman provides holds for Lamu but her overall thesis seems insightful. Eastman quotes a Swahili proverb that she places in gender context: "a slave talks; a freeman acts." Indeed, women do engage in considerable talk and they remember the "stories" from the past (oral traditions); but women also wrote poetry in Arabic script—and some of these women were descendants of slave women.

28. Patricia W. Romero, "Does being 'sexy' keep a marriage going in Lamu (Kenya)," paper presented at the African Studies Association, November, 1991.

29. Suad Joseph, "Brother/Sister Relationships: Enrichment in the Reproduction of Arab Patriarchy," Paper presented at seminar on Gender and the Middle East, Johns Hopkins University, November, 1991.

30. References to poets and poetry as "Swahili" are made in the cultural context.

31. See Patricia W. Romero (ed)., Emily Ruete's *Memoir of an Arabian Princess* (trans and reprint New York, 1989). Born Salme Said in Zanzibar in about 1840, Ruete was taught to read and write Arabic script by a private tutor. As early as 1778, a Dutch shipper visiting Zanzibar commented on "public schools" there where Arabic was among the subjects taught. Robert Ross (ed)., "Dutch on the Swahili Coast" Pt. I., 483. Along with a number of women, some slaves were taught to read and write and served as scribes to their upperclass masters.

32. "Utendi wa Mwana Kupona" in Ali A. Jahadhmy (ed)., *Anthology of Swahili Poetry* (London, 1975) 29-41. Ann Biersteker reads irony into Mwana Kupona's advice, suggesting that in part, the poetess is actually making fun of men. While it is true that poetry written by Swahili women often contains elements of hidden humor and irony, this poem represents much of the advice women of the aristocracy actually passed on their daughters from the early twentieth century on. See Ann Biersteker, "Language, Poetry, Power: A Reconsideration of '*Utendi wa Mwana Kupona*'" in Kenneth W. Harrow (ed)., *Faces of Islam in African Literature* (New York, 1991), 68-71. Mwana Kupona married Sheikh Mataka at Siyu. Her daughter, to whom the poem was written, was Nana Shee wa Bwana Mataka. Nana Shee married a Lamu man, Abdalla Komo and bore a daughter, Siti wa Binti Shee. Siti married an el Hussein sharif from the Comoro Islands and gave birth to a son, Mohammed bin Ahmed el Hussein. His son, Ahmed bin Mohammed Badawy el Hussein was still living in Mombasa in 1991. (Private communication from Sheikh Ahmed Jahadhmy, Muscat, 1991).

33. In the 1880s Lamu women were unveiled. See John Haggard's letters to his mother and sisters, January-July, 1884. Stigand refers to Lamu women as going under the

tentlike cover at the turn of the century. But, Pamela Scott, a white woman born and raised in Kenya, remembers visiting Lamu in the late 1920s, and women then went unveiled. Yet in the 1930s they were using the *shiraa*.

34. Kirk to Haggard, 13 December 1883. Zanzibar National Archives.

35. Mrs. Charles E. B. Russell (ed)., *General Rigby, Zanzibar and the Slave Trade with Journals, Dispatches, Etc* (London, 1935) 332. The British were equally unfavorably impressed with Arab men in Zanzibar and in Lamu. Missionary Charles New called them the most "useless being upon the coast of Africa. . . ." See Charles New, *Life Wanderings and Labours in East Africa* (London, 1874) 59-60.

36. H. Greffulhe, "Voyage de Lamoo a Zanzibar," *Bulletin de la Societe' de Geographie et d'Etudes Coloniale de Marseilles* II (1878) 212. Lt. Jack Haggard, British Consul in Lamu in 1884, moved into the stone house previous occupied by M. Greffulhe. Lt. John G. Haggard Mss. British Empire 465 (4) 13 December 1883 Rhodes House, Oxford.

37. Lyndon Harries, *Swahili Poetry*, (Oxford, 1962), 54, 57.

38. Shabaan Robert, "Utenzi Wa Hati" in Ali A. Jahadhmy, *Anthology*, 21.

39. Frederick Jackson, *Early Days* 22.

40. Sayyid Abdallah, *Al-Inkishafi* translated and edited by Sayyid Abdallah A. Nasir (Nairobi, 1972), 28-29.

41. Mrs. Charles E. B. Russell (ed)., *General Rigby,* 332. Bhacker, *Trade and Empire* 192-3.

42. For comparisons with Muscat and elsewhere in the Indian Ocean world, see Colvin H. Allen Jr., "The Indian Merchant Community of Masqat" *School of Oriental and African Studies Bulletin* 44 (1981) 39-53; R. D. Bathurst, "Maritime Trade and Imamate Government" in Derek Hopwood (ed)., *The Arabian Peninsula, Society and Politics* (London, 1972); Edward A. Alpers, "Moqdisho in the 19th Century: A Regional Perspective" *International Journal of African Historical Studies* 24 (1983) 442; Frederick Cooper, *Plantation Slavery on the East Coast of Africa* (New Haven, 1977) 32. For a lovely composite description of the Arab city see Albert Hourani, *A History of the Arab Peoples* (Cambridge, 1991); and K. N. Chadhouri, *Trade and Civilization* 100-09.

43. John G. Haggard to father, October 13, 1884, 87/1.

44. For an older but still valuable account of the spice trade in the Indian Ocean, see Auguste Toussaint (translated by June Guicharnaud), *History of the Indian Ocean* (Chicago, 1966) 178-80.

45. C. R. Rigby to Secretary of State for India April 6, 1860, L/P and S/9/38 IOL.

46. Bennett and Brooks (eds)., *New England Merchant Traders* 434. Even in the early years of the Civil War, Americans conducted a rather heavy trade with East Africa mostly through Zanzibar. Captain Playfair reported back to Britain for the years 1862- to July 1863 the Americans imported 27,179 (Pounds Sterling) worth of goods; but by mid-1863 and through 1864, their imports were reduced to only 9,552 (Pounds Sterling). "Year End Report" 17 April 1865 L/PAS/9/42 IOL. For opium, see Stigand, *Land of Zinj*, 155. For an increase in East African coastal trade, see Beverly Brown and Walter T. Brown, "East AFrican Trade Towns: A Shared Growth" in Arens (ed)., *A Century of Growth*, 183.

47. "Lamoo: Report of Ships and Merchandise by the American Consul at Zanzibar" L488 National Archives. The American consul does mention hides and ivory as leaving Zanzibar earlier which indicates that trade items from coastal East Africa were

being transshipped from there. Annual Report, Lamu, 1873-74 2915 Box 105 Institute of Commonwealth Studies. The Somalis were actually in residence at Shela at this time and fears of warfare were mentioned in the annual report. Ill will has existed between the Somalis and the local Lamu people over time. During some parts of the nineteenth century, Somalis were not allowed to enter Lamu at all.

48. Ahmed Hamard Al-Maamiry, *Oman and East Africa* (New Dehli, 1979) says the *siwa* originated in Summaria or Assyria. Appendix II, 141. Hamo Sasoon, *The Siwas of Lamu* (Nairobi, 1975). C. A. Petley, an agriculturalist and later Lamu hotelier, recorded the local and often repeated oral tradition claiming the ivory siwa, which originally came from Pate, was made by a sharif of the Jamal al Layl family "seven hundred years ago" in Pate. See C. A. Petley, "The Lamu Siwa" manuscript in Lamu Museum.

49. Elmawhali in this case almost certainly refers to the al Maawyia family who owned considerable property. Written by his slave by order of Nasir bin Sulieman bin Nasir bin Saif Elmawhali, 1860. DC/LAM/3/2 LMU/Political Record Book V5 KNA.

50. This document was written "by order of Muhidin bin Shaik." DC/LAM/3/2 LMU/Political Record Book V5 KNA

51. This is not to say that Horton is incorrect in suggesting the old stonehouses he found in Shanga were architecturally influenced by Red Sea contacts—and especially in terms of the building materials. What I do propose, however, is that the "modern" two and three story Swahili houses found in Lamu were architecturally influenced by styles in Gujarat. For long time trade between India and East Africa see Edward A. Alpers, "Gujarat and the Trade of East Africa 1500-1800" *International Journal of African Historical Studies* IX:1 (1976) 22-44. See Patricia W. Romero, "Possible Sources for the Origin of Gold as an Economic and Social Vehicle for Women in Lamu (Kenya)" *Africa* 57:3 (1987) 363-76. The design of the arches, for instance, are India influenced. See also Romero, "Art and Material Culture." Interviews in Mombasa included Kesharji Ratlansey Dhutia, October 13, 1975; Husseinali A. Hussein, October, 1975. Husseinali's grandfather came to Zanzibar from Cutch in 1860. His wife's grandfather grew up in Lamu, where his Bohra family settled years before—in the mid-nineteenth century. Both men believed that architecture in the Old Town of Mombasa was Gujararti influenced as well. See Linda Wiley Donley, "The Social Uses of Swahili Space and Objects" Ph.D. thesis Cambridge, 1984.

52. Usam Ghaidan, *Lamu: A Study of the Swahili Town* (Nairobi, 1975) 83. James Kirkman, *Men and Monuments on the East African Coast* (London, 1964). See Romero, "Possible Sources for the Origin of Gold" 369. Building construction in Zanzibar was very similar to Lamu suggesting similar influences from the Indian Ocean and Persian Gulf. See also Ulrich Malisius, *The Stone Town of Zanzibar* (Zanzibar, 1985).

53. Ghaidan, *Lamu* 35, doubts the existence of a wall around Lamu town. But Ali Abdalla al Maawyia, Sheikh Ahmed Jahadhmy, and Mohammed BuSaid all remembered seeing remnants of the wall in their boyhood. It was supposed to have marked off the town proper from the north and the south, with the gate near what is today's Langoni.

54. See Albert Hourani, *A History* 123. It was traditional in the Arab world for cemeteries to be located outside the walls of cities

55. This manner of building would account for problems with stairs that Ghaidan mentions. See Usam Ghaidan, *Lamu: A Study in Conservation* (Nairobi, 1976), 55.

Traditions supplied by Lamu women. The Indian community in Muscat, confined as it was to a small area, practiced the same sort of expansion. According to Gray ". . . houses are three and four storeys high . . .while elsewhere in Muscat houses were never more than two storeys." See Leisl Graz, *The Omanis*, 117. In Zanzibar, houses were "designed for an extended family" as well. See Malisium, *The Stone Town*, 57.

56. William Webb to the Secretary of State, Zanzibar, May 11, 1861 National Archives. Webb noted that every year "about 20,000 African slaves were exported from Kilwa [with] many going to Lamu." Of this number the majority would have gone to work in the shambas on the mainland; nevertheless, some would have gone straight into domestic service. Others, on the mainland, would have been brought into domestic service, with their places taken by the new arrivals. "Every year" in this case is at least between 1860 and 1865, when Webb sends the same summary of the slave trade to Washington. Spatial concerns in African houses have only recently come under scrutiny.

57. Ali Abdalla al Maawyia, interview, 1989; 1990. Ali Abdalla and his family live in the house on plot 488 which was originally that of Bwana Zaidi. A daughter of Mohammed al Maawyia lives in his house. Another son in another of the six houses. Daughters of Mohammed al Maawyia, interviews 1980-1991. One daughter showed me all the houses and where the bridges used to be across the roadway. All informants described each of these houses as being added to, bit by bit, as the family increased and required more space. In the late 1980s a daughter of Ali Abdalla and her husband added a third story apartment to Bwana Zaidi's house—keeping with the tradition of "going up." See Ghaidan, *A Study in Conservation*, 56.

58. Lamu women, 1980-1991. For Zanzibar see Emily Ruete, *Memoir*, 20.

59. Jackson, *Early Days*, 17.

60. John Haggard to his father, September 29, 1884 86/1 Rhodes House. Haggard again referred to the Maltese cross in another letter to his brother, Will (September 27, 1884, 85/1) He bought two of these Lamu chairs that had the Maltese cross inlaid in them, and sent them to his novelist brother, Rider.

61. Haggard to Will 85/1.

62. Jan Vansina, *Art in History: An Introduction to Method* (London, 1984) 196. Usam Ghaidan, *Lamu*, 133-35. Romero, "Material Culture."

63. Emily Ruete, *Memoir* 20. Ghaidan, *Lamu*, 56. Recently, and to illustrate change in fashions in home decorating styles, pictures of the patriarch of the family, or in some cases pictures of the entire family, are found on display in the niches.

64. Eva Wiesauer, "Reshnitzte Eingangstore an der Ostafrikanischen Kuste" in *Ethnohistorische Blatter* 12 (1976) copy in Lamu Museum. Wiesauer believed the influences were Arabian, Persian and Indian. She found the same types of carved doors running from Mogadishu to Delagoa Bay. See also Hourani, *The Arabs*, 126-27.

65. J. J. Adie, "Zanzibar 'Arab' Chests," *Guide to Zanzibar* (London, 1912), 117-120. The chests were said to have been designed in Surat and Bombay; and in Zanzibar, they were believed to be of Lamu design.

66. For Oman, see Landen, *Oman Since*, 32-33. For Lamu, interviews with Abdalla Skanda, Sheikh Ahmed Jahadhmy, Mohammed BuSaid. Mohammed BuSaid's male ancestors came to Lamu as Liwalis in mid-nineteenth century. The Jahadhmy family claims residence in Lamu before Sultan Said moved his capital to Zanzibar, or before about 1840.

Chapter 3

1. C. S. Nicholls, *The Swahili Coast* 71, 378. Graz, *The Omanis* ll0. Of the Omanis who settled in East Africa, many returned after the 1964 revolution in Zanzibar. They were recognized by clan leaders, given land by the government, and some moved into important positions because of their advanced education. Many of these Omani "returnees" were descendants of the nineteenth century settlers who intermarried with local woman of African ancestry.

2. David Cohen has written about how "marriages articulate the working networks of social activity rather than the residual categories of corporate identity." David Cohen, "Reconstructing a Conflict in Bunafu" in Joseph C. Miller (ed)., *The African Past Speaks* (Hamden CN, 1980) 209. There are conflicting views on classification of marriage on the Swahili Coast. See Peter J. Leinhardt (ed)., *The Medicine Man* (London, 1969) 28-37 for Tanganyika. See also Francoise Le Guennec-Coppens, *Femmes Voilees de Lamu (Kenya):Variations Culturelles et Dynamiques Sociales* (Paris, 1983). Coppens (and others) dwells on the high level of social stratification in Lamu. As the following chapters will disclose, Lamu society is much more flexible than previous researchers (myself included) had noted.

3. Norman R. Bennett, "Americans in Zanzibar" *Tanganyika Notes and Records* 56 (1961) 103. N. Isaac Traves *Adventures in Eastern Africa* (London, 1836) remarked on Lamu as a "free port" in the 1830s but "few have visited it except the enterprising Americans whose star spangled banner may be seen streaming in the wind where other nations, not excepting even my own country, would not deign to traffic."

4. C. F. Beckingham, Personal communication, October, 1991. See Landen, *Oman Since* 43. Jadeusz Lewicki, "The Ibadhites in Arabia and Africa" *Journal of World History* XIII (1971) 3-81.

5. D. F. Eickelman, "Religious Tradition, Economic Domination and Political Legitimacy" *Revue de L'Occident Muslim* 29 (1980) 17-30.

6. J. S. Trimingham, *Islam in East Africa* (Oxford, 1964) 81.

7. Mwalimu Harith Saleh, interview, February, 1982. Sheikh Ahmed Jahadhmy, interview, 1982. Jahadhmy also noted that the Sultan appointed qadis in Zanzibar who were Sunni; and a Sunni qadi in Mombasa. See Pouwels, *Horn and Crescent* 63-96 for details pertaining to religious matters on the northern Kenya coast. See also B. G. Martin, "Notes on Some Members of the Learned Classes of Zanzibar and East Africa in the Nineteenth Century" *African Historical Studies* IV:3 (1971) 525-545. Martin's expertise is especially informative on the Hadramis. Although Knappert's interpretation of conversion does not appear to hold in the case of the Ibhadi in Lamu, see Jan Knappert, "The Theme of Conversion" 177-88. Amiji, *Asiatic Bias* (71) notes that incorporating one group into another is an African custom. In this the Omanis incorporated the religious persuasion; and the Africans the "idea" of being Arab. Esmail, "Towards a History of Islam" 47-58. Aziz Esmail makes a cogent argument for self image as a factor in conversion. See Bernard Lewis, *Race and Slavery in the Middle East* (New York, 1990) and *Race and Color in Islam* (New York, 1971) for Arab attitudes towards black Africans. While color may have dictated superiority in the Arab world, in coastal East Africa the Arabs cohabited with African women, thus color was no longer a sign of stigma; and even the blackest of coastal people often refer to themselves as "Arab" because of ancestry traced back through the father.

8. Extracts from Diary of Richard Thornton, 99 Fort Jesus, Mombasa. Interview Sheikh

Ahmed Jahadhmy, l980. Jahadhmy's mother, an al Maawyia, was born in Mecca in the late 1880s.

9. Mwalimu Harith Saleh, interview, 1990.
10. Lamu Political Record Book 78, l860 KNA. For an excellent summary of the different persuasions of Islam on the coast, see J. N. D. Anderson, "Appendix B" *Islamic Law in Africa* (London, l970) 322; see also l07-l0.
11. C. S. Nicholls, *The Swahili Coast* 271. The son of Khamis ibn Othman also went to school in England. This must be the first WaAmu man trained abroad and says something about the quality of education available through tutors, including that of English. The documents that are on record in the Kenya National Archives for this period are all written in English translation by slaves in Zanzibar.
12. Captaine de Vaisseau Guillain, mss and notes, O. I. 523; O.I. 10.43 "Missions 1839-1854". Guillain, "Muscate et Zanzibar 1838-41 A. O. I. 6; Guillain, "Possessions britanniques 1820-1893" A.O. I. 34, National Archives l'Ancien Ministiere d'Outre Mer, Paris. These conflicts between Lamu and Pate were the last armed battles that they fought.
13. Ahmed Khatib, interview, January 1990, l991. There are other examples of dropping clan names that will come later. As to the negative reasons for dropping a clan name, the venerated Habib Saleh, a Sharif who plays a dominant role in nineteenth century Lamu, was said to have divorced a pregnant wife because he did not believe the child she carried was his. This man, now dead, was never allowed to use the surname nor the clan name of Jamal al-Layl—although paternity was always questionable and many believed Abdalla Kadara was the son of Habib Saleh [see chapter four]. Another example of name dropping concerned that of Bwana Zaidi, the leader in the Battle of Shela. The "Chronicle of Lamu" refers to him as Bwana Zaidi Mnguumi. Mngumi was added to indicate Zaidi's intelligence and cleverness. (Mohammed Jahadhmy, 1990).
14. J. M. Grey, "Zanzibar and the Coast 1840-1884" in Roland Oliver and Gervase Mathew (eds)., *History of East Africa* I (London, 1963), 236.
15. Reports from Naval Officers, Box 165 ICS.
16. Lamu women, interviews, l989. These women were descendants of the former owner, and the story was handed down by the old women to their daughters and on to granddaughters, until the generation of women born in the l930s who were my informants.
17. For a broader picture of events in this period, see G. S. Graham, *Great Britain in the Indian Ocean 1810-1850* (London, 1967); C. S. Nicholls, *The Swahili Coast*; Sir Reginald Coupland, *The British Anti-Slavery Movement* (Oxford, 1938) and *The Exploitation of East Africa 1856-1890* (Cambridge, 1967). See also "Richard D. Wolff, "British Imperialism and the East African Slave Trade" *Science and Society* 36 (1972) 443-62.
18. For a brief survey of the BuSaid family until the death of his grandfather, see Rudolph Said-Ruete, "Dates and References to the History of Al Bin Said dynasty 1741-1856" *Journal of Royal Central Asian Society* 18 (1931) 233-255.
19. The British briefly considered placing Rudolph Said-Ruete, son of Salme, on the throne after Ali died. At that time Ruete was a military officer in the German army. Portal to Barrington, FO 84/2077.
20. Patricia Romero Curtin, "Lamu (Kenya), Slave Trade, and British Efforts to Suppress" *Slavery and Abolition* 7 (1986) 148-59. Although this chapter merely

touches on the East African slave trade, much of the material that follows comes from the above article. For an important work on the East African trade, see William Gervase Clarence-Smith (ed)., *The Economics of the Indian Ocean and Red Sea Trades in the 19th Century* (London, 1989). For references to Lamu, see Clarence-Smith, "Introduction" 1-19.

21. Mrs. Charles E. B. Russell, *General Rigby* 94.
22. Graham, *Great Britain*, 181.
23. The French supported Bargash in his attempt to overthrow Majid soon after the latter assumed the Zanzibari throne. This was due to their resentment over Britain's attempts to pressure them out of the trade, and thus out of the slaves they required for their Indian Ocean island plantations. Bhacker, *Trade and Empire* (18-19) argues that Rigby put Majid on the throne. See Romero Curtin, "British Efforts to Suppress" 151. See also R. W. Beachey, *The Slave Trade of Eastern Africa* (London, 1976) which covers the subject extensively; and Ylvisaker, *Lamu in the Nineteenth Century*, 111-13.
24. Rigby to Secretary of State for Bombay L/P&S/9/37 IOL.
25. Majid to Rigby, 25 July 1861, L/P&S/9/38 IOL. In fact Majid was prescient. British pressures on ending the slave trade turned the Sultan's Arab followers against him, as was also the case with the Indians who continued in the trade. The split between the Sultans and their followers consequently pushed the Zanzibari rulers further into the British fold. See Richard D. Wolff, *The Economics of Colonialism* (New Haven, 1974) 34.
26. L/P&S/a37 IOL. See also Ylvisaker, 112-13. Dumping slaves was an all too common practice. See Captain G. L. Sullivan, *Dhow Chasing in Zanzibar Water* (London, 1873).
27. Romero Curtin, "British Efforts to Suppress" 152.
28. Ward to Secretary of State, 19 May, 1861, General Records of Department of State 468-4 Record GP 59, National Archives of the United States of America (NA).
29. L/P&S/18/890 IOL. Most of the Indians were from Gugarat which was under the native ruler, the Rao of Cutch. Although the British pressured him to abolish the trade and end slavery, both continued illegally.
30. Abdul Shariff makes the point that class interests dictated cooperation between Arab and Indian. While a Marxist interpretation may explain the close relations that characterized these communities during the period of the Ocean going trade, and later the caravan trade, the very human element of desire to continue profits and mutual hostility to the British may have provided their tendency to bond. Abdul Sheriff and Ed Ferguson, *Zanzibar Under Colonial Rule* (London, 1991) 13.
31. Zanzibar was controlled by the India Office until 1883: after that the Foreign Office took over.
32. Churchill to the Duke of Argyll, Secretary of State for India, 21 January 1869 L/P&S/18/890 IOL. See also Joseph E. Harris, *The African Presence in Asia* (Evanston, 1971) 12-13. Harris held that there were only a few Indians dealing directly in the trade—and those were from Cutch. However, others were financing from behind the scenes. For a Marxist interpretation of relations between Indians and the British, see Lawrence Sakarai, "Indian Merchants in East Africa: Part I. The Triangular Trade and the Slave Economy" *Slavery and Abolition* 1 (1980) 292-39. See also Correspondence with British Representatives, Box 105 Institute of Commonwealth Studies (ICS), London.

33. Holmwood to Captain Prideaux, 17 Nov. 1874, Box 105 ICS.
34. J. G. Malcolm to Dr. Kirk, Box 163 ICS. Ylvisaker refers to the liwali as Sud bin Ungu, but this must have been Suud bin Hamed since she places him in Lamu in 1874. See Marguerite Ylvisaker, "Shamba na Konde: Land Use in the Hinterland of the Lamu Archipelago 1865-1895) l0. Unpublished paper Ft. Jesus Library.
35. According to John Haggard, who knew McCausland, the chief of Faza was responsible for his death. "Journal" April 23, 1884, Rhodes House, Oxford. See also J. R. Colomb, *Slave Catching in the Indian Ocean* (New York, l969).
36. Reports from Naval Officers Inclosure 1 in No. 181 ICS. See A. Sheriff, *Slaves, Spices and Ivory in Zanzibar: Economic Integration of East Africa into the World Economy* (London, 1987) ll0. Bhacker, *Trade and Empire* 69.
37. Sheikh Ahmed Jahadhmy, personal communication, May 1992.
38. Romero Curtin, "British Efforts to Suppress" 153. This incident was still remembered in oral traditions in Lamu as late as l985. Frederick Cooper points out that there was no way to separate the legal from the illegal trade in the l870s. And certainly no way to measure how many died because the trade was illegal after 1873. See Cooper, *Plantation Slavery*, ll7.
39. Kirk report to Bombay, Box l05 ICS.
40. The British were still destroying Arab dhows as late as 1890 when they believed them to be carrying slaves. See FO 84/2059; FO 84/l725; FO 84/l729.
41. The only attempts to provide numbers for the slave trade in Lamu were figures based on imports onto the island from 1866-1877 and these seem much too high. In 1866-1867 they estimate that 5,039 came directly to Lamu. And in 1873-1874 when evidence suggests the trade was coming to a halt, they estimate that 5,550 arrived there. In addition they state that in 1870-1871, 2,637 came to Lamu from Zanzibar. See Esmond B. Martin and T.C.I. Ryan, "A Quantitative Assessment of the Arab Slave Trade in East Africa 1770-1896" *Kenya Historical Review* 5 (1977) 71-91. Henry Churchill gives numbers of registered slaves leaving Zanzibar for all areas in the Sultan's domains at 4,500 in 1855-57. These figures represented the numbers on which two Maria Theresa dollars tax was paid. L/P&S/18b/150 IOL.
42. Holmwood Report, Box 163 ICS.
43. R. W. Beachey, *The Slave Trade of Eastern Africa* (London, 1976), 190-91. See also Oskar Karstedt, *Der WeiBe Kampf um Afrika* I (Berlin, 1937), 192-94.
44. Jackson, *Early Days in East Africa* 91. For the slave trade from central Africa, see Edward Alpers, *Ivory and Slaves in East Central Africa: Changing Patterns of International Trade to the later Nineteenth Century* (London, 1975). See also Gwyn Campbell, "The East African Slave Trade 1861-95: The Southern Complex" *International Journal of African Historical Studies* 22 (1989) 1-26.
45. Lamu women informants, interviews, January-February, l981. See also Patricia Romero Curtin, "Laboratory for the Oral History of Slavery: The Island of Lamu on the Kenya Coast" *American Historical Review* 88:4:l983:862.
46. Sharon Stichter, *Migrant Labour in Kenya: Capitalism and the African Response, 1895-1975* (London, 1982), 1-2.
47. Holmwood Report C Box l05 ICS.
48. Beachey, *The Slave Trade* 197-98. Lamu women, interviews, l980-85. I knew and delighted in a former slave woman who became *suria* (free and equal) after she provided her BuSaid owner with a child. This woman will figure in later chapters, but there is no question of her having been captured as a slave when but a child and

brought into Lamu. Her owner raised her from childhood and soon after she reached puberty, he "put her inside" the house and made her his mistress. Unfortunately both this woman and the son of that relationship died within 6 days of each other in the spring of 1990. He was 80. She claimed to be over 100.

49. John Haggard to Will September 3, 84/3. See Sir John Gray, "The British Vice-Consulate at Kilwa Kivinji, 1884-85" *Tanganyika Notes and Records* 51:1958:175. Gray says that Haggard was then a Lieutenant whose orders to Lamu were issued 9 October 1883; and his responsibility was to "watch the slave trade." Haggard's brother, Will, was an official in the Foreign Office and often Haggard would write long letters to him in which he discussed issues of importance, especially in terms of the German presence in 1885. J. E. Haggard also conveyed back to Will personal impressions of British authorities in East Africa. For instance, when Kirk was about to leave, John wrote Will that he thought Holmwood, an administrator in Zanzibar, "was incompetent" to succeed. Kirk was often "lazy" and did not stir out of Zanzibar was much as Haggard would have liked—this opinion delivered to Will in another letter.

50. Haggard to Kirk, June, 1884; September, 1884. Zanzibar National Archives.

51. John Kirk FO 84/1724.

52. Kirk [FO 84/1725]. These were Maria Theresa dollars: four dollars equalled one Pound Sterling; and four and one-half German Crowns in the 1870s-1880s.

53. John Haggard to mother, July 6, 1884.

54. John Haggard to Will, July, 1884, 79/1.

55. John Haggard to The Rev. Charles Maddison Green, April 10, 1885, 95/1.

56. Frederick Jackson, *Early Days*, 23.

57. Haggard to Will, May 1, 1884 73/2.

58. John Haggard to father 3 June 1884 75/1.

59. Frederick Jackson, *Early Days*, 13-14. Suud's four brothers were also employed in high posts by the Sultan of Zanzibar. Clive's "History" is somewhat inaccurate in that he gives the date of Suud bin Hamed reappointment as 1884 (120). Sheikh Ahmed Jahadhmy, personal communication, 1991.

60. Haggard to Will, July 10, 1884, 79/1.

61 Haggard to Will, July 10, 1884, 79/2.

62. Haggard to father July 30, 1884, 81/1.

63. John Haggard to father, 24 December 1883, 67/1.

64. Derek Nurse, "History from Linguistics: The Case of the Tana River" *History in Africa* 10 (1983) 225.

Chapter 4

1. For an short study of the *watoro*, see Jonathon Glassman, "The runaway slave in coastal resistance to Zanzibar: the case of the Witu Sultanate," M. A. Thesis, University of Wisconsin, 1983. For activities on the mainland, see also Marguerite Ylvisaker, *Lamu in the Nineteenth Century*, passim. Salim Kheri, interviews, January-February, 1981. Ali Abdalla Skanda, interviews, January-May, 1980.

2. Holmwood Report C Box 105 ICS.

3. DC LMU/3/10 KNA; Sheikh Ahmed Jahadhmy, interview, 1980. Mohammed bin Ali al Busaid, interview, 1983. Sharif Abdalla Salim, interview, Mombasa, 1980.

4. Glassman, "The Runaway Slave in Coastal Resistance to Zanzibar" 72-73.

5. John Haggard to mother, July 6, 1884, 76/1.
6. Arthur Hardinge [FO 84/1725]
7. Salim Kheri, interviews, January-February, 1981. Ali Abdalla Skanda, interviews, January-May, 1980. The *watoro*, however, were examples of slaves who did not accept the paternalistic system established by their Muslim owners. For slave opposition to the social order, see Frederick Cooper, "Islam and Cultural Hegemony: The Idealogy of Slaveowners on the East African Coast," in Paul E. Lovejoy, (ed)., *The Idealogy of Slavery in Africa* (Beverly Hills: 1981), 277.
8. FO 84/1725. Haggard to Will April 27, 1884 85/1. Ylvisaker covers this period (122-43) in depth. See also Galbraith, *Mackinnon and East Africa* 121-22; and Prosser Gifford and Louis B. Roger, *Britain and Germany in Africa* (New Haven, 1967).
9. The house, which contains the name Denhardt written in Arabic script obove the portal, has been reconstructed with some funding from Germany.
10. Sheikh Ahmed Jahadhmy, personal communication, July, 1991.
11. FO 84/1934; Sheikh Ahmed Jahadhmy, personal communication, August 1991. Morton believes that Suud bin Hamed's defeat was probably "deliberate." The attack was opposed by many of the WaAmu because of their kinship ties with the Nabahany. Jahadhmy says this was not the case, some sympathies did rest with Simba, but these were based on anti-British feelings. The WaAmu were caught in the middle: losing their slaves to Simba on the mainland, and their rights to the British in Zanzibar. See Fred Morton, *Children of Ham:Freed Slaves and Fugitive Slaves on the Kenya Coast 1873-1907* (Boulder, 1990).
12. Sheikh Ahmed Jahadhmy, personal communication, 1991, said the two were not related. John Horace Clive, "A Short History of Lamu" unpublished manuscript, Mss/Afr/51273 Rhodes House, presents a different interpretation of the killing, but the results were the same: Suud bin Hamed did not admit involvement.
13. Frederick Jackson, *Early Days*, 14.
14. Among the families with whom Abdalla bin Hamid's descendants married was that of Bwana Zaidi, whose family claimed to come from Syria and whose "history" he recorded in "The Lamu Chronicle."
15. Kirk to FO October 9, 1884 FO 84/1775
16. B\P&S\18\B150a IOL; FO documents list Suud bin Hamed as Liwali from 1870 until 1883; reappointed later thay year through fall of 1884; and then briefly Liwali in 1889. [FO 84/2058]. Sheikh Ahmed Jahadhmy, personal communication, August 22, 1991. According to Sheikh Ahmed, Suud bin Hamed was born in Oman, and after posted to Lamu married Mwana Baraka, a cousin of his father's. After she died, his *suria* gave birth to Ahmed bin Suud, Khalifa bin Suud, Sheikha binta Suud, and Aisha binta Suud. All of these children left Lamu but the house in which they lived with their father, which is now a partial ruin, is still called Bait Suud.
17. Kirk to FO, June 4, 1885. [FO 84/1726] See Karl Peters, *New Light on Dark Africa: Being a Narrative of the German Emin Pasha Expedition*, (London, 1891). Karl Peters was later a model for the National Socialists in Germany. For a full account of events surrounding the Sultanate of Witu and German activities in the area see Marguerite Ylvisaker, *Lamu in the Nineteenth Century*.
18. Edward Rodwell, Sunday *Standard*, November 13, 1983. See also Sir Frederick Jackson, *Early Day in East Africa* 223-25.
19. Haggard to Charles Maddison, April 10, 1885, 95/1.
20. Kirk to FO. FO 84/1725.

21. See M. J. DeKiewiet, "History of the Imperial British East Africa Company 1876-1895" Ph.D. thesis University of London, 1965. See also Galbraith, *Mackinnon and East Africa.*

22. Marie de Kiewiet Hemphill, "The British Sphere, 1884-91" in Roland Oliver and Gervase Mathew (eds)., *History of East Africa* I (London, 1968), 393. See also the William Mackinnon Papers, Box 63, School of Oriental and African Studies, University of London. Mackinnon sent his agent, George Mackenzie, to Lamu several times between December 1888 and February 1889 to keep tabs on the German activity in both Lamu and Witu.

23. George Mackenzie to William Mackinnon, Mackinnon papers, January, 1891, Box 63. See also Galbraith, *Mackinnon and East Africa* 89-103. Galbraith refers to negotiations with the chief of Lamu but he must have meant the liwali, as there was no "chief" until the British installed one later in the twentieth century.

24. L. W. Hollingsworth, *Zanzibar under the Foreign Office 1890-1913* (London, 1953), 19-22. J. W. Gregory, *The Foundation of British East Africa*, London, 1901, 123-43. John Flint, "The Witu Background to Partition and Colonial Opposition," in Roland Oliver and Gervase Mathews (eds)., *History of East Africa* I (London, 1968), 352-90. The Germans in Lamu did not abandon their efforts to take over the area despite the treaty. The Denhardts stayed on in Witu, serving as advisors to the Sultans; and they kept their Lamu house, with increasing numbers of Germans joining them. In the 1890s a new feud between Britain and Germany raged when Germans in Lamu opened a post office and attempted to force British agents and subjects to pay postal duties to them, despite postage having been paid at point of origin. The correspondence concerning the post office alone took on major diplomatic proportions and involved even Lord Salisbury, Cabinet Minister for the Foreign Office. See GPO Post 105 Public Notices and Instructions to Postmasters, 1840-1890, No. 20; Post 51, Overseas Mails, Contracts, Sea 1722-1923, No. 96, 1898; Post 29, Packet Minutes: Documents, 1811-1920 Packet 212p/1889 "Lamoo German Postal Agency Assimilated to Postal Union. Thanks to Anne Thurston for providing me with photocopies of the post office squabbles. See also correspondence between C. B. Euan-Smith, Consul General Zanzibar to R. Simons, Consul General Lamu, April-September 1890, Zanzibar National Archives. Thanks to Abbas Ibrahim Sanya, Zanzibar National Archives for copies of this correspondence. See [FO 84/2059].

25. John Horace Clive, "A Short History".

26. "The Chronicle of Lamu" 31.

27. J.S. Sandy's June 7, 1889, Lamu Box 13, Zanzibar National Archives.

28. Later, the British, too, accused the Germans of tampering with their mail. 7 January 1892 Box 63 1b IBEA Papers.

29. Extract from a letter from Mr. Sandy's Br. Consular Agent Lamu, to Col. Euan-Smith, dated 13 February 1889. Zanzibar National Archives.

30. Lamu Political Record Book, LMU/8, KNA. FO 84/2039. The record, however, is inaccurate. Sandys is called Roger; and his date of death is given as 1888. Actually Sandys died at the age of 32 on 31st August 1889. Thanks are due to Dr. Roland Minor of Lamu, who checked the tombstone and provided the correct name and date of death.

31. Portal to Simons, September 18, 1881, Zanzibar National Archives. Simons was appointed with no pay but did receive free housing and was allowed to collect a percentage of the "actual fees collected from stamps."

259

32. R. Simons to Col. Euan-Smith, November, 1889. Zanzibar National Archives.
33. John Horace Clive, "A Short History." According to Clive, "the watch was a gold half-hunter on the back of which was a large W in diamonds and inside the lid an engraving of the Kaiser, complete with helmet and fiercely upturned moustache. . . . Some forty five years later the watch was handed over to one of the widows of Hamed bin Suud who were practically destitute . . . to my horror it was valued at 6.10.0 - the gold was rolled, the diamonds were clippings and His Imperial Majesty had obviously been trying to buy support on the cheap." See also Galbraith, *Mackinnon and East Africa* 121-22.
34. Copy 70 in Nl52, April 13. Zanzibar National Archives.
35. R. E. Simons to Euan-Smith, September 4, 1890, Zanzibar National Archives.
36. Clive, "A Short History." See Ylvisaker, *Lamu in the Nineteenth Century* 149-51.
37. R. W. Pigott to Consul General, Zanzibar, September 17, 18, 21, 29. Clive, "A Short History."
38. Sir G. H. Portal, "Diary-Zanzibar, 1891-92"; Portal Letters, Zanzibar, March-December, 1892; Portal letters to Lady Alice, 1891-92. Mss. Afr. S. 105 Rhodes House, Oxford. Thanks to Anne Thurston for providing me with copies of this correspondence.
39. Portal to Lady Alice, n. d.; Portal to Sir Percy Anderson, May 10, 1892. Mss. Afr S.106. Rhodes House
40. Sheikh Ahmed Jahadhmy, 1991.
41. G. H. Portal to Lord Rosebery. Mss. Afr. S.105. Rhodes House.

Chapter 5

1. See Ibrahim Sundiate, "Twentieth Century Reflections on Death in Zanzibar" *International Journal of African Historical Studies* 20 (1987) 45-60. See also Gerald W. Hartwig and K. David Patterson (eds)., *Disease in African History* (Chapel Hill, 1978); Patricia W. Romero, "Whose Medicine: Some Problems Understanding Health and Healing in Lamu," paper presented at the Lamu Museum, 1989.
2. Haggard to Ellen Maddison Green, March 15, 1884, 70/1. Haggard to father July 30, 1884, 81/1. The vaccination, he wrote, was not going to take although his arm was very sore. Hartwig and Patterson, *Disease* (7) mention the difficulty "visitors to the Swahili coast" encountered because of the difference in the African disease environment.
3. Haggard to mother, July 14, 1884 71/1; to Will, March, 1885, 94/1; and to father, July, 1884. Thanks to Dr. Mark E. Gann for information pertaining to bladder conditions and the French catheter.
4. Richard F. Burton, *First Footsteps in East Africa* (London, 1860), 549. See also Eugenia Herbert, "Smallpox Inoculation in Africa," *Journal of African History* 4(1981)539-59.
5. See R. F. Eberlie, "The German Achievement in East Africa," *Tanganyika Notes and Records* 55 (1960) 207.
6. John Haggard to mother, December 13, 1883 476/6.
7. Christie, *Cholera Epidemics in East Africa* 273. The slave traders took diseases into the interior, including those that afflicted animals. See Hartwig and Patterson, *Disease* 25-45. See also Good, "Man, Mileau, and the Disease Factor," *Disease* 46-87.
8. Haggard to Mother, December 13, 1883, 67/1. Frederick Jackson, *Early Days*, 11.

9. Christie, *Chlorea Epidemics*, xiii.
10. Frederick Jackson, *Early Days*, 9. With the influx of people from the Bajun islands and the mainland, in the late 1980s poor people were again using the beach areas in front of the mud and wattle houses as a public toilet. See Hartwig and Patterson, *Disease*, 15.
11. Stigand, *Land of Zinj*, 156.
12. For abortifacients elsewhere on the Swahili coast see G. H. Becker (ed)., translation by B. G. Martin, "Materials for the Understanding of Islam in German East Africa," *Tanganyika Notes and Records*, 67 (1968) 36-57. Interviews with Lamu women, 1980-90.
13. Haggard to mother July 6, 1884, 76/l. In terms of the relationship between drought and smallpox, see G. H. Hartwig, "Smallpox in the Sudan," *International Journal of African Historical Studies* 14 (1981) 14-18.
14. Haggard to Will, September 3, 1884, 77/l. Haggard believed the reason he did not succumb was because of a pot of carbolic acid he kept in the center of his house.
15. Frederick Jackson, *Early Days*, 22.
16. Christie, *Cholera Epidemics*, xii-xiii, lll, 147. Burton, *Zanzibar* 176. Christie wrote that the first outbreak of cholera in East Africa was in 1821. But Dr. D. A. Henderson believes that "true chlorea could not have been before 1831." Interview, Baltimore, April, 1988.
17. Christie, *Cholera Epidemics*, 25.
18. While the locals in Lamu were becoming more hostile to both Zanzibari and British interference in their affairs, and though they feared problems again with the Somalis, John Kirk blithely assured the Foreign Office that the Sultan (and then indirectly the British officers) was totally in control of his coastal possessions—"one may walk along the coast without any weapon if provided with the Sultan's letter from the southern extremity of his dominions to Lamu." John Kirk to FO, July, 1885 FO 84/2059. Ylvisaker, *Lamu in the Nineteenth Century* (123) noted that the Hindu murdered in 1874 was thought to have been killed by a Bajun who lived in Lamu on a pension from the Sultan, his slave, and others.
19. Frederick Jackson, *Early Days*, 21. The long held British view of Arab superiority over Africans is illustrated in the following quote from John Kirk, "Since earliest ages of the Mohammedan era and probably long before . . . .[there was] rule by successive waves of northern races of Arab and Persian origin . . . .Nowhere in history do we find a trace of a native ruling race though numerous barbarian invasions have for a time crushed progress and civilization in the trading centers established by those foreign settlers." John Kirk to FO, July, 1885, [FO 84/2059]
20. Mrs. C. E. Russell, *General Rigby* 352.
21. Mohammed bin Ali BuSaid, interview, December, 1988. Lamu women, interviews, 1980-91.
22. Stigand, *Land of Zinj*, (48 n.) commented on the immorality (as he saw it) in Lamu during his visit early in the twentieth century. For an excellent insights into homosexuality in Mombasa, see Gill Shepherd, "Rank, gender, and homosexuality: Mombasa as a key to understanding sexual options," in Patricia Caplan (ed)., *The Cultural Construction of Sexuality* (London, 1987) 240-70. For the a description of the female slave as prostitute see Jean-Pierre Olivier De Sardan, "The Songhay-Zarma Female Slave: Relations of Production and Ideological Status" in Claire G. Robertson and Martin A. Klein (eds)., *Women and Slavery in Africa* (Madison, 1983)

130-43. See also Deborah Pellow "Sexuality in Africa" *Trends in History* 4 (1990) 71-96. For transsexuals and transvestites see John Money, "The Transformation of Sexual Terminology: Homosexuality in Sexological History," *Siecus Report* 19 (1991), 10-13. Money coined the term "gynemimesis" (13) to define "woman miming" which was most often the type of disorder openly flaunted in Lamu before independence.

23. Clemens Denhardt, "A History of Manda and Patta by Clemens Denhardt submitted to R. Simons, April 9, 1890." Zanzibar National Archives.

24. F. Hamerick Douglas, acting British Consular Agent to Euan-Smith, April 29, 1890 with the translated "genealogy-history" provided by Mohammed bin Hamed attached. Mzee Nabahani, from whom Mohammed bin Hamed garnered the dates of rule, was uncertain about one sultan, claiming he ruled "for a few months." He seems to have garbled the "history" badly but perhaps the inaccuracies were purposely conveyed by the "historian" Mohammed bin Hamid. See Chapter One and the Nabahany claims to arrival in Pate in the sixteenth century.

25. See Vail, *The Creation of Tribalism*, Introduction. In this case, Vail's interpretation fits. Placing people in "tribal" categories and labeling them at this time added to the confusion as to "who were the WaSwahili."

26. Ahmed Mohammed Jahadhmy, in *Tarika ya Amu* (16) lists the then ruling families of Lamu by their nisba. Those people, who were descended from "Bwana Mbekeya", included members of the Mahdali sharifan group—in this instance, descent is traced through the mother's line, which was often the case in Lamu, when the mother was freeborn and of "good family." See the Appendix. Bwana Zaidi was descended from Bwana Mwenyemui's line. Both of these families were regarded as being members of the aristocracy.

27. T. Hammerick Douglas Acting British Consular Agent to Col. Euan-Smith, May 1, 1890. Zanzibar National Archives.

28. Sheikh Ahmed Jahadhmy, personal communication, January, 1992. The Indians from Gujarat continued to speak their native language which they taught their children. For some, the Bajun are people from Faza and Siyu. For others, they are all the people who dwell on Pate island as well as Siyu, Faza, Kisingitni and the islands further north.

29. Ali Abdalla al Maawyia, interview, 1983. Fadhil al Maawyia, interview, 1985. A. A. Skanda, interview, 1980. Mohammed and Sheikh Ahmed Jahadhmy, interviews, Lamu, 1994. Sharif Abdalla Salim al Hussein, interview, Mombasa, 1981. See Jahadhmy, *Tarikhi ya Amu* 15-16. Middleton, *The World of the Swahili* (93) is correct in stating that the sharifu were mostly marginal in Lamu, but the al Hussein sharifs do not fall in this category as is clear throughout this study. See also Middleton, 90-100 and especially his chart of descent groups, 94. See Clive, "A Short History"; Prins, *Didemic Lamu* passim.; and el Zein, *The Sacred Meadows* (4-18 and 23-26) who drew heavily on Prins. The Skanda family, who were in Lamu by the end of the nineteenth century, claimed they were "WaFamao" and were regarded by other Afro-Arabs in Lamu as "WaFamao" but were not included in Jahadhmy's listing of old families in the several *mta*.

30. "Proclamation issued at Mombasa 1 January, 1892" Box 63 1b IBEA Papers.

31. Mackinnon Papers, box 63.

32. Box 63 1A IBEA Papers. One man, "Aboo Baker bin Mohammed" sold a piece of land on the seafront to the IBEA. This land eventually became the property on which Smith Mackenzie built its wholesale business after the IBEA went out of business.

33. Oscar Baumann, *In Deutsch-Ostafrika: Wahrend des Aufstandes* (Wein und Olmutz, 1890), 9-14.

34. W. W. A. Fitzgerald, *Travels in British East Africa, Pemba and Zanzibar* (London, 1898).

35. Fitzgerald, *Travels,* 394-96.

36. Rigby to India Office May 1, 1860 L/PAS/9/37 IOL. Fitzgerald, *Travels,* 379-83.

37. Fitzgerald, *Travels*, 393. Talbot-Smith, "History." Sheikh Ahmed Jahadhmy, interviews, 1980; Ali Abdalla al Maawyia, interviews, 1980-81; Mohammed bin Ali BuSaid, interview, 1983.

38. Fitzgerald, *Travels*, 407.

39. A. Whyte, "Travels on the Kenya Coast, 1903" CO 1534 Parliamentary Papers.

40. L. Talbot-Smith, "Short History of Tanaland" LMU/6 KNA

41. Report of W. H. During to the British Counsel, Zanzibar, November, 1883. Zanzibar National Archives.

42. See Bruce Berman and John Lonsdale, *Unhappy Valley: Conflict in Kenya and Africa Book One: State and Class* (Athens, 1992) 94. Although their study is primarily concerned with the interior of Kenya, and particularly the Kikuyu, Lonsdale refers to British attempts to promote settlers for "the reproduction of settler capitalism."

43. Sir Arthur H. Hardinge, *A Diplomatist in the East* (London, 1928), 143.

44. Hardinge, *Diplomatist*, 143-146. See also A. T. Matson, "The Freelanders: Cautionary Tale of a Social Idea" *Kenya Weekly News*, 7 August 1959. For Circassian concubines, see Romero (ed)., *Memoirs*, 12 *et passim*. For a riotous fictional account of this group see J. D. F. Jones, *Freeland* (London, 1994).

45. Hardinge, *Diplomatist* 119.

46. For a theoretical treatment of Britain's colonial policy in Kenya see Bruce Berman, *Control and Crisis in Colonial Kenya* (London, 1990). While there is little evidence that religious revivals in Lamu came about at this time, it is possible that some of the unexplained resistance there may have had backing from the conservative sharifs, who would have seen British control inimical to their own growing powers especially among the poor. For elsewhere on the coast, see B. G. Martin, "Muslim Politics and Resistance to Colonial Rule: Shaykh Uwaya B. Muhammed el-Barawi and the Qadariya Brotherhood in East Africa," *Journal of African History* X (1969) 471-486. T. O. Ranger, however, in looking at Christian central Africa found that religious movements were not necessarily an early manifestation of anti-colonialism. See T. O. Ranger, "Religious Movements and Politics in Sub-Saharan Africa," *African Studies Review* 29:2 (1986) 1-70. For a brief reappraisal of arguments pertaining to resistance, see Frederick Cooper, "Conflict and Connection: Rethinking Colonial African History" *American Historical Review* 99 (1994) 1516-1545. As an example of how colonial policies in Kenya differed between coast and upcountry, taxes levied in 1901 were accepted in "kind" if no money was available. This was never the case in Lamu, where money was required from the outset. See Robert L. Tignor, *The Colonial Transformation of Kenya: The Kamba, Kikuyu and Masai from 1900-1901* (Princeton, 1976) 8.

47. Freeman-Grenville, personal communication, November 27, 1981.

Chapter 6

1. These stories were embellished on by two strangers from Mombasa visiting in Lamu

in November, 1984, who said that some sharifs had continued this policy until quite recently in Mombasa. A chief qadi there had finally "put an end of Hadrami sharif exploitation in Mombasa" in the 1970s. Qadi el Farsi "preached that sharifs were not different from other men and gradually their 'powers' eroded" although many people from the Lamu archipelago continued going to a Lamu sharif in Mombasa's old town for medical treatment. For Tanganyika see C. H. Becker (trans. B. G. Martin), "Materials for Understanding Islam in German East Africa" 61.

2. Leroy Vail says ethnic consciousness in Africa is "a new phenomenon, an ideological construct, usually in the twentieth century. This concept was "helped along" by sociologists, anthropologists, and political scientists who were, in the main, studying particular groups at the "time they found them." (3) As a port city, albeit one located on the East Coast of Africa, Lamu differs from most of the models included in Vail's edited volume. In migrations came from so many areas, with each group carrying their cultural baggage that, at least in the nineteenth century, caused them to be labelled as distinct ethnic groups. In some cases migrants differed from the locals because of religion—the Indians were Hindu or Shi'ites; and the African slaves were traditionalists until they were converted to Islam, although most clung to some of their traditional beliefs even then. Those from the Comoro Islands, were referred to as Comoro people; and the Hadrami were called by what was then the Hadramaut (and then Yemen). Later, Christian Pokomo and Giriama were among others who came in. As to the indigenous Swahili community—whoever they may have been—the commonality was culture and religion. Class appears to have been dominant, however, if we look at the traditions featuring the body washing Yumbili. See Leroy Vail (ed)., *The Creation of Tribalism* "Introduction" 1-19.

3. Abdalla bin Ali, interview, 1980. Sheikh Ahmed Jahadhmy, interview, 1980. Lamu women, interviews, 1980. This family, however, is also said to be the one for whom the Damascus claim is made. Later, there were splits within the al Maawyia family. One branch claimed to be religious; and the other were said to be interested in business. No one knows exactly when these divisions took place, but the family of the Khatib of the Jumaa Mosque in the 1980-1990's, claim to be al Maawyia's who came in from Witu.

4. Captain Thomas Boteler, *Narrative of a Voyage of Discovery to Africa and Arabia*, II (London, 1840), 384.

5. B. G. Martin, "Notes on Members of the Learned Classes of Zanzibar and East Africa" 531-33. A branch of this sharifan family migrated to Zanzibar in the late nineteenth century. After the 1964 revolution, a descendant who was a religious scholar much revered for his piety, settled in Lamu where he died in 1991.

6. See Helen Brown, "Three Kilwa Coins" 3-4.

7. Gill Shepherd, "The Making of the Swahili: A View from the South End of the East African Coast" *Paiduma* 28 (1982) 142-44. See H. Neville Chittick, "The 'Shirazi' Colonization of East Africa" *Journal of African History 6 (1965) 275-92.*

8. Sharif Abdalla bin Salim, interview, 1980. For more on the early history of these Hadrami sharifan (and other) families, see R. B. Sergeant, *The Portuguese off the South Arabian Coast: Hadrami Chronicles* (London, 1963); "The Saiyids of Hadramawt: An Inaugural Lecture delivered on 5 June 1956, School of Oriental and African Studies, University of London (SOAS Library). Saleh Badawi correctly claimed to be related to the Mahdali sharifs, and perhaps the connection was lost on el Zein, who believed he had found members of this Sharifan family in Lamu in the

1960s. Considering that all legitimate sharifs were related to each other—no matter how millions there are—obviously there is a distant relationship to the Mahdali family, whose lineage el Zein traced only fifteen generations beyond the Prophet Mohammed. See Hamid M. el Zein, *The Sacred Meadows: A Structural Analysis of Religious Symbolism in an East African Town* (Evanston, 1974). According to Sheikh Ahmed Jahadhmy, personal communication January 21, 1992, the Mahdali sharifs were the first remembered to have come to the Lamu area. See also Marina A. Tolmacheva, "Group Identity."

9. William Hichens, "Introduction" to Sayyid Abdallah A. Nasir, *Al Inkishafi* (Nairobi, 1972), 9. Tolmacheva, *Pate Chronicle*, 63-64.

10. Hitchens gives the dates for Sharif Abdalla bin Ali as 1720-1820, but according to the dates on the tombstone, he must have lived in Pate during the late sixteenth century. Personal correspondence from Thomas H. Wilson, 1995.

11. Sharif Abdalla bin Salim said his al Hussein forebears came to Pate island in the seventeenth century because the people there were very respectful of sharifs and receptive to their presence. Sharif Abdalla's branch of the family moved to Lamu sometime early in the nineteenth century. Sharif Abdalla's father was born there as was he. Interviews with Sharif Abdalla bin Salim, Mombasa, 1980, 1981, 1982, 1983, 1985.

12. Sheikh Ahmed Jahadhmy, interview, 1994. Ahmed Jahadhmy's second wife, Sharifa, was a sister to Jahi. Ali Ahmed Jahadhmy, interview Mombasa, 1994.

13. Ali Abdalla Jahadhmy, interview, Mombasa, January 1983. See Ingraham, *Zanzibar and its History and Peoples* (London, 1931), 152, who erroneously noted that the immigration of Hadramis began when the Sultan brought them into guard his forts; but Ingraham seemed to be correct in adding that the Hadramis had severed all connections with their home country.

14. See for instance Pouwels, "Tenth Century Settlement of the East African Coast: The Case for Qarmatian/Isma'ili Connexions" 65-74.

15. The major schools of Islamic law are the Hanafi, Maliki, Shafi, and Hanbali. See J. N. D. Anderson, *Islamic Law in Africa* 81-109. There is a tremendous body of literature on Islam in East Africa. For some references see Becker (trans. B. G. Martin), "Materials for Understanding of Islam in German East Africa" where Martin talks about the conflict between Muslim scholars and pagan superstitions. J. S. Trimingham, *Islam in East Africa* 81-84. J. S. Trimingham, "The Phases of Islamic Expansion and Islamic Culture Zones in Africa" in I. M. Lewis (ed)., *Islam in Tropical Africa* (London, 1966) 127-43; T. Cuyler Young, "East Africa and Classical Islam: some remaining research problems in relationships" *Transafrican Journal of History* 2:2 (1972) 3-10; Aziz Esmail, "Towards a History of Islam in East Africa" *Kenya Historical Review* 3 (1975) 147-58; Randall Pouwels, *Horn and Crescent: Traditional Islam and Cultural Change on the East African Coast* (Cambridge, 1987). British colonial official W. H. Ingraham, *Zanzibar: Its History and Peoples*, 190, believed that "The Sunnis are the people who have mixed much with savages. They mix religion with noisy play and make a great show of it." For the "conflict" between the Shirazi and the Arabs, see A. H. J. Prins, *Didemic Lamu*. For a confusing and controversial, yet valuable study of religion in Lamu see Abdul Hamid M. el Zein, *The Sacred Meadows*. Finally, for a sketch of the pre-Colonial background, see Ahmed Idha Salim, "The Impact of Colonialism Upon Muslim Life in Kenya" *Journal of the Institute of Muslim Minority Affairs* 1 (1979) 60-66.

16. Abdulla S. Bujra, *The Politics of Stratification: A Study of Political Change in a*

South Arabian Town (Oxford, 1971). Interestingly, Bujra makes no reference to his own ties to Hadramaut; nor does he mention that he grew up in a home where the father spoke the Hadrami form of Arabic to which Bujra refers in his book. I was able to ascertain that his grandfather, a Bedouin, came from a small town in the interior, similar to Hureidah. el Zein drew on Bujra's findings in Hureidah in the *Sacred Meadows* see especially 128 *et passim.*

17. Bujra, *The Politics of* xiii. The complexities within and between these castes are much greater than I have indicated here. See 46-53 *et passim.*

18. el Zein, *The Sacred Meadows, passim.* James de Vere Allen, "Lamu Town" 3; Francoise Le Guennec-Coppens, "Les Masharifu Majalilil a Lamu (Kenya) *Annuaire des Pay de l'Ocean Indien* VI (1979) 92-95. For criticism of el Zein's Lamu findings, see Patricia Romero Curtin, "The Sacred Meadows: A Case Study of 'Anthropologyland' VS. 'Historyland'" *History in Africa* 9 (1982) 339-46. See chapter nine.

19. Bujra, *The Politics of* 13-53. For anyone studying the social structure of contemporary Lamu, and especially religious differences among the Sunni community, Bujra's book is required reading. el Zein, whose *Sacred Meadows* set off a storm of controversy when it arrived in Lamu. Mwalimu Harith Saleh and others believe that Bujra may have been indirectly influential on el Zein's interpretations because of recommendations on Lamu informants. el Zein, of course, wrote critically concerning the Jamal al Layl sharifs who are most representative of the characteristics described for the sharifs in Hadramaut.

20. See C. H. Becker, B. G. Martin, (trans and ed. of Becker), "Materials for the Understanding of Islam" 48. Also Martin, 51, talks about the influence of the Hadrami in the Muslim religion on the East African coast.

21. Bujra, *Politics of* 93-114. See also R. F. Murphy, "The Structure of Parallel Cousins" *American Anthropologist* I (1959) 69-82. See R. Levy, *The Social Structure of Islam* (Cambridge, 1957). Robert Bertram Sergeant, "The Hadrami Network" in Lombard et Aubin (eds)., *Marchands* 147-54.

22. L. W. C. Van Beers, *Le Hadhramout et les colonies Arabes dans L'Archipel Indien* (Batavia, 1886), Plate V, 188. In addition, see UNESCO, *Cultural Newsletter*, 3 (1985) 2-3; Richard F. Nyrop, Beryle Lieff Benderly, Lorraine Newhouse Carter, *Area Handbook for the Yemens* (Washington, D.C., 1977).

23. Hadrami women, interviews, September, 1985. Sharif Abdalla bin Salim al Hussein, Mombasa, 1981. Ali Mukaka, interview, Lamu, 1989. Bradford G. Martin, *Muslim Brotherhoods in the Nineteenth Century* (Cambridge, 1976), 172, noted that in Zanzibar, too, Hadrami migrated in to "do menial tasks" late in the reign of Sultan Said. Sailing dhows had been going between the Hadramaut and East Africa for centuries. See R. B. Sergeant, "Hadramaut to Zanzibar: The Pilot-Poem of the Nakhudha Said Ba Tayi of A. Hami" *Paiduma* 28 (1982), 120. See also Allen Villiers, *Sons of Sinbad* (New York 1964), 50, who referred to Hadrami smugglers in East African ports. Villiers also mentioned the "wandering" Hadrami traders.

24. Ibuni Saleh, *A Short History of the Comorians in Zanzibar* (Dar es Salaam, 1936), 6-7.

25. Christie, *Cholera Epidemics* 332.

26. Martin, *Muslim Brotherhoods*, 152-54. B. G. Martin, "Arab Migrations to East Africa" *International Journal of African Historical Studies* 7:3 (1974) 379. For Madagascar see Philippe Oberle', *Provinces Malgaches* (Antanarivo, 1976).

27. Abdalla Kadara on "Habib Saleh" Lmu 23.3.76 (Lamu Museum Library); Sharif Hassan Badawy, interview, Lamu, March, 1980; Sheikh Ahmed Jahadhmy, February, 1980; Sharif Abdalla bin Salim el Hussein, interview, Mombasa, May, 1980. See Peter Lienhardt, "The Mosque College of Lamu and Its Social Background," *Tanganyika Notes and Records* 53 (1959) 229-42. See also el Zein, *Sacred Meadow*, 117-24.

28. Sharif Abdalla bin Salim, 1980. See Le Guennec Coppens, "Les Masharifu" 91-102.

29. Abdalla Kadara, "Habib Saleh" says he did not like living in town.

30. Abdalla Kadara, "Habib Saleh"; Sharif Abdalla bin Salim, 1980; Sheikh Ahmed Jahadhmy, 1980. Ali Skanda, interview with Sharif Saleh Badawi, 1981 (tape in possession of the author). Ali Abdalla al Maawyia, interview, January, 1983. Mohammed al Hussein, interview, Mombasa, October, 1985. According to Mohmamed "the al Hussein gave the land but after they kept away from him [Saleh]. The el Hussein have "kept clear of further divisions among the Jamal al Layl sharifs" and almost all had left Lamu by the 1980s, although the divisions within the Jamal al Layl family have continued.

31. James de Vere Allen, "Lamu Town" 26.

32. Some controversy has developed as to whether the poor and uneducated—including slaves—recited the Maulidi KiSwahili in Lamu before Habib Saleh introduced the Maulidi al Habshi. Sharif Abdalla Salim al Hussein said there was a "Swahili maulidi" and it was meant for "those who did not know Arabic." Some slaves knew Arabic. Some of the old families did not. As time passed, "many of the old families did not know more than the basic Qur'an in Swahili" and these people continued saying the Maulidi KiSwahili. Interview, Mombasa, 1980.

33. Abdalla Kadara, "Habib Saleh."

34. Ali Skanda to Sharif Saleh, taped interview; Sheikh Ahmed Jahadhmy, interview, 1980. Peter Lienhardt, "The Mosque College" 229-42. For an interesting interpretation of the WaFamao, see Marina Tolmacheva, "Group Identity."

35. Hassan Badawy, 1980. The old daughter of Habib Saleh ran a *madrassa* for poor, mostly ex-slave and Hadrami women until just a year or so before she died. Like her father and siblings, this woman was thought to have special "baraka" and healing powers were also ascribed to her.

36. See chapter one. Lamu informants, including a descendant of Habib Saleh, 1980, 1981.

37. See Alan Boyd, "To Praise the Prophet: A Processional Symbolic Analysis of 'Mauld': A Muslim Ritual of Lamu, Kenya" Ph.D. thesis, Indiana University, 1981. See also B. G. Martin, "Notes on Members of the Learned Classes" (538-39) for Sharif Abdalla bin Mohammed bin Kathin al Kindi whose early religious training was in Lamu. His "cleverness brought him to the attention of the Jamal al Layl sharifs" in Lamu sometime in his youth (c.1902). The patronage of Habib Saleh "ensured his advancement as a scholar" where he became one "of the most popular and influential teachers in Zanzibar." Sharif Abdalla bin Salim remembered the controversies over the tambourines being played in the mosque; as did Sheikh Ahmed Jahadhmy, interviews, 1980.

38. Stigand, *Land of Zinj* (156) noted a "little leprosy" still visible in Lamu when he visited there in 1912.

39. James Christie, *Cholera Epidemics*, 330-31.

40. Hatim Amiji, "The Asian Communities" in James Kritzeck and William H. Lewis (eds)., *Islam in Africa* (New York, 1969) 142-68.

41. Robert G. Gregory, *India and East Africa* (Oxford, 1971), 37. Sir Bartle Frere, however, believed the Indian community was undercounted.

42. Mzee Shamsuddin, interview, January, 1981. See Hatem Amiji, "The Asian Communities" in James Kritzeck and William H. Lewis (eds)., *Islam and Africa* (New York, 1969) 141-81. Hatim Amiji, "The Bohras of East Africa *Journal of Religion in Africa* 7 (1976) 27-40. Jean-Claude Penrad, "La presence isma'ilienne en Afrique de l'est" in Denys Lombard et Jean Aubin (eds)., *Marchands et hommes d'affaires asiatiques dans l'Ocean Indien et la Mer de Chine 13e-20e siecles* (Paris, 1988) 221-35.

43. See Moojan Momen, *An Introduction to Shi'a Islam: The History and Doctrines of Twelver Shi'ism* (New Haven, 1985) 56. See also Patricia W. Romero, "A glimpse at the East African Bohra and the reformers" paper presented at the African Studies Association, 1995.

44. For the spread of Islam to the Comoro Islands, see Pierre Verin, "L'Introduction de L'Islam aux Comores Selon les Traditions Orales" *Paiduma* 28 (1982) 193-99.

45. Verin, "L'Introduction de L'Islam aux Comores selon les Traditions Orales," 193-99. But there are controversies among the Bohra as to whether the Dawoodi Bohra were there that early.

46. For the Indian communities see Hatim M. Amiji, "Some Notes on Religious Dissent in Nineteenth Century East Africa" *African Historical Studies* IV: (1970) 603-16; Hatim M. Amiji, "The Bohras of East Africa" 27-61. Robert G. Gregory, *Indians in East Africa* ; H. M. Morris, *Indians in Uganda*; J. Christie, *Cholera Epidemics* 335-37; Abdul Sheriff, *Slaves, Spices and Ivory Economic Integration of East Africa into the World Economy* (London, 1987). Shariff says that there were a few Indian adventurers in East Africa in 1811 but by 1850 about 2,000—Hindu financiers and both Hindu and Muslim merchants. For background in Gujarat, see W. Ivanow, *A Guide to Ismaili Literature* (London, 1933); and P. Hardy, *The Muslims in British India* (Cambridge, 1972).

47. Bhacker, *Trade and Empire* 72-4.

48. John Kirk to FO, November, 1870. FO 84/2059.

49. Abdul Hussein, interview Lamu, October, 1985.

50. Hussein A. Husseinali, interview, Mombasa, 1985. Husseinali's Lamu wife was taken by her family to this shrine when she was a child of seven or, in the 1930s. See Patricia W. Romero, "The East African Bohra." See also Juma Premji Rupani, *Trade in Africa and the Asian Community* (Bombay, 1937). J. de V. Allen, *Lamu Town* 26, has no date for the Bohra Mosque; an estimate of "late 19th century" for the Ithnasharia Mosque; and guesses that Jamatkhana, the Ismaili Mosque, was much older than the date of 1942 which appeared on the entry gate.

51. See Gwen Campbell, "The Structure of Trade in Madagascar 1750-1810" *Journal of African Historical Studies* 26 (1993) 130-131.

52. Lamuwalla, interview, LaReunion, February, 1986. Christie, *Chlorea Epidemics*, 344, referred to the style of dress which characterized the Bohra, noting that they "are the only class in Zanzibar, with the exception of the Persians, who wear a kind of trouser."

53. Husseinali A. Hussein interview, Mombasa, October, 1985; January, 1986. For the growth of Mombasa see Karim Kassam Janmohammed, "A History of Mombasa, c. 1895-1939: Some Aspects of Economic and Social Life in an East African Port Town During Colonial Rule" Ph.D. thesis, Northwestern University, 1978.

54. Interview Mombasa, January, 1990. The Ithnasharia Mosque is still run by trustees and includes some African congregants. No Indian members of the community reside in Lamu. The Ismaili Mosque, which was located on the seafront, was sold by the current Aga Khan in 1985 and was torn down in 1990. The last remaining member of that community married an Afro-Arab woman and converted to Sunni Islam.
55. Christie, *Chlorea Epidemics*, 336-39.
56. Christie, *Chlorea Epidemics*, 342-43.
57. Bakaraly, Chef du Bohra, Tamatave, believed that the custom of chewing betel nut leaves originated in India and was carried by Indian traders throughout the Indian Ocean diaspora. Interview, January, 1986, Tamatave, Madagascar.
58. Christie, *Chlorea Epidemics*, 344-353.

Chapter 7

1. Euan-Smith to Foreign Office, January 9, 1890. FO 84/2059
2. Clive "A Short History"; L. Talbot Smith, "History of Tanaland." For differences between the northern coast and Bagamoyo, see Jonathan Glassman, *Feasts and Riot: Revelry, Rebellion and Popular Consciousness on the Swahili Coast 1856-88* (New York, 1995); and Allen, *Swahili Culture* 201. For slavery in Africa, see Igor Kopytoff and Suzanne Miers, eds., *Slavery in Africa: historical and anthropological perspectives* (Madison, 1977), 73-74 *et passim.*
3. Simons to Euan-Smith, November 1890, Zanzibar National Archives.
4. R. Simons to Col. Euan-Smith, July 28, 1891. Zanzibar National Archives.
5. Jackson, *Early Days* 353-55. For an economic assessment of Lamu's decline, see Ylvisaker, *Lamu, passim.* See also Ahmed Ibna Salim, "The Impact of Colonialism" 63; A. I. Salim, *Swahili Speaking*, 100. A.I. Salim and I are in agreement that the end of the slave trade and slavery (1907) were responsible for the decline.
6. Sheikh Ahmed Jahadhmy, interview, 1980.
7. Jackson, *Early Days* 355.
8. Box 631A Mackinnon Papers.
9. P. A. Memon and Esmond B. Martin, "The Kenya Coast: An anomaly in the Development of an 'Ideal Type' Colonial Spatial-System," *Kenya Historical Review* 4:2 (1976) 196.
10. Testimony of Sir Ali bin Salim before the Carter Commission, *Kenya Land Commission* III (Nairobi, 1934) 2718.
11. Ali Mukakaa, interview, Lamu, 1985. Salim Kheri, interview, 1983. Ali Abdalla al Maawyia, interview, 1981. Sheikh Ahmed Jahadhmy, interviews, 1980-82. Abdalla Skanda, interviews, 1980, Sharif Abdalla Salim, interview Mombasa, 1980.
12. Sheikh Ahmed Jahadhmy, interview, 1980. Abdalla Skanda, interview, 1980. Carter Land Commission, *Kenya Land Commission*, 2214-17. See chapter nine.
13. Sheikh Ali Ahmed Jahadhmy to author, 1994.
14. Interviews with Lamu women, 1989, 1990, 1994. Middleton, *World of the Swahili* (99) agrees that residence is uxorilocal but says he saw no examples of matrilineal descent in Lamu. See, however, Knappert, *Four Centuries of Swahili Verse* (London, 1979) 5 who disagrees. See also Nurse and Spear, *The Swahili.* Knappert and Nurse and Spear claim that the Swahili were matrilineal. It is possible that the Swahili descent patterns blended with those of the Arabs who came in, rather than being sub-

sumed by Arab emphasis on tracing their lines exclusively through males. See also Bhacker, *Trade and Empire*.

15. Sheikh Ali Ahmed Jahadhmy.

16. Thomas Wilson, personal communication, April, 1992.

17. Sharif Abdalla Salim al Hussein, interview, Mombasa, 1980. Patricia W. Romero, "The Problems of Studying Witchcraft in Lamu, Kenya" paper presented at the Berkshire Conference on the History of Women, June, 1990.

18. See Jonathan Glassman, "The Runaway Slave" for more on the *Watoro*.

19. Ali Mukakaa, interview, 1985. Salim Kheri, interview, 1983. Lamu ex-slave women and their descendants, interviews 1981-90. Among the several works concerned with witchcraft and spirit possession, see Lienhardt (ed)., *The Medicine Man et passim;* and Linda L. Giles, "Spirits, Class, and Status in Swahili Society: The *Habeshia* and *Kibuki* Spirit Cults in Zanzibar Town" paper presented at the American Anthropological Association meeting, November, 1989. Giles found that in recent times men as well as women were active in spirit possession cults and that those of slave descent were not more likely than free born to be members of these cults. Giles research reenforces my own surface findings in Lamu, although Lamu informants claim that spirit possession and witchcraft had their origins in the slave community.

20. Patricia W. Romero, "Whose Medicine: Traditional *versus* Western Practices in Lamu." Ex-slave female informants, interviews, 1981-85.

21. The District Commissioner for Lamu reported in 1909 that the oldest son supervised the mainland plantations.; KNA LMU/ll. Ylvisaker, *Lamu in the Nineteenth Century*, 82, drew the same conclusion. But, on the island shambas, masters more often came, sometimes even joining their slaves in harvesting as the slave population decreased.

22. Fred J. Berg found a slightly different pattern for slave workdays, see Berg, "Mombasa under the BuSaidi Sultanate: The City and its Hinterlands in the Nineteenth Century" Ph.D. thesis University of Wisconsin, 1971, 175. See also Ylvisaker, *Lamu in the Nineteenth Century*, 58; and Cooper, *Plantation Slavery*, 153-212.

23. See el Zein, *The Sacred Meadows*, 244. Ali Mukakaa, interview, 1985; Sheikh Ahmed Jahadhmy, interview, 1980; Mohammed Jahadhmy, interviews, 1980-90. I am much indebted to Mohammed Jahadhmy for information pertaining to the operation of these island shambas.

24. Cooper, *Plantation Slavery*, 190-95. But Cooper cautioned that slave army may be too strong a term, although he did find that "military service was part of the generalized expectations masters had of their dependents." Personal communication, November, 1981.

25. Talbot-Smith, "History." Abdalla Skanda, interview, 1983.

26. Provincial Commissioners's Report, Tanaland, 1909-10, KNA.

27. Lamu women informants, interviews, 1980-90.

28. Talbot-Smith, "History" and District Commissioner Reports, LMU/ll KNA. A. J. H. Prins also wrote about the low birth rate among slave people: *Swahili-Speaking Peoples of Zanzibar*, 24. Margaret Strobel, "Slavery and Reproductive Labor" in Klein and Robertson (eds)., *Woman and Slavery* 111-29. Patricia W. Romero, "Does Being 'Sexy' Keep a Marriage Going in Lamu, Kenya." Gill Shepherd, "Rank, gender and homosexuality" 240-70. It is possible that Lamu women were passionless as a way of controlling their reproduction of children (see Caplan, 4). Lamu woman informants, 1980-90. See also E. R. Toledano, "Slave Dealers, Women, Pregnancy

and Abortion: The story of a Circassian Slave Girl in Mid-Nineteenth Century Cairo" *Slavery and Abolition* 2 (1981) 53-68.

29. "Mama Khadija" in Romero (ed)., *Life Histories* (148-51) talks about how hard she had to work during the years she chose to remain in slavery to the al Maawyia family. Khadija was born in 1919, nine years after slavery legally ended but did not consider herself "free" until Chief Mohammed died in the mid-1950s. Meillassoux refers to how dehumanizing slavery was for women in Africa. See Claude Meillassoux, "Female Slavery" in Klein and Robertson, *Woman and Slavery* 64-65.

30. Lamu ex-slave women and their descendants, interviews, 1982-85.

31. Lamu ex-slave women informants, 1981. Mohammed bin Ali BuSaid, 1982. See also T. O. Ranger, *Dance and Society in Eastern Africa* (Berkeley, 1975) 16-30. Margaret Strobel, *Muslim Women in Mombasa* (New Haven, 1978) 157-8; and Alan Boyd, "The Musical Instruments of Lamu" *Kenya Past and Present* 9 (1978) 3-8.

32. Talbot-Smith, "History."

33. Sheikh Ahmed Jahadhmy, interview, 1980, 1994. Lamu women, including "Mama Khadija" and ex-slave Samoe (now deceased), 1980-85. Azziz bin Mohammed, interview, Mombasa, 1986. Mohammed bin Abdalla, interview, Mombasa, 1986. Fateh Hila, interview, 1990.

34. Burton, *Zanzibar City* 1:466 reported that slave captains enjoyed wide responsibilities in Zanzibar. Cooper, "Treatment of Slaves" 94, 98, also noted that slaves farther down the coast owned property which, at their deaths, reverted to their owners. A. A. Skanda, interview, 1980. In fact, profits accrued to slave seaman in larger amounts than would be the case in freedom, when they had to support themselves and, as a consequence, drew advances which kept them in perpetual debt. See chapter eight.

35. Cooper found this to be true further south in the Mombasa area as well: "Negroid features are not the clear and highly visible indication of inferiority they are in the Americas." See Frederick Cooper, "The Treatment of Slaves on the Kenya Coast in the 19th Century," *Kenya Historical Review* II (1973) 97.

36. Morton has criticized both Cooper and myself for characterizing slavery as benign. Cooper and I arrived at our interpretations independent of each other. Each of us conducted careful fieldwork in our respective locales, although Cooper preceded me to the coast by several years. Our findings were similar even though they reflected our independent research—his in the area of Mombasa and Malindi, and mine in Lamu. The similarities in our findings reenforce the interpretations of treatment on the Kenya coast running from Mombasa to Lamu. They do not cast us in the role of apologists, and neither Cooper or I claim that all slaves were uniformly well treated. By comparison, coastal East African slaves were generally better treated than those in the Americas. Morton, whose archival research was centered primarily on the missionary operated (i.e. abolitionist) refuge for slaves at Rabai, naturally encountered documents that emphasized harsh treatment. See Morton, *Children of Ham*, Chapter One; Cooper, "Treatment of Slaves" 89-103; and Romero Curtin, "The Island of Lamu" especially 875-76.

37. Lamu ex-slave women and their descendants, interviews, 1980-90.

38. Ex-slave women, interviews, 1981.

39. Ali Mukakaa, interview, 1985. Ex-slave women and their descendants, 1985.

40. el Zein, *The Sacred Meadows* (31) stated that suria were not regarded as having the same status. He seemed never to have interviewed any of the Lamu Afro-Arab or ex-slave women, otherwise he could not have drawn that conclusion.

41. Information on divorce rates is contained in the Annual Reports of the District Commissioner, Lamu, 1909-63, KNA. Many Lamu informants referred to unhappy marriages. Even Afro-Arab women testified to their beliefs that concubines were "loved" and wives tolerated or discarded. Romero, "Does Being 'Sexy'"; Strobel, *Mombasa Women*, 44-48.
42. Margaret Strobel, Khadija Ali, interview, Mombasa, 1980; Zachia Abdalla, interview, Mombasa, 1980; Ali Salim, interview, Mombasa, 1980. These informants agreed that *unyago* was "African" in origin and did not in Lamu.
43. This informant figures in the genealogies as "A".
44. Igor Kopytoff suggested that female slaves long attached to a family were viewed as kin. See Kopytoff and Miers (eds)., *Slavery in Africa* 73-74. See also Strobel, *Mombasa Women*, 137-47.
45. Unnamed British district officer, as quoted in Berg, "Mombasa under the BuSaidi" 169.

Chapter 8

1. Ali Abdalla Jahadhmy, interview Mombasa, May, 1980.
2. Lamu Political Record Book III D.C. Report 1910 KNA.
3. For a similar development in Mombasa, see Karim Kassam Jonmohammed, "A History of Mombasa c. 1895-1939" Ph.D. thesis, Northwestern University, 1971, 134-136 *et passim*.
4. Pamela Scott, interview, Lamu, June, 1989.
5. Willis argues that local IBEA officials "were staunch opponents of the abolition of slavery until legal abolition was forced on them in 1907. Unfortunately, his single source is an IBEA official whose views may, or may not, have reflected those of the majority of British officials in positions of importance on the coast in 1907. See Willis, *The Making of the Mijikenda*, 83 and n. 18, 83.
6. Patricia W. Romero, "Where Have all the Slaves Gone: Emancipation and Post-Emancipation in Lamu, Kenya" *Journal of African History* 27 (1986) 497-512. Much of the material in this chapter dealing with emancipation and exslaves comes from this article. See also Tanaland Provincial Commissioner's Report, 1912-13, KNA; Frederick Cooper, *From Slaves to Squatters: Plantation Labor and Agriculture in Zanzibar and Coastal Kenya 1890-1925* (New Haven, 1980).
7. This amounted to Pounds Sterling 15,000 or 75,000 U.S. dollars.
8. Talbot-Smith "History" mentions that the owners generally provided for their aged slaves. Ex-slaves and their descendants agreed that most of them were taken care of, although not often very well, until their deaths. After emancipation, for those slaves who stayed on, most were supported the rest of their lives.
9. Handling Over Reports LMU/9 1910-1924 KNA. Freedom also meant for some loss of fictive kinship for slaves. See, for instance, David Northrup, "The Ideological Context of Slavery in Southeastern Nigeria in the 19th Century" in Paul Lovejoy (ed)., *The Ideology of Slavery in Africa* (Beverly Hills, 1981) 118-19.
10. Talbot-Smith, "History."
11. Clive, "History." Talbot-Smith, "History."
12. Ali Abdalla Jahadhmy, interview, June, 1980. Ex-slave and slave descendants, Lamu, 1983-90.

13. Sharif Hassan Bawady, interview, 1981.
14. Sharif Abdalla bin Salim al Hussein, interview, 1980. Sheikh Ali Jahadhmy, interview, 1994.
15. Somoe Ali, interview, 1981. This woman was mistreated by her daughter, who moved into her house and who spat at me each time I entered during our several interviews.
16. The role of religious indoctrination in a Muslim society is not to be underestimated. Miers found that some captured slaves actually "gave thanks for their capture and conversion." See Suzanne Miers, *Britain and the Ending of the Slave Trade* (London, 1975) n.6 Frederick Cooper disagrees. See "Islam and Cultural Hegemony: The Ideology of Slave owners on the East African Coast" in Lovejoy (ed)., *The Ideology of Slavery* 247-77. Cooper's studies were made in the much larger areas of Malindi and Mombasa, where intimacy between slave holders and slaves may not have been as great as was the case between many in Lamu. But, on Pemba, another island community, slaves also stayed on. See Moses D. E. Ndwulia, *Britain and Slavery in East Africa* (Washington, 1974) 192.
17. Lamu women informants, some of whom were products of unions between concubines and free men in the 1920s and 1930s. See Romero Curtin, "Laboratory" 859; and Tanaland Provisional Commissioner's Report, LMU/O, 1924 KNA.
18. Lamu Political Record Book III D.C. Report 1910 KNA.
19. Ali Abdalla Skanda, taped interview with Sharif Saleh, 1982. Tape in the possession of the author.
20. "Mama Khadija" interview, 1981.
21. Interview, Lamu, 1985. Lamu women, interviews, 1985.
22. R. Skene, "Arab and Swahili Dances and Ceremonies" *Journal of the Royal Anthropological Institute of Great Britain and Ireland 47* (1917) 413-34. Caplan found that on Mafia Island the jinns were not so much condemned by the Qur'anic teachers as those from the land. See Pat Caplan, *Choice and Constraint in a Swahili Community* (London, 1975) 101. See also Linda Giles, "Spirits, Class and Status" copy of paper in possession of the author.
23. Skene, "Arab and Swahili Dances" 480. Skene included a number of different dances pertaining to spirit possession and all of them featured women as the possessed. Linda L. Giles, "The Dialectic of Spirit Possession: A Cross Cultural Dialogue" *The Mankind Quarterly* XXIX (1989) 243-65. Patricia W. Romero, "The Problems of Studying Women as Witches and Diviners in Lamu, Kenya" paper presented at the Berkshire Conference on Women's History, 1990. The pioneering study of women power and spirit possession is Edward A. Alpers, "'Ordinary Household Chores': Ritual and Power in a 19th-Century Swahili Women's Spirit Possession Cult" *International Journal of African Historical Studies* 17:4 (1984) 677-702. For further down the East African coast, see Mtoro bin Mwinyi and other Swahili Persons, *The Customs of the Swahili People (Desturi za Waswahili)* J.W.T. Allen (ed and trans)., (Berkeley, 1981).
24. "Ghosts and spirits" LMU Political Record Book III KNA.
25. Personal observations, Lamu, 1980-1988. Indian, Afro-Arab, Hadrami, and ex-slave women, Lamu, 1989. According to Lamu informants, the Prophet Mohammed, before the Qur'an was revealed to him, also suffered ill effects from the "evil eye." This story is substantiated in Alfred Guillaume, *New Light on the Life of Muhammad* (Manchester, 1960) 29.

273

26. Lamu women, interviews. Ahmed Khatib, interview, 1989.
27. This woman said her African grandmother was "a witch" and used to perform the dance. Kubrakhai Mohammedbhai, now living in Mauritius, remembered *kayambi* from Mombasa. For witchcraft and sorcery, see Middleton, *World of the Swahili*, 74 *et passim.*
28. "Mama Khadija" interview, 1981.
29. Skene, "Arab and Swahili Dances" 413, 415, 419.
30. Lamu women, 1982. In 1979, in the last month of the Swahili year, several small sailing vessels capsized off the tip of Shela, resulting in the deaths of numbers of Lamu women, none of whom could swim.
31. Lamu women, 1983.
32. CD/LMU/1/5/KNA.
33. Lamu Political Record Book III KNA. This was also supported by former owners who talked about their mothers, sisters, and even wives who wove mat bags and rugs, and sewed *kofia*. But, ex-slave women also talked about earning money in this way and of passing some of their profits on to their formers owners.
34. Ahmed Salim, "The Impact of colonialism upon Muslim life in Kenya," *Muslim Minority Affairs* I (1979) 60-66.
35. Salim (*Swahili-Speaking Peoples*) 53, noted that banditry was a cause of considerable concern after emancipation.
36. Ex-slave woman, interview, November, 1983. This woman thought she was born about 1900, and she said she had been set free by the British when she was a child and before she joined her father, a runaway, on the mainland. Upperclass woman, interview, November, 1983. See Clive, "A Short History."
37. DC/LMU/1/5 KNA.
38. Clive, "A Short History."
39. Report of Messrs. Ainsworth and Hollis, copy loaned to author by Edward Rodwell.
40. The R. E. Skene Papers, housed at the University of California, Los Angeles (UCLA) and covering the year and one half that he was posted in Lamu contain over 1,000 documents, ranging from copies of old, mostly unimportant, telegrams to his terse reports on social and economic conditions in Lamu. Much of the material in the sections that follow comes directly from the Skene papers, xerox copies of which were supplied me by UCLA. In some instances, especially where numbers of documents are mentioned, I have not used specific citations.
41. LMU425/16 9 May 1911 KNA. Ahmed Idha Salim, "'Native or Non-Native?' The Problem of Identity and the Social Stratification of the Arab-Swahili of Kenya" *Hadith* 6 (1976) 65-85.
42. R. Skene to Seif bin Abdalla, 13 April 1911 UCLA.
43. These statistics represent marriages for Tanaland Province and thus are indicative of how few actual marriages and divorces were officially recorded. Tanaland Provincial Report, MF 1840, KNA.
44. Clive, "A Short History."
45. Mzee A. A. Skanda to Sharif Saleh, taped interview in possession of the author.
46. PC Report 1912-13 LMU KNA.
47. Lamu District, Annual Report, March 1911, Skene Papers, UCLA.
48. R. Skene to The Registrar, High Court, Mombasa, June, 1911, Skene Papers.
49 R. Skene to The Ag. Provincial Commissioner, Lamu, 31 May 1911. R. Skene to the Mudir of Mkenumbi, 13 January, 1911, Skene Papers.

50. DC Report, 1911. Copies of letters from Fatuna [sic] binti Mohomed to Skene 23 December 1910, Skene Papers. Sheikh Ahmed Jahadhmy, personal communication, January, 1992.
51. See chapters two and six.
52. Talbot-Smith, "History."
53. R. Skene to Messrs. Sheriff Jaffer and Company, 19 June 1911, Skene Papers. For Whitten's arrival in Lamu, see T. Ainsworth Dickens, "History" and Clive, "A Short History." Whitten became a justice of the peace and later was awarded "the Jubilee and Coronation medal." According to Clive, Whitten returned to England only once, otherwise spent thirty eight years "running" in Lamu.
54. See DC Reports, Lamu, 1920s and 1930s, KNA. See copies of documents pertaining to the court case in Bombay 1911, Skene Papers.
55. DC/LMU/l/5 KNA.
56. PC Report LMU 1912-13 KNA. Sheikh Ahmed Jahadhmy, personal communication, January, 1912. Ali Abdalla Skanda to Sharif Saleh.
57. Sharif Abdalla Salim al Hussein, interview, 1980.
58. DC/LMU/1/5 KNA. A. H. J. Prins, *Swahili Speaking Peoples* 70.
59. PC Report 1916-17 Tanaland KNA.
60. Tanaland Provincial Report MF 1840 KNA.
61. Tanaland Provincial Report, MF 1840 KNA.
62. Sharif Abdalla Salim, interview, 1980. Sharif Abdalla married an aunt of political scientist, Ali Mazrui. See chapter eleven.
63. PC Tanaland 1916-17 KNA. Abdalla Ali Skanda, interviews, 1980; Sharif Abdalla bin Salim, interviews, 1980-81. Ahmed Khatib, who spoke with numbers of wazee in Lamu who refused to talk to me on the subject of slavery, interviews, 1989-91.
64. Lamu ex-slave and free women, interviews, 1980-91.
65. See Romero Curtin, "Weddings in Lamu." See also Strobel, *Mombasa Women passim*. In 1985 a taxi driver who had been a policeman in Lamu told me about the long history of smuggling which characterized those who he labelled the Hadrami merchants. See Villiers, *Sons of Sinbad* 89-92, for a description of smugglers further up the coast.
66. Silks were frequently listed on the list of imports into Lamu, thus duties and taxes were also paid in addition to whatever materials may have been smuggled in. See DC Reports for Lamu 1913-20 KNA.
67. Sharif Abdalla bin Salim, interviews, 1981.
68. Talbot-Smith, "History."

Chapter 9

1. DC LAM/2/3 LMU Political Record Book KNA.
2. PC/Coast 1/1/165 KNA.
3. PC/Coast I/1/1/165 KNA. Dickens wrote his "history" of Lamu during the final months he was posted there, providing the basis for the longer and more detailed history for Clive's "A Short History."
4. Coast Province 1912-1929 20/151/22/177 Pt. S KNA
5. DC LMU/KT1.2 KNA
6. Leila Abdalla to author, based on interviews with members of the old families in

Lamu, 1982.

7. Lamu woman, interview 1982. Although she repeatedly referred to the Hindus, the Bohra also loaned money. Later so did the Hadrami, who found ingenious ways to get around the prohibition against usury.

8. Some members of the Jevanjee family were posted in Lamu from the turn of the twentieth century. Their East African base was originally Zanzibar from 1820, but the family's interests spread throughout the Indian Ocean world. Huseina Yusuf Ali Currumjee Jevanjee, interview, Mauritius, l986.

9. DC LMU 1/3/ KNA. Copy in the possession of the author.

10. R. Skene purchased the land; and DC Isaacs built the "school." It is unclear exactly what kind of school this was since European style education did not begin in Lamu until the 1920s (see chapter nine). DC/LMU/3/2 Political Record Book #5 KNA.

11. DC LMU KTl.2 KNA

12. PC/Coast 1/1/165 KNA. In 1923 the Lamu and Tana River Districts were put under the administration of the Lamu DC. These shifts in district responsibilities, in conjunction with the constant change in administrators, made reporting even more difficult.

13. DC LMU/9 KNA. Mohammed bin Ali BuSaid, interview, 1981. Kiki Dastoor, interview, Lamu, 1985. Mohammed Jahadhmy, interview, 1980.

14. PC/Coast/1/1/238 KNA. No explanation was given for listing "married men" nor are the women identified as to their marital status.

15. Mohammed Jahadhmy, interview, 1980.

16. DC LMU/1/2 KNA.

17. Edward Rodwell to the author, personal communication, 1991.

18. DC LAM/1/2 KNA. See Romero, "Where Have all the Slaves Gone."

19. DC LMU/1/2/ KNA; Clive, "A Short History."

20. Charles Chenevix Trench, *Men Who Ruled Kenya* (London, 1993) 175.

21. DC LMU/1/3 KNA.

22. DC LMU/1/2 KNA.

23. DC LMU/1/2 KNA.

24. Sharif Abdalla Salim, interview, 1980. See similar attitudes and behavior in Morocco, see Allen R. Meyers, "Class, Ethnicity, and Slavery: The Origins of the Moroccan 'Abid'" *International Journal of African Historical Studies* 10 (1977) 436.

25. See Miers and Kopytoff (eds)., "Intro." *Slavery in Africa* 74.

26. Fatuma Abdalla, interview, Mombasa, 1982.

27. L. Talbot Smith, "A Short History of Tanaland" DC/LAM/3/1 KNA. One ex-slave woman recalled the woodcarving "Lamu made chairs and furniture. . . . There were no woodcarving shops in Lamu. After slaves stopped carving in their masters homes (in the 1930s) the industry died out." Afro-Arab informants recalled some furniture being carved in the courtyard in front of the fort in the 1930s.

28. DC/LAM/3/2 Political Record Book KNA.

29. "Mama Khadija" and another old ex-slave woman, interviews, 1983. See Patricia Romero, "Gold as an Economic Vehicle."

30. Ex-slave women, interviews, 1983-84. See Romero, "Mama Khadija" and "Where Have all the Slaves Gone" for more details about the roles of slaves and ex-slaves in post-emancipation Lamu.

31. LMU/9 Handing Over Report KNA.

32. See Chapter nine.

33. Sharif Hassan Badawy, interview.
34. Abdalla bin Ali, interview, 1985. Mohammed bin Ali, interview, 1982. Lamu women.
35. Margaret Strobel, *Mombasa Women* (156-57) believes *lelemama* came to Mombasa in the late nineteenth century. When queried, however, all Lamu informants insisted *lelemama* came to Lamu only in the 1920s and directly from Zanzibar.
36. Binta Arafa, member of "Kingi" to Leila binta Ali Giansiracusa, Lamu, 1981. Personal communication, Leila binta Ali to author, 1981. At that time Leila was my research assistant in Lamu.
37. Informants, who read passages from Rangers book, disagree with his view that the competitions were representative of political and social divisions within the town. They were reflective, however, of class differences between those who stayed on, and those who chose freedom. See T. O. Ranger, *Dance and Society in Eastern Africa 1890-1970* (Berkeley, 1975) 75-78.
38. This woman was the former slave of Mohammed al Maawyia who, she said, was a "religious man with a position in the town." He did not like the bands, did not like the costumes, and believed the competition was unhealthy. Since his "slaves were the ones who took care of his shambas, he agreed" that they could hold some of their competitions there, and he also provided tea as part of their celebration.
39. DC LAM/1/2 KNA; DC/LMU/1/3 KNA.
40. Lamu ex-slave women, interviews, 1983. Sharif Abdalla Salim, interview, 1981. For Bajun prostitutes see Janet Bujra, "Production, property, prostitution: Sexual politics in Atu" *Cahiers d'etudes africaines* XVII (1975) 13-39. See also Strobel, *Mombasa Women.* "Mama Khadija" interview, 1982.
41. Lamu woman, interview, 1985.
42. Lelimama was still being danced in Lamu in the 1950s. Prins (*The Swahili Speaking Peoples* 112) said he participated in one lelimama dance that lasted three hours in 1957.
43. Lamu women, 1981.
44. T. O. Ranger, *Dance and Society* (78) noted cowboy hats at the dances he saw in Lamu. Ahmed Nabahany, interview, Mombasa, 1980.
45. Lamu women, interviews, 1983. Lamu men to Leila binta Adballa, 1981.
46. Fateh Hila, interview, 1989.

Chapter 10

1. Abdalla Kadara, "Habib Swaleh" LMU 23.3.76 Lamu Library.
2. Sharif Hassan Badawy, Sharif Badawy Jamal al Layl, Sharif Saleh Hassan, interviews, Lamu, 1980. See el Zein, *The Sacred Meadows passim.*
3. Sharif Saleh Hassan, interview, 1981; Sharif Hassan Badawy, taped interview, 1980.
4. B. G. Martin, "Notes on Members" 538-9. Martin refers to el Kindi having been born in Mkumoni, the area most associated with the patrician class. See el Zein, *The Sacred Meadows* (72-74). for what he believed to be the extent of Habib Saleh's reputation beyond Lamu District.
5. B. G. Martin, "Notes on Members" 543. August Nimtz, who draws on el Zein, Trimingham, and on Lienhardt for Lamu, paints a much different picture for the development of a sufi order elsewhere on the coast. See August H. Nimtz, Jr., *Islam and Politics in East Africa: The Sufi Order in Tanzania* (Minneapolis, 1980); J. Spencer Trimingham, *Islam in the Sudan* (London, 1949) 987-95. Guennec-Coppens

has written a highly derivative but inaccurate article on the role of the Jamal al Layl sharifs in Lamu. She leans heavily on el Zein, and Abdalla Kadara, although she also draws from Lienhardt's study of the Riyadha Mosque. Guennec-Coppens, "Les Masharifu Jamalilil" 91-102. el Zein, *The Sacred Meadows* (72) says that Habib Saleh refused to issue invitations to the Riyadha. The family and other Afro-Arab informants refute this claim. They believe el Zein was incorrectly informed by Abdalla Kadara. Peter Lienhardt, "The Mosque College" (38), however, referred to the "family" of Habib Saleh who promoted themselves on the basis of the "Alawiyya Tariqa." For sufism within Sunni Islam, see A. J. Arbery, *Sufism: An Account of the Mystics in Islam* (London, 1963). The Lamu Afro-Arabs and Hadrami followed the Shafi' school of Islam. For Muslim schools of law in East Africa, see J. N. D. Anderson, *Islamic Law* 322. See n.15 Chapter 6.

6. For obvious reasons it is difficult to cite particular informants, but they include a woman from Mombasa who grew up in Lamu and who witnessed the changes in the Riyadha Mosque over the period from 1920 and on. For much of the information that comes from informants in this section and later, I shall be forced to mention only "informants" and will not be able to provide specific names. In the case of Habib Saleh's sons and later descendants using the "Alawiyya tariqa" to promote them- selves ring true according to any number of informants, but are refuted by members of the family. See Peter Lienhardt, "The Mosque College" 38.

7. For similar rites in North Africa, see Vansina, *Art in History* 211-12.

8. Nyrop, *et al* (eds)., *Area Handbook for the Yemen* 74. A. J. H. Prins, *Didemic Lamu passim*. In this case, the "didemic" refers to a division between the Hadrami and the Arabs.

9. Kiki Dastoor, interview, Lamu, 1986.

10. This was an Afro-Arab man, but he was backed up in his testimony by several of the women, including Hadrami.

10. el Zein, *The Sacred Meadows* 61, 68.

12. DC/LMU/5/6 KNA. Fundamentalist is not an altogether appropriate term but because it has made its way into the lexicon in describing revivalist and literal inter- pretations of the Qur'an, as well as those Muslims are who are influenced by reli- gious authorities elsewhere, I have chosen to use it.

13. Sharif Ali al Beidh, interview, Mambrui, May, 1980. el Zein, *The Sacred Meadows* (74) incorrectly states that Habib Saleh refused to issue licenses to other sharifs, keeping instead the Alawiyya to himself and his direct progeny.

14. DC LMU/5/2/1 KNA. Lamu informants. For the unique Lamu mosque architecture, including the Riyadha, see Peter S. Garlake, *The Early Islamic Architecture of the East African Coast* (London, 1966), 75.

15. By the mid-1970's another, but more serious, rift took place within the Riyadha. This was an outgrowth of a quarrel between some of Badawy's acknowledged sons (see Appendix). Two brothers left and founded the Swofaa Mosque, which is located near the police barracks in what was then an open shamba area. Habib Saleh's Riyadha went through a period of decline—although the congregation clung to "The Maulidi" celebrations that continued to draw thousands on the last day of the month marking the birth of the Prophet Mohammed. Ironically, in the power struggles that ensued the schism between brothers, the sympathies of the old families tended to flow in the direction of the Riyadha Mosque.

16. Abdalla Bujra, *The Politics of* 76, 115.

17. Altogether, between 1988 and 1991, I interviewed five elderly Hadrami women, and one female Bajun woman regarding the Hadrami community. Perhaps because of the memories of el Zein's *The Sacred Meadows*, Hadrami men were unwilling to be interviewed. Also, they may have been unwilling to discuss matters such as their finances which many guard closely, including keeping matters such as income from their wives.
18. "Mama Khadija" 1983. See chapter twelve.
19. These were not registered with the Qadi and could run from a night or two to long term clandestine relations between men and their illegal "wives."
20. Romero Curtin, "The Sacred Meadows" 341. el Zein, *The Sacred Meadows* 261, 268. Romero Curtin, "Weddings in Lamu" 145. Romero, "Mama Khadija" 148-49. Romero, "Does Being Sexy Keep a Marriage Going in Lamu." Lamu informants. Mombasa informants (including descendant of Habib Saleh). Sharif Abdalla Salim, interview, Mombasa 1980, said secret marriages took place in Mombasa as well as in Lamu.
21. Sharif Saleh Hassan, interviews, 1980-91.
22. Sheikh Ahmed Jahadhmy, interview, 1981. Sharif Abdalla Salim al Hussein, interview, 1981. For the maulidi see Boyd, "In Praise of the Prophet." Peter Seitel, "Cultural Implications of the Eclipse of 16 February 1980 in Lamu, Kenya" *Archaeostronomy* 6 (1983) 134-40.
23. Sharif Abdalla Salim, interview, 1980.
24. LMU/8 Political Record Book KNA; DC/LMU/KTI.2.1 KNA. See also F. LeGuennec-Coppens, "Les Hadrami: Une des Composantes des Populations Swahili de l'Afrique Orientale" *Recheres Pedagogie Culturelle* (1984) 23-27.
25. A. C. M. Mullins, DC Lamu, 1935 Mss. Afr. 360 (5) Rhodes House. In Mombasa, the Hadramis were active in the informal economy and performed many of the same functions as in Lamu. See Karim Jonmohammed, "A History of Mombasa" 176.
26. Hadrami women and Afro-Arabs, interviews.
27. In 1985 I met and interviewed this woman. I was the first European with whom she had spoken. Although she had been in Lamu for fifty plus years, she had remained mostly hidden in her home because of her illegal status upon entry. In 1985 she said there were only two tattooed women left in Lamu, the other having come in at about the same time and in the same way, and also living in isolation.
28. Lamu informants said the Comoro men made dresses for women in Lamu. These were shipped back to the islands and sold by kinsmen.
29. Hadrami women, interviews. Not all latter day Hadrami have married into their own community, as was also the case with the Afro-Arabs and others. See Romero, "Mama Khadija" (146, 153) who in the 1940s married a Hadrami man among her several husbands.
30. DC LMU/2/2 KNA. Hadrami woman, interview, 1985. This "sharif"-auctioneer received a five percent commission on selling mostly Somali cattle, but also engaged in buying and selling other items for profit.
31. Abdalla Mackenzie and Mohammed Jahadhmy, interviews, 1986.
32. Lamu male informants, 1985-86. The largest exodus of Indians occurred at independence in 1964-65. Some WaPate, who had already come in, also rented their shops and began small businesses.
33. The Christian Missionary Society briefly ran a school in 1915-16 but few students were allowed to attend. This is probably the school Isaacs reported being construct-

ed in 1911. Tanaland Provincial Report, KNA.
34. Ali Abdalla to Sharif Saleh, taped interview.
35. Sharif Hassan Badawy, taped interview.
36. DC/LMU/13KNA
37. DC/LMU/5/8 KNA. This particular squabble lasted into 1935. The Bohra remained prickly about their passageway. On one occasion in the 1940s, the Bohra engaged in actual combat with some intruders.
38. Lmu/9 Handing Over Report KNA. Actually the slaughterhouse was a bone of contention among the Afro-Arabs, too. The liwali resented its presence so close to his mosque.
39. DC/LMU/2/1 KNA.
40. Kiki Dastoor, interview Lamu, 1984. Shabar Ebrimjee, interview, Lamu, 1985.
41. For Gujarati Indians and their migrations, see Jacques Nemo, "La dispora gujarati musulmane dans Sud-ouest de l'Ocean Indien" *Recherche pedagogie et culture* XX (1984) 64-76.
42. Kesharji Ratlansey Dhutia, interview, Mombasa, 1985. Also, Gorariydas Raoawi, 90 years old in 1985, was another Lamu Bhattia who moved to Mombasa. Interview, Mombasa.
43. Esmailjee Hasanbahi, interview, Mombasa, 1985.
44. The Goolamhusein family hardware business was founded in Lamu by this man and one of his brothers in 1892 and is the oldest "hardware house on the coast." *Tarikhud-Daiel-Ajal* 1392 A.H. (Mombasa, 1972), 14.
45. For Carrimjee family, see chapter seven.
46. Cross cousin marriages are preferred among the Shi'a. Nemo, *Musulmans de la Re'union* 32. Nemo says that mixed marriages are rare but that if cousin marriage is not possible, Gujarati Indians marry into their clan or caste. See also Romero, "Gold as a Vehicle."
47. The name had changed to Mohamdbhai. Indians, like the Swahili, often change family names. Interviews with Taherally, his wife, daughter, daughter-in-law (a doctor), and son, Goolam, Mauritius, 1986, 1990.
48. James Christie, *Chlorea Epidemics*, 330-31.
49. Kesharji Ratlansey Dhutia and Gorariydas Raoawi, interviews, Mombasa. Fatah Hila, interview, Lamu, 1985.
50. Kubrabai and Taherally Mohammedbhai, interview, 1986. Fateh Hila Ebrimjee, interview, Lamu, 1990.
51. Fateh Hila, interview.
52. Kubrabai Mohammedbhai to Zeinab Mohammedbhai, personal communication to author, 1990.
53. Kiki Dastoor, interview, 1985.
54. Kubrabai Mohammedbhai, 1990.
55. Kubrabai, interview. Lamu women, interviews, 1981. For similar practices in Mombasa, see Sarah Mirza and Margaret Strobel (eds and trans) *Three Swahili Women: Life Histories from Mombasa* (Bloomington, 1989) 41, 43, 76-78, 101.
56. Huseina Yusuf Ali Carrimjee (interview) made several trips to Mecca where she encountered Lamu Bohra. Kubrabai and Taherally, interview.
57. Kiki Dastoor, interview.
58. Husseinali A. Hussein, interview, 1986. For the reformist view, see Asghar Ali Engineer, *The Bohras* (Sahibabad, 1980) 165-217. For the split in East Africa, 213-

15.

59. Member of the Dawoodi Bohra Goolamhusein family, interview, Lamu, 1985. See Hatim Amiji, "The Bohras of East Africa" *Journal of Religion in Africa* 27 (1980) 25-27.

60. Ismaili man who did not wish to be named. Interview, Lamu, 1985.

61. DC/LMU/2/1 KNA.

Chapter 11

1. *Kenya Land Commission* III 2473-76.

2. *Kenya Land Commission* 2617.

3. Sheikh Ahmed Jahadhmy, interview, 1980. Sharif Abdalla Salim, interview, 1980. Mohammed bin Ali BuSaid, interview, 1981. Mama Fatuma (whose husband was alive and involved at that time), interview, 1981. *Kenya Land Commission* 2618.

4. (Sir) Philip Mitchell, *African Afterthoughts* (London, 1954) 145.

5. Sheikh Ahmed Jahadhmy, interview, 1980.

6. Clive, "A Short History."

7. *Kenya Land Commission* 2637.

8. *Kenya Land Commission*, 2611-12.

9. *Kenya Land Commission* 2611. Also, in the maze that represents these land claims over nearly two decades, references to the *watoro* problems tended to get left out of the records.

10. *Kenya Land Commission* 2638.

11. Michael Blundell, *A Love Affair with the Sun* (Nairobi, 1994) 89.

12. *Kenya Land Commission* 2640.

13. Sir Ali's suggestion that the Germans and then the customs duties at Witu began the economic decline is the major theme presented in Ylvisaker, *Lamu in the Nineteenth Century passim.*

14. Copies of land titles provided by Sheikh Ali Ahmed Jahadhmy. In 1974 the family sold Hamed bin Said's Mambrui land to an African. (Copy of document in the possession of the author). Between 1963 and 1969 the surveys were finally completed. The WaAmu then were able to sell the land they were awarded, or the Indian merchants were able to title the lands they held mortgages on, some for over fifty years. See Ghaidan, *Lamu: A Study in Conservation* 111.

15. Sharif Abdalla Salim, 1981. Sheikh Ali Ahmed Jahadhmy, 1994. In the 1970s and on, land that had not been foreclosed by the Indian mortgage holders, was slowly being sold off by descendants of the original claimants. In the case of a plot belonging originally to Mohammed Al Maawyia, most of his children were still alive and directly shared the profits—according to Muslim law which meant that the women received only one-third of each full share accorded to the men. Some families had grown drastically in numbers: the Witu plot that belonged to Ali Jahadhmy's family was sold for over one million Kenya shillings, but the profits were subsequently divided among a surviving member of the third generation (Ali), and the multiple descendants of his nine siblings.

16. Ali Bin Abdalla, interview, 1982.

17. Lamu women, interviews.

18. Sheikh Ahmed Jahadhmy, interview, 1980. Sharif Abdalla Salim, interview, 1980. Sheikh Ali Jahadhmy, interview, 1994. See Jahadhmy's *Anthology of Swahili Poetry.*

19. It is these riddles which may have influenced Ann Biersteker's interpretation of Mwana Kupona's poem. See Beirsteker, "Language, Poetry, and Power" 59-60.
20. Abdalla A. Skanda, interview, 1980. For linkages between Swahili poetry with Egypt and Arabia, see Harold Scheub, "African Oral Traditions and Literature" *African Studies Review* 28 (1985) 23. See also J. W. T. Allen, *Tendi: Six Examples of Swahili Classical Verse* (New York, 1971); Jan Knappert, *Traditional Swahili Poetry: An Investigation into the Concepts of East African Islam as Reflected in the Utenzi Literature* (Leiden, 1967); Marina Tolmacheva, "The Arabic Influence on Swahili Literature" *Journal of African Studies* 5 (1978) 223. Tolmacheva stresses the African influence on the poetry. See also Carol Eastman, "Women, Slaves, and Foreigner."
21. Abdalla A. Skanda, 1980.
22. An Indian teacher ran the school for six years and was followed by Ahmed Mohammed Jahadhmy, who had been on the board as well as teacher. In 1947 Jahadhmy when the staff of the new government sponsored day school before accepting an appointment as Mudir on the mainland. LMU/12/6 Political Record Book KNA.
23. LMU 12/8/1 KNA.
24. Sheikh Ahmed Jahadhmy, Fatia Jahadhmy, Mohammed Jahadhmy, interviews, 1981.
25. DC LMU/1/3 KNA. The night school reached the height of enrollment in 1939 with 59 boys and 6 girls. For girls and education in Mombasa, see Strobel, *Mombasa Women* 101-25.
26. Mohammed Jahadhmy, interview, 1980.
27. One of Skanda's daughters became the first headmistress of Lamu Primary School, which was built on land donated by another Afro-Arab, Mohammed Farthi. A.A. Skanda, interview.
28. LMU/8/ Political Record Book KNA. The subject matter was basically the same innocuous domestic science, and even that received criticism from a visiting British supervisor who, oddly, felt the teach was unqualified.
29. Sheikh Ali Jahadhmy, interview.
30. DC LMU/12 KNA; DC LMU/2/14/5/KNA. Lamu women, including one of the women who had been stoned, 1980. The teacher was Zena Mohammed Fadhil; and ironically her father was among the critical WaAmu who signed a petition to the government requiring religious instruction. In the aftermath of Kenyan independence, Jahadhmy, still taking the lead in promoting for education for girls, donated land in one of his shambas, for what came to be the Lamu Girls Harambee School.
31. DC/LMU/12 KNA.
32. H. J. Simpson, District Commissioner in 1958, Mss. Afr. 5930 Rhodes House.
33. Salim Khamis to "The English by Radio" 23 October 1953, File E 6/15 BBC Written Archives Centre, Reading.
34. Sharif Hassan Badawy, 1980.
35. Sharif Hassan, interview; Sharif Saleh Hassan, interview, 1980.
36. DC LMU/17KNA
37. LMU/8 Political Record Book, KNA.
38. Lamu women who were associated with both N'nalalo (1753) and Bwana Fadhil Mosques. Interviews 1981.
39. The editors and translators of this document suggest that the Somali family may have been in residence in Lamu for four generations. Although that is possible, Lamu informants believe it is likely that the Somali were at Shela and the document was

recorded in Lamu. Sharif Abdalla Salim al Hussein, interview, 1982. Sheikh Ahmed Jahadhmy, interview, 1982. J. O. Hunwick and R. S. O'Fahey, *Documents Pertaining to Lamu and the WAFQ Commission* #6 by the *Fontes HIstoriae Africanae* (Evanston, 1981) 35-36.

40. In 1980 Jeffrey Romero conducted a survey of Lamu stonehouses. Of seventy-three names listed as owners in one *mtaa*, twenty-seven were women (including one European). Several more showed joint ownership of men and women. Some were owned by Indians, who do not title property to women; and some were listed as WAFQ properties. Philip Kitane later carried out a house-to-house survey for the Lamu Museum. He reported that "Lamu women mostly own their own houses" and numbers of them refused him and his team entry. During the survey they found many houses with more than one woman, and often women and children." Interview, Lamu, 1985. We have seen that the patricians employ aspects of matrilineage in Lamu. In some cases, this practice includes brothers taking on financial responsibility for sisters children, as well as managing their affairs.

Chapter 12

1. Trench, *Men Who Ruled Kenya*, 110.
2. Abdalla Mackenzie and Abdalla al Maawyia, interview, 1989.
3. DC LMU/124; DC LMU/17 KNA.
4. George Adamson, *My Autobiography*, 50.
5. DC LMU/17 KNA.
6. DC LMU/3/2 KNA. Jane Clive vaccinated the Lamu women in that year. The British were not as efficient in the matter of containing smallpox as the Germans during the colonial era. See Eberlie, "The German Achievement in East Africa" 207.
7. K. D. Patterson, "Disease and Medicine in African History: A Bibliographical Essay" *History in Africa* I (1974) 141-48.
8. Ann Beck, *Medicine, Tradition and Development in Kenya and Tanzania 1920-1970* (Waltham, 1981) 22.
9. DC LMU/3/8 KNA.
10. LMU/1/2 Political Records Book KNA.
11. DC LMU/1/2 KNA.
12. Feierman suggests that women can control fertility when they want to. In the nineteenth century, communal care was more available than later when the community was depopulated of extended family. The less family members to care for the elderly, the greater need for more children. Feierman's findings elsewhere would seem to apply to Lamu where low birth rates were reported earlier in the century. Steven Feierman, "Struggles for Control: The Social Roots of Health and Healing in Modern Africa" *African Studies Review* 28 (1985) 73-148. See also Niles Newton, "Population Limitation in Crosscultural Perspective (I) Patterns of Contraception" *Journal of Reproductive Medicine* 1 (1968) 343-54.
13. DC LMU/7 KNA. Lamu women, interviews, 1983, 1889.
14. DC LMU 1/2; DC LMU/7 KNA.
15. "Miss Grey's Arab School" in Mombasa was the source of this study. Copy in the possession of Edward Rodwell. Dr. Monica Puress, interview, Mombasa, 1994, was conducting a study of hookworm among pregnant women for the Centers on Disease Control, Atlanta.

16. LMU/3 Political Record Book.
17. DC LMU 1/2 KNA.
18. DC LMU/1/2 KNA.
19. See chapter four for earlier references to homosexuality.
20. Edward Rodwell, interview, 1983; Sharif Abdalla Salim, taped interview, 1983.
21. Lamu male informant, 1990.
22. Lamu women, 1980; Mohammed BuSaid, interview, 1985.
23. Edward Rodwell, interview, 1991. See also Gill Shepherd, "Rank, gender and homosexuality" 267. See also John Money, "The Transformation of Sexual Terminology: Homosexuality in Sexological History" *Siecus Report* 19 (1991) 10-13; William Davenport, "Sex in Cross Cultural Perspective" in Frank A. Beach (ed)., *Human Sexuality in Four Perspectives* (Baltimore, 1977) 153. In Guinea, for instance, Davenport reported that more Muslims than Christians practiced homosexual behavior at some time in their lives.
24. Elspeth Huxley, *Out in the Midday Sun* (New York, 1987) 204.
25. Lamu women, interviews, 1989. Edward Rodwell, interview, Mombasa, 1990.
26. Edward Rodwell, "Focus on the Coast" n. d. copy in the possession of the author.
27. Ahmed Khatib, who received a Whitten bursary, interview, Lamu, 1990.
28. Pamela Scott, interview.
29. Edward Rodwell, 1990. According to Rodwell, Lamu was "known as a mecca for homosexuals, including any numbers of district commissioners who were posted there." Petley died in 1957. (DC LMU/15 KNA).
30. DC LMU/13 KNA.
31. Pamela Scott, interview, Lamu, 1989; Leonard Scard, interview, Lamu, 1985. Kiki Dastoor, 1986.
32. Leonard Scard, 1985.
33. Lamu women, 1984. See Unni Wikan, *Behind the Veil in Arabia:Women in Oman* (Baltimore, 1982) 168-86.
34. Dr. John Money, interview, Baltimore, 1990.
35. DC LMU/2/14/5 KNA.
36. Thomas H. Wilson, interview, 1981. Lamu ex-slave women, 1985. See Gordon M. Wilson, in "Mombasa Social Survey" copy in the possession of the author. Wilson elaborated on the effects of early homosexual encounters for young boys. He believed there were no long range psychological danger to young boys between the ages of 8 and 15 years, although he saw problems of a sociological nature. This study was conducted in the 1950s.
37. Janet M. Bujra, "Production, Property, Prostitution" 13-39. Thomas Wilson (1982) commented that it was common knowledge that some homosexuals in Lamu procured for prostitutes and shared lodgings in Langoni.
38. Janet Bujra, "a Bajuni village" 6.
39. Sheikh Ali Jahadhmy, interview, 1980.
40. Janet Bujra, "a Bajuni village" 52.
41. Sharif Saleh Hassan, interview.
42. Sharif Abdalla Salim, interview, 1982.
43. The old alliance that marked relations between the Nabahany and the Mazrui in the early nineteenth century recurred in Mombasa during the twentieth when a few members of both families, with Bajun allies, assumed positions of leadership in the Old Town and over Fort Jesus Museum.

44. Romero Curtin, "Weddings in Lamu" 143. The Hadrami bride unravels her hair while on "display" rotating her head from side to side and back and forth. I was incorrect in 1983 when I wrote about the "highly stratified Lamu society" that had characterized the findings of others who preceded me—and who were also incorrect. See Francoise Le Guennec-Coppens, "Stratification Sociale et Division Sexuelle dan la Communalite' Swahili de Lamu (Kenya) *Ethnographie,* 85 (1981) 139-150; Coppens, *Femme,* passim. el Zein, *The Sacred Meadows* failed to notice that it was religious differences more than elitism that separated the Hadrami and others from the *waungwana.* Romero Curtin, "Laboratory" 865. See Strobel, *Mombasa Women* (156-181) for social change there. See also Mizra and Strobel, *Life Histories.*
45. Lamu women, interviews, 1980, 1981, 1983. For vugo dancing in sexual context elsewhere, see Carol A. Campbell and Carol M. Eastman, "*Ngoma*: Swahili Adult Song Performance in Context" *Ethnomusicology* XXII (1984) 467-95.
46. Romero, "Weddings" 144 *et passim.* M. Arens, "The WaSwahili: The Social History of an Ethnic Group" *Africa* 43 (1973) 426-38. Arens correctly notes that some Swahili extended the henna to legs and arms. The Hadrami often do this in Lamu. A. I. Salim, *Kenya's People of the Coast* (London, 1978) 29-30. For body decoration as art, Brain, *The Decorated Body*; Vansina, *Art History in Africa* 73.
47. Elspeth Huxley, *The Sorcerer's Apprentice* (London, 1948) 23.
48. Lamu women, interviews, 1980, 1981. See Marc Swartz, *The Way the World is: Cultural Processes and Social Relations among the Mombasa Swahili* (Berkeley, 1991), for an anthropological study of social change in Mombasa.

Chapter 13

1. DC LMU/l/3 KNA.
2. DC LMU/l/3 KNA. Dastoor died during the War. Whitten was later decorated for his services.
3. Clive, "A Short History."
4. Muslihi Abdalla, interview, Lamu, 1983. Lamu women, 1983.
5. Sheikh Ahmed Jahadhmy, interview 1995.
6. Sheikh Ahmed Jahadhmy, 1980. Mohammed bin Ali BuSaid, 1980. Mohammed Jahadhmy, 1980. See Jahadhmy *Maisha Yunga* 25.
7. Muslihi Abdalla, 1983.
8. Clive, "A Short History."
9. Lamu women, interviews, 1994. Many of the women were curious about the refugees, having heard old wives tales concerning their "tails and horns."
10. DC LMU/l/3 KNA.
11. DC LMU/1/3 KNA.
12. Among those salaried was Ahmed Basheikh, whose name is another example of how family names were dropped: originally he was an al Bakri.
13. DC LMU/1/2 KNA.
14. DC LMU/1/3 KNA.
15. DC LMU/1/3 KNA.
16. For a partial view of political activity among the Bajun, see Janet Bujra, "An Anthropological Study of Political Action in a Bajuni Village" Ph.D. University of London, 1968.

17. DC LMU/2/2 KNA.
18. Mohammed Jahadhmy, 1980.
19. DC LMU/9 KNA.
20. Sharif Abdalla Salim, 1980. See Salim, *Swahili Speaking Peoples* 212-15.
21. DC LMU/2/2 KNA.
22. DC LMU/7 KNA.
23. DC LMU/15 KNA.
24. DC LMU/12 KNA.
25. Janet Bujra, "a Bajuni Village" 9.
26. Janet Bujra, "a Bajuni village" 23.
27. For the Bajun as a fishing culture in mid-twentieth century, see V. L. Grottanelli, *Pescatori dell'Oceano Indiano* (Rome, 1965).
28. Prins, *Swahili Speaking Peoples* (11) found the Muslims there doing menial work in 1957.
29 DC LMU/7 KNA.
30. See Romero, "Mama Khadija" 149-50.
31. DC LMU/7 KNA.
32. Patricia Romero Curtin, "Generations of Strangers: The Kore of Lamu" *International Journal of African Historical Studies* 18 (1985) 455-471. Romero Curtin, Weddings in Lamu" 149-152. For Kore marriages within the ex-slave community, see Romero, "Mama Khadija." For the Kore as descendants of the Maasai, see B. Heine and R. Vossen, "The Kore of Lamu: A Contribution to Maa Dialectology" *Afrika und Ubersee* LXII (4) 272-288.
33. Romero, "Mama Khadija" 150, 153.
34. Ali bin Mohammed interview, Lamu, 1982.
35. Lamu informant, interview, 1985.
36. Sharif Abdalla Salim, 1983.
37. A. I. Salim, *Swahili Speaking peoples* 214.
38. The product of this marriage is the well known singer Sol Davis who took his mother's maiden name.
39. Sharif Abdalla, 1980. In 1955 he went to London to take part in negotiations that led eventually to Kenyan independence. The next year he returned, taking two of his wives, and met the Queen.
40. Salim, 197.
41. Sharif Abdalla, 1980.
42. DC LMU/17 KNA.
43. H. J. Simpson, mss.
44. Although none of these makes the specific argument for the Pokomo and Giriama, Nurse and Spear place them in the proto-Sabaki speaker group whose language formed the Bantu basis for KiSwahili. Derek Nurse and Thomas Spear, *The Swahili* 52-55. Allen argues that the Pokomo were mixed with the Orma and others. The Orma, too, returned to Lamu in some small numbers following World War II. See James DeVere Allen, *Swahili Origins* 90-96.
45. This quote, which ended John Clive's "History" in the 1930s was still appropriate when the WaAmu became part of the Republic of Kenya in 1963.

Bibliography

ARCHIVES AND SPECIAL COLLECTIONS

Africa:
Ft. Jesus Museum Library
Lamu Museum Library
Kenya National Archives (Nairobi)
Private Papers of Edward Rodwell (Mombasa)
National Archives of Zanzibar

United States:
Essex Institute (Massachusetts)
National Archives (Washington D. C.)
University of California, Los Angeles

France:
Archives de l'Ancien Ministere d'Outre-Mer (Paris)

Mauritius:
The National Archives

The United Kingdom:
House of Commons, *Parliamentary Papers*
Foreign Office FO84 series
Institute of Commonwealth Studies (London)
School of Oriental and African Studies, University of London
India Office Library and Records
Rhodes House, Oxford
Papers of:
    John Clive
    John Haggard
    G. H. Portal
    H. J. Simpson

BBC Written Archives Centre, Reading

INTERVIEWS

Lamu:
47 women across ethnic and class lines beyond those named below
Binta Arafa
Mwalimu Harith Saleh
Sharif Hassan Badaway
Sharif Saleh Hassan
Ahmed Khatib
Salim Kheri
Fateh Hil Ebrimjee
Shabar Ebrimjee
Homi Dastoor
Kiki Dastoor
Ismaili man
"Mama Khadija"
Somoe Ali
Mushali Abdalla
Mama Fatuma
Mohamed bin Ali BuSaid
Ali bin Mohamed BuSaid
Fadhil al Maawyia
Ali Abdalla al Maawyia
Mohdamed al Maawyia
Abdul Nassir Skanda
Ali Aballa Skanda (taped by Sharif Saleh)
A. A. Skanda
Ali Mukaka
Sheikh Ahmed bin Mohamed Jahadhmy
Mohamed bin Ahmed Jahadhmy
Mzee Shamsuddin
Abdalla Mackenzie
Ahmed Basheikh
Sharif Badawy Jamal-al-Layl
Abdul Hussein
Ali bin Salim
Abdalla Kadara
Philip Katane
Sharif Mohamed al Hussein
Aziz Fumo Bakari
Leonard Scard
Pamela Scott
Thomas Wilson

Mambrui:
Sharif Ali al Beidh

Mombasa:
Sharif Abdalla Salim el Husein
Sharif Muhdar Kitame
Jaffer Panjur
Azziz Mohamed
Ahmed Nabahany
Sharif Abdalla Tiab
Sharif Nassir Abdalla
Sharif Abdulrahman Tiab
Murtza Hasseinali
Aisha Suud
Fatia binta Mohamed
Husseinali A. Hussein
Kesharji Ratlansey Dhatia
Gorariydas Raoawi
Esmailjee Hasanbahi
Sheikh Ali Abdalla Jahadhmy
Fatuma Abdalla
Mohamed bin Abdalla
Dr. Monica Puress of Centers for Disease Control, Atlanta, Georgia

Madagascar:
Akbaraly-Chef du Bohra Tamatave

Mauritius:
Huseina Yusuf Ali Carrimjee
Carrim Carrimjee
Kubrabhai Mohamedbhai
Taherally Mohamedbhai
Zeinab Mohamedbhai (correspondence 1986-93)

La Reunion:
Dr. Kolchoy Firoze
"Lamuwala" and other members of the Bohra Congregation, St. Denis

Baltimore:
Dr. Mark E. Gann
Dr. Donald A. Henderson
Dr. John Money

NEWSPAPERS

East African Standard (later) *The Standard*
Kenya Weekly News

MEMOIRS AND PUBLISHED WORKS

Adamson, George, *An Autobiography*: *My Pride and Joy* (London, 1965).
Adie, J.J., *Guide to Zanzibar* (London, 1912).
Allen, Colvin H. Jr., "The Indian Merchant Community of Masqat" *School of Oriental and African Studies Bulletin* 44 (1981) 39-53.
Allen, James DeVere, *Swahili Origins*: *Swahili Culture and the Shungwaya Phenomenon* (London, 1993).
———, *Lamu Town*: *A Guide* (Mombasa, n.d.).
——— and Thomas H. Wilson, *Swahili Houses and Tombs of the Coast of Kenya* (London, 1979).
Allen, J.W.T., *Tendi*: *Six Examples of Swahili Classical Verse* (New York, 1971).
Amiji, Hatim, "The Asiatic Bias in the Historiography of the East African Coast" *Journal of African Studies* 10 (1983) 66-72.
———, "The Bohra of East Africa" *Journal of Religion in Africa* 27 (1980) 25-32.
———, "Some Notes on Religious Dissent in Nineteenth Century East Africa" *African Historical Studies* IV (1970) 603-16.
———, "The Asian Communities" in James Kritzeck and William H. Lewis (eds)., *Islam in Africa* (New York, 1969) 142-68.
Arnoldi, Mary Jo, "The Artistic Heritage of Somalia: *African Arts* VIII (1984) 148-52.
Alpers, Edward A., "Ordinary Household Chores: Ritual and Power in a 19th Century Swahili Spirit Possession Cult" *International Journal of African Historical Studies* 17 (1984) 677-702.
———, "Moqdisho in the 19th Century: A Regional Perspective" *International Journal of African Historical Studies* 24 (1983) 441-59.
———, "Gujarat and the Trade of East Africa 1500-1800" *International Journal of African Historical Studies* IX (1976) 22-44.
———, *Ivory and Slaves*: *Changing Patterns of International Trade in East Central Africa in the Later Nineteenth Century* (Berkeley, 1975).
———, "Trade, State and Society Among the Yao in the 19th Century" *Journal of African History* 10 (1969) 405-20.
Arbery, A.J., *Sufism*: *An Account of the Mystics of Islam* (London, 1963).
Arens, W., "Changing Patterns of Ethnic Identity and Prestige in East Africa" in W. Arens, (ed)., *A Century of Change in East Africa* (The Hagae, 1976) 65-75.

Anderson, J.N.D., *Islamic Law in Africa* (London, 1970).

Al-Bakariy, Shaibu Faraji bin Hamed, "The Chronicle of Lamu" [Khabari Lamu] (Collected by Abdallah bin Hamed Wali of Lamu) William Hichens (ed. and trans.), *Bantu Studies* 12 (1938)

Bate, Kelly William, "Family History: Some Answers, Many Questions" *Oral History Review* 16 (1988) 127-30.

Bathurst, R.D., "Maritime Trade and Imamate Government" in Derek Hopwood, (ed)., *The Arabian Peninsula, Society of Politics* (London, 1972).

Baumann, Oscar, *In Duetsch-Ostafrika: Wahrend des Aufstandes* (Wein and Olmutz, 1890).

Beachey, R.W., *The Slave Trade of Eastern Africa* (London, 1976).

Beck, Ann, *Medicine, Tradition and Development in Kenya and Tanzania 1920-1970* (Waltham, 1981).

Beckingham, C.F., "The Reign of Ahmed bin Said Imam of Oman" *Journal of the Royal Asiatic Society* XVIII (1941) 257-60.

Bennett, Norman R. and George E. Brooks, (eds)., *New England Merchants in Africa: A History Through Documents 1802-1865* (Boston, 1965).

———, "Americans in Zanzibar" *Tanganyika Notes and Records* 56 (1961) 93-108.

Berg, Fred J., "Mombasa under the Busaid Sultanate: the City and its Hinterlands in the Nineteenth Century" Ph.D. Thesis, University of Wisconsin, 1971.

Berman, Bruce and John Lonsdale, *Unhappy Valley: Conflict in Kenya and Africa Book One: State and Class* (Athens, 1992).

———, *Control and Crisis in Colonial Kenya* (London, 1990).

Bhacker, Reda M., *Trade and Empire in Muscat and Zanzibar: Roots of British Domination* (London, 1992).

Biersteker, Ann, "Language, Poetry, Power: A Reconsideration of 'Utendi wa Mwana Kupona'" in Kenneth W. Harrow (ed)., *Faces of Islam in African Literature* (New York, 1991) 68-71.

de Blis, Harm, J., *Mombasa: An African City* (Evanston, 1968).

Blundell, Michael, *A Love Affair with the Sun* (Nairobi, 1994).

Boteler, Thomas (Captain), *Narrative of a Voyage of Discovery to Africa and Arabia* II (London, 1840).

Boxer, C. R. (ed)., *Further Selections From the Tragic History of the Sea 1559-1565* (Cambridge, 1968).

———, *Race Relations in the Portuguese Colonial Empire 1415-1825* (Oxford, 1963).

———, and Carlos de Azevedo, *Fort Jesus and the Portuguese in Mombasa* (London, 1960).

Boyd, Alan, "To Praise the Prophet: A Processional Symbolic Analysis of 'Maulidi': A Muslim Ritual of Lamu, Kenya" Ph.D. Thesis, Indiana

University, 1980.

Brain, Robert, *The Decorated Body* (New York, 1980).

Brooks, George, "The *Signares* of Saint-Louis and Goree" in Nancy J. Hafkin and Edna G. Bay, (eds)., *Women in Africa* (Stanford, 1976) 19-44.

Brown, Helen, "Three Kilwa Coins" *Azania* XXVI (1991) 1-4.

Brown, Walter Thaddeus, "A Pre-Colonial History of Bagamoyo: Aspects of the Growth of an East African Town" Ph.D. Thesis, Boston University, 1971.

Bujra, Abdalla A., *The Politics of Stratification*: *A Study of Political Change in a South Arabian Town* (Oxford, 1971).

Bujra, Janet, "An Anthropological Study of Political Action in a Banuni Village" Ph.D. thesis, University of London, 1968.

_____ "Production, Property, Prostitution: Sexual Politics in Atu" *Cahiers d'e-tudes Africaines* XVII (1975) 13-39.

Burton, Richard F., *Zanzibar City, Island and Coast* I (London, 1872).

————, *First Footsteps in East Africa* (London, 1860).

Campbell, Carol A. and Carol M. Eastman, "*Ngoma*: Swahili Adult Song Performance in Context" *Ethnomusicology* XXII (1984) 467-95.

Campbell, Gwyn, "Crisis of Faith and Colonial Conquest: The Impact of Disease in Late Nineteenth Century Madagascar" *Cahier d'Etudes africaines* 11-3 (1992) 409-53.

Caplan, Pat, and Françoise Le Guennec-Coppens, *Les Swahili entre Afrique et Arabie* (Paris, 1991).

_____ "The Structure of Trade in Madagascar 1750-1810" *Journal of African Historical Studies* 26 (1993) 130-131.

————, "The East African Slave Trade 1861-95: The Southern Complex" *International Journal of African Historical Studies* 22 (1989) 1-26.

————, "Madagascar and the Slave Trade 1810-1895" *Journal of African History* 22 (1981) 203-27.

Carter Land Commission, *Kenya Land Commission* (Nairobi, 1934).

Chaudhuri, K.N., *Asia Before Europe*: *Economy and Civilization of the Indian Ocean From the Rise of Islam to 1750* (Cambridge, 1990).

————, *Trade and Civilization in the Indian Ocean*: *An Economic History From the Rise of Islam to 1750* (Cambridge, 1985).

Chittick, Neville, "Sewn Boat in the Western Indian Ocean, and a Survival in Somalia" *International Journal of Nautical Archaeology* 9 (1980) 21-23.

————, "East African Trade With the Orient" in D.S. Richards (ed)., *Papers in Islamic History* II *Islam and the Trade With Asia* (Oxford, 1970) 97-103.

Christie, James, *Chlorea Epidemics in East Africa* (London, 1876).

Clarence-Smith, William Gervase (ed)., *The Economics of the Indian Ocean and Red Sea Trades in the 19th Century* (London, 1989).

Clive, J.H., "A Short History of Lamu" Typescript Rhodes House.

Cohen, David, "Reconstructing a Conflict in Bunafo" in Joseph Miller, (ed)., *The*

African Past Speaks (Hamden CT. 1980) *221*-239.

Colombo, J.R., *Slave Catching in the Indian Ocean* (New York, 1969).

Constantin, F., "Social Stratification on the Swahili Coast: From Race to Class" *Africa* 59 (1989) 145-61.

Cooper, Frederick, "Conflict and Connection: Rethinking Colonial History" *American Historical Review* 99 (1994) 1516-1545.

————, *On the African Waterfront: Urban Disorder and Transformation of Work in Colonial Mombasa* (New Haven, 1987).

————, "The Treatment of Slaves on the Kenya Coast in the 19th Century" *Kenya Historical Review* II (1973) 89-103.

————, "Islam and Cultural Hegemony: The Ideology of Slave Owners on the East African Coast" in Paul Lovejoy (ed)., *The Ideology of Slavery in Africa* (Beverly Hills, 1981) 247-77.

————, *From Slaves to Squatters: Plantation Labor and Agriculturein Zanzibar and Coastal Kenya 1890-1925* (New Haven, 1980).

————, *Plantation Slavery on the East Coast of Africa* (New Haven, 1977).

Coupland, R., *The Exploitation of East Africa 1856-1890* (Cambridge, 1967).

————, *East Africa and its Invaders* (Oxford, 1938).

Davenport, William, "Sex in Cross Cultural Perspective" in Frank A. Beach (ed)., *Human Sexuality in Four Perspectives* (Baltimore, 1977).

DeKiewiet, "History of the Imperial British East Africa Company 1876-1895 Ph.D. Thesis, University of London 1965.

Denhardt, Clemens, "A History of Manda and Patta" typescript 1890 Zanzibar National Archives.

Dickins, T. Ainsworth, "Recent History" typescript KNA.

Donley, Linda Wiley, "The Social Uses of Swahili Space and Objects" Ph.D. Thesis, Cambridge University, 1984.

Doughty, Charles M., *Travels in Arabia Deserta* (reprint, London, 1933).

Eastman, Carol, "Women, Slaves and Foreigners: African Cultural Influences and Group Processes in the Formation of Northern Swahili Coastal Society" *International Journal of African Historical Studies* 23 (1988) 1-20.

————, "Who Are the WaSwahili" *Africa* 41 (1971) 228-36.

Eberlie, R.F., "The German Achievement in East Africa" *Tanganyika Notes and Records* 55 (1960) 155-207.

Eickelman, D.F., "Religious Tradition, Economic Domination and Political Legitimacy" *Revue de L'Occident Muslim* 29 (1980) 17-30.

Engineer, Asghar Ali, *The Bohras* (Sahibabad, 1980).

Esmail, Aziz, "Towards a History of Islam in East Africa" *Kenya Historical Review* 3 (1975) 147-58.

Feierman, Steven, "Struggles for Control: The Social Roots of Health and Healing in Modern Africa" *African Studies Review* 28 (1985) 73-148.

Fitzgerald, W.W.A., *Travels in British East Africa, Pemba and Zanzibar*

(London, 1898).

Flint, John, "The Witu Background to Partition and Colonial Opposition" in Roland Oliver and Gervase Mathew (eds)., *History of East Africa* I (London, 1968).

Freeman-Grenville, G.S.P., "Lamu" in *The Encyclopedia of Islam* (Leiden, 1983) 633.

———, (ed and trans)., *The Mombasa Rising Against the Portuguese 1631 From Sworn Evidence* (London, 1980).

———, *The French at Kilwa* (Oxford, 1965).

———, *The Medieval History of the Coast of Tanganyika* (Berlin, 1962).

Galbraith, John, *Mackinnon and East Africa 1878-1895* (Cambridge, 1972).

Ghaidan, Usam, *Lamu: A Study of the Swahili Town* (Nairobi, 1975).

———, *Lamu: A Study in Conservation* (Nairobi, 1976).

Gibbs, H.R. (ed)., *Ibn Battuta, Travels in Asia and Africa 1325-1354* (London, 1939).

Gifford, Prosser and Louis W. Roger, *Britain and Germany in Africa* (New Haven, 1967).

Giles, Linda, "The Dialectic of Spirit Possession: A Cross Cultural Dialogue" *The Mankind Quarterly* XXIX (1989) 243-65.

Glassman, Jonathan, *Feasts and Riot: Revelry, Rebellion and Popular Consciousness on the Swahili Coast 1856-88* (New York, 1995).

———, "The Runaway Slave in Coastal Resistance to Zanzibar: The Case of the Witu Sultanate" M.A. Thesis, University of Wisconsin, 1983.

Good, Charles M., "Man, Mileau and the Disease Factor: Tick-Borne Relapsing Fever in East Africa" in Gerald W. Hartwig and K. David Patterson (ed)., *Disease, in African History* 46-87.

Gray, John (Sir), "The British Vice-Consulate at Kilwa Kivinji, 1884-85" *Tanganyika Notes and Records* 51 (1958) 174-194.

Graham, G. S., *Great Britain and the Indian Ocean 1810-1850* (New Haven, 1967).

Graz, Leisl, *The Omanis: Sentinels of the Gulf* (London, 1982).

Great Britain Admiralty, I.D. 1189 *A Manual of Portugal in East Africa* (London, 1920).

Greffulhe, H., "Voyage de Lamoo 'a Zanzibar" *Bulletin de la Societe' de Geographie et d'etudes Coloniales de Marseille* ii (1878) 327-60.

Gregory, J.W., *The Foundation of British East Africa* (London, 1901).

Gregory, Robert G., *South Asians in East Africa: An Economic and Social History 1890-1980* (Boulder, 1993).

———, *India and East Africa* (Oxford, 1971).

Grey, J.M., "Zanzibar and the Coast 1840-1884" in Oliver, Roland and Gervase Matthew, *History of East Africa* I (London, 1963).

Grossett-Grange, H., "La Cote Africaine dan Routiers Nautiques Arabes au

Moment des Grand De'couvertes" *Routiers Nautiques* XXX (1971) 1-35.

Grottanelli, V.L., *Pescatori dell'Oceano Indiano* (Rome, 1965).

Guennec-Coppens, Françoise Le and Pat Caplan, *Les Swahili entre Afrique et Arabie* (Paris, 1991).

————,"Stratification Sociale et Division Sexuelle dans la Communalite' Swahili de Lamu (Kenya) *Ethnographie"* 85 (1981) 139-50.

————, "Les Masharifu Majalilil a Lamu (Kenya)" *Annuaire des Pay de l'Ocean Indian VI* (1979) 92-95.

Guillain, M., *Documents Sur 'Histoire de l'Afrique Orientale* I (Paris, 1856).

Guillaume, Alfred, *New Light On the Life of Muhammad* (Manchester, 1960).

Halls, C., "Dutch Navigation of the East African Coast" *Tanganyika Notes and Records* 67 (1967) 39-48.

Hardinge, Arthur H. (Sir), *A Diplomatist in the East* (London, 1928).

Hardy, P., *The Muslims in British India* (Cambridge, 1972).

Harries, Lyndon, *Swahili Poetry* (Oxford, 1962).

Harris, Joseph, *African Prescence in Asia*: *Consequences of the East African Slave Trade* (Evanston, 1971).

Hartwig, G.H., "Smallpox in the Sudan" *International Journal of African Historical Studies* 14 (1981) 14-18.

————, and K. David Patterson (eds)., *Disease in African History* (Chapel Hill, 1978).

Heine, B., and R. Vossen, "The Kore of Lamu: A Contribution to Maa Dialectology" *Afrika und Ubersee* LXII (1983) 272-88.

Hemphill, Marie de Kiewiet, "The British Sphere 1884-91" in Roland Oliver and Gervase Matthews (eds)., *History of East Africa* I (London, 1968).

Henige, David, *Oral Historiography* (London, 1982).

Herbert, Eugenia, "Smallpox Inoculation in Africa" *Journal of African History* 4 (1981) 539-59.

Hichens, William, *Al Inkishafi* (Nairobi, 1972).

Hinks, Peter, *The Folklore of Jewellery* (London, forthcoming).

Hollingsworth, L.W., *Zanzibar and the Foreign Office 1890-1913* (London, 1953).

Horton, Mark, "The Swahili Corridor and the Southern African Iron Age" paper presented at University of London, School of Oriental and African Studies, Nov. 1986.

————, "Early Muslim Trading Settlements on the East African Coast: New Evidence from Shanga" *Antiquaries Journal* 68 (1986) 290-323.

———— and C.M. Clark, "Zanzibar Archaeological Survey 1984-5" Ministry of Information, Culture and Sports. (Zanzibar, 1985)

————, "The Early Settlement of the Northern Kenya Coast" Ph.D. Thesis, University of Cambridge, 1984.

Hourani, Albert, *A History of the Arab Peoples* (Cambridge, MA., 1991).

————, *The Ottoman Background of the Modern Middle East* (London, 1970).

Huntingford, G.W.B., (ed. and trans)., *The Periplus of the Erythraean Sea* (London, 1980).

Hunwick, J.O., and R.S. O'Fahey, *Documents Pertaining to Lamu and the WAFQ Commission #6* (Evanston, 1981).

Huxley, Elspeth, *Out in the Midday Sun* (New York, 1987).

————, *The Sorcerer's Apprentice* (London, 1948).

Ingrams, W.H., *Zanzibar: Its History and Peoples* (London, 1931).

Israel, Jonathan I., *Dutch Primacy in World Trade 1585-1740* (New York, 1989).

Ivanow, W., *A Guide to Ismaili Literature* (London, 1933).

Jackson, Frederick (Sir), *Early Days in East Africa* (London, 1930).

Jahadhmy, Ali A. (ed)., *Anthology of Swahili Poetry* (London, 1975).

Al-Jahadhmy, Ahmed Muhammad Ahmed, *Maishu Yungu* (Muscat, 1989).

————, *Tarikhi Ya Amu* (Muscat, 1991).

Jones, J.D.F., *Freeland* (London, 19941)

Jonmohamed, Karim Kassam, "A History of Mombasa c. 1895-1939" Ph.D. Thesis, Northwestern University, 1971.

Joseph, Suad, "Brother/Sister Relationships: Enrichment in the Reproduction of Arab Patriarchy" paper presented at Johns Hopkins University, November, 1991.

Kadara, Abdalla, "Habib Saheh" Typescript Lamu Museum.

Karstadt, Oskar, *Der Weisse Kampf Um Afrika* I (Berlin, 1937).

Kelly, J.B., *Britain and the Persian Gulf 1795-1880* (Oxford, 1968).

————, *Kenya Trade and Supplies Bulletin* IX (1959).

Kirkman, James, *Men and Monuments on the East African Coast* (London, 1964).

————, *The Arab City of Gedi: Excavations at the Great Mosque, Architecture and Finds* (London, 1954).

Klein, Martin A. (ed)., *Breaking the Chains: Slavery, Bondage Emancipation in Modern Africa and Asia* (Madison, 1993).

Knappert, Jan, *Four Centuries of Swahili Verse* (London, 1979).

————, "The Theme of Conversion in Swahili Literature" in N. Levtzion (ed)., *Conversion and Islam* (New York, 1979) 177-88.

————, *Traditional Swahili Poetry: An Investigation into the Concepts of East African Islam as Reflected in Utenzi Literature* (Leiden, 1967).

Kupona, Mwana, *Utendi* in Ali A. Jahadhmy, Ali A. (ed)., *Anthology of Swahili Poetry* (London, 1975) 29-41.

Landen, Robert Geran, *Oman Since 1856: Disruptive Modernization in a Traditional Arab Society* (Princeton, 1967).

Lane, Frederick C., *Venice: A Maritime Republic* (Baltimore, 1973).

Leinhardt, Peter J. (ed)., *The Medicine Man* (London, 1969).

————, "The Mosque College of Lamu and Its Social Background" *Tanganyika*

Notes and Records 53 (1959) 229-42.

Levathes, Louise, *When China Ruled the Seas*: *The Treasure Fleet of the Dragon Throne 1405-1433* (New York, 1994).

Levy, R., *The Social Structure of Islam* (Cambridge, 1957).

Lewicki, Jadeusz, "The Ibadhites in Arabia and Africa" *Journal of World History* XIII (1971) 3-81.

Lewis, Bernard, *Race and Color in Islam* (New York, 1971).

———, *Race and Slavery in the Middle East* (New York, 1990).

Al-Maamiry, Ahmed Hamard, *Oman and East Africa* (New Dehli, 1979).

Mangot, J.S., "The Immigrant Communities: The Asians" in D.A. Low and Alison Smith (eds)., *History in East Africa* (Oxford, 1976).

Malisius, Ulrich, *The Stone Town of Zanzibar* (Zanzibar, 1985).

Martin, B.G., *Muslim Brotherhoods in the Nineteenth Century* (Cambridge, 1976).

———, "Notes on Some Members of the Learned Classes of Zanzibar and East Africa in the Nineteenth Century" *African Historical Studies* IV (1971) 525-545.

———, "Muslim Politics and Resistance to Colonial Rule: Shaykh Uwaya B. Muhammed el-Barawi and the Qadariya Brotherhood in East Africa" *Journal of African History* X (1969) 471-486.

———, "Materials for the Understanding of Islam in German East Africa" *Tanganyika Notes and Records* 67 (1968) 53-67.

Martin, Esmond B. and T.C.I. Ryan, "A Quantitative Assessment of the Arab Slave Trade in East Africa 1770-1896" *Kenya Historical Review* 5 (1977) 71-91.

Al-Mazrui, Sheikh al-Amin bin 'Ali, *The History of the Mazru'i Dynasty of Mombasa* translated and annotated by J. McL. Ritchie (Oxford, 1995).

Mazrui, Alamin M. and Ibrahim Noor Shariff, *The Swahili: Idiom and Identity of an African People* (Trenton, NJ, 1994).

McCall, Daniel F., *Africa in Time Perspective*: *A Discussion of Historical Reconstruction from Unwritten Sources* (New York, 1969).

McKim, Wayne, "House Types in Tanzania: A Century of Change" *Journal of Cultural Geography* 6 (1985) 51-78.

McPherson, Kenneth, "Processes of Cultural Interchange in the Indian Ocean Region: An Historical Perspective" *The Great Circle* 6 (1979) 78-92.

Meillassoux, Claude, "Female Slavery" in Martin Klein and Claire Robertson (eds)., *Women and Slavery in Africa* (Madison, 1983) 49-66.

Meyers, Allen R., "Class, Ethnicity, and Slavery: The Origins of the Moroccan 'Abid'" *International Journal of African Historical Studies* 10 (1977) 427-442.

Memon, P.A., and Esmond P. Martin, "The Kenya Coast: An anomoly in the development of an 'Ideal Type' Colonial Spatial-System" *Kenya Historical*

Review 4 (1976) 186-196.

Middleton, John, *The World of the Swahili: An African Mercantile Civilization* (New Haven, 1992).

Miers, Suzanne and Igor Kopytoff (eds)., *Slavery in Africa: Historical and Anthropological Perspectives* (Madison, 1977) 101.

———, *Britain and the Ending of the Slave Trade* (London, 1975).

Miller, Joseph E. (ed)., *The African Past Speaks* (Hamden CT, 1980).

Mitchell, (Sir) Philip, *African Afterthoughts* (London, 1954).

Mizra, Sarah and Margaret Strobel, (eds. and trans)., *Three Swahili Women: Life Histories from Mombasa* (Bloomington, 1989).

Money, John, "The Transformation of Sexual Terminology: Homosexuality in Sexological History" *Siecus Report* 19 (1991) 10-13.

Morris, H.S., *The Indians in Uganda* (London, 1968).

Morton, R.F., "Slaves, Fugitives, and Freed Men on the Kenya Coast, 1873-1907" Ph.D. Thesis, Syracuse University, 1976.

Mungeam, J., *Kenya: Selected Historical Documents 1884-1923* I (Nairobi, 1978).

Murphy, R.F., "The Structure of Parallel Cousins" *American Anthropologist* I (1959) 79-82.

Mwinyi, Mtoro bin, *The Customs of the Swahili People (Desturi Za Waswahili)* J.W.T. Allen (ed. and trans). (Berkeley, 1981).

Ndwulia, Moses D.E., *Britain and Slavery in East Africa* (Washington, DC, 1974).

Nemo, Jacques, "Le dispora Gujarati Musulmane dans Sud-ouest de l'Ocean Indien" *Recherche Pedagogie et Culture* (1984) 64-76.

New, Charles, *Life Wanderings and Labours in East Africa* (London, 1874).

Newitt, M.D.D., "East Africa and Indian Ocean Trade: 1500-1800" in Ashin Das Gupta, and M.N. Pearson (eds)., *India and the Indian Ocean 1500-1800* (Calcutta, 1987) 201-23.

———, "The Comoro Islands in Indian Ocean Trade Before the 19th Century" *Cahiers d'Etudes Africaine* XXXIII (1974) 139-65.

Newton, Niles, "Population Limitation in Crosscultural Perspective (I) Patterns of Contraception:" *Journal of Reproductive Medicine* I (1968) 343-54.

Nimtz, August H., *Islam and Politics in East Africa: The Sufi Order in Tanzania* (Minneapolis, 1980).

Northrup, David, "The Ideological Context of Slavery in Southeastern Nigeria in the 19th Century" in Paul Lovejoy (ed)., *The Ideology of Slavery in Africa* (Beverly Hills, 1981) 101-122.

Nunes, Antonio, *Luiro dos Pesos da Ymdia e assy Medidas e Mohedas escripto em 1554* (Lisboa, 1868).

Nurse, Derek and Thomas J. Hinnebusch, *Swahili and Sabaki: A Linguistic History* (Berkeley, 1993).

————, "A Linguistic Reconstruction of Swahili Origins" *Azania* 18 (1983) 127-50.

————, "History From Linguistics: The Case of the Tana River" *History in Africa* 10 (1983) 207-238.

Nyrop, Richard F., Beryle L., Benderly, Lorraine N. Carter, *Area Handbook for the Yemens* (Washington, DC, 1977).

Pellow, Deborah, "Sexuality in Africa" *Trends in History* 4 (1990) 71-96.

Penrad, Jean-Claude, "La Presence Isma'ilienne en Afrique de l'est" in Denys Lombard et Jean Aubin (eds)., *Marchands et hommes d'affaires asiatiques dans l'Ocean Indien et al Mer de Chine 13e-20e siecles* (Paris, 1988).

Peters, Karl (Dr.), *The Eldorado of the Ancients* (London, 1902).

————, *New Light on Dark Africa: Being A Narrative of the German Emin Pasha Expedition* (London, 1891).

Petley, C.A., "The Lamu Siwa" Typescript, Lamu Museum.

Platt, V.B., "The East Africa India Company and the Madagascar Slave Trade" *William and Mary Quarterly* XXVI:3 (1969) 15-39.

Pouwels, Randall L., "Reflections on Historiography and Pre-Nineteenth Century History from the Pate Chronicles" *History in Africa* 20 (1993) 263-96.

————, "Swahili Literature and History in the Post-Structuralist Era" *International Journal of African Historical Studies* 25 (1992) 261-83.

————, *Horn and Crescent: Cultural Change and Traditional Islam on the East African Coast* (Cambridge, 1987).

————, "Tenth Century Settlement of the East African Coast: The Case for Qarmation Ismaili Connections" *Azania* XI (1974) 65-74.

Prins, A.H.J., "The *Mtepe* of Lamu, Mombasa and the Zanzibar Sea" *Paiduma* 28 (1982).

————, *Didemic Lamu: Social Stratification and Spatial Structure in A Muslim Maritime Town* (Groningen, 1971).

————, *Sailing From Lamu: A Study of Maritime Culture* (Assen, 1965).

————, "Uncertainities in Coastal Cultural History: The 'Ngalawa' and the 'Mtepe'" *Tanganyika Notes and Records* 53 (1956) 207-212.

Ranger, T.O., "Religious Movements and Politics in Sub-Saharan Africa" *African Studies Review* 29 (1986) 1-70.

————, *Dance and Society in Eastern Africa 1890-1970* (Berkeley, 1975).

Ricks, T.M., "Persian Gulf Seafaring and East Africa: Nineth to Twelfth Centuries" *International Journal of African Historical Studies* 3 (1970) 339-57.

Risso, Patricia, "Muslim Identity in Maritime Persian Gulf/Indian Ocean Region" *International Journal of Middle Eastern Studies* 21 (1989) 381-92.

————, *Oman and Muscat: An Early Modern History* (New York, 1986).

Romero Curtin, Patricia, "Lamu (Kenya) Slave Trade, and British Efforts to Suppress" *Slavery and Abolition* 7 (1986) 148-59.

———, "Generations of Strangers: The Kore of Lamu" *International Journal of African Historical Studies* 18 (1985) 455-71.

———, "Laboratory for the Oral History of Slavery: The Island of Lamu on the Kenya Coast" *American Historical Review* 88 (1983) 858-82.

———, "The Sacred Meadows: A Case Study of 'Anthropologyland' *vs.* 'Historyland'" *History in Africa* 9 (1982) 339-46.

Romero, Patricia, "A Glimpse at the East African Bohra and the Reformers" paper delivered at the African Studies Association 1995.

———"Does Being 'Sexy' Keep a Marriage Going in Lamu" paper delivered at the African Studies Association, 1992.

———, "The Problems of Studying Women as Witches and Diviners in Lamu, Kenya" paper presented at Berkshire Conference on Women's History, 1990.

———, "Whose Medicine: Some Problems in Understanding Health and Healing in Lamu, Kenya" paper presented at the Lamu Museum, 1989.

——— (ed)., *Life Histories of African Women* (London, 1988).

———, "Possible Sources For the Origin of Gold as an Economic and Social Vehicle For Women in Lamu (Kenya)" *Africa* 57 (1987) 364-376.

———, "Where Have all the Slaves Gone: Emancipation and Post-Emancipation in Lamu, Kenya" *Journal of African History* 27 (1986) 497-512.

———, "Weddings in Lamu, Kenya: An Example of Social and Economic Change" *Cahier d'Etudes Africaines* 94 (1984) 131-155.

Ross, Robert (ed)., "The Dutch on the Swahili Coast 1776-1778: The Slaving Journals; Part I, II" *International Journal of African Historical Studies* 19 (1986). (Part I 305-60) (Part II 479-506).

Ruete, Emily, *Memoirs of An Arabian Princess of Zanzibar*, Patricia W. Romero (ed)., (New York, 1989).

Rupani, Juma Premji, *Trade in Africa and the Asian Community* (Bombay, 1937).

Russell, (Mrs.) Charles E.B. (ed)., *General Rigby, Zanzibar and the Slave Trade With Journals, Dispatches, etc.* (London, 1935).

Said-Ruete, Rudolph, "Dates and References to the History of Al Bin Said dynasty 1741-1856" *Journal of Royal Central Asian Society* 18 (1931) 233-55.

Sakari, Lawrence J., "Indian Merchants in East Africa Part I. The Triangular Trade and the Slave Economy" *Slavery and Abolition* 1 (1980) 292-39.

———"Merchants in East Africa Part II: British Imperialism and the Transformation of the Slave Economy" *Slavery and Abolition* VI (1982) 2-30.

Saleh, Ibuni, *A Short History of the Comorians in Zanzibar* (Dar-es-Salaam, 1936).

Salim, A.I., "The Elusive Mswahili: Some Reflections on his Culture and Identity" in J. Maw, and D. Parkin, (eds)., *Swahili Language and Society*

(Vienna, 1985) 215-27.

————, (ed)., *State Formation in East Africa* (New York, 1985).

————, "The Impact of Colonialism Upon Muslim Life in Kenya" *Journal of the Institute of Muslim Minority Affairs* I (1979) 60-66.

————, "The Impact of Colonialism on Muslim Life in Kenya" *Muslim Minority Affairs* I (1979) 60-66.

————, *Kenya's People of the Coast* (London, 1978).

————, "Native or Non-Native? The Problem of Identity and Social Stratification of the Arab-Swahili of Kenya" *Hadith* 6 (1976) 65-85.

dos Santos, Joao, *Ethiopia Oriental* (Lisboa, 1609).

Sasoon, Hamo, *The Siwas of Lamu* (Nairobi, 1975).

Sayyid Abdallah, *Al-Inkishafi* (Nairobi, 1972).

Scheub, Harold, "African Oral Traditions and Literature" *African Studies Review* 28 (1985) 1-72.

Seitel, Peter, "Cultural Implications of the Eclipse of 16 February 1980 in Lamu, Kenya" *Archaeostronomy* 6 (1983) 134-40.

Serjeant, R.B. and Ronald Lewcock, (eds)., *San:—a: An Arabian Islamic City* (London, 1983).

————, "Hadramaut to Zanzibar: The Pilot-Poem of the Nakhudha Said Ba Tayi of al Hami" *Paiduma* 28 (1082) 109-128.

————, *The Portuguese Off the South Arabian Coast: Hadrami Chronicles* (Oxford, 1963).

Shepherd, Gill, "Rank, Gender and Homosexuality: Mombasa as a Key to Understanding Sexual Options" in Patricia Caplan (ed)., *The Cultural Construction of Sexuality* (London, 1987) 240-70.

————, "The Making of the Swahili: A View From the South End of the East African Coast" *Paiduma* 28 (1982) 142-44.

Shariff, Abdul and Ed Ferguson (eds)., *Zanzibar Under Colonial Rule* (London, 1991).

————, *Slaves, Spices and Ivory in Zanzabar: Economic Integration of East Africa into the World Economy* (London, 1987).

Shell, Robert C.-H., *Children of Bondage: A Social History of the Slave Society at the Cape of Good Hope 1652-1838* (Johannesburg, 1994).

Sinclair, Paul J.J., "Archaeology in Eastern African History: An Overview of Current chronological Issues" *Journal of African History* 32 (1991) 179-220.

Skene, R., "Arab and Swahili Dances and Ceremonies" *Journal of the Royal Anthropological Institute of Great Britain and Ireland* 47 (1917) 413-34.

Spear, Thomas, *Traditions and Their Interpretation: The Mijikenda of Kenya* (Athens, 1982).

————, *Kenya's Past: An Introduction to Historical Method in Africa* (Longman, 1981).

————, "Oral Traditions" Whose History?" *History in Africa* 8 (1981) 163-79.

Stichter, Sharon, *Migrant Labour in Kenya: Capitalism and the African Response* (London, 1982).

Stigand, J.H. (Capt.), *The Land of Zinj* (London, 1913).

Strandes, Justus, *The Portuguese Period in East Africa* (trans. Nairobi, 1961).

Strobel, Margaret, *Mombasa Women* (New Haven, 1979).

———— and Sarah Mirza (eds)., *Three Swahili Woman: Life Histories from Mombasa, Kenya* (Bloomington, 1989).

Sundiata, Ibrahim, "Twentieth Century Reflections on Death in Zanzibar" *International Journal of African Historical Studies* 20 (1987) 45-60.

Sullivan, Captain G.L., *Dhow Chasing in Zanzibar Waters* (London, 1873).

Sutton, J.E.G., "The Settlement of East Africa" B.A. Ogot, and J.A. Kiernan, (eds)., *Zamani: A Survey of East African History* (Nairobi, 1968) 69-99.

————, *The East African Coast: An Historical and Archaeological Review* (Nairobi, 1966).

Swartz, Marc J., *The Way the World Is: Cultural Processes and Social Relations Among the Mombasa Swahili* (Berkeley, 1991).

Talbot-Smith, "Short History of Tanaland" Typescript, KNA.

Talib, Yusof A., "Etudes sur le diaspora des peuples arabes dans l'Ocean Indien." *Diogenes*, July-Sept: (1980) 39-54.

Thornton, Richard, "Diary of..." Typescript, Ft. Jesus Library.

Tolmacheva, Marina, "Essays in Swahili Geographical Thought" in (eds)., Rose-Marie Beck, Thomas Geider, Werner Graebner, *Swahili Forum II* (Koln, 1995) 1-40.

————, "Sur la cote swahelie aux frontieres naturelles et culturelles de la civilisation" (ed)., Sylvie Devers *Pour Jean Malaurie* (Paris, 1960) 435-47.

————, (ed)., *Pate Chronicle* (East Lansing, 1993).

————, "Ibn Battata on Women's Travel in the Daral-Islam" in Bonnie Frederick, and Susan H. McLeod, (eds)., *Women and the Journey: The Female Travel Experience* (Pullman, 1993) 119-40.

————, "Group Identity in Swahili Chronicles" paper presented at the African Studies Association Meeting, 1991.

————, "They Came From Damascus, Syria: A Note on Traditional Lamu Historiography" *International Journal of African Historical Studies* 12 (1979) 259-69.

————, "The Arabic Influences on Swahili Literature" *Journal of African Studies* 5 (1978) 223-243.

————, "The Origin of the Name 'Swahili'" *Tanzania Notes and Records* 77 and 78 (1976) 27-38.

Trimingham, J.S., "The Arab Geographers and the East African Coast" in H. Neville Chittick, and Robert I. Rotberg, (eds)., *East Africa and the Orient* (London, 1975) 115-46.

————, "The Phases of Islamic Expansion and Islamic Culture Zones in Africa" in I.M. Lewis (ed)., *Islam in Tropical Africa* (London, 1966) 127-43.

————, *Islam in East Africa* (Oxford, 1964).

————, *Islam in the Sudan* (London, 1949).

Toledano, E.R., "Slave Dealers, Women, Pregnancy and Abortion: The Story of a Circassian Slave Girl in Mid-Nineteenth Century Cairo" *Slavery and Abolition* 2 (1981) 53-68.

Toussaint, Auguste, *History of the Indian Ocean* (Chicago, 1966). UNESCO, *Cultural Newsletter* 3 (1985).

Van Beers, L.W.C., *Le Hadhramout et les Colonies Arabes dans L'Archipel Indien* (Batavia, 1886).

Vail, Leroy (ed)., *The Creation of Tribalism in Southern Africa* (London, 1989).

Vansina, Jan, *Living with Africa* (Madison, 1994).

————, *Oral Traditions as History* (Madison, 1985).

————, *Art in History: An Introduction to Method* (London, 1984).

————, R. Mauny, and L.V., Thomas (eds)., *The Historian in Tropical Africa* (London, 1966).

Villiers, Allen, *Sons of Sinbad* (New York, 1964).

Voeltzlow, Alfred, "Geschich der Witu Inseln" *Reise in Ostafrika* (Stuttgart, 1923).

Waddy, Charis, *Women in Muslim History* (London, 1980).

Werner, Alice, "A Swahili History of Pate" *Journal of the Royal Asiatic Society* 14 (1915) 280-299.

Whitley, Wilfred, *Swahili: The Rise of a National Language* (London, 1969).

Wiesauer, Eva, "Reshnitzte Eingangstore an der Ostafrikanischen Kuste" *Ethnohistorische Blatter* 12 (1976) 4-18.

————, "DeKortechiken und Ornamate an Holzobjekten der Ost-Afrikanischen Kuste. Ein beitrag zum Kunsthandwerk der Suaheli Under Beruck-Sichtigung ethnohistoris cher Quellen" Ph.D. Thesis, Universitat Wien 1976.

Wikan, Unni, *Behind the Veil in Arabia: Women in Oman* (Baltimore, 1982).

Willis, Justin, *Mombasa, the Swahili, and the Making of the Mijikenda* (Oxford, 1993).

Wilson, Gordon M., "Mombasa Social Survey" Typescript, Edward Rodwell Archive.

Wilson, Thomas H., "Takwa: An Ancient Swahili Settlement on the Lamu Archipelago" (pam). n.d.

Wolff, Richard D., *The Economics of Colonialism* (New Haven, 1974).

————, "British Imperialism and the East African Slave Trade" *Science and Society* 36 (1972) 443-62.

Wright, T.H., "Early Seafarers of the Comoro Islands" *Azania* 19 (1984) 13-60.

Whyte, A., "Travels on the Kenya Coast" PP Colonial Office.

Ylvisaker, Marguerite, "The Ivory Trade in the Lamu Area" *Paiduma* 28 (1982)

221-32.

———, *Lamu in the Nineteenth Century: Land, Trade and Politics* (Boston, 1979).

———, Shamba na Konde: Land Use in the Hinterland of the Lamu Archipelago 1865-1895" Typescript, Ft. Jesus Library (Mombasa).

Young, T. Cuyler, "East Africa and Classical Islam: Some Remaining Research Problems in Relationships" *Transafrican Journal of History* 2 (1972) 3-10.

el Zein, Hamid M., *The Sacred Meadows: A Structural Analysis of Religious Symbolism in an East African Town* (Evanston, 1974).

Index